Working with Arabic Prepositions

Working with Arabic Prepositions: Structures and Functions is a reference book focusing on Arabic prepositions, their structure and usage.

The system of Arabic prepositions is complex, and the textbook aims to assist students at the lower intermediate to advanced level understand it in an accessible way. This is an area in which students can experience great difficulty, and the aim of this book is to explain clearly the structures and functions of Arabic prepositions and their usage in Modern Standard Arabic and media Arabic. Drills and exercises are provided to enable readers to practice what they have learned in the chapters.

This book will be an ideal source of information for undergraduate students studying Arabic, as well as graduate studies and additional courses in the major dialect areas, and a very useful resource for teachers of Arabic as a foreign language.

Ronak Husni has taught Arabic language, modern and classical literature, gender studies, translation and cultural studies in a number of universities in the UK, including St. Andrews, Durham and Heriot-Watt University over the course of twenty-four years. Her main area of research is classical and modern Arabic literature, applied translation studies, gender studies and Arabic as a foreign language. Her study and translation of the Tunisian reformer Al-Qasim al-Haddad's seminal book *Muslim Women in Law and Society* won her the 2007 World Award of the President of the Republic of Tunisia for Islamic Studies. She is currently a professor of Arabic and Translation Studies at the American University of Sharjah.

Aziza Zaher has taught Arabic language and translation for more than twenty years in a number of higher education institutions in Egypt and the UK. Her research interests are teaching Arabic as a foreign language, systemic functional linguistics and critical discourse analysis. She is currently Assistant Professor of Arabic at the School of Modern Languages and Cultures at Durham University, and she received Durham University's Excellence in Learning and Teaching Award in 2018.

Working with Arabic Prepositions
Structures and Functions

Ronak Husni and Aziza Zaher

LONDON AND NEW YORK

First published 2020
by Routledge
2 Park Square, Milton Park, Abingdon, Oxon OX14 4RN

and by Routledge
52 Vanderbilt Avenue, New York, NY 10017

Routledge is an imprint of the Taylor & Francis Group, an informa business

© 2020 Ronak Husni and Aziza Zaher

The right of Ronak Husni and Aziza Zaher to be identified as authors of this work has been asserted by them in accordance with sections 77 and 78 of the Copyright, Designs and Patents Act 1988.

All rights reserved. No part of this book may be reprinted or reproduced or utilised in any form or by any electronic, mechanical, or other means, now known or hereafter invented, including photocopying and recording, or in any information storage or retrieval system, without permission in writing from the publishers.

Trademark notice: Product or corporate names may be trademarks or registered trademarks, and are used only for identification and explanation without intent to infringe.

British Library Cataloguing-in-Publication Data
A catalogue record for this book is available from the British Library

Library of Congress Cataloging-in-Publication Data
A catalog record for this book has been requested

ISBN: 978-1-138-29763-0 (hbk)
ISBN: 978-1-138-29761-6 (pbk)
ISBN: 978-1-315-09910-1 (ebk)

Typeset in Times New Roman
by Apex CoVantage, LLC

Contents

Introduction   viii

1   The basics of Arabic prepositions   1

Definition of Arabic prepositions 2
Importance of prepositions 2
Functions of prepositions 3
Classifications of prepositions 4
Constructions involving prepositions 4
Case marking of prepositional phrases 7
Locative adverbs 9
The importance of prepositions for foreign-language learning 10

2   One-letter prepositions   11

11 البَاء
29 اللَّام
39 الكَاف
44 وَاو وبَاء وتَاء القَسَم

3   Two-letter prepositions   46

46 مِنْ
69 عَنْ
79 فِي
93 كَي

4   Three-letter prepositions   98

98 إلَى
107 عَلَى
121 خَلَا / عَدَا

مُنْذُ *124*
رُبَّ *126*

5 Four-letter prepositions   130

حَتَّى *130*
حَاشَا *133*

6 Locative adverbs   136

بَيْنَ *138*
عِنْدَ *140*
مَعَ *144*
لَدَى *146*
بَعْدَ / قَبْلَ *148*
خِلَالَ *152*
قُرْبَ *153*
نَحْوَ *154*
Adverbs of time 156
إِبَّانَ *156*
أَبَدَ *157*
أَثْنَاءَ *157*
إِثْرَ *158*
أَنَاءَ *158*
غَدَاةَ *158*
Adverbs of place 159
أَمَامَ / قُدَّامَ *159*
خَلْفَ / وَرَاءَ *160*
تَحْتَ *162*
فَوْقَ *163*
دَاخِلَ *165*
خَارِجَ *165*
إِزَاءَ *166*
تِجَاهَ *166*
جَانِبَ *167*
وَسْطَ *168*

7 Analysis of examples of errors by students   169

Introduction 169
Examples of errors by students 169

Deletion of prepositions 170
Substitution of prepositions 176
Addition of prepositions 182
Conclusion 185

Glossary of common verbs with prepositions	186
Answer key	217
Bibliography	223
Index	227

Introduction

Working with Arabic Prepositions: Structures and Functions is a reference book focusing on Arabic prepositions, their structure and usage. It illustrates the structures and functions of Arabic prepositions with authentic examples from Arab media. The book is intended for learners with intermediate to advanced knowledge of Arabic. Teachers and researchers may also find some aspects of this book useful.

This book benefits from most Arabic and English grammar texts that deal with Arabic prepositions in particular or Arabic grammar in general, such as those by Cantarino (1974–1976), Ryding-Lentzner (1977), Carter (1981), Murādī (1983), Ibn al-Sarrāj (1985), Abbās (1996), al-Farahīdī (2003), Buckley (2004), Ryding (2005), Wright (1967) and Ibn Jinnī (2013), among others. The examples cited in this book are adapted from various sources, including Arabic newspapers and news websites and the Arabic corpus (http://arabicorpus.byu.edu/), as well as examples created by the authors.

In this book, we discuss the structures and functions of Arabic prepositions, explain their usage and analyze how students of Arabic as a foreign language use prepositions in their writing, as well as suggesting ways of improving this. Moreover, we provide a glossary of common verbs with prepositions and particles.

Chapter 1, 'The basics of Arabic prepositions', provides background information on the structures and functions of Arabic prepositions. It presents definitions of Arabic particles and prepositions and a brief discussion of their functions and what different grammar schools say about them. The chapter also explains the structures of prepositional phrases, their case marking and functions in Arabic sentences. Moreover, the importance of prepositions for foreign-language learning is highlighted.

Chapter 2, 'One-letter prepositions', covers one-letter prepositions (/ تَاء القَسَم / وَاو القَسَم / الكَاف / اللَّام / البَاء). It discusses the main and subsidiary functions of each preposition, giving a selection of contextual examples that illustrate each function. It also presents common constructions in which each preposition is used and a list of fixed expressions for common prepositions. At the end of the chapter, some exercises can be found to enable readers to understand and practice what they have learned in the chapter.

Chapter 3, 'Two-letter prepositions', deals with two-letter prepositions (/ كَيْ / مُذْ
مِنْ / فِي / عَنْ). It discusses the main and subsidiary functions of each preposition, with a selection of contextual examples that illustrate each function. It also presents common constructions in which each preposition is used and a list of fixed expressions for common prepositions. At the end of the chapter, there are some exercises to enable readers to understand and practice what they have learned in the chapter.

Chapter 4, 'Three-letter prepositions', focuses on three-letter prepositions (/ رُبَّ
مُنْذُ / عَدَا / خَلَا / عَلَى / إِلَى). It discusses the main and subsidiary functions of each preposition, with a selection of contextual examples that illustrate each function. It also presents common constructions in which each preposition is used and a list of fixed expressions for common prepositions. Finally, the chapter includes some exercises to enable readers to understand and practice what they have learned in the chapter.

Chapter 5, 'Four-letter prepositions', concentrates on four-letter prepositions (حَاشَا / حَتَّى). It discusses the main and subsidiary functions of each, with a selection of contextual examples to illustrate each function. It also presents common constructions in which each preposition is used. This chapter also ends with exercises to help readers understand and practice what they have learned.

Chapter 6, 'Locative adverbs', covers locative adverbs (الظُّرُوف). These are traditionally divided into adverbs of time (ظُرُوف الزَّمَانِ) and adverbs of place (ظُرُوف المَكَانِ), with a particular focus on those that function in a way similar to prepositions. This category of words is called 'semi-prepositions'. Their functions and a selection of contextual examples that illustrate each function are given, along with common constructions in which they appear.

Chapter 7, 'Analysis of examples of errors by students', analyzes the performance of students in using prepositions, with a focus on their writing at intermediate and advanced levels. Errors in the use of prepositions by learners of Arabic as a foreign language are presented along with corrections.

The 'Glossary of common verbs with prepositions' includes a bilingual list of common Arabic verbs with prepositions and their translation to illustrate the meanings.

The 'Answer key' provides answers to the exercises presented in the book.

1 The basics of Arabic prepositions

Arab grammarians divide words into three categories of nouns (أَسْمَاء), verbs (أَفْعَال) and particles (حُرُوف). Nouns (الأَسْمَاء) are words that refer to objects, whether concrete or abstract; verbs (الأَفْعَال) are words that refer to events associated with a certain time frame in the past, present or future; and particles (الحُرُوف) are words that do not belong to either of the categories or nouns or verbs and that have a linking function. Particles include prepositions, conjunctions, interjections and so on. Arabic particles are divided into several categories. However, the exact name of each category has not been agreed on by scholars and grammarians in the field (Versteegh, 1997a: 76–77). Particles (الحُرُوف) in general are divided into two types. The first is (حُرُوف المَبَانِي), denoting letters of the alphabet, and this category is also referred to as (حُرُوف الهَجَاء), a term used by both Kufa and Basra schools of grammar. The second type of particle is called (حُرُوف المَعَانِي), a name which was used primarily by the Basra school of grammar.

Arab grammarians mention various different lexical meanings of the word (حَرْف); among them, for example, Ibn Jinnī, who states that these three letters in any stretch of text denote the boundary and edge of something (Ibn Jinnī, 2001: 15). Furthermore, Ibn Fāris states that (حَرْف) has three meanings: (1) border or the edge of something, such as a sword; (2) to deviate and depart from something; and (3) a surgical probe (Ibn Fāris, 1972: 42). Al-Murādī, on the other hand, defines (حَرْف) as 'border' or 'part of', and in a grammatical context, this is appropriate because the particle (حَرْف) is indeed part of any given speech (al-Murādī, 1992: 24–25). The number of particles in Arabic has been debated by grammarians; some count fifty or ninety-five particles, whereas al-Murādī counts one hundred (ibid: 25).

Some Arab grammarians have long debated the appropriateness of the use of the terms (حَرْف) or (أَدَاة). While some have preferred the term (أَدَاة), others have rejected it on the grounds that traditional Arab grammarians insist that words consist of (اِسْم وفِعْل وحَرْف) 'noun, verb and particle', and thus, they do not mention the word (أَدَاة) (Sībawayhi, 1988 al-Kitaab: Vol.1, P. 419). Meanwhile, the Kufa school used (أداة pl. أَدَوات) for particles, perhaps to differentiate them from the letters of the alphabet (حُرُوف المَبَانِي). Unlike the Basra school, the Kufa school believed that particles do not represent any meaning in themselves and that only when used in conjunction with other words or phrases do they impart meaning.

Definition of Arabic prepositions

Arab grammarians have not agreed on an exact definition of prepositions (حُرُوف الجَر). They have defined prepositions as a subcategory of particles (الحُرُوف) and define particles as 'words that do not have a meaning in themselves, but that have a linking function with other parts of speech' (Louchene, 2006: 11). In general, particles (الحُرُوف) are defined as 'words that have a grammatical function but which do not belong to the noun or verb classes or their derivatives' (Badawi, Carter and Gully, 2014: 862). Therefore, it can be said that prepositions (حُرُوف الجَر) can be defined in terms of their function as well as their meaning.

Preposition (حَرْف الجَر) literally means 'particle of attraction'. Other less commonly used names for the same category are: (حُرُوف الإِضَافَة) 'particles of annexation', (حُرُوف الخَفْض) 'particles of depression' and (حُرُوف الكَسْر) 'particle of genitives'. In general, Arabic prepositions are a closed category that includes up to twenty particles. The Arabic prepositions that are agreed on by all grammarians are البَاء، ومِنْ، وإِلى، وعَنْ، وعَلى، وفِي، والكَاف، ولَام القَسَم، ووَاو القَسَم وتَاء القَسَم،) (ومُذْ، ومُنْذُ، ورُبَّ، وحَتَّى، وخَلَا، وعَدَا، وحَاشَا).

In addition, certain Arabic dialects have identified further prepositions in addition to this list, such as (كي ومَتَى) in the dialect of Hudhail and (لَعَلَّ) in the dialect of ꜥuqail. Moreover, in Modern Standard Arabic (MSA), (مَعَ) is sometimes viewed as a preposition, although Sibawayh classifies it as a locative adverb (ظَرْف) (Sibawayh I: 177). In this volume, we concentrate on the Arabic prepositions agreed on by all grammarians and deal with (مَعَ) under the category of locative adverbs (الظُّرُوف). Some Arabic prepositions are considered to be archaic in their usage and are only found in very limited contexts in MSA, for example, (خَلَا وحَاشَا). Some others, such as (كي ومَتَى ولَعَلَّ), are considered to be prepositions only by Ibn Malik, with only very few examples of their usage in poetry in certain old Arabic dialects.

Prepositions are, typically, words that reveal relationships between their objects and other words in sentences. Wright (1896) states that prepositions originally designated relations of place, but subsequently relations of time were accepted and then other types of relation too, such as of instrument, manner, reason, source or accompaniment. In addition, prepositions can be used figuratively.

Importance of prepositions

Prepositions are very important for the structure of writing and speech. They are a basic building block of sentences with an important cohesive function. In a study undertaken by al-Khūlī on the frequency of different word categories, it was revealed that nouns make up 58% of words in the sample, particles

31% and verbs 11%. So, particles make up around one-third of Arabic texts. Prepositions make up approximately 14.1% of Arabic texts, and 44.5% of all particles in the sample (al-Khūlī, 1998: 30). The same study also revealed that nouns in the genitive case are more common than nouns in the nominative and accusative cases. Nouns in the genitive case make up 61.8% of the total, in the accusative 9.6% and in the nominative 18.5%. Genitive nouns that occur after prepositions make up 24.4% of all nouns; that is, nouns that occur after a preposition are more frequent than nominative and accusative nouns in the sample. This means that of every four nouns we use, one will be genitive after a preposition, and of every seven words we use, there will be one preposition. This is evidence of the prevalence and importance of prepositions in Arabic syntax. Semantically, prepositions have significant cohesive functions that link other parts of the sentence.

Functions of prepositions

Ḥasan (1960: 2:434) explains the functions of a preposition in two ways. First, prepositions add new meanings to a sentence, as in the following:

| ذَهَبَ الرَّجُلُ. | The man went. |
| ذَهَبَ الرَّجُلُ إلى الحَديقَةِ. | The man went to the park. |

Second, prepositions link verbs with the following nouns so that, through prepositions, a nontransitive verb passes on to an object, as in the following:

| سَافَرَ صَديقي. | My friend traveled. |
| سَافَرَ صَديقي مِنَ القَرْيَةِ إلى المَدينَةِ بالسَّيَّارَةِ. | My friend traveled from the village to the city by car. |

Moreover, a transitive verb can assume a new meaning with a preposition, as in the following:

| عُدْتُ المَريضَ. | I visited the patient. |
| عُدْتُ إلى البَيْتِ. | I returned home. |

Sometimes prepositions have other stylistic functions in a sentence, such as denoting emphasis, for example, in (لَسْتُ بِنَائِمٍ), 'I am not asleep'. The preposition here is used for emphasis, and it literally means 'indeed' or 'surely'. Prepositions can also refer to other relationships, such as denoting some of a whole relationship; for example, (أَكَلْتُ مِنَ الطَّعَامِ), 'I ate some food'. In this volume, the semantic relationships created by each preposition are discussed in detail. This includes the overarching meanings and relevant subsidiary meanings for each preposition as explained by Arab and Western grammarians.

Classifications of prepositions

Arabic prepositions can be classified as true prepositions (حُرُوف الجَر الأَصْلِيَّة), redundant prepositions (حُرُوف الجَر الزَائِدَة) and a quasi-redundant preposition (حَرْف الجَرّ شِبْه الزَّائِد).

1 True prepositions (حُرُوف الجَر الأَصْلِيَّة) add a new meaning to the sentence in which they appear. They cannot be preceded by other prepositions. Moreover, only a true preposition can combine with a verb to create a verb–preposition idiom.
2 Redundant prepositions (حُرُوف الجَر الزَائِدَة) do not add any new meaning to the sentence. They are used for emphasis, and they can be deleted without affecting the meaning.
3 A quasi-redundant preposition (حَرْف الجَرّ شِبْه الزَّائِد) adds a limited meaning, such as (رُبَّ) which means *perhaps*.

Prepositions in Arabic can also be subdivided according to their form as separable or inseparable:

1 Separable prepositions are made up of two or more letters, and they stand alone as independent words and are not attached to other nouns, for example, (مِنْ) and (إِلَى).
2 Inseparable prepositions are made up of one letter, and they are always prefixed to a noun, such as in (البَاء) and (الكَاف) (Abdel Nasser, 2013: 67).

Prepositions can also be classified according to their categories as follows:

1 Particles only, for example, مِنْ، إِلَى، حَتَّى، فِي، البَاء، اللَّام، رُبَّ، وَاو القَسَم، تَاء القَسَم
2 Particles as well as nouns, such as عَلَى، عَنْ، الكَاف، مُذْ، مُنْذُ
3 Particles as well as verbs, like حَاشَا، عَدَا، خَلَا

Prepositions can also be classified according to the types of words that can follow them:

1 Prepositions that can be followed by nouns only: مُنذُ، مُذْ، حَتَّى، الكاف، رُبَّ
2 Prepositions that can be followed by nouns referring to God only: وَاو القَسَم، تَاء القَسَم
3 Prepositions that can be followed by nouns and pronoun suffixes: مِنْ، إِلَى، عَنْ، عَلَى، فِي، البَاءُ، اللَّام

Constructions involving prepositions

In prepositional phrases, the preposition occurs as the first part of the phrase, and the second part is either a noun or a similar word functioning as the object of the preposition. For example, in the sentence (وَضَعَ الكِتَابَ عَلَى الطَّاوِلَةِ.), the word (عَلَى) is the preposition, and (الطَّاوِلَةِ) is its object. However, other constructions are also possible after a preposition, including pronoun suffixes, interrogatives, relative pronouns and so on. Buckley (2004) lists constructions that can occur after a preposition.

Prepositions are mainly followed by nouns, such as in the following:

سَافَرْنَا بِالطَّائِرَةِ.	We traveled by plane.
وَصَلْتُ إِلَى الجَامِعَةِ.	I arrived at the university.
تَجَمَّعَتِ الطُّيُورُ عَلَى الشَّجَرَةِ.	The birds gathered on the tree.

Prepositions can be followed by pronoun suffixes, such as in the following:

نَظَرْتُ إِلَيْهَا.	I looked at her.
أَعْتَمِدُ عَلَيْهِمْ.	I depend on them.
رَحَّبُوا بِنَا.	They welcomed us.

Prepositions can be followed by interrogative pronouns. It should be noted here that the interrogative (ما) becomes shortened after prepositions to (مَ), as in the following:

لِمَ العَجَلَةُ؟ (لِمَ = لِ+مَا)	Why do you rush?
عَمَّ تَسْتَفْسِرُ؟ (عَمَّ = عَنْ+مَا)	What do you inquire about?
بِكَمْ هَذَا الكِتَابُ؟	How much is this book?
لِمَنِ المِعْطَفُ الأَسْوَدُ؟	Who owns the black coat?

Prepositions can be followed by demonstrative pronouns, as in the following:

اِسْتَمِعْ إِلَى هَذِهِ المُحَاضَرَةِ!	Listen to this lecture!
سَكَنْتُ فِي ذَلِكَ البَيْتِ.	I lived in that house.
هَلْ سَمِعْتَ عَنْ هَذَيْنِ الشَّخْصَيْنِ؟	Did you hear about these two people?

Prepositions can be followed by relative pronouns. The relative pronoun (ما) is not shortened after prepositions, unlike with the interrogative, as in the following:

وِفْقًا لِمَا أَعْلَنَتْهُ الحُكُومَةُ	According to what the government announced
لِمَنْ يُهِمُّهُ الأَمْرُ	To whom it may concern
يَجِبُ خَلْقُ فُرَصِ عَمَلٍ لِلَّذِينَ لَا يَجِدُونَ عَمَلًا.	Job opportunities must be created for those who cannot find work.

6 The basics of Arabic prepositions

Prepositions can be followed by locative adverbs (الظُّرُوف), as in the following:

اِخْتَرْتُكِ مِنْ بَيْنِ جَمِيعِ الطُّلَّابِ.	I chose you from all students.
لَمْ أُقَابِلْهَا مِنْ قَبْلُ.	I have not met her before.
جَاءَ مِنْ هُنَاك إِلَى هُنَا.	He came from there to here.

Prepositions can be followed by a nominal sentence preceded by (أَنَّ) or a verbal sentence preceded by (أَنْ), as in the following:

تَأَكَّدْتُ مِنْ أَنَّ الأُسْتَاذَة مُنَى هِيَ المُشْرِفَةُ عَلَى بَحْثِي.	I made sure that Professor Mona is the supervisor of my research.
اِعْتَرَفَ المُجْرِمُ بِأَنَّهُ هُوَ مُرْتَكِبُ الجَرِيمَةِ.	The offender admitted that he was the perpetrator of the crime.
لَا بُدَّ مِنْ أَنْ أُعِيدَ الكِتَابَ إِلَى المَكْتَبَةِ.	I have to return the book to the library.
فَكَّرْتُ فِي أَنْ أُسَافِرَ إِلَى أَمْرِيكَا، ولَكِنَّنِي غَيَّرْتُ رَأْيِي.	I thought about traveling to America, but I changed my mind.

The prepositional phrase (preposition and noun or equivalent) is a complete unit that can be placed in different positions in the sentence, as in the following:

أَسْتَذْكِرُ دُرُوسِي فِي المَسَاءِ.	I revise my lessons in the evening.
فِي المَسَاءِ أَسْتَذْكِرُ دُرُوسِي.	I revise my lessons in the evening.

In certain instances, it is necessary to begin the sentence with the prepositional phrase; for example,

1. if the prepositional phrase is a fronted predicate and the subject of the sentence is indefinite, such as the following:

فِي المَدْرَسَةِ تَلَامِيذُ كَثِيرُونَ.	There are lots of pupils in the school.
لِلأَدِيبِ عِشْرُونَ رِوَايَةً.	The author wrote twenty novels.

2. if the prepositional phrase is a fronted predicate and the subject contains a pronoun that refers back to the prepositional phrase, as in the following:

فِي البَابِ مِفْتَاحُهُ.	The door has its key.
عَلَى الطَّالِبِ اسْتِذْكَارُ دُرُوسِهِ.	The student has to revise his lessons.

3. if it is part of an interrogative:

لِمَنْ هَذِهِ السَّيَّارَةُ؟	Who owns this car?
بِكَمْ اِشْتَرَيْتَ الكِتَابَ؟	How much did you pay for the book?

Moreover, there are some instances in which it is better to begin the sentence with a prepositional phrase, for example, to give it prominence and highlight its meaning:

مِنْ أَجْلِ أُسْرَتِي، هَاجَرْتُ خَارِجَ بَلَدِي.	For the sake of my family, I left my home country.
هَاجَرْتُ خَارِجَ بَلَدِي مِنْ أَجْلِ أُسْرَتِي.	I left my home country for the sake of my family.

Case marking of prepositional phrases

Prepositions are uninflected (مَبْنِيّ) and thus have fixed endings.

Some prepositions end in (سُكُون):

مِنْ – عَنْ – مُذْ – كَيْ

خَرَجْتُ مِنْ غُرْفَتِي.	I left my room.
تَكَلَّمَت الأُسْتَاذَة عَنْ حَضَارَةِ الشَّرْقِ الأَدْنَى.	The professor talked about the civilization of the Near East.
لَمْ أَرَ خَالَتِي مُذْ شَهْرَيْنِ.	I have not seen my aunt for two months.
أَدْرُسُ كَيْ أَنْجَحَ.	I study so as to succeed.

It should be noted that if (مِنْ) and (عَنْ) are followed by the definite article (ال), the final vowel is substituted as follows: (مِنْ) becomes (مِنَ), and (عَنْ) becomes (عَنِ), moreover, (مُذْ) becomes (مُذِ), such as in the following:

عَادَ الوَلَدُ مِنَ المَدْرَسَةِ.	The boy returned from school.
سَأَلَ الرَّجُلُ عَنِ الوَقْتِ.	The man asked about the time.
لَمْ أَسْتَرِحْ مُذِ الصَّبَاحِ.	I have not rested since morning.

The following prepositions should also end in (سُكُون); however, it cannot be pronounced, as they all end in long vowels:

إِلَى – عَلَى – خَلَا – عَدَا – حَاشَا – حَتَّى – فِي

سَافَرَ صَدِيقِي إِلَى قَرْيَتِهِ.	My friend traveled to his village.
جَلَسْنَا عَلَى مَقَاعِدَ مُرِيحَةٍ.	We sat on comfortable seats.
حَضَرَ الجَمِيعُ خَلَا جَمَالٍ.	Everyone came except Jamal.
أَجَبْتُ عَلَى كُلِّ الأَسْئِلَةِ عَدَا سُؤَالٍ.	I answered all the questions except one.
زُرْتُ جَمِيعَ أَجْزَاءِ المَدِينَةِ حَاشَا الجُزْءِ الغَرْبِيِّ.	I visited all parts of the city except the western part.
قَرَأْتُ الرِّوَايَةَ حَتَّى نِهَايَتِهَا.	I read the novel until its end.
سَأُرَاجِعُ دُرُوسِي فِي المَكْتَبَةِ.	I will revise my lessons in the library.

Some prepositions end in (فَتْحَة):

رُبَّ ـ وَ (واو القسم) ـ تَ (تاء القسم) ـ كَ (كاف التشبيه)

رُبَّ ضَارَّةٍ نَافِعَةٌ.	A harmful thing may turn out to be useful.
أَنْتَ طَوِيلٌ كَأَخِيكَ.	You are as tall as your brother.
وَاللهِ لَأَنْصُرَنَّ الحَقَّ.	I swear by God to support what is right.

One preposition ends in (ضَمَّة):

مُنْذُ

مَا أَكَلْتُ مُنْذُ أَمْسِ.	I have not eaten since yesterday.
وَصَلْتُ لَنْدَن مُنْذُ يَوْمَيْنِ.	I arrived in London two days ago.

Two prepositions end in (كَسْرَة):

بِ (البَاء) / لِ (اللَّام)*

خَتَمْتُ كَلِمَتِي بِالسَّلَامِ عَلَى الحَاضِرِينَ.	I concluded my speech by greeting the audience.
تَوَجَّهْتُ لِلْمَدِينَةِ لِشِرَاءِ اِحْتِيَاجَاتِي.	I went to town to buy what I needed.
سَيَصِلُ الرَّئِيسُ لِلْمُؤْتَمَرِ بِالسَّيَّارَةِ.	The president will come to the conference by car.

*It should be noted that لِ (اللَّام) ends in (فَتْحَة) if its object is a pronoun suffix, other than *me* (يَاء المُتَكَلِّم); for example, لَهُ، لَهَا، لَنَا، لَكُمْ.

شَرَحَتْ لِي وِجْهَةَ نَظَرِهَا.	She explained her point of view to me.
شَرَحَتْ لَهُ وِجْهَةَ نَظَرِهَا.	She explained her point of view to him.
شَرَحَتْ لَكُمْ وِجْهَةَ نَظَرِهَا.	She explained her point of view to you.

Nouns following prepositions are always in the genitive case (مَجْرُور). If a preposition or semi-preposition is followed by a personal pronoun, it becomes a pronoun suffix instead. When the object of a preposition is an uninflected word such as a demonstrative, it remains invariable, as in (عَنْ ذَلِكَ), 'about that'. Genitive nouns following prepositions can be marked in different ways.

If the noun is indefinite singular, feminine plural or short broken plural, it is marked by (تَنْوِين الكَسْر):

سَكَنْتُ فِي بَيْتٍ كَبِيرٍ.	I lived in a large house.
سَكَنْتُ فِي بُيُوتٍ كَبِيرَةٍ.	I lived in large houses.
اِسْتَمْتَعْتُ بِأُغْنِيَاتٍ قَدِيمَةٍ.	I enjoyed classical songs.

If the noun is definite singular, feminine plural or short broken plural, it is marked by (الكَسْرَة):

سَكَنْتُ فِي البَيْتِ الكَبِيرِ.	I lived in the large house.
سَكَنْتُ فِي البُيُوتِ الكَبِيرَةِ.	I lived in the large houses.
اِسْتَمْتَعْتُ بِالأُغْنِيَاتِ القَدِيمَةِ.	I enjoyed the classical songs.

If the noun is sound masculine plural, it is marked by (اليَاء) as part of the suffix (ـيْنَ):

اِسْتَمَعْتُ إِلَى مُطْرِبِيْنَ لُبْنَانِيِّيْنَ.	I listened to Lebanese singers.
اِسْتَمَعْتُ إِلَى المُطْرِبِيْنَ اللُّبْنَانِيِّيْنَ.	I listened to the Lebanese singers.

If the noun is dual, it is marked by (اليَاء) as part of the final suffix (ـيْنِ):

تَعَرَّفْتُ عَلَى طَالِبَيْنِ جَدِيدَيْنِ.	I met two new students.
تَعَرَّفْتُ عَلَى الطَّالِبَيْنِ الجَدِيدَيْنِ.	I met the two new students.

If the noun is a diptote (مَمْنُوع مِنَ الصَّرْفِ), such as a broken plural with three or more syllables, a superlative, or many types of proper nouns, it is marked by (الفَتْحَة) without nunation if it is indefinite, since it belongs to the category of diptotes (المَمْنُوع مِنَ الصَّرْفِ). It should be noted that if the noun is definite, it takes normal case marking (الكَسْرَة).

دَرَسَتْ فِي مَدَارِسَ وَمَعَاهِدَ مِصْرِيَّةٍ.	She studied at Egyptian schools and institutes.
دَرَسَتْ فِي المَدَارِسِ وَالمَعَاهِدِ المِصْرِيَّةِ.	She studied at the Egyptian schools and institutes.
عَمِلْنَا فِي مَشَارِيعَ جَدِيدَةٍ.	We worked on new projects.
عَمِلْنَا فِي مَشَارِيعِ الحُكُومَةِ الجَدِيدَةِ.	We worked on new government projects.
ذَهَبْنَا إِلَى مِصْرَ مَعَ فَاطِمَةَ وَحَمْزَةَ.	We went to Egypt with Fatima and Hamza.
سَافَرْتُ إِلَى فِلَسْطِينَ حَيْثُ صَلَّيْتُ فِي المَسَاجِدِ القَدِيمَةِ وَذَهَبْتُ إِلَى كَنَائِسَ أَثَرِيَّةٍ.	I traveled to Palestine where I prayed in the old mosques and went to ancient churches.

Locative adverbs

Certain locative adverbs (الظُّرُوف) share some characteristics with prepositions, as they are always followed by genitive nouns. These are called semi-prepositions, and some people do not distinguish between common locative adverbs, such as

(بَيْنَ), 'between'; (عِنْدَ), 'at'; and (مَعَ) 'with', and prepositions. Locative adverbs can be classified as adverbs of time (ظُرُوف الزَّمَانِ), adverbs of place (ظُرُوف المَكَان) or adverbs of time and place (ظُرُوف المَكَانِ والزَّمَانِ).

Locative adverbs are derived from trilateral lexical roots, and therefore they are grammatically considered to be a type of noun, and the genitive noun that follows them is considered part of an iḏāfa construction, such as (عِنْدَ البَيْتِ), 'at the house'; (قَبْلَ الفَجْرِ), 'before dawn'; (بَعْدَ الظُّهْرِ), 'afternoon'; (بَيْنَ المَكَاتِبِ), 'between the offices'; and (مَعَ أَصْدِقَائِي), 'with my friends'. Whereas prepositions are uninflected, some locative adverbs can take case inflections.

The importance of prepositions for foreign-language learning

Prepositions are very challenging for students of Arabic as a foreign language who find it difficult to choose and use prepositions correctly. Ryding (2005: 367) states that the usage of prepositions can be highly idiomatic and may not correspond to their English equivalents. Therefore, learners of Arabic as a foreign language often make errors when using prepositions, and they need guidance on their uses and the structures that involve them.

In both Arabic and English, some prepositions may have several meanings that change according to the semantic and/or pragmatic context of the sentence. Some prepositions are used specifically with certain nouns, verbs and adjectives as fixed expressions. One difference between Arabic and English is that, while a preposition might be vital in an Arabic sentence, it may not be needed in an English sentence and vice versa. Moreover, the meaning and usage of prepositions in English may differ significantly from Arabic. Therefore, one should not assume direct equivalence between prepositions in English and in Arabic.

2 One-letter prepositions

This chapter deals with prepositions that are made up of one letter. They are classified as inseparable prepositions, as they cannot exist autonomously but have to be joined to the words that follow them, thus appearing as prefixes to them. This class of prepositions includes الْبَاء and تَاء الْقَسَمِ, الْكَاف, اللَّام, وَاو الْقَسَمِ.

الْبَاء

الْبَاء is one of the most commonly used prepositions in Arabic. According to *A Frequency Dictionary of Arabic* (2011), it is the sixth-most commonly used word in Arabic. It is used to serve many functions and can be translated into English in several ways, as 'in', 'at', 'on', 'with', 'for' and 'by', among others.

الْبَاء *in context*

> أَعْمَلُ أُسْتَاذَةً بِجَامِعَةِ الْقَاهِرَةِ، وَهِيَ جَامِعَةٌ مَرْمُوقَةٌ تَقَعُ فِي مَدِينَةِ الْقَاهِرَةِ بِمِصْرَ. يَبْدَأُ يَوْمِي عِنْدَ الْفَجْرِ بِالصَّلَاةِ، ثُمَّ أَتَنَاوَلُ الْفَطُورَ وَأَذْهَبُ إِلَى عَمَلِي بِالسَّيَّارَةِ. أَقْضِي الصَّبَاحَ عَادَةً فِي التَّدْرِيسِ، ثُمَّ أَتَنَاوَلُ غَدَائِي بِمَطْعَمِ الْكُلِّيَّةِ. وَأَقْضِي فَتْرَةَ بَعْدَ الظُّهْرِ فِي الِاجْتِمَاعَاتِ الرَّسْمِيَّةِ وَالْأَعْمَالِ الْأَكَادِيمِيَّةِ. وَلِأَنَّنِي أَهْتَمُّ كَثِيرًا بِالْأَدَبِ الْعَرَبِيِّ، فَإِنَّنِي أَقْضِي كَثِيرًا مِنْ وَقْتِي بِالْمَكْتَبَةِ أَقُومُ بِالْقِرَاءَةِ وَالتَّرْجَمَةِ. أَقْضِي نَهَارِي فِي الْعَمَلِ وَفِي الْمَسَاءِ أَنْشَغِلُ بِرِعَايَةِ أُسْرَتِي.
>
> I am a professor at Cairo University, a great university located in Cairo, Egypt. My day begins at dawn by praying; then I have breakfast and go to work by car. I usually spend the morning teaching; then I have lunch at the faculty restaurant. I spend the afternoon in formal meetings and academic work. Because I am very interested in Arabic literature, I spend much of my time reading and translating at the library. I spend my day at work, and in the evening, I am busy caring for my family.

Notes on the usage of الْبَاء *in context*

In this paragraph, الْبَاء is used with locative functions to indicate time and place (بِجَامِعَةِ الْقَاهِرَةِ، بِمِصْرَ، بِالْمَسَاءِ). It is also used with an instrumental function to indicate a means of transport (بِالسَّيَّارَةِ), and it is used alongside various different verbs to indicate transitivity (أَقُومُ بِالقِرَاءَةِ، أَنْشَغِلُ بِرِعَايَةِ أُسْرَتِي), among other functions. It is very important to note that, due to the wide array of meanings associated with this preposition, it is necessary to try to understand it in context.

In the following section, some of the common functions of the preposition are discussed and examples are given.

Functions of البَاء

البَاء is used with a locative function to indicate place. In this sense, it means 'in' or 'at', as in the following examples:

أَقِيمُ بِدُبَيّ وَأَدْرُسُ بِجَامِعَةِ زَايِدَ.	I live in Dubai and study at Zayed University.
تَزَايَدَتْ أَعْدَادُ مُسْتَخْدِمِي مَوْقِعِ "فيسبوك" لِلتَّوَاصُلِ الاِجْتِمَاعِيّ بِالمِنْطَقَةِ العَرَبِيَّةِ.	The number of Facebook users in the Arab region has increased.
تَحْرِصُ بَعْضُ الدُّوَلِ الغَرْبِيَّةِ عَلَى الوُجُودِ العَسْكَرِيِّ المُبَاشِرِ بِالخَلِيجِ العَرَبِيِّ.	Some Western countries are keen to have a direct military presence in the Arabian Gulf.
تَدَفَّقَ المُوَاطِنُونَ الأُرْدُنِيُّونَ عَلَى القَصْرِ المَلَكِيِّ بِعَمَّانَ.	Jordanian citizens flocked to the royal palace in Amman.

Note

According to Wright (1896), although both (في) and (البَاء) can be used to serve the locative function and both can be translated as either 'in' or 'at', there is a slight difference between them, since (في) has the sense of 'contained within', while (البَاء) has the sense of 'close to'. In Modern Standard Arabic, the two prepositions are interchangeable when expressing the locative function.

Note

According to Cantarino (1974–1976), when (البَاء) is used with a locative function, it is often associated with larger geographical areas, such as in (مُحَادَثَاتُ السَّلَامِ بِالشَّرْقِ الأَوْسَطِ), 'Middle East peace talks'.

البَاء is used to indicate time. In this sense it can mean 'in', 'at' or 'on', such as in the following:

سَهِرْتُ بِاللَّيْلِ وَعَمِلْتُ بِالنَّهَارِ.	I stayed up at night and worked in the day.

One-letter prepositions 13

يَتَحَوَّلُ المَكَانُ بِاللَّيْلِ إِلَى مَكَانٍ لِلرُّعْبِ نَظَرًا لِلظَّلَامِ الشَّدِيدِ الَّذِي يُحِيطُ بِالمِنْطَقَةِ.	At night, the place turns into a sight of horror, due to the darkness that engulfs the area.
أُقِيمَتْ مُبَارَاةٌ ضِمْنَ الدَّوْرِيِّ الأُرْدُنِيِّ لِكُرَةِ القَدَمِ بِالسَّاعَةِ الخَامِسَةِ مِنْ مَسَاءِ يَوْمِ الجُمْعَةِ.	A match in the Jordanian football league was held at five o'clock on Friday.
لَا يَتَضَمَّنُ الجَدْوَلُ الجَدِيدُ إِقَامَةَ 4 مُبَارَيَاتٍ بِيَوْمٍ وَاحِدٍ.	The new schedule does not include four matches being held on one day.

البَاء is used to indicate attachment or proximity.

أَمْسَكْتُ بِيَدِ أُمِّي وَنَحْنُ نَعْبُرُ الشَّارِعَ.	I held my mother's hand as we crossed the street.
مَرَرْتُ بِمَكْتَبِ البَرِيدِ.	I passed by the post office.
يَعْمَلُ كُلُّ فَرْدٍ بِجَانِبِ الدَّوْلَةِ.	All individuals work alongside the state.
رَسَمَ الرَّئِيسُ مَلَامِحَ الخِطَّةِ لِإِقَامَةِ الدَّوْلَةِ الفِلَسْطِينِيَّةِ مُسْتَبْعِدًا المَنَاطِقَ الَّتِي يَنْوِي الاِحْتِفَاظَ بِهَا بِأَيْدِي إِسْرَائِيلَ.	The president outlined the plan for establishing a Palestinian state, excluding areas he intends to keep in Israel's hands.

البَاء is used with instruments used to perform a certain task. In this sense, it means 'with' or 'by', such as in the following:

أَكَلْتُ الحَلْوَى بِالمِلْعَقَةِ.	I ate the dessert with a spoon.
ذَهَبَتْ صَدِيقَتِي إِلَى عَمَلِهَا بِالسَّيَّارَةِ.	My friend went to her work by car.
كَتَبْتُ بِالقَلَمِ.	I wrote with a pen.
قَامَ بِإِغْلَاقِ الغُرْفَةِ بِقُفْلٍ كَبِيرٍ.	He closed the room with a big lock.

Note

Concerning the use of (البَاء) with instruments, it is also used in the expression (بسم الله), 'in the name of God', which is used by Muslims at the beginning of different activities, such as eating and working.

بِسْمِ الله أَكُلْ!
In the name of God, I eat!

بِسْمِ الله نَبْدَأُ!
In the name of God, we begin!

Also relevant to this is the same usage in the expression (أَعُوذُ بِالله), which means 'I seek God's refuge'.

الْبَاء is used with certain intransitive verbs to make them transitive, such as in the following:

قَامَ الْمُحَقِّقُ بِالْمَهَمَّةِ.	The investigator undertook the mission.
جَاءَ الطُّلَّابُ بِالْكُتُبِ إِلَى قَاعَةِ الْمُحَاضَرَاتِ.	Students brought the books to the lecture theater.
بَدَأَ الْمُنَظِّمُونَ الْحَفْلَ بِعَزْفِ السَّلَامِ الْوَطَنِيِّ.	Organizers began the event by playing the national anthem.
اِلْتَحَقَ بِجَامِعَةِ الْقَاهِرَةِ.	He joined Cairo University.

> **Note**
>
> The verbs (قَامَ and جَاءَ) are both intransitive, but when they are followed by (الْبَاء), they become transitive and assume new meanings. For example, (قَامَ) means 'to get up' (قَامَ الرَّجُلُ), but when it collocates with (الْبَاء) it means 'to undertake' (قَامَ الرَّجُلُ بِالْمَهَمَّةِ). (جَاءَ) means 'to come' (جَاءَ الرَّجُلُ), but when it collocates with (الْبَاء), it means 'to bring' (جَاءَ الرَّجُلُ بِالطَّعَامِ).

الْبَاء is used to indicate cause and justification. In this sense, it means 'of', 'for' or 'by', as in the following:

مَاتَ الْكَلْبُ بِالْجُوعِ.	The dog died of hunger.
دَخَلُوا السِّجْنَ بِالسَّرِقَةِ.	They were imprisoned for stealing.
كَانَ النَّاسُ هُنَاكَ يَمُوتُونَ بِسَرَطَانِ الرِّئَةِ.	People there were dying of lung cancer.
تُوُفِّيَ السَّائِقُ بِالسَّكْتَةِ الْقَلْبِيَّةِ.	The driver died of a heart attack.

الْبَاء is used to indicate compensation and exchange. In this sense, it means 'for' or 'with', as in the following:

اِشْتَرَيْتُ الْكِتَابَ بِدِرْهَمَيْنِ.	I bought the book for two dirhams.
اِسْتَبْدَلَ الْمَاءَ بِاللَّبَنِ.	He replaced milk with water.
بِيعَ بِرْمِيلُ النِّفْطِ بِأَكْثَرَ مِنْ 80 دُولَارًا.	A barrel of oil was sold for more than USD 80.
اِسْتَبْدَلَ مُصْطَفَى كَمَالْ أَتَاتُورْك بِالْحَرْفِ الْعَرَبِيِّ فِي اللُّغَةِ التُّرْكِيَّةِ الْحَرْفَ اللَّاتِينِيَّ!	Mustafa Kemal Ataturk replaced Arabic letters with Latin letters in Turkish!

الْبَاء is used to indicate accompaniment. In this sense, it means 'with', as in the following:

سَافَرَ بِأُسْرَتِهِ.	He traveled with his family.
اِشْتَرَيْتُ الْبَيْتَ بِأَثَاثِهِ.	I bought the house with its furniture.

One-letter prepositions 15

اِنْتَقَلَ بِأُسْرَتِهِ لِلْإِقامَةِ فِي الشَّقَّةِ الجَديدَةِ.	He moved with his family to stay in the new apartment.
هَرَبَ بِزَوْجَتِهِ وابْنَتِهِ إِلى بَريطانْيا.	He fled with his wife and daughter to Britain.

البَاء is used to express the attributes of someone or something, as in the following:

اِنْتَظَمَتْ صُفوفٌ طَويلَةٌ مِنَ المُواطِنينَ بِالمَلابِسِ التَّقْليدِيَّةِ.	There were long queues of citizens in traditional clothes.
تَمَّ تَصْويرُ الحِصانِ بِسِرْجِهِ وَلِجامِهِ.	The horse was photographed with its saddle and bridle.
المَقْصودُ هُنا هُوَ مِنْطَقَةُ الشَّرْقِ الأَوْسَطِ بِكُلِّ أَبْعادِها الجُغْرافِيَّةِ.	What is meant here is the Middle East, with all its geographical dimensions.
كانَ الثَّمَنُ يُساوي نَحْوَ دولارٍ واحِدٍ بِأَسْعارِ أَرْبَعينَ عامًا مَضَتْ.	The price was equivalent to about one dollar at the prices of forty years ago.

البَاء is used to express the manner of undertaking an action. In this sense, it is generally translated as an adverb, as in the following:

فَتَحَ البابَ بِقُوَّةٍ.	He opened the door forcefully.
لا أَحَدَ يَسْتَطيعُ الإِجابَةَ بِوُضوحٍ عَلى هَذِهِ التَّساؤُلاتِ.	No one can answer these questions clearly.
لَنْ تَسْتَطيعَ الدَّوْلَةُ تَقْديمَ الكَثيرِ مِنَ الخَدَماتِ الأُخْرى الَّتي اعْتادَ المُواطِنُ الحُصولَ عَلَيْها بِالمَجَّانِ.	The state will not be able to provide many of the services that the citizen is accustomed to obtaining free of charge
كانَ صاروخانِ قَدْ سَقَطا بِطَريقِ الخَطَأِ.	Two missiles were dropped by mistake.

البَاء is used in oaths. In this sense, it means 'by', such as in the following:

أَقْسَمَ بِاللهِ.	He swore by God.
أُقْسِمُ بِاللهِ العَظيمِ أَنْ أَقولَ الحَقَّ وَلا شَيءَ إِلَّا الحَقَّ.	I swear by Almighty God to say the truth and nothing but the truth.

Notes on the usage of البَاء

البَاء is used with a directional function in expressions, such as in (بِاتِّجاهِ), 'toward', or (بِمُحاذاةِ), 'along', as in the following:

قَرَأْتُ عَنْ تاريخِ المَسيرَةِ الكُبْرى بِاتِّجاهِ الشَّمالِ.	I read about the history of the great march to the north.

16   One-letter prepositions

يُمْكِنُ أَنْ يُؤَدِّيَ اِنْخِفَاضُ اليُورُو إِلَى زِيَادَةِ السِّيَاحَةِ بِاتِّجَاهِ أُورُوبَا.
The decline of the euro could lead to an increase in tourism to Europe.

كَانَ يَقُودُ سَيَّارَتَهُ بِمُحَاذَاةِ الشَّاطِئِ.
He was driving his car along the beach.

سَارَتِ القَوَارِبُ بِمُحَاذَاةِ النَّهْرِ وَهِيَ تَحْمِلُ عَلَى مَتْنِهَا أَلْفَ شَخْصٍ.
The boats sailed along the river, carrying a thousand people on board.

When البَاء is used with (قَبْلَ) and (بَعْدَ), it indicates the time period before or after an event, such as in the following:

سَيَبْدَأُ عَمَلُ اللَّجْنَةِ رَسْمِيًّا قَبْلَ اِنْطِلَاقِ البُطُولَةِ بِشَهْرٍ.
The committee's work will begin officially a month before the start of the championship.

وَصَلَ اللَّاعِبُونَ قَبْلَ مَوْعِدِ المُبَارَاةِ بِسَاعَاتٍ.
The players arrived hours before the match.

قَبْلَ بِدَايَةِ المِهْرَجَانِ بِأُسْبُوعٍ اِتَّصَلَ بِي المَسْؤُولُونَ عَنْ تَنْظِيمِهِ.
A week before the start of the festival, its organizers contacted me.

لَمْ تُعْرَضِ المَسْرَحِيَّةُ إِلَّا بَعْدَ وَفَاةِ الكَاتِبِ بِسَنَتَيْنِ.
The play was only shown two years after the writer's death.

البَاء is used to express adjacency in expressions such as (بِجَانِبِ) or (بِجِوَارِ), which mean 'next to' or 'near', such as in the following:

تَمَّ تَخْصِيصُ مَسَاحَةِ أَرْضٍ وَاسِعَةٍ بِجِوَارِ السُّوقِ لِلتَّوَسُّعَاتِ المُسْتَقْبَلِيَّةِ.
A large area of land near the market was allocated for future expansion.

وُجُودُهُ بِجِوَارِ زَوْجَتِهِ هُوَ الَّذِي حَالَ دُونَ عَوْدَتِهِ إِلَى وَطَنِهِ.
His presence next to his wife prevented him from returning home.

أُنْشِئَتِ المَكْتَبَةُ الَّتِي حَوَتْ 700 أَلْفِ مُجَلَّدٍ بِجَانِبِ قَصْرِ بَطْلَيْمُوس.
The library, which had 700,000 volumes, was set up next to the palace of Ptolemy.

جَلَسْتُ عَلَى آخِرِ مَقْعَدٍ بِجَانِبِ النَّافِذَةِ.
I sat on the last seat by the window.

البَاء collocates with some verbs expressing making a demand or asking, such as the following:

نَادَى الإِعْتِصَامُ بِإِسْقَاطِ النِّظَامِ.
The sit-in called for the overthrow of the regime.

طَالَبَ القَرَارُ 524 بِاِنْسِحَابِ إِسْرَائِيلَ مِنْ جَنُوبِ لُبْنَانَ كَإِحْدَى قَوَاعِدِ عَمَلِيَّةِ السَّلَامِ.
Resolution 524 called for Israel's withdrawal from southern Lebanon as a basis for the peace process.

الْبَاء collocates with some verbs expressing threatening, such as in the following:

| هَدَّدَ حِزْبُ العَمَلِ بِالإنْسِحَابِ مِنْ حُكُومَةِ الوَحْدَةِ الوَطَنِيَّةِ. | The Labour Party threatened to withdraw from the national unity government. |
| تَوَعَّدَ مُعَمَّرُ القَذَّافِي بِمُهَاجَمَةِ أَيِّ هَدَفٍ مَدَنِيٍّ أَوْ عَسْكَرِيٍّ. | Muammar Gaddafi had vowed to attack any civilian or military target. |

الْبَاء collocates with some verbs expressing saying, as in the following:

لَمْ يَتَحَدَّثِ المَسْؤُولُ بِأَيِّ جَدِيدٍ.	The official did not speak of anything new.
لَمْ يَنْطِقْ بِكَلِمَةٍ طَيِّبَةٍ بِشَأْنِ التَّكَامُلِ الأُورُوبِّيِّ.	He has not uttered a good word about European integration.
تَكَلَّمَ بِالسِّيَاسَةِ مُبَكِّرًا.	He talked about politics early.
اِعْتَرَفَ المُتَّهَمُ بِارْتِكَابِ الجَرِيمَةِ.	The defendant pleaded guilty to the crime.

الْبَاء collocates with some verbs expressing fame or reputation, such as in the following:

| هُوَ مُحَامٍ وكَاتِبٌ مِصْرِيٌّ اِشْتَهَرَ بِلَقَبِ مُحَامِي الجَمَاعَاتِ الإسْلامِيَّةِ. | He is an Egyptian lawyer and writer known as 'the lawyer of Islamic groups'. |
| عُرِفَ الرَّئِيسُ بِتَوَاضُعِهِ وَمَحَبَّتِهِ لِلجَمِيعِ. | The president was known for his humility and love for all. |

الْبَاء is used with certain negative particles to mean 'without', as in the following:

أَعْلَنَتْ مُنَظَّمَةُ "أَطِبَّاء بِلا حُدُودٍ" أَنَّ المَدَنِيِّينَ الصُّومَالِيِّينَ مَا يَزَالُونَ الضَّحَايَا الرَّئِيسِيِّينَ لِلمَعَارِكِ.	Doctors Without Borders announced that Somali civilians continue to be the main victims of the fighting.
تَتِمُّ المُوَافَقَاتُ الرَّسْمِيَّةُ لإقَامَةِ بَعْضِ المَشَارِيع بِغَيْرِ دِرَاسَاتٍ لِلمَنَاطِقِ الجُغْرَافِيَّةِ وَالمَوَاقِعِ الأَثَرِيَّةِ.	Official approval for the establishment of some projects are given without prior study of the geographical areas and archaeological sites.
مَا زَالَ المَرْكَزُ بِدُونِ كَوَادِرَ وبِدُونِ خُطَّةِ عَمَلٍ.	The center is still without cadres and without a plan of action.

الْبَاء is used with the word (المِئَة) to express a percentage, as in the following:

| يَسْتَهْلِكُ قِطَاعُ الصِّنَاعَةِ 5 بِالمِئَةِ فَقَطْ مِنَ المِيَاهِ. | Industry consumes only 5 percent of the water. |
| التَّبَادُلُ التِّجَارِيُّ مَعَ دُوَلِ الشَّرْقِ الأَوْسَطِ يُعَادِلُ 25 بِالمِئَةِ مِنْ إِجْمَالِي النَّاتِجِ المَحَلِّيِّ الأَمْرِيكِيِّ. | Trade with the Middle East is equivalent to 25 percent of the US gross domestic product. |

18 One-letter prepositions

الْبَاء is used in the construction (أَفْعِلْ بِـ) to express an exclamation, as in the following:

أَكْرِمْ بِالْأَسَاتِذَةِ!	How honorable the teachers are!
أَكْرِمْ بِالْعَرَبِ!	How generous Arabs are!

الْبَاء is used with expressions such as (نَفْس), (ذَات) and (عَيْن) for emphatic identification, as in the following:

وَقَّعَ الْمُؤَلِّفُ الْكِتَابَ بِنَفْسِهِ.	The author himself signed the book.
مَطْلُوبٌ مِنَ الْمُتَرْجِمِ أَنْ يُتَرْجِمَ عَمَلًا أَدَبِيًّا بِعَيْنِهِ.	The translator is required to translate a particular literary work.
كَيْفَ تَكُونُ الثَّقَافَةُ بِذَاتِهَا مَوْرِدًا؟	How can culture in itself be a resource?

الْبَاء is used after (هَيَّا) and (هَلُمَّ) to call someone to move, as in the following:

هَيَّا بِنَا يَا مُحَمَّدُ!	Come on, Mohammed!
هَلُمُّوا بِنَا!	Come on! Let's go!

الْبَاء is used after (إِذَا) to express surprise, as in the following:

وَإِذَا بِرِجَالِ الْأَمْنِ دَاخِلَ الصَّالَةِ يُقَرِّرُونَ إِغْلَاقَ الْأَبْوَابِ.	Suddenly, security men inside the hall decided to shut the doors.
بَعْدَمَا كَانَتِ الْأَنْبَاءُ تُشِيرُ إِلَى أَجْوَاءٍ إِيجَابِيَّةٍ وَإِذَا بِهَا تَنْقَلِبُ إِلَى تَأَزُّمٍ.	After the news indicated a positive atmosphere, it turned into a crisis.

الْبَاء is used in some negative constructions to introduce the predicate after a negative particle, as in these examples:

لَيْسَ بِخَافٍ عَلَيْكُم ضَعْفُ مُسْتَوَى الْمَعْرِفَةِ الْعَامَّةِ لَدَى الْمُوَاطِنِ الْعَادِيِّ.	The weak level of general knowledge of the average citizen is not hidden from you.
لَيْسَ بِجَدِيدٍ أَنَّ ظَاهِرَةَ أَطْفَالِ الشَّوَارِعِ وَالْأَطْفَالِ الْجَانِحِينَ تَرْجِعُ أَسَاسًا إِلَى تَمَزُّقِ الْأُسْرَةِ.	It is not new that the phenomenon of street children and delinquent children is mainly due to broken families.
لَيْسَ بِالْأَمْرِ الطَّبِيعِيِّ تَحْدِيدُ يَوْمٍ مُعَيَّنٍ بِاعْتِبَارِهِ الْيَوْمَ الَّذِي وُلِدَ فِيهِ تَيَّارٌ أَدَبِيٌّ أَوْ فَنِّيٌّ.	It is not normal to identify a specific day as the time when a literary or artistic movement was born.
لَسْتُ بِحَاجَةٍ لِأَنْ أَعْتَذِرَ عَنْ انْتِمَائِي السِّيَاسِيِّ.	I do not need to apologize for my political affiliation.

One-letter prepositions

الْبَاء is used after (مَاذَا) to ask what is the matter and to describe the condition of a person, such as in the following:

مَاذَا بِكَ؟	What's the matter with you?
مَا بِي مَنْ شَيءٍ.	Nothing.
هَلْ أَنْتَ بِخَيْرٍ؟	Are you well?
أَنَا بِأَحْسَنِ حَالٍ.	I am very well.

الْبَاء can be used to denote the meanings of other prepositions. This phenomenon is called (التَّضْمِين), and although it is not common in modern usage, we can find many examples in the Qur'an and classical poetry, as in the following:

(عَيْنًا يَشْرَبُ بِهَا عِبَادُ اللهِ) *(76:6)	"A fountain whereat drink the servants of God"*	الباء is used with the same meaning as مِن.
(فَاسْأَلْ بِهِ خَبِيرًا) (25:59)	"Ask any informed of Him!"	الباء is used with the same meaning as عَن.
(وَمِنْ أَهْلِ الْكِتَابِ مَنْ إِنْ تَأْمَنْهُ بِقِنْطَارٍ يُؤَدِّهِ إِلَيْكَ) (3:75)	"And of the People of the Book is he who, if thou trust him with a hundredweight, will restore it thee"	الباء is used with the same meaning as عَلى.

(For verses from the Qur'an, we have opted for Arberry's translation)

الْبَاء can also be used for emphasis, as in the following:

(قُلْ كَفَىٰ بِاللَّهِ شَهِيدًا بَيْنِي وَبَيْنَكُمْ) (17:96)	"Say: 'God suffices as a witness between me and you'"

In this example (الْبَاء) is redundant; that is, if it is deleted, the basic meaning does not change. However, it serves to emphasize meaning.

In sum, الْبَاء has a number of functions, including attachment, accompaniment, transitivity, causality, exchange and in oaths, among others. Moreover, it collocates with various verbs and may include the meanings of other prepositions in traditional texts such as the Qur'an.

Notes on translation

In accordance with the many functions that الْبَاء serves, it can be translated into English in many different ways, as 'in', 'at', or 'by', and 'for', among others. Moreover, in some contexts it does not appear directly in the translation. The following examples illustrate some of these possible translations.

وُلِدَ السَّيَّابُ فِي قَرْيَةٍ بِالعِرَاقِ.	As-Sayyab was born in a village in Iraq.
مَاذَا بِيَدِكَ؟	What's in your hand?
هَلْ سَنَتَقَابَلُ بِالعُطْلَةِ؟	Will we meet in the holiday?
حَضَرَ صَدِيقِي الحَفْلَ بِالمَلَابِسِ الرَّسْمِيَةِ.	My friend attended the ceremony in formal wear.
زَارَ الوَلَدُ جَدَّتَهُ بِالمَسَاءِ.	The boy visited his grandmother in the evening.
مَرَّتْ وَالِدَتِي بِالسُّوقِ.	My mother passed by the market.
وَقَفْنَا بِالبَابِ وَانْتَظَرْنَاكُمْ.	We stood by the door and waited for you.
اِهْتَدَى المُسَافِرُونَ القُدَمَاءُ بِالنُّجُومِ.	Ancient travelers were guided by the stars.
زَادَتْ أَرْبَاحُ الشَّرِكَةِ بِنِسْبَةِ 10 بِالمِئَةِ.	The company's profits increased by 10 percent.
فَتَحْتُ البَابَ بِالمِفْتَاحِ.	I opened the door with the key.
اِسْتَقْبَلْنَا الضُّيُوفَ بِالإِبْتِسَامِ.	We met the guests with a smile.
هُمْ مَعْرُوفُونَ بِكَرَمِهِمْ.	They are known for their generosity.
اِلْتَحَقَ أَخِي بِالجَيْشِ.	My brother joined the army.
قَامَتْ الجَامِعَةُ بِتَكْرِيمِ الأَوَائِلِ.	The university honored the best students.
أَمَرَ المُحَافِظُ بِرَصْفِ الطَّرِيقِ.	The governor ordered the paving of the road.
لَا تَخْرُجْ بِسُرْعَةٍ.	Do not go out quickly.
أَنَا أَكْبَرُ مِنْكَ بِسَنَةٍ وَاحِدَةٍ.	I am one year older than you.
أُحِبُّ أَنْ أَطْبُخَ طَعَامِي بِنَفْسِي.	I like to cook my own food.

البَاء with pronoun suffixes

البَاء can be followed by a noun or a pronoun. When joined to a pronoun, it becomes a prefix, and the pronoun becomes a suffix. The following section shows how different pronouns appear after the preposition.

بِهِمَا	البَاء + هُمَا		بِي	البَاء + أَنَا	
بِنَا	البَاء + نَحْنُ		بِكَ	البَاء + أَنتَ	
بِكُمْ	البَاء + أَنْتُم		بِكِ	البَاء + أَنْتِ	
بِكُنَّ	البَاء + أَنْتُنَّ		بِهِ	البَاء + هُوَ	
بِهِمْ	البَاء + هُمْ		بِهَا	البَاء + هِيَ	
بِهِنَّ	البَاء + هُنَّ		بِكُمَا	البَاء + أَنْتُمَا	

One-letter prepositions 21

اِتَّصَلُوا بِي فِي عَمَلِي.	They called me at work.
مَرْحَبًا بِكَ أَيُّهَا الأَخُ!	Welcome, Brother!
الصُّورَةُ تُذَكِّرُنِي بِهِ دَائِمًا.	The photo always reminds me of him.
كَانَتِ الْإِنْتِخَابَاتُ غَيْرَ دِيمُوقْرَاطِيَّةٍ وَفَازَ بِهَا مُؤَيِّدُو الْحُكُومَةِ.	The elections were undemocratic, and government supporters won.
لَا عَجَبَ فِي أَنْ تَفْتَرِقَ بِكُمَا السُّبُلُ بَعْدَ الزِّيَارَةِ الأُولَى.	It is no wonder that you parted ways after the first visit.
اِلْتَقَى الوَزِيرُ مَعَ اللَّاعِبَاتِ لِلتَّرحِيبِ بِهِنَّ.	The minister met with the players to welcome them.

البَاء with interrogatives and conjunctions

البَاء with interrogatives

البَاء + مَاذَا = بِمَ

بِمَ تَسْتَمْتِعُ فِي يَوْمِ الْعُطْلَةِ؟	What do you enjoy at the weekend?
بِمَ تُفَسِّرُ زِيَادَةَ الأَسْعَارِ؟	How do you explain the price increase?
بِمَ تَتَمَيَّزُ هَذِهِ الْمِنْطَقَةُ؟	What distinguishes this area?

البَاء + مَنْ = بِمَنْ

بِمَنْ تَهْتَمُّ؟	Who do you care about?
بِمَنْ تَأَثَّرْتَ؟	Who has affected you?
بِمَنْ تُرَحِّبُونَ فِي الْحَفْلِ؟	Who is welcome to attend the party?

البَاء + كَمْ = بِكَمْ

بِكَمْ هَذَا الكِتَابُ؟	How much is this book?
بِكَمْ قَمِيصُكَ؟	How much is your shirt?
بِكَمِ الدَّرَاجَةُ الجَدِيدَةُ؟	How much is the new bike?

البَاء with conjunctions

البَاء + مَا = بِمَا

ذَكَّرَنِي بِمَا نَسِيتُهُ.	He reminded me of what I forgot.
أَشْعُرُ بِمَا تَشْعُرُ بِهِ.	I feel what you feel.
تَحَسَّنَتِ الْمُؤَشِّرَاتُ الْإِقْتِصَادِيَّةُ، بِمَا فِي ذَلِكَ مُتَوَسِّطُ دَخْلِ الفَرْدِ.	Economic indicators, including average per capita income, improved.

One-letter prepositions

البَاء + مَنْ = بِمَنْ

The accident resulted in the death of ten people, including the driver.	أَسْفَرَ الحَادِثُ عَنْ مَقْتَلِ عَشَرَةِ أَشْخَاصٍ بِمَنْ فِيهِمْ السَّائِقُ.
The president does not care about anyone who disagrees with him.	لَا يَهْتَمُّ الرَّئِيسُ بِمَنْ يَخْتَلِفُ مَعَهُ فِي الرَّأْيِ.
The meeting will be held with the members who attended.	سَيُعْقَدُ الاِجْتِمَاعُ بِمَنْ حَضَرَ مِنَ الأَعْضَاءِ.

Fixed expressions with البَاء

In sum, the experience of the revolution has hardly left a democratic legacy.	بِاخْتِصَارٍ، تَجْرِبَةُ الثَّوْرَةِ لَمْ تَتْرُكْ تُرَاثًا دِيمُوقْرَاطِيًّا يُذْكَرُ.	in sum	بِاخْتِصَارٍ
Security forces dispersed the demonstration using force.	قَامَتْ قُوَّاتُ الأَمْنِ بِتَفْرِيقِ التَّظَاهُرَةِ بِاسْتِخْدَامِ القُوَّةِ.	using	بِاسْتِخْدَامِ
This situation has left an impact throughout all of the Middle East.	هَذَا المَوْقِفُ تَرَكَ أَثَارَهُ فِي مِنْطَقَةِ الشَّرْقِ الأَوْسَطِ بِأَسْرِهَا.	all of	بِأَسْرِهِ
The spokesperson for the US State Department issued important statements.	صَدَرَتْ تَصْرِيحَاتٌ هَامَّةٌ عَلَى لِسَانِ النَّاطِقِ الرَّسْمِيِّ بِاسْمِ وِزَارَةِ الخَارِجِيَّةِ الأَمْرِيكِيَّةِ.	For/in the name of	بِاسْمِ
Large-scale production is not in the best interest of producing countries in the long term, considering that oil is a limited resource.	الإِنْتَاجُ الكَبِيرُ لَيْسَ فِي مَصْلَحَةِ الدُّوَلِ المُنْتِجَةِ فِي المَدَى الطَّوِيلِ بِاعْتِبَارِ أَنَّ النِّفْطَ ثَرْوَةٌ مَحْدُودَةٌ.	considering	بِاعْتِبَارِ
The hostage wants to return to his family as quickly as possible.	يُرِيدُ الأَسِيرُ أَنْ يَعُودَ إِلَى أَهْلِهِ بِأَقْصَى سُرْعَةٍ مُمْكِنَةٍ.	as fast as possible	بِأَقْصَى سُرْعَةٍ
The UN Security Council unanimously approved a resolution that would end the crisis in Lebanon.	وَافَقَ مَجْلِسُ الأَمْنِ بِالإِجْمَاعِ عَلَى إِصْدَارِ قَرَارٍ مِنْ شَأْنِهِ أَنْ يُنْهِيَ الأَزْمَةَ فِي لُبْنَانَ.	unanimously	بِالإِجْمَاعِ

One-letter prepositions 23

بِالأَخَصّ	especially	دَعَا البَيَانُ إِلَى ضَرُورَةِ التَّحَرُّكِ السَّرِيعِ وَالفَعَّالِ لِتَحْقِيقِ السَّلَامِ مِنْ قِبَلِ رَاعِيي السَّلَامِ وَبِالأَخَصِّ الوِلَايَاتُ المُتَّحِدَةُ الأَمْرِيكِيَّة.	The statement called for the necessity of rapid and effective action to achieve peace by the sponsors of peace, especially the USA.
بِالإِضَافَةِ إِلَى	in addition to/ as well as	يَشْمُلُ البَرْنَامَجُ زِيَادَةَ فُرَصِ تَعْلِيمِ الفَتَيَاتِ وبَرَامِجَ مَحْوِ الأُمِّيَّةِ، بِالإِضَافَةِ إِلَى أَنْشِطَةِ التَّوْعِيَةِ الصِّحِّيَّةِ والثَّقَافِيَّةِ.	The program includes increasing girls' education opportunities and literacy programs, as well as health and cultural awareness activities.
بِالأَغْلَبِيَّة	by the majority	أَقَرَّ مَجْلِسُ الشَّعْبِ بِالأَغْلَبِيَّةِ مَشْرُوعَ المُوَازَنَةِ عَنِ السَّنَةِ المَالِيَّةِ المُقْبِلَةِ.	The majority of the People's Assembly approved the draft budget for the next fiscal year.
بِالإِمْكَانِ	possible	أَصْبَحَ بِالإِمْكَانِ اجْتِذَابُ المُشَاهِدِ العَرَبِيِّ بِأَعْمَالٍ تَنْطَلِقُ مِنَ الهَوِيَّةِ العَرَبِيَّةِ.	It became possible to attract Arab viewers to works based on Arab identity.
بِالتَّأْكِيدِ	certainly	بِالتَّأْكِيدِ لَا تُوجَدُ سِيَادَةٌ مِن دُونِ اسْتِقْلَالٍ.	There is certainly no sovereignty without independence.
بِالتَّالِي	Therefore	مِنْ عَوَامِلِ الاسْتِقْرَارِ والأَمْنِ فِي المِنْطَقَةِ القَضَاءُ عَلَى جَمِيعِ أَسْلِحَةِ الدَّمَارِ الشَّامِلِ، وَبِالتَّالِي يَجِبُ نَزْعُ السِّلَاحِ الشَّامِلِ والكَامِلِ فِي الشَّرْقِ الأَوْسَطِ.	One of the factors of stability and security in the region is the elimination of all weapons of mass destruction, and therefore, comprehensive and complete disarmament in the Middle East must be achieved.
بِالتَّعَاوُنِ مَعَ	in collaboration with	بِالتَّعَاوُنِ مَعَ الوَكَالَةِ الأَمْرِيكِيَّةِ لِلتَّنْمِيَةِ، تَمَّ افْتِتَاحُ شَبَكَةِ مُرَاقَبَةِ جَوْدَةِ هَوَاءِ القَاهِرَةِ.	In cooperation with the US Development Agency, a Cairo Air Quality Control Network was inaugurated.

بِالذَّاتِ	especially	كَيْفَ تُقَيِّمُونَ التَّقَدُّمَ الَّذِي حَدَثَ عَلَى صَعِيدِ العَلَاقَاتِ الثُّنَائِيَّةِ بَيْنَ المَمْلَكَةِ المُتَّحِدَةِ وَمِصْرَ، وَبِالذَّاتِ عَلَى المُسْتَوَى الِاقْتِصَادِيِّ؟	How do you assess the progress that has been made in the bilateral relations between the UK and Egypt, especially at the economic level?
بِالرَّغْمِ مِنْ (أَنَّ)	although	يَرَى مَانْدِيلَا أَنَّهُ بِالرَّغْمِ مِنْ أَنَّ الأَدْيَانَ لَا يَزَالُ يَتِمُّ إِسَاءَةُ اسْتِخْدَامِهَا غَالِبًا، إِلَّا أَنَّ هَذِهِ الأَدْيَانَ لَهَا قُوَّةٌ كُبْرَى فِي التَّوْحِيدِ وَجَلْبِ الِاحْتِرَامِ لِلْآخَرِينَ.	Mandela thinks that, although religions are still often misused, these religions have a great power to unite people and bring respect to others.
بِالضَّبْطِ	exactly	بِالضَّبْطِ فِي تَمَامِ السَّاعَةِ 8 مَسَاءً تَلْمَعُ سَمَاءُ دُبَيّ بِمُخْتَلَفِ أَلْوَانٍ وَأَشْكَالِ الأَلْعَابِ النَّارِيَّةِ.	At exactly 8 p.m., the Dubai sky glimmers with various colors and forms of fireworks.
بِالضَّرُورَةِ	necessarily	إِنَّنِي لَا أَبْحَثُ بِالضَّرُورَةِ عَنْ جَوَابٍ.	I'm not necessarily looking for an answer.
بِالطَّبْعِ	of course	وَبِالطَّبْعِ لَنْ يَرَى السَّائِحُ كُلَّ مَعَالِمِ المَدِينَةِ بِمُجَرَّدِ النَّظَرِ عَبْرَ نَوَافِذِ الحُجْرَةِ.	Of course, the tourist will not see all the landmarks of the city just by looking out of the windows of the room.
بِالعَكْسِ	vice versa	اِقْتَرَحَ الوَزِيرُ تَرْجَمَةَ بَعْضِ الكُتُبِ مِنَ العَرَبِيَّةِ إِلَى العِبْرِيَّةِ وَبِالعَكْسِ.	The minister suggested translating some books from Arabic into Hebrew and vice versa.
بِالعَكْسِ	on the contrary	كَانَ البَعْضُ يَخْشَى أَنَّ رَفْعَ حَالَةِ الطَّوَارِئِ سَيُؤَدِّي إِلَى خَلَلٍ فِي الأَمْنِ، وَلَكِنْ بِالعَكْسِ فَإِنَّ رَفْعَ حَالَةِ الطَّوَارِئِ أَدَّى إِلَى تَعْزِيزِ الأَمْنِ فِي البِلَادِ.	Some feared that lifting the state of emergency would lead to a security imbalance, but on the contrary, lifting the state of emergency has strengthened security in the country.
بِالفِعْلِ	indeed	عَارَضَتْ مِصْرُ بِالفِعْلِ الغَزْوَ العِرَاقِيَّ لِلْكُوَيْتِ.	Indeed, Egypt has opposed Iraq's invasion of Kuwait.

بِالقَطْعِ	certainly	سَيُؤَثِّرُ هَذَا الإِجْرَاءُ بِالقَطْعِ عَلَى المُوَاطِنِينَ.	This measure will certainly affect the citizens.
بِالمُقَابِلِ	in contrast/ in return	تَصِلُ اسْتِثْمَارَاتُ الأُرْدُنِيِّينَ فِي دُوَلِ الخَلِيجِ إِلَى حَوَالَي 4 بَلَايِينَ دُولَارٍ، وَبِالمُقَابِلِ، فَإِنَّ اسْتِثْمَارَاتِ هَذِهِ الدُّوَلِ فِي الأُرْدُنِ تَتَجَاوَزُ 12 بِلْيُونَ دُولَارٍ.	Jordanian investments in the Gulf countries amount to about USD 4 billion. In contrast, the investments of these countries in Jordan exceed USD 12 billion.
بِالنِّسْبَةِ إِلَى —	for —	بِالنِّسْبَةِ إِلَى الحُكُومَةِ، يُعْتَبَرُ الأَمْنُ أَكْثَرَ أَهَمِّيَّةً مِنَ التَّنْمِيَةِ الاقْتِصَادِيَّةِ.	For the government, security is more important than economic development.
بِانْتِظَامٍ	regularly	تَتَعَرَّضُ إِيرَانُ بِانْتِظَامٍ لِهَزَّاتٍ أَرْضِيَّةٍ مُدَمِّرَةٍ؛ إِذْ إِنَّ كُلَّ أَرَاضِيهَا تَقْرِيبًا عَلَى خَطِّ الزَّلَازِلِ.	Iran is regularly hit by devastating quakes, with almost all of its territory on the seismic line.
بِجَانِبِ	beside/ alongside	شَهِدَ العَامُ المُنْصَرِمُ اتِّفَاقَاتٍ آسْيَوِيَّةً كَانَ مِحْوَرُهَا الصِّينَ بِجَانِبِ الهِنْدِ وَرُوسْيَا وَبَاكِسْتَانَ.	The past year has seen Asian agreements centered on China alongside India, Russia and Pakistan.
بِجِدِّيَّةٍ	seriously	مِنَ المَفْرُوضِ عَلَيْنَا أَنْ نُفَكِّرَ بِجِدِّيَّةٍ فِي وَضْعِ خُطَّةٍ لِتَقْدِيمِ ثَقَافَتِنَا إِلَى العَالَمِ.	We must seriously consider a plan to bring our culture to the world.
بِحَاجَةٍ إِلَى	in need of	المَرَافِقُ الأَسَاسِيَّةُ بِحَاجَةٍ إِلَى تَطْوِيرٍ أَوْسَعَ لِتَلْبِيَةِ الإِقْبَالِ المُتَوَقَّعِ عَلَى السِّيَاحَةِ.	The infrastructure needs to be further developed to meet the expected demand for tourism.
بِحَسْبِ	according to	بِحَسْبِ الكَاتِبِ، لَا تَخْتَلِفُ الجَمَاعَاتُ الدِّينِيَّةُ الأُصُولِيَّةُ اليَوْمَ عَنْ مَثِيلَتِهَا أَوَاخِرَ أَيَّامِ العَرَبِ فِي الأَنْدَلُسِ.	According to the author, religious fundamentalist groups today are no different from those of late Arab days in Andalusia.
بِحَقٍّ	truly	تُعْتَبَرُ المَرْأَةُ المِصْرِيَّةُ بِحَقٍّ رَائِدَةَ نِسَاءِ العَالَمِ العَرَبِيِّ، فَهِيَ أَوَّلُ مَنْ تَعَلَّمَتْ وَعَمِلَتْ فِي كُلِّ المَجَالَاتِ.	Egyptian women are truly considered the pioneers of Arab women, as they were the first to get education and work in all fields.

26 *One-letter prepositions*

Concerning Arab–Israeli peace, the United States was not a true sponsor of peace and was always biased toward Israel.	بِخُصُوصِ السَّلامِ العَرَبِيِّ-الإِسْرَائِيلِيِّ، لَمْ تَكُنْ الوِلاَيَاتُ المُتَّحِدَةُ رَاعِيًا حَقِيقِيًّا لِلسَّلامِ وَكَانَتْ دَوْمًا مُتَحَيِّزَةً إِلَى جَانِبِ إِسْرَائِيلَ.	concerning	بِخُصُوصِ
But I am optimistic, because otherwise one cannot work in the field of bilateral relations with other countries.	وَلَكِنَّنِي مُتَفَائِلٌ، إِذْ بِخِلافِ ذَلِكَ يَتَعَذَّرُ عَلَى المَرْءِ أَنْ يَعْمَلَ فِي مَيْدَانِ العَلاقَاتِ الثُّنَائِيَّةِ مَعَ الدُّوَلِ الأُخْرَى.	otherwise	بِخِلافِ
Modern technology in turn has become a standard of progress and a goal for nations and peoples.	أَصْبَحَتِ التَّكْنُولُوجْيَا الحَدِيثَةُ بِدَوْرِهَا مِعْيَارًا لِلتَّقَدُّمِ وَغَايَةً لِلأُمَمِ وَالشُّعُوبِ.	in turn	بِدَوْرِهِ
Without freedom of opinion and expression, the press becomes worthless.	بِدُونِ حُرِّيَةِ الرَّأْيِ وَالتَّعْبِيرِ تُصْبِحُ الصَّحَافَةُ بِلا قِيمَةٍ.	without	بِدُونِ
Thus, Ahmed Zewail is considered the founder of the field of femtochemistry.	وَبِذَلِكَ، يُعْتَبَرُ أَحْمَد زُويل هُوَ مُؤَسِّسُ مَجَالِ الفِيمْتُو كِيمْيَاء.	thus	بِذَلِكَ
Although in the life of nations war is an exceptional event, preparedness for war is in fact a daily task.	بِرَغْمِ أَنَّ الحَرْبَ فِي حَيَاةِ الأُمَمِ تُعْتَبَرُ حَدَثًا اسْتِثْنَائِيًّا، لَكِنَّ الاسْتِعْدَادَ لَهَا فِي الحَقِيقَةِ هُوَ عَمَلُ كُلِّ يَوْمٍ.	despite/although	بِرَغْمِ
In the 1970s, oil prices multiplied nearly fourfold because of the Arab oil embargo.	فِي السَّبْعِينِيَّاتِ تَضَاعَفَتْ أَسْعَارُ النِّفْطِ حَوَالَي أَرْبَعَ مَرَّاتٍ بِسَبَبِ الحَظْرِ العَرَبِيِّ لِلنِّفْطِ.	because of	بِسَبَبِ
Increased defense spending raised the alarm about rising poverty rates.	زِيَادَةُ الإِنْفَاقِ الدِّفَاعِيِّ دَقَّتْ أَجْرَاسَ الخَطَرِ بِشَأْنِ تَزَايُدِ مُعَدَّلاتِ الفَقْرِ.	concerning	بِشَأْنِ
Interest rates fell sharply in 1989 under pressure from the United States.	انْخَفَضَتْ أَسْعَارُ الفَائِدَةِ بِشِدَّةٍ عَامَ 1989 تَحْتَ ضُغُوطٍ مِنَ الوِلاَيَاتِ المُتَّحِدَةِ.	strongly	بِشِدَّةٍ

One-letter prepositions 27

بِشَرْطِ	provided that	أَكَّدَ وَزِيرُ الْخَارِجِيَّةِ اسْتِعْدَادَ مِصْرَ لِلتَّعَاوُنِ الْإِقْلِيمِيِّ بِشَرْطِ تَحْقِيقِ تَقَدُّمٍ فِي عَمَلِيَّةِ السَّلَامِ.	The foreign minister confirmed Egypt's readiness for regional cooperation provided that progress is made in the peace process.
بِشَكْلٍ	in a — way	لَمْ تَتَمَكَّنِ الْمُنَظَّمَةُ مِنَ التَّحَقُّقِ بِشَكْلٍ مُسْتَقِلٍّ مِنْ عَدَدِ الضَّحَايَا.	The organization has not been able to verify independently the number of victims.
بِصُورَةٍ	in a — way	الْأَحْدَاثُ الَّتِي تَقَعُ فِي الْبِلَادِ الْعَرَبِيَّةِ الْأُخْرَى، تَنْعَكِسُ بِصُورَةٍ مُبَاشِرَةٍ أَوْ غَيْرِ مُبَاشِرَةٍ عَلَى أَوْضَاعِ الْأُرْدُنِ.	Events in other Arab countries are reflected directly or indirectly in the conditions in Jordan.
بِطَبِيعَةِ الْحَالِ	of course	بِطَبِيعَةِ الْحَالِ، إِنَّ الْخَوْضَ فِي الْمُسْتَقْبَلِ لَا يَعْنِي إِنْكَارَ الْحَاضِرِ.	Of course, talking about the future does not mean denying the present.
بِغَرَضِ	for the purpose of	يَتِمُّ الْاسْتِيرَادُ بِغَرَضِ التَّصْنِيعِ وَإِعَادَةِ التَّصْدِيرِ.	Importation is conducted for the purpose of manufacturing and re-export.
بِغَضِّ النَّظَرِ عَنْ	regardless of	يَجِبُ أَنْ تَشْمَلَ بَرَامِجُ الدِّرَاسَةِ التَّقْلِيدِيَّةِ فِي الْمَدَارِسِ وَالْجَامِعَاتِ الْكَثِيرَ مِنَ الْعُلُومِ الْإِنْسَانِيَّةِ بِغَضِّ النَّظَرِ عَنِ التَّخَصُّصِ.	Traditional study programs at schools and universities should include a lot of the humanities regardless of specialization.
بِغَيْرِ	without	كَانَ يُسَافِرُ بِغَيْرِ حَقِيبَةٍ.	He was traveling without a suitcase.
بِفَضْلِ	thanks to	بِفَضْلِ سِيَاسَةِ تَنَوُّعِ مَصَادِرِ الدَّخْلِ، اسْتَطَاعَتْ مِصْرُ أَنْ تَمْتَصَّ الْآثَارَ السَّلْبِيَّةَ لِانْخِفَاضِ عَائِدَاتِ السِّيَاحَةِ.	Thanks to the income diversification policy, Egypt was able to absorb the negative effects of low tourism revenues.
بِقَصْدِ	with the intention of	يَحْتَكِرُ بَعْضُ التُّجَّارِ السِّلَعَ بِقَصْدِ رَفْعِ الْأَسْعَارِ غَيْرِ الْمُبَرَّرِ.	Some traders monopolize goods with the intention of unjustifiably raising prices.

28 One-letter prepositions

بِكَافَّةِ	in all	مِنَ الضَّرُورِيِّ تَعْزِيزُ التَّعَاوُنِ الدَّوْلِيِّ تَحْتَ رِعَايَةِ الأُمَمِ المُتَّحِدَةِ مِنْ أَجْلِ مُكَافَحَةِ الإِرْهَابِ بِكَافَّةِ أَشْكَالِهِ.	It is necessary to strengthen international cooperation under the auspices of the United Nations to combat terrorism in all its forms.
بِلَا	without	حَاوَلْنَا بِلَا جَدْوَى!	We tried with no use!
بِمَا فِي ذَلِكَ	including	يَجِبُ أَنْ تَكُونَ عَلَاقَاتُ مِصْرَ وَالوِلَايَاتِ المُتَّحِدَةِ مُسْتَقِلَّةً عَنْ أَيِّ دَوْلَةٍ أُخْرَى بِمَا فِي ذَلِكَ اِسْرَائِيلُ.	The relations between Egypt and the United States must be independent of any other state, including Israel.
بِمَثَابَةِ	act as	كَانَتِ المُحَاضَرَةُ بِمَثَابَةِ وَصِيَّةٍ لِحَيَاةٍ أَفْضَلَ.	The talk acted as a recommendation for a better life.
بِنَفْسِ	in the same	نَسْتَطِيعُ حِمَايَةَ حُدُودِنَا بِنَفْسِ التَّكْنُولُوجِيَا مِنْ أَيَّةِ أَمْرَاضٍ أَوْ أَوْبِئَةٍ يُمْكِنُ أَنْ تَنْتَقِلَ إِلَيْهَا مِنْ دُوَلٍ مُجَاوِرَةٍ.	With the same technology, we can also protect our borders from any diseases or epidemics that can be transmitted from neighboring countries.
بِهَدَفِ	with the aim of	بِهَدَفِ إِقَامَةِ مِنْطَقَةِ تِجَارَةٍ حُرَّةٍ مَعَ الوِلَايَاتِ المُتَّحِدَةِ، ثَانِي أَكْبَرِ شَرِيكٍ تِجَارِيٍّ لِمِصْرَ، سَيَنْتَهِي البَلَدَانِ قَرِيبًا مِنْ وَضْعِ اتِّفَاقٍ يُعَزِّزُ الاِسْتِثْمَارَاتِ الأَمْرِيكِيَّةَ فِي مِصْرَ.	With the aim of establishing a free-trade zone with the United States, Egypt's second-largest trading partner, the two countries will soon conclude an agreement that will enhance US investments in Egypt.
بَهَذِهِ الطَّرِيقَةِ	in this way	بِهَذِهِ الطَّرِيقَةِ عَرَفَ شَمْبِلْيُون حَقِيقَةَ الكِتَابَةِ الهِيرُوغْلِيفِيَّةِ بِأَنَّ عَلَامَاتِهَا لَيْسَتْ كُلَّهَا رَمْزِيَّةً وَلَيْسَتْ كُلُّهَا أَبْجَدِيَّةً.	In this way, Champollion knew the truth of hieroglyphic writing: that its marks were not all symbolic and not all alphabetic.
بِوَاسِطَةِ	by	يَتِمُّ نَقْلُ الخُضَرِ مِنَ المَغْرِبِ إِلَى أُورُوبَّا بِوَاسِطَةِ الشَّاحِنَاتِ.	Vegetables are transported from Morocco to Europe by truck.

اللَّام

اللَّام is one of the most commonly used prepositions in Arabic. According to *A Frequency Dictionary of Arabic* (2011), it is the fifth-most commonly used word in Arabic. The meaning of اللَّام is closely connected to the meaning of إِلَى. They can be used interchangeably in some contexts; however, the main difference, according to Wright (1898), is that إِلَى is used more in contexts that express more concrete relations than اللَّام, which is used in more abstract contexts. It is used to serve many functions and it can be translated into English in several ways, including 'for' and 'to', among others.

> **Note**
>
> It should be noted that, when اللَّام comes at the beginning of a word with the definite article الـ, the first letter of the definite article is deleted; for example,
>
> لِ + الجَامِعَة = لِلجَامِعَة
>
> لِ + المَدِينَة = لِلمَدِينَة

اللَّام *in context*

مُنِحَتْ جَائِزَةُ نُوبِل لِلسَّلَام لِعَام 2018 لِلعِرَاقِيَّةِ نَادِيَة مُرَاد، بِفَضْلِ جُهُودِهَا لِإنْهَاءِ اسْتِخْدَامِ العُنْفِ الجِنْسِيِّ كَسِلَاحٍ فِي الحَرْب. وُلِدَتْ نَادِيَة مُرَاد عَامَ 1993 فِي قَرْيَةِ كُوجُو لِعَائِلَةٍ مِنَ الإيزِيدِيِّينَ. دَخَلَتْ قُوَّاتُ دَاعِش لِقَرْيَتِهَا عِنْدَمَا كَانَتْ فِي عُمْرِ التَّاسِعَةَ عَشَرَ وَجَمَعُوا الإيزِيدِيِّينَ ومِنْ بَيْنِهم نَادِيَة. وَلَكِن بَعْدَ سِتَّةِ أَشْهُرٍ اسْتَطَاعَتْ نَادِيَة الهَرَبَ وَتَمَكَّنَتْ مِنْ دُخُولِ مُخَيَّمٍ لِلَّاجِئِيْنَ فِي شَمَالِ العِرَاقِ. ثُمَّ اتَّصَلَتْ بِمُنَظَّمَةٍ تُسَاعِدُ الإيزِيدِيِّينَ أَتَاحَتْ لَهَا السَّفَرَ لِشَقِيقِهَا فِي أَلْمَانِيَا. وَهُنَاكَ نَشَطَتْ نَادِيَةُ لِتَوْضِيحِ الجَرَائِمِ التِي تَعَرَّضَ لَهَا الإيزِيدِيّونَ وَلِلمُطَالَبَةِ بِمُعَاقَبَةِ تَنْظِيمِ دَاعِش.

The Nobel Peace Prize for 2018 has been awarded to the Iraqi Nadia Murad for her efforts to end the use of sexual violence as a weapon of war. Nadia Murad was born in 1993 in Kuju village to a family of Yezidis. When she was 19 years old, Islamic State fighters attacked her village and rounded up the Yezidis, including Nadia. But six months later, Nadia was able to escape and managed to enter a refugee camp in northern Iraq. She then contacted an organization that helped Yezidis, which allowed her to travel to her brother in Germany. There, Nadia was active in explaining the crimes to which the Yezidis had been subjected and demanding the punishment of the Islamic State organization.

Notes on the usage of اللَّام *in context*

اللَّام is used for specification, for example, (جَائِزَةُ نُوبِل لِلسَّلَام), and for purpose, as in (جُهُودِهَا لِإنْهَاءِ اسْتِخْدَامِ العُنْفِ). It is also used with the meaning of *to*, as in (دَخَلَتْ قُوَّاتُ دَاعِش لِقَرْيَتِهَا) and is used alongside different verbs, for example, (أَتَاحَتْ لَهَا). Due to the wide array of meanings associated with this preposition, it needs to be understood in context.

Functions of اللَّام

اللَّام is used with a locative function to express a destination or direction of movement, as in the following:

يَخْرُجُونَ لِلْمُجْتَمَعِ بِتَعْلِيمٍ ثَانَوِيٍّ أَوْ جَامِعِيٍّ.	They go out into society with secondary or university education.
بَعْدَ سَنَوَاتٍ مِنَ الغُرْبَةِ، عُدْنَا لِأَرْضِ الوَطَنِ.	After years of living abroad, we returned to our homeland.
وَصَلْتُمْ لِلْجَامِعَةِ مُتَأَخِّرِينَ.	You arrived late to the university.
عَادَ السَّائِحُونَ لِلْعَاصِمَةِ بَعْدَ قَضَاءِ يَوْمَيْنِ فِي الرِّيفِ.	The tourists returned to the capital after spending two days in the countryside.

اللَّام is used with a temporal function to relate an event to a point in time, as in the following:

فِي اليَوْمِ التَّالِي لِوُصُولِي زُرْتُ أَعْمَامِي وَعَمَّاتِي.	The day after my arrival, I visited my uncles and aunts.
اِحْتَفَلَ العَالَمُ بِانْتِهَاءِ الأَلْفِيَّةِ الثَّانِيَةِ لِمِيلَادِ السَّيِّدِ المَسِيحِ.	The world celebrated the end of the second millennium of Christ's birth.
فِي الذِّكْرَى السَّنَوِيَّةِ لِرَحِيلِ الشَّاعِرِ، عُقِدَتْ نَدْوَةٌ فِي المَرْكَزِ الثَّقَافِيِّ العَرَبِيِّ.	On the anniversary of the poet's death, a symposium was held at the Arab Cultural Centre.
بَنَى المُسْلِمُونَ مَدِينَةَ البَصْرَةِ فِي السَّنَةِ الرَّابِعَةَ عَشْرَةَ لِلْهِجْرَةِ.	Muslims built the city of Basra in the fourteenth year of the Hijra.

اللَّام is used with a temporal function to express for how long an event lasted, as in the following:

اِسْتَمَرَّ زَوَاجُهُمَا لِمُدَّةِ 50 سَنَةً.	Their marriage lasted for 50 years.
زَجَّ الرَّئِيسُ بِالمُعَارِضِينَ فِي السُّجُونِ لِسِنِينَ طَوِيلَةٍ.	The president imprisoned his opponents for many years.
اِسْتَمَرَّ إِغْلَاقُ آبَارِ النَّفْطِ اللِّيبِيَّةِ لِشُهُورٍ بِسَبَبِ الحَرْبِ الأَهْلِيَّةِ.	Libya's oil wells have been closed for months by civil war.
عَمَّتْ مُظَاهَرَاتٌ أَنْحَاءَ الصِّينِ لِلْيَوْمِ الثَّانِي عَلَى التَّوَالِي.	Demonstrations were held across China for the second day in a row.

اللَّام is used to introduce the indirect object or beneficiary of a verb, as in the following:

الزِّيَارَةُ أَتَاحَتْ لَهُ فُرْصَةَ الِاسْتِمْتَاعِ بِمُشَاهَدَةِ مَجْمُوعَاتٍ رَائِعَةٍ مِنَ الشِّعَابِ المَرْجَانِيَّةِ.	The visit gave him the opportunity to enjoy watching wonderful formations of coral reefs.

One-letter prepositions 31

لَمْ تَسْمَحِ الدَّوْلَةُ العُثْمَانِيَّةُ لِأُورُوبَا سِوَى بِعَلَاقَاتٍ تِجَارِيَّةٍ.	The Ottoman Empire only allowed trade relations with Europe.
طَلَبْنَا لَكُمْ وَجَبَاتٍ سَاخِنَةً وَمَشْرُوبَاتٍ.	We ordered hot meals and drinks for you.
أَعْطَى القَانُونُ الجَدِيدُ لِلْمَرْأَةِ حَقَّ التَّرَشُّحِ إِلَى البَرْلَمَانِ.	The new law gave women the right to be elected to the parliament

اللَّام is used to ascribe something to someone or to something else, as in the following:

المَكْتَبَةُ لِلْقِرَاءَةِ.	The library is for reading.
تَمَّ تَعْيِينُ قَائِدٍ جَدِيدٍ لِلْجَيْشِ.	A new commander of the army has been appointed.
أَنْشَأَتِ الحُكُومَةُ مَعَارِضَ لِلْأَحْيَاءِ المَائِيَّةِ.	The government established exhibitions of aquatic creatures.
نَنْوِي تَأْسِيسَ رَابِطَةٍ لِلْمُثَقَّفِينَ العَرَبِ فِي الشَّتَاتِ.	We aim to establish an association of Arab intellectuals in the diaspora.

اللَّام is used to express possession, as in the following:

لِلتَّعْلِيمِ أَهَمِيَّةٌ كَبِيرَةٌ فِي المُجْتَمَعَاتِ العَرَبِيَّةِ.	Education has great importance in Arab societies.
لِي أَرْبَعَةُ إِخْوَةٍ وَأُخْتٌ وَاحِدَةٌ.	I have four brothers and one sister.
كَانَ لِلْعَنْبَرِ الأَنْدَلُسِيِّ سُوقٌ رَائِجَةٌ فِي حَوْضِ البَحْرِ المُتَوَسِّطِ.	The Andalusian amber had a popular market in the Mediterranean Basin.
كَانَ لِلدِّعَايَةِ العُثْمَانِيَّةِ ضِدَّ الاحْتِلَالِ الفَرَنْسِيِّ صَدَى لَدَى المِصْرِيِّينَ.	The Ottoman propaganda against the French occupation resonated with the Egyptians.

اللَّام is used to express giving possession, as in the following:

جَعَلَ الإِسْلَامُ لِلْمُسْلِمِينَ تَحِيَّتَهُمُ الخَاصَّةَ.	Islam gave Muslims their own greeting.
هُنَاكَ عِدَّةُ عَوَامِلَ جَعَلَتْ لِلسُّعُودِيَّةِ دَوْرًا خَاصًّا فِي البِلَادِ العَرَبِيَّةِ.	There are several factors that gave Saudi Arabia a special role in Arab countries.
أَعْطَى سُقُوطُ صَدَّامِ حُسَيْنٍ لِإِيرَانَ فُرْصَةً ذَهَبِيَّةً لِبَسْطِ نُفُوذِهَا إِلَى مَا وَرَاءَ حُدُودِهَا.	The fall of Saddam Hussein gave Iran a golden opportunity to extend its influence beyond its borders.
أَعْطَى القَانُونُ لِأَيِّ مَجْمُوعَةٍ مِنَ المُوَاطِنِينَ حَقَّ تَشْكِيلِ الأَحْزَابِ.	The law gave any group of citizens the right to form parties.

32 *One-letter prepositions*

اللَّام is used to express intention or purpose, as in the following:

سَافَرْتُ إِلَى الْقَرْيَةِ لِزِيَارَةِ عَائِلَتِي.	I traveled to the village to visit my family.
اِجْتَمَعَتْ الْوُفُودُ لِمُنَاقَشَةِ الاِتِّفَاقِيَّةِ.	The delegations met to discuss the agreement.
الْفَنَادِقُ الْكُبْرَى تَتَنَافَسُ لِجَذْبِ مَزِيدٍ مِنَ السُّيَّاحِ.	Major hotels compete among themselves to attract more tourists.
كَانَ الْفَاطِمِيُّونَ يُحَاوِلُونَ الاِسْتِيلَاءَ عَلَى بِلَادِ الشَّامِ لِتَثْبِيتِ أَقْدَامِهِمْ فِي الْمِنْطَقَةِ.	The Fatimids were trying to seize the Levant to stabilize their rule in the region.

Note

When اللَّام is used to express purpose, it can either be a preposition followed by a genitive noun or an adverbial particle followed by a verb in the subjunctive mood, such as in the following:

سَافَرْنَا إِلَى مِصْرَ لِمُشَاهَدَةِ الأَهْرَامَاتِ.
سَافَرْنَا إِلَى مِصْرَ لِنُشَاهِدَ الأَهْرَامَاتِ.

اللَّام can be used to express a reason or cause, for example, in the following:

تَوَقَّفَتْ السَّيَّارَةُ لِنَفَادِ الْوُقُودِ.	The car stopped because the fuel ran out.
تَغَيَّبَتْ عَنِ الْمُحَاضَرَةِ لِمَرَضِهَا.	She was absent from the lecture because of her illness.
غَرِقَتْ الْقَرْيَةُ لِارْتِفَاعِ مُسْتَوَى مِيَاهِ الْبَحْرِ.	The village drowned due to a high level of seawater.
تَوَقَّفَتْ حَرَكَةُ السِّيَاحَةِ فِي الْبَلَدِ لِانْدِلَاعِ الْحَرْبِ الأَهْلِيَّةِ.	The tourism movement in the country stopped due to the outbreak of civil war.

اللَّام is used to express deserving or 'having the right to', as in the following:

الْحَمْدُ لِلَّهِ.	Thank God.
الْجَائِزَةُ لِلْفَائِزِ.	The prize is for the winner.
حُرِّيَّةُ التَّعْبِيرِ حَقٌّ لِكُلِّ الْبَشَرِ.	Freedom of expression is the right of all people.

اللَّام is used with some verbs expressing saying or explaining to refer to the person who is being spoken to, as in the following examples:

قُلْتُ لَكُمُ الْحَقِيقَةَ كَامِلَةً.	I told you the whole truth.
أَكَّدَتْ لَهُمُ الطَّبِيبَةُ أَنَّ الْوَرَمَ حَمِيدٌ.	The doctor assured them that the tumor is benign.

One-letter prepositions

شَرَحْتُ لَهُ المُشْكِلَةَ وَأَوْضَحْتُ لَهُ طُرُقَ حَلِّهَا.	I explained to him the problem and ways to solve it.

اللَّام is used to express giving permission to someone, as in the following:

لَكَ أَنْ تَعِيشَ هُنَا بِأَمَانٍ.	You can live here safely.
مَا كَانَ لَكَ أَنْ تَبْقَى هُنَا لَوْلَا حِمَايَتُنَا.	You would not have been here without our protection.

Notes on usage

In transactions, (اللَّام) is used to denote a creditor while (عَلَى) is used for a debtor, as in the following:

لَنَا نِصْفُ المِيرَاثِ وَلَكُمُ النِّصْفُ.	We have half the inheritance and you have half.
لِي عَلَيْكَ أَلْفُ جُنَيْهٍ.	You owe me a thousand pounds.
لَكَ الأَمْرُ وَعَلَيَّ الطَّاعَةُ.	You command and I obey.

اللَّام can be used before the name of an author, director or composer, as in the following:

تُقَدِّمُ الجَامِعَةُ الأَمْرِيكِيَّةُ بِبَيْرُوتَ مَسْرَحِيَّةً لِلْكَاتِبِ وليم شكسبير.	The American University in Beirut presents a play by William Shakespeare.
شَاهَدْنَا فِيلْمَ "المُومْيَاء"، لِلْمُخْرِجِ شَادِي عَبْدِ السَّلَامِ.	We watched *Mummy* by Shadi Abdel Salam.
هَلْ قَرَأْتَ دِيوَانَ "الكِتَاب"، لِلشَّاعِرِ أُدُونِيس؟	Have you read *The Book* by the poet Adonis?

In a fixed expression, when preceded by (هل) and followed by a pronoun suffix, (اللَّام) is used to inquire about willingness to undertake an action, as in the following:

هَلْ لَكَ أَنْ تُعْطِينَا المَوْقِفَ الأَمْرِيكِيَّ الحَقِيقِيَّ حِيَالَ تِلْكَ القَضِيَّةِ؟	Can you tell us the real US position on this issue?
هَلْ لَكِ أَنْ تَشْرَحِي لِي وِجْهَةَ نَظَرِكِ؟	Can you explain to me your point of view?
هَلْ لَكُمْ فِي رُكُوبِ الخَيْلِ؟	Do you like to ride horses?

اللَّام can be used after (مِنْ أَيْنَ), and it can be followed by a noun or a pronoun suffix, as in the following:

مِنْ أَيْنَ لَكَ هَذَا؟	Where did you get this?
مِنْ أَيْنَ لَكِ هَذَا الثَّوْبُ الجَمِيلُ؟	Where did you get this beautiful dress?
مِنْ أَيْنَ لِلنَّاسِ بِكُلِّ هَذَا التَّفَاؤُلِ؟	Where do people get all this optimism?

اللَّام can be used after (ما) and is often followed by a pronoun suffix to ask, 'What is the matter?', as in the following:

مَا لَكَ؟	What is the matter with you?
مَا لَهُمْ؟	What is the matter with them?

اللَّام is used to express an exclamation in the expression (يا لَ). It is voweled with fatḥa, and it is used to seek help, as in the following:

يا لله لِلضُّعَفَاءِ!	Oh God! Please help the vulnerable!
يَا لَزَيْدُ!	Oh Zayd!

اللَّام is used to express an exclamation in the expression (عَجِبْتُ لِ), as in the following:

عَجِبْتُ لِمَا قَالَهُ.	I was amazed at what he said!
عَجِبْتُ لِدَعْمِ الغَرْبِ لِبَعْضِ الدِّكْتَاتُورِيِّينَ.	I was amazed at the West's support for some dictators.

اللَّام is used to mark a person for whom permission is granted, with verbs such as (أَجَازَ), (سَمَحَ) and (رَخَّصَ), as in the following:

سَمَحَ لِي وَالِدِي بِقِيَادَةِ سَيَّارَتِهِ.	My father allowed me to drive his car.
أَجَازَ الدُّسْتُورُ لِلْمُوَاطِنِينَ حَقَّ التَّظَاهُرِ السِّلْمِيِّ.	The constitution granted citizens the right to peaceful demonstration.

اللَّام can occur as a redundant preposition that can be deleted without affecting the meaning. However, although it is redundant, it serves to emphasize the meaning, as in the following:

شَكَرْتُ وَالِدَيَّ.	I thanked my parents.
شَكَرْتُ لِوَالِدَيَّ.	I thanked my parents.
الله عَالِمٌ مَا فِي الغُيُوبِ.	God knows what is unknown to people.
الله عَالِمٌ لِمَا فِي الغُيُوبِ.	God knows what is unknown to people.

One-letter prepositions 35

اللَّام can be used to manipulate a genitive construction (الإضافة) so that the first noun can remain undefined or can be modified by an adjective or to make a long genitive construction shorter, as in the following:

وَجَدْتُ صُورَةً لِأُسْرَتِي.	I found a photo of my family.
وَجَدْتُ صُورَةً قَدِيمَةً لِأُسْرَتِي.	I found an old photo of my family.
الهَدَفُ الأَوَّلُ لِمَشْرُوعِ مُوَازَنَةِ الحُكُومَةِ هُوَ سَدَادُ الدُّيُونِ الخَارِجِيَّةِ.	The main goal of the government budget proposal is to repay foreign debts.

> **Note**
>
> Long genitive constructions can be ambiguous when followed by adjectives, as there might be more than one noun that the adjective could potentially refer to, as in the following:
>
> هَدَفُ مَشْرُوعِ مُوَازَنَةِ الحُكُومَةِ الأَوَّلُ
>
> In this sentence, the adjective (الأَوَّلُ) can potentially describe either (هَدَفُ) or (مَشْرُوعِ). However, ل can be used to shorten the iḍāfa construction and to modify the appropriate noun with the adjective, thus removing ambiguity, as in
>
> الهَدَفُ الأَوَّلُ لِمَشْرُوعِ مُوَازَنَةِ الحُكُومَةِ

اللَّام is used with the demonstratives (ذَلِكَ) or (هَذَا) to make the expressions (لِذَلِكَ) or (لِهَذَا), which mean 'thus' or 'for this reason', as in the following:

المَرَضُ لَا يَنْتَقِلُ مِنْ إِنْسَانٍ إِلَى آخَرَ وَلِذَلِكَ لَا تُوجَدُ خُطُورَةٌ فِي التَّعَامُلِ مَعَ المَرِيضِ.	The disease does not spread from person to person, and therefore, there is no danger in interacting with the patient.
وَصَلْتُ البَلَدَ مِنْ أُسْبُوعٍ فَقَطْ وَلِذَلِكَ لَا أَسْتَطِيعُ إِرْشَادَكَ.	I arrived in the country just a week ago, so I cannot guide you.
انْسَحَبَ الوَفْدُ السُّودَانِي مِنَ المُفَاوَضَاتِ، وَلِهَذَا تَمَّ تَأْجِيلُ الجَلْسَةِ لِلْغَدِ.	The Sudanese delegation withdrew from negotiations, so the meeting was postponed for tomorrow.

اللَّام is used with (أَنَّ), to make (لِأَنَّ), which means 'because', as in the following:

تَرَاجَعَ الاقْتِصَادُ لِأَنَّ السِّيَاسَاتِ الاقْتِصَادِيَّةَ فَاشِلَةٌ.	The economy is deteriorating because economic policies are failing.
أَعْجَبَنِي هَذَا الكِتَابُ لِأَنَّهُ يُعَبِّرُ عَنْ أَفْكَارٍ إِيجَابِيَّةٍ.	I liked this book because it expresses positive ideas.
تَوَقَّفَتِ المُفَاوَضَاتُ لِأَنَّ جَمِيعَ الأَطْرَافِ تَرْفُضُ المُصَالَحَةَ.	Negotiations have been stalled because all parties reject reconciliation.

Notes on translation

اللام can be translated in different ways according to the context of its usage. The following examples illustrate some of the different ways of translating it.

ذَهَبْنَا لِلْمَدِينَةِ.	We headed for the city.
وَهَبَ الْبَيْتَ لِأَبْنَائِهِ.	He gave his children the house.
لَهُمْ أَصْدِقَاءُ كَثِيرُونَ.	They have many friends.
قَالَ لِي الْحَقِيقَةَ.	He told me the truth.
سَمَحُوا لَنَا بِالدُّخُولِ.	They let us in.
لَكَ أَنْ تُغَادِرَ.	You can leave.
يَا لَلْعَجَبِ!	Oh, the wonder!
بَدَأْتُ التَّدْرِيسَ فِي السَّنَةِ التَّالِيَةِ لِتَخَرُّجِي.	I started teaching the year after my graduation.
اِنْتَظَرْنَا لِيَوْمَيْنِ قَبْلَ السَّفَرِ.	We waited for two days before traveling.
فَتَحْنَا مَصْنَعًا لِمَلَابِسِ الْأَطْفَالِ.	We opened a children's clothes factory.
طَلَبَ مُقَابَلَتِي لِأَمْرٍ عَاجِلٍ.	He asked to see me about an urgent matter.
وَقَعَ لِي حَادِثٌ بَسِيطٌ.	I had a minor accident.
أَعْدَدْنَا لَكُم الْعَشَاءَ.	We prepared dinner for you.
أُحِبُّ قِرَاءَةَ قِصَصٍ لِنَجِيب مَحْفُوظ.	I like reading the stories of Naguib Mahfouz.
قَرَّرَتْ عَدَمَ الْحُضُورِ لِمَرَضِهَا.	She decided not to come, due to her illness.
مَا لَكَ؟	What's the matter with you?

اللام with pronoun suffixes

When اللام is joined to a pronoun, the pronoun becomes a suffix, and the pronunciation of (اللام) changes from (لِ) to (لَ), with the exception of the suffix (ي), 'me'. The following table shows how different pronouns appear after the preposition.

لَهُمَا	اللام + هما	لِي	اللام + أنا
لَنَا	اللام + نحن	لَكَ	اللام + أنتَ
لَكُم	اللام + أنتم	لَكِ	اللام + أنتِ
لَكُنَّ	اللام + أنتن	لَهُ	اللام + هو
لَهُم	اللام + هم	لَهَا	اللام + هي
لَهُنَّ	اللام + هنّ	لَكُمَا	اللام + أنتما

لَمْ تُتَحْ لِي الفُرْصَةُ لِلتَّعَرُّفِ عَلَى الجَمِيعِ.	I did not have the chance to get to know everyone.
نَحْنُ نُعَبِّرُ عَنْ آرَائِنَا حِيَالَ القَضَايَا الَّتِي تُشَكِّلُ أَهَمِيَّةً بِالنِّسْبَةِ لَنَا كَقَضَايَا حُقُوقِ الإِنْسَانِ.	We express our views on issues that are important to us, such as human rights issues.

Art has an important mission.	الفَنُّ لَهُ رِسَالَةٌ هَامَّةٌ.
Her husband brought her a precious gift.	أَحْضَرَ لَهَا زَوْجُهَا هَدِيَّةً ثَمِينَةً.
In the novel, there are two fundamental issues with important cultural and political connotations.	فِي الرِّوَايَةِ قَضِيَّتَانِ أَسَاسِيَّتَانِ لَهُمَا دَلَالَاتٌ ثَقَافِيَّةٌ وَسِيَاسِيَّةٌ مُهِمَّةٌ.

اللام with interrogatives and conjunctions

اللام with interrogatives

اللام + مَا = لِمَ
اللام + مَاذَا = لِمَاذَا

Why are you surprised?	لِمَ العَجَبُ؟
Why negotiate?	لِمَ التَّفَاوُضُ؟
Why did universities raise tuition fees?	لِمَاذَا قَامَتِ الجَامِعَاتُ بِرَفْعِ رُسُومِ الدِّرَاسَةِ؟
Why have the political situations in the Middle East deteriorated?	لِمَاذَا تَدَهْوَرَتِ الأَوْضَاعُ السِّيَاسِيَّةُ فِي الشَّرْقِ الأَوْسَطِ؟

اللام + مَنْ = لِمَنْ

Whose book is this?	لِمَنْ هَذَا الكِتَابُ؟
For whom do the bells toll?	لِمَنْ تَدُقُّ الأَجْرَاسُ؟
To whom is your message directed?	لِمَنْ تُوَجِّهُ رِسَالَتَكَ؟
Who will be awarded the prize?	لِمَنْ سَتُمْنَحُ الجَائِزَةُ؟

اللام with conjunctions

اللام + ما = لِمَا

The government should listen to what protesters say.	عَلَى الحُكُومَةِ أَنْ تُنْصِتَ لِمَا يَقُولُهُ المُحْتَجُّونَ.
According to what is being prepared, the elections will not take place in a democratic atmosphere.	وِفْقًا لِمَا يَجْرِي الإِعْدَادُ لَهُ، لَنْ تَتِمَّ الِانْتِخَابَاتُ فِي جَوٍّ دِيمُوقْرَاطِيٍّ.

اللام + مَن = لِمَنْ

The grant applicant must be a recent graduate with excellent grades.	يُشْتَرَطُ لِمَنْ يَتَقَدَّمُ لِلْحُصُولِ عَلَى المِنَحِ أَنْ يَكُونَ مُتَخَرِّجًا حَدِيثًا بِتَقْدِيرٍ مُمْتَازٍ.
Awards were given to those who deserve them.	أُعْطِيَتِ الجَوَائِزُ لِمَنْ يَسْتَحِقُّونَهَا.

38   One-letter prepositions

Fixed expressions with اللام

English	Gloss	Arabic	Prep
Projects have been established to benefit from groundwater in the desert.	for / to	أُقِيمَتْ مَشْرُوعَاتٌ لِأَجْلِ الاسْتِفَادَةِ مِنَ المِيَاهِ الجَوْفِيَّةِ فِي الصَّحْرَاءِ.	لِأَجْلِ
It is necessary to empower women in society for economic, political and social considerations.	for considerations	مِنَ الضَّرُورِيِّ تَمْكِينُ المَرْأَةِ فِي المُجْتَمَعِ لِاعْتِبَارَاتٍ اقْتِصَادِيَّةٍ وَسِيَاسِيَّةٍ واجْتِمَاعِيَّةٍ.	لِاعْتِبَارَاتٍ
The election results were cancelled because voter turnout was under 50 percent of the total number of registered voters.	because	تَمَّ إلْغَاءُ نَتَائِجِ الانْتِخَابَاتِ لِأَنَّ نِسْبَةَ مُشَارَكَةِ النَّاخِبِينَ كَانَتْ أَقَلَّ مِنْ خَمْسِينَ فِي المِئَةِ مِنْ مَجْمُوعِ المُسَجَّلِينَ.	لِأَنَّ
Fortunately, there was no one in the building when the fire broke out.	fortunately	لِحُسْنِ الحَظِّ لَمْ يَكُنْ هُنَاكَ أَحَدٌ فِي البِنَايَةِ حِينَ انْدَلَعَ الحَرِيقُ.	لِحُسْنِ الحَظِّ
It was raining too heavily, so traffic was disrupted.	so	هَطَلَتِ الأَمْطَارُ غَزِيرَةً جِدًّا؛ لِذَا تَعَطَّلَتْ حَرَكَةُ مُرُورِ السَّيَّارَاتِ.	لِذَا
Income from foreign tourism increased last year, and thus, overall economic performance improved.	thus	زَادَ الدَّخْلُ مِنَ السِّيَاحَةِ الخَارِجِيَّةِ فِي العَامِ المَاضِي، وَلِذَلِكَ تَحَسَّنَ الأَدَاءُ الاقْتِصَادِيُّ بِشَكْلٍ عَامٍ.	لِذَلِكَ
Unfortunately, the political experience in most Arab countries seems to lack democracy and transparency.	unfortunately	لِسُوءِ الحَظِّ، تَبْدُو التَّجْرِبَةُ السِّيَاسِيَّةُ فِي أَغْلَبِ بُلْدَانِ المِنْطَقَةِ العَرَبِيَّةِ تَفْتَقِرُ إِلَى الدِّيمُوقْرَاطِيَةِ والشَّفَافِيَّةِ.	لِسُوءِ الحَظِّ
The economic recession will not last forever.	forever	الرُّكُودُ الاقْتِصَادِيُّ لَنْ يَسْتَمِرَّ لِلْأَبَدِ.	لِلْأَبَدِ
Unfortunately, there was not enough awareness of the real causes of the problem, so the solutions were unrealistic.	unfortunately	لِلْأَسَفِ لَمْ يَكُنْ هُنَاكَ وَعْيٌ كَافٍ بِالأَسْبَابِ الحَقِيقِيَّةِ لِلْمُشْكِلَةِ، فَكَانَتِ الحُلُولُ غَيْرَ وَاقِعِيَّةٍ.	لِلْأَسَفِ
I've just left the meeting.	just	خَرَجْتُ لِلتَّوِّ مِنَ الاجْتِمَاعِ.	لِلتَّوِّ
The government's position has become extremely awkward after discussing its human rights record.	very / extremely	أَصْبَحَ مَوْقِفُ الحُكُومَةِ حَرِجًا لِلْغَايَةِ بَعْدَ مُنَاقَشَةِ سِجِلِّ حُقُوقِ الإنْسَانِ فِي البَلَدِ.	لِلْغَايَةِ

One-letter prepositions 39

Mathematics and algebra books were translated from Arabic into Latin in the twelfth century AD.	تُرْجِمَتْ كُتُبُ الحِسَابِ وَالجَبْرِ مِنَ العَرَبِيَّةِ إِلَى اللَّاتِينِيَّةِ فِي القَرْنِ الثَّانِي عَشَرَ لِلْمِيلَادِ.	AD	لِلْمِيلَادِ
Arab culture was promoted during the first three centuries of the Hijra.	تَعَزَّزَتِ الثَّقَافَةُ العَرَبِيَّةُ خِلَالَ القُرُونِ الثَّلَاثَةِ الأُولَى لِلْهِجْرَةِ.	of the Hijra	لِلْهِجْرَةِ
The player was not able to train because of his injury, so he had to postpone the game.	لَمْ يَكُنِ اللَّاعِبُ قَادِرًا عَلَى مُمَارَسَةِ تَدْرِيبَاتِهِ بِسَبَبِ إِصَابَتِهِ، وَلِهَذَا اُضْطُرَّ إِلَى تَأْجِيلِ المُبَارَاةِ.	for this reason	لِهَذَا
I waited for you for a long time.	اِنْتَظَرْتُكُم لِوَقْتٍ طَوِيلٍ.	for a long time	لِوَقْتٍ طَوِيلٍ
The country was colonized for a long time.	خَضَعَ البَلَدُ لِلِاسْتِعْمَارِ لِزَمَنٍ طَوِيلٍ.	for a long time	لِزَمَنٍ طَوِيلٍ
China has come close to reaching the World Cup finals for the first time in its history.	اِقْتَرَبَتِ الصِّينُ مِنْ بُلُوغِ نِهَائِيَّاتِ كَأْسِ العَالَمِ لِكُرَةِ القَدَمِ لِلْمَرَّةِ الأُولَى فِي تَارِيخِهَا.	for the first time	لِلْمَرَّةِ الأُولَى
At first glance, the judge looks like he is thirty years old.	لِلْوَهْلَةِ الأُولَى يَبْدُو القَاضِي وَكَأَنَّهُ فِي الثَّلَاثِينَ مِنْ عُمْرِهِ.	at first glance	لِلْوَهْلَةِ الأُولَى
We did not think for a moment about the consequences of our decision.	لَمْ نُفَكِّرْ لِلَحْظَةٍ فِي عَوَاقِبِ قَرَارِنَا.	for a moment	لِلَحْظَةٍ

الكَاف

Most grammarians classify الكَاف as a preposition, as it is made up of one letter; however, some grammarians argue that it can be classified as a noun that is formally undeveloped. الكَاف has few usages in Arabic, mainly to express similarity. It is a synonym of (مِثْل), and it means 'as' or 'like'. It cannot be followed by a pronoun suffix.

الكاف *in context*

فِي عَمَلِي كَمُصَوِّرٍ صَحَفِيٍّ، أُسَافِرُ كَمَا أُرِيدُ، فَأَنَا كَالطَّيْرِ المُهَاجِرِ أَتَنَقَّلُ مِنْ مَكَانٍ إِلَى مَكَانٍ طَوَالَ العَامِ. وَفِي عَمَلِي، زُرْتُ قَارَّاتٍ كَثِيرَةً كَأَمْرِيكَا وَأُورُوبَا وَإِفْرِيقْيَا وَآسِيا كَمَا لَوْ كُنْتُ بِلَا وَطَنٍ أَوْ عُنْوَانٍ أَوْ كَأَنَّ العَالَمَ هُوَ وَطَنِي. وَيُعَزِّزُ هَذَا

الشُّعُورُ حُبِّي لِلتَّرْحَالِ، كَمَا أَنَّنِي وَحِيدٌ بِلَا أَهْلٍ، فَلَا يَرْبِطُنِي بِوَطَنِي الأُمِّ إِلَّا بَعْضُ الذِّكْرَيَاتِ الْبَعِيدَةِ.

> In my work as a news photographer, I travel as I want. I am like a migrant bird; I move from place to place throughout the year. In my work, I visited many continents, such as America, Europe, Africa and Asia, as if I had no homeland or address, or as if the world was my homeland. This feeling is strengthened by my love for travels; moreover, I am a lonely person with no family and nothing connects me to my homeland except some distant memories.

Notes on the usage of الكَاف in context

The preposition الكَاف is used in limited contexts, particularly to express similarity, as in (عَمَلِي كَمُصَوِّرٍ), and it can be used to express 'in the capacity of', such as in (أَنَا كَالطَّيْرِ), and when giving examples, for example, in (قَارَاتٍ كَثِيرَةً كَأَمْرِيكَا وَأُورُوبَا). It is also used in some compounds, such as (كَمَا، كَأَنَّ).

Functions of الكَاف

الكَاف is used to express similarity, as in the following cases:

سَيَظَلُّ الإِصْلَاحُ الدِّيْمُوقْرَاطِيُّ فِي الْعَالَمِ الْعَرَبِيِّ كَالسَّرَابِ.	Democratic reform in the Arab world will continue to look like a mirage.
تَفَاقَمَتِ الْمُشْكِلَةُ كَكُرَةِ الثَّلْجِ.	The problem snowballed.
أَخَذَتِ الشَّائِعَاتُ تَنْتَشِرُ كَالنَّارِ فِي الْهَشِيمِ.	Rumors spread like wildfire.
أَعْرِفُ صَدِيقَتِي كَكِتَابٍ مَفْتُوحٍ.	I know my friend like an open book.

الكَاف is also used in similes, such as the following:

تَارِيخُ الْحِزْبِ نَظِيفٌ كَالثَّلْجِ.	The history of the party is as clear as ice.
أَنْتَ بَطِيءٌ كَالسُّلَحْفَاةِ.	You are as slow as a tortoise.

الكَاف is used to express roles and positions, with the meaning of 'as' or 'in the capacity of'. In this sense, it is often followed by a noun that expresses a role, as in the following:

كَأَمِينٍ عَامٍ لِلْمُنَظَّمَةِ الدَّوْلِيَّةِ، أَعْرَبَ عَنْ قَلَقِهِ مِنْ قَمْعِ التَّظَاهُرَاتِ السِّلْمِيَّةِ.	As secretary-general of the international organization, he expressed concerns about the suppression of peaceful demonstrations.
هَذَا أَوَّلُ مَقَالٍ لِي أَكْتُبُهُ كَرَئِيسٍ لِلتَّحْرِيرِ.	This is the first article I write as editor-in-chief.

يُدْرِكُ كِبَارُ ضُبَّاطِ الْقُوَّاتِ الْمُسَلَّحَةِ أَنَّهُمْ لَنْ يَسْتَطِيعُوا تَنْصِيبَ جِنِرَالٍ آخَرَ كَرَئِيسٍ لِلْبِلَادِ.	Senior military officers know that they will not be able to install another general as president.
كَسَفِيرٍ لِمِصْرَ فِي السُّودَانِ أَحْلُمُ بِأَنْ تَكُونَ الْعَلَاقَاتُ بَيْنَ الْبَلَدَيْنِ عَلَى أَحْسَنِ وَجْهٍ.	As an ambassador from Egypt in Sudan, I dream that relations between the two countries will be at their best.

الكاف is used to elaborate or give examples, in the sense of 'like' or 'such as', as in the following:

هَلْ وَصَلَ الْإِنْسَانُ أَحَدَ الْكَوَاكِبِ كَالْمِرِّيخِ أَوْ عُطَارِدٍ؟	Have humans reached planets like Mars or Mercury?
تَطَوَّرَتْ أَنْشِطَةُ التَّرْجَمَةِ مِنَ اللُّغَاتِ الْأَجْنَبِيَّةِ إِلَى اللُّغَاتِ الشَّرْقِيَّةِ كَالْفَارِسِيَّةِ وَالْأُرْدُو وَالتُّرْكِيَّةِ.	Translation activities from foreign languages into Eastern languages such as Persian, Urdu and Turkish have developed.
تَمَّ الْكَشْفُ عَنْ مَعَادِنَ كَالرَّصَاصِ وَالزِّئْبَقِ وَالزَّرْنِيخِ فِي الْأَسْمَاكِ.	Minerals such as lead, mercury and arsenic have been detected in fish.
يَنْبَغِي عَلَى الْحُكُومَةِ تَوْفِيرُ الْمُسْتَلْزَمَاتِ الْأَسَاسِيَّةِ كَالتَّعْلِيمِ وَالنَّقْلِ وَالْمُوَاصَلَاتِ وَالزِّرَاعَةِ وَالصِّنَاعَةِ وَالْمِيَاهِ وَالْكَهْرُبَاءِ.	The government should provide basic necessities such as education, transport, communications, agriculture, industry, water and electricity.

Notes on usage

الكاف is used with the conjunction (أنّ) to make (كأنّ), which means 'as if', as in the following:

كَأَنَّ الْهَيْمَنَةَ الْأَمْرِيكِيَّةَ لَا تَكْفِي حَتَّى تُضَافُ إِلَيْهَا الْهَيْمَنَةُ الْفَرَنْسِيَّةُ.	As if American hegemony was not enough, now there is also French hegemony.
كَأَنَّ أَدَبَ الْأَطْفَالِ لَمْ يُحَقِّقْ أَيَّ تَقَدُّمٍ فِي الْعَالَمِ الْعَرَبِيِّ.	As if children's literature did not achieve any progress in the Arab world.
كَأَنَّ الزَّمَنَ تَوَقَّفَ.	As if time stopped.
كَأَنَّ الْفَضِيحَةَ الَّتِي تَعْصِفُ بِالْحُكُومَةِ لَيْسَتْ كَافِيَةً.	As if the scandal in the government is not enough.

الكاف is used with the demonstrative pronoun (ذَلِكَ) to make (كَذَلِكَ), which means 'also' or 'as well as', as in the following:

تَمْتَلِكُ مِنْطَقَةُ الشَّرْقِ الْأَوْسَطِ ثُلْثَيِ الْاِحْتِيَاطِيِّ الْعَالَمِيِّ مِنَ النَّفْطِ وَكَذَلِكَ ثُلْثَ الْاِحْتِيَاطِيِّ الْعَالَمِيِّ مِنَ الْغَازِ الطَّبِيعِيِّ.	The Middle East has two-thirds of the world's oil reserves and also one-third of the world's natural gas reserves.

غَالِبِيَّةُ الْمَحَاصِيلِ وَخُصُوصًا الْخُضْرَوَاتِ وَكَذَلِكَ الْفَوَاكِهَ تَتَطَلَّبُ الْكَثِيرَ مِنَ الْمِيَاهِ.

The majority of crops, especially vegetables and fruits, require a lot of water.

حَظِيَتْ بَغْدَادُ بِاهْتِمَامِ الرَّحَّالَةِ وَالْمُؤَرِّخِينَ الْمُسْلِمِينَ وَكَذَلِكَ عَدَدٍ مِنَ الْمُسْتَشْرِقِينَ الْأُورُوبِيِّينَ.

Baghdad has attracted the attention of Muslim travelers and historians as well as a number of European orientalists.

تَسْعَى سِيَاسَاتُ دُوَلِ مَجْلِسِ التَّعَاوُنِ الْخَلِيجِيِّ وَكَذَلِكَ الدُّوَلِ الْعَرَبِيَّةِ الْأُخْرَى إِلَى إِقَامَةِ أَفْضَلِ الْعَلَاقَاتِ الْمُمْكِنَةِ مَعَ الْغَرْبِ.

The policies of the GCC and other Arab countries seek to establish the best possible relations with the West.

الكاف is used with the indefinite relative pronoun (مَا) to make (كَمَا), which is very common in usage in Arabic in the sense of 'as' or 'as well as'. (كَمَا) can be followed by a number of constructions, such as in the following:

- كَمَا can be followed by a verb, such as in

طَالَبَتِ الْمُنَظَّمَةُ بِوَقْفِ الْعُدْوَانِ فَوْرًا، كَمَا طَالَبَتْ بِرَفْعِ الْحِصَارِ الْمَفْرُوضِ عَلَى الْبَلَدِ.

The organization called for an immediate end to the aggression as well as an end to the siege imposed on the country.

كَمَا أَظْهَرَتِ النَّتَائِجُ أَنَّ 90% يُؤَيِّدُونَ السِّيَاسَةَ الْاِقْتِصَادِيَّةَ وَبَرْنَامَجَ الْإِصْلَاحِ الْاِقْتِصَادِيِّ.

The results also showed that 90% support economic policy and the economic reform program.

يَحْكِي لِي جَدِّي التَّارِيخَ كَمَا شَاهَدَهُ.

My grandfather tells me the history as he had seen it.

كَمَا تَعْلَمُ فَإِنَّ مُنَظَّمَةَ الْوَحْدَةِ الْإِفْرِيقِيَّةِ تَوَلَّتْ هَذِهِ الْمَسْأَلَةَ وَحَدَثَ تَقَدُّمٌ فِي جُهُودِهَا.

As you know, the Organization of African Unity has taken up this issue and progress has been made in its efforts.

- كَمَا can be followed by a complete nominal sentence, as in the following:

يَجِدُ الزَّائِرُ فِي الْأَمَاكِنِ السِّيَاحِيَّةِ الْمُهِمَّةِ أَسْمَاءً عَرَبِيَّةً كَمَا هُوَ الْحَالُ فِي مَزَارِ الْقِدِّيسِ نَاعُومٍ.

Visitors to important tourist attractions find Arabic names as they do in the San Na'om Shrine.

سَتَجِدُ تِلْكَ الْقُوَى فِي الْجَيْشِ خِيَارًا أَفْضَلَ مِنَ الْإِسْلَامِيِّينَ، كَمَا هُوَ الْوَضْعُ فِي الْحَالَةِ الْجَزَائِرِيَّةِ.

These forces will find the army a better option than the Islamists, as is the case in Algeria.

مَنَعَ الْحُكَّامُ الْجُدُدُ الْبَنَاتِ مِنَ التَّوَجُّهِ إِلَى الْمَدَارِسِ، كَمَا هُوَ مُطَبَّقٌ فِي الْمَنَاطِقِ الْأَفْغَانِيَّةِ الْأُخْرَى.

The new rulers have prevented girls from going to school, as is the case in other Afghan areas.

هُنَاكَ بُلْدَانٌ وَضَعَتْ نَفْسَهَا تَحْتَ مِظَلَّةِ الْإِمْبْرِيَالِيَّةِ الْغَرْبِيَّةِ، كَمَا الْحَالُ فِي هُونْغ كُونْغ وَتَايْوَانَ وَكُورِيَا الْجَنُوبِيَّةِ.

There are countries that have placed themselves under the umbrella of Western imperialism, as in Hong Kong, Taiwan and South Korea.

One-letter prepositions 43

- كَمَا can be followed by a noun or a pronoun. It is worth noting that this single noun or pronoun often represents a contracted sentence, as in the following:

إِنَّنِي إِمَّا أَنْ أَقْبَلَ الْعَمَلَ كَمَا هُوَ أَوْ أَرْفُضَهُ.	I either accept the work as it is or reject it.
اِبْتَعَدَتِ الْقِيَادَةُ الْفِلَسْطِينِيَّةُ، كَمَا الْقِيَادَاتُ الْعَرَبِيَّةُ الْأُخْرَى، عَنِ الْأَهْدَافِ الْاِسْتِرَاتِيجِيَّةِ.	The Palestinian leadership, like other Arab leaders, has moved away from strategic objectives.
التَّرْجَمَةُ الْكَامِلَةُ، كَمَا الْحَقِيقَةُ الْمُطْلَقَةُ، شَيْءٌ لَا وُجُودَ لَهُ.	A perfect translation, as absolute truth, is something that does not exist.
هِيَ تُخَاطِبُ الْإِسْرَائِيلِيِّينَ كَمَا الْعَرَبَ.	It speaks to the Israelis as well as the Arabs.

- كَمَا can be followed by a prepositional phrase, as in the following:

فِي الْمِنْطَقَةِ الْعَرَبِيَّةِ، كَمَا فِي سَائِرِ الْمَنَاطِقِ فِي الْعَالَمِ، يَبْرُزُ مَوْضُوعُ الْأَقَلِّيَّاتِ فِي النِّقَاشَاتِ الثَّقَافِيَّةِ وَالسِّيَاسِيَّةِ وَالْاِجْتِمَاعِيَّةِ.	In the Arab region, as in other regions of the world, the issue of minorities is highlighted in cultural, political and social debates.
فِي الْبِلَادِ الْعَرَبِيَّةِ كَمَا فِي بَقِيَّةِ الْعَالَمِ، لَا تَزَالُ التَّنْمِيَةُ تُشَكِّلُ مِحْوَرًا أَسَاسِيًّا لِلسِّيَاسَاتِ.	In the Arab countries as well as in the rest of the world, development remains a central focus of policies.
يَرَى الْاِتِّحَادُ الْأُورُوبِيُّ أَنَّ عَمَلِيَّةَ السَّلَامِ هِيَ فِي مَصْلَحَةِ إِسْرَائِيلَ كَمَا فِي مَصْلَحَةِ الْفِلَسْطِينِيِّينَ.	The European Union believes that the peace process is in the interests of Israel and in the interests of Palestinians.
بَلَدُنَا فِي خِدْمَةِ السَّلَامِ فِي الشَّرْقِ الْأَوْسَطِ كَمَا فِي بَقِيَّةِ أَنْحَاءِ الْعَالَمِ.	Our country is in the service of peace in the Middle East as in the rest of the world.

- كَمَا can be followed by (لو) to make a hypothetical statement, and it then means 'as if', as in the following:

كَانَتِ الْإِنْفِجَارَاتُ هَائِلَةً حَتَّى أَنَّنَا شَعَرْنَا كَمَا لَوْ كَانَ هُنَاكَ زِلْزَالٌ.	The explosions were so huge that we felt as if there was an earthquake.
كُنْتُ أَتَصَرَّفُ كَمَا لَوْ كُنْتُ مَرِيضَةً.	I was acting as if I were sick.
يَبْدُو الْأَمْرُ كَمَا لَوْ أَنَّ لَعْنَةً تُلَاحِقُ الْبِلَادَ.	It looks as if a curse is afflicting the country.
أَتَكَلَّمُ كَمَا لَوْ كُنْتُ أَهْمِسُ مَعَ نَفْسِي.	I speak as if I were whispering to myself.

الكاف cannot be followed by pronoun suffixes.

44   One-letter prepositions

وَاو وبَاء وتَاء القَسَم

An oath (القَسَم) is used to emphasize a statement and to remove any doubt in the mind of the recipient. The oath is expressed by three particles (وَاو وبَاء وتَاء القَسَم). They are followed by God or words that refer to Him. An oath requires a complement (جواب القَسَم), which can be either a nominal or a verbal sentence.

وَاللهِ لَأَفْعَلَنَّ الخَيْرَ.
تَاللهِ لَأَفْعَلَنَّ الخَيْرَ.
بِاللهِ لَأَفْعَلَنَّ الخَيْرَ.

By God, I will do good deeds!

وَرَبِّ الكَعْبَةِ إِنَّ الحَقَّ مُنْتَصِرٌ.
تَرَبِّ الكَعْبَةِ إِنَّ الحَقَّ مُنْتَصِرٌ.
بِرَبِّ الكَعْبَةِ إِنَّ الحَقَّ مُنْتَصِرٌ.

By the Lord of the Ka'ba, truth will prevail!

This chapter presented the main functions and structures involving one-letter prepositions. The following section presents some exercises to help the learners practice some of the information presented in the chapter.

Exercises

I What is the function of the prepositions in the underlined words in the following sentences?

1 تَحَوَّلَ لِدِراسَةِ التَّاريخِ.
2 دَرَسَتْ فِي الجَامِعَةِ الأَمْريكِيَّةِ بِبَيْرُوتَ.
3 دَمَّرَ المُحْتَلُّونَ المَدينَةَ بِكَامِلِهَا.
4 عَمِلَ بِالتِّجَارَةِ أَثْنَاءَ وُجُودِهِ بِدِمَشْقَ.
5 عَمِلَ وَالِدِي مُدِيرًا عَامًّا لِلآثَارِ.
6 كَانَ يَتَصَرَّفُ كَزَعِيمٍ.
7 كَانَ يَزُورُنا بِالأَعْيَادِ.
8 لَنَا عَائِلاتٌ كَبِيرَةٌ.
9 مَا زَالَ يَذْكُرُ مَدْرَسَتَهُ بِدِقَّةٍ.
10 المُفَاوَضَاتُ السِّيَاسِيَّةُ سَتُتيحُ لِلأَطْرافِ حَلَّ الأَزْمَةِ.

II Choose the correct preposition to complete these sentences.

1 بَعْدَ سَنَوَاتٍ طَوِيلَةٍ مِنَ الغُرْبَةِ، عَادَ (ب، ك، ل) بِلادِهِ.
2 تَسْتَوْرِدُ مُعْظَمُ البُلْدَانِ العَرَبِيَّةِ مَوَادَّ غِذَائِيَّةً (ب، ك، ل) سَدِّ حَاجَاتِ السُّكَّانِ.
3 تَشْتَهِرُ شَوَاطِئُ البَحرِ الأَحْمَرِ (ب، ك، ل) كَثْرَةِ الأَمَاكِنِ الصَّالِحَةِ (ب، ك، ل) مُمَارَسَةِ رِيَاضَةِ الغَوْصِ.

4 تَلَقَّيْنَا دَعْوَةً (ب، ك، ل) حُضُورِ حَفْلِ زِفَافِ ابْنِ أَخِي.

5 قَامَ الجَيْشُ (ب، ك، ل) حَمَلَاتٍ كَبِيرَةٍ دَاخِلَ البِلَادِ (ب، ك، ل) مُكَافَحَةِ الإِرْهَابِ.

6 قَامَ الوَزِيرُ (ب، ك، ل) زِيَارَةٍ رَسْمِيَّةٍ (ب، ك، ت) شَخْصِيَّةٍ سِيَاسِيَّةٍ بَارِزَةٍ.

7 مِيزَانُ القُوَى قَدْ تَحَوَّلَ (ب، ك، ل) صَالِحِ إِيرَان (ب، ك، ل) دَوْلَةٍ ذَاتِ نُفُوذٍ قَوِيٍّ.

8 هَاجَمَتْ قُوَّاتُ الأَمْنِ المُتَظَاهِرِينَ (ب، ك، ل) صُورَةٍ عَنِيفَةٍ.

9 الوِلَايَاتُ المُتَّحِدَةُ (ب، ك، ل) قِيَادَةِ الرَّئِيسِ تَسْعَى (ب، ك، ل) تَحْقِيقِ مَكَاسِبَ سِيَاسِيَّةٍ فِي الشَّرْقِ الأَوْسَطِ.

10 وُلِدَ الكَاتِبُ فِي قَرْيَةٍ صَغِيرَةٍ، (ب، ك، ل) أُسْرَةٍ مَيْسُورَةِ الحَالِ.

III Make sensible sentences with the phrases in the columns below.

	A		1
بِكُلِّيَّةِ العُلُومِ بِجَامِعَةِ الإِسْكَنْدَرِيَّةِ.	A	تُنَادِي الأُمَمُ المُتَّحِدَةُ	1
لِعَدَدٍ هَائِلٍ مِنَ السَّائِحِينَ.	B	عَقَدَ البَرْلَمَانُ جَلْسَةً طَارِئَةً	2
بِتَسْوِيَةٍ نِهَائِيَّةٍ لِقَضِيَّةِ السَّلَامِ فِي الشَّرْقِ الأَوْسَطِ.	C	التَحَقَ أَحْمَدُ زُوَيْل	3
كَسِلَاحٍ يُسْتَخْدَمُ فِي الحِفَاظِ عَلَى مَصَالِحِ العَرَبِ فِي المُجْتَمَعِ الدَّوْلِيِّ.	D	أَصْبَحَتِ الغُرْقَةُ مَقْصِدًا	4
لِمُنَاقَشَةِ تَطَوُّرَاتِ الأَزْمَةِ الاقْتِصَادِيَّةِ.	E	تَكَلَّمَ العَرَبُ عَنِ النَّفْطِ	5

IV Translate the following sentences into English.

1 ظَهَرَتْ تَرْجَمَةُ الكِتَابِ بِاللُّغَةِ العَرَبِيَّةِ لِلْمَرَّةِ الأُولَى فِي العَامِ 1904.

2 يُحِبُّ الأَبُ أَبْنَاءَهُ وَيَرْتَبِطُ بِهِمْ ارْتِبَاطًا قَوِيًّا.

3 هَذِهِ الرَّاقِصَةُ تَبْدُو كَفَرَاشَةٍ جَمِيلَةٍ.

4 كَمَا يَعْرِفُ الجَمِيعُ، الكِتَابُ مُؤَلَّفٌ مِنْ ثَلَاثَةِ أَجْزَاءٍ.

5 تَمَّ دَفْعُ تَعْوِيضَاتٍ لِلضَّحَايَا.

V Translate the following sentences into Arabic.

1 Why do you study Chinese?
2 The president gave the team prizes.
3 Most Arab people struggle to secure a living.
4 I assure you that the book is in the library.
5 It was as if the beautiful past had returned.

3 Two-letter prepositions

مِنْ

مِنْ is one of the most frequently used prepositions in Arabic. According to *A Frequency Dictionary of Arabic* (2011), it is the fourth-most commonly used word in Arabic. It has numerous functions and can be translated as 'of' or from', among other terms. It is mainly used to designate the starting point of a departure from a place.

مِنْ *in context*

> سَافَرَ عَلِيٌّ مِنْ بَغْدَادَ إِلَى البِصرةِ مِنْ أَجْلِ الْحُصُولِ عَلَى عَمَلٍ يَرْتَزِقُ مِنْهُ، وَكَذَلِكَ هَرَبًا مِنَ الْحَالَةِ الْأَمْنِيَّةِ الْمُتَرَدِّيَةِ فِي الْعَاصِمَةِ، وَمِنْ حُسْنِ حَظِّهِ حَصَلَ عَلَى وَظِيفَةٍ فِي شَرِكَةٍ كَانَ صَاحِبُهَا بَغْدَادِيَّ الْأَصْلِ، وَمِنَ الْمِنْطَقَةِ نَفْسِها الَّتِي كَانَ يَسْكُنُ فِيهَا عَلِيٌّ. كَانَ عَلِيٌّ يَعْمَلُ مِنَ الصَّبَاحِ الْبَاكِرِ حَتَّى السَّابِعَةِ مِنْ مَسَاءِ كُلِّ يَوْمٍ، لَمْ يُعَانِ مِنَ الْوَحْدَةِ لِأَنَّهُ صَادَقَ الْكَثِيرَ مِنَ النَّاسِ الطَّيِّبِينَ فِي الْعَمَلِ، وَادَّخَرَ بَعْضًا مِنَ الْمَالِ، فَاسْتَطَاعَ أَنْ يُرْسِلَ مَبْلَغًا مِنَ الْمَالِ كُلَّ شَهْرٍ لِوَالِدَيْهِ. وَبَعْدَ فَتْرَةٍ اسْتَقَرَّتْ ظُرُوفُهُ، وَخَاصَّةً مِنَ النَّاحِيَةِ الْمَادِّيَّةِ، بَعْدَ ثَلَاثِ سَنَوَاتٍ مِنَ الْعَمَلِ قَرَّرَ عَلِيٌّ أَنْ يَتَزَوَّجَ مِنِ امْرَأَةٍ مِنْ مَعَارِفِ أَحَدِ أَصْدِقَائِهِ فِي الْعَمَلِ، وَاسْتَقَرَّ عَلِيٌّ أَخِيرًا فِي الْبَصرَةِ.
>
> Ali traveled from Baghdad to Basra in order to get a job and to escape the deteriorating security conditions in the capital. He was lucky to get a job in a company whose owner was of Baghdadi origin and from the same area where Ali himself lived. Ali was working from early morning until seven in the evening. He did not suffer from loneliness because he befriended several kind people at work and saved some money, so he could send a sum of money each month to his parents. After a period of time, his situation stabilized, especially in terms of finances. After three years of work, Ali decided to marry a woman who was an acquaintance of one of his friends at work. Ali eventually settled in Basra.

Notes on the usage of مِنْ *in context*

In this paragraph, مِنْ is used to fulfill several functions. It is used to denote departure from a place, as in (مِنْ بَغْدَادَ). It is also used as part of a collocation with verbs,

Two-letter prepositions 47

as in (يَرْتَزِقُ مِنْهُ، لَمْ يُعَانِ مِنَ الْوَحْدَةِ، يَتَزَوَّجُ مِنْ). Other functions of مِنْ in the text are to explain the cause behind an action, as in (هَرَبًا مِنْ); temporal departure, as in (مِنَ الصَّبَاحِ); and with weight and quantity, as in (بَعْضًا مِنْ) and (مَبْلَغًا مِنْ).

> **Note**
>
> When the preposition مِنْ is followed by a word that begins with the definite article (ال), the final voweling changes; (السُّكُون) on the (نْ) changes to (الفَتْحَة), as in (مِنَ الْبَيْتِ) and (مِنْ بَيْتٍ) or (مِنَ الْمَكْتَبَةِ) and (مِنْ مَكْتَبَةٍ).

Functions of مِنْ

مِنْ is used to designate a starting point or the point of departure from a place, as in the following cases:

خَرَجَ الطَّالِبُ مِنَ الصَّفِّ.	The student came out of the class.
وَقَعَ الْكِتَابُ مِنْ يَدَيْهِ.	The book dropped from his hands.
وَصَلَتْ صَدِيقَتِي الْيَوْمَ مِنْ بَيْرُوتَ.	My friend has arrived from Beirut today.
هَذِهِ رِسَالَةٌ مِنْ عَلِيٍّ إِلَى صَدِيقِهِ مَحْمُودٍ.	This is a message from Ali to his friend Mahmoud.
سَافَرَ عَلِيٌّ مِنْ بَغْدَادَ إِلَى الْمَوْصِلِ.	Ali traveled from Baghdad to Mosul.

مِنْ is also used to indicate a temporal starting point as in the following:

كَانَتْ غَائِبَةً مِنَ الضُّحَى إِلَى الْمَسَاءِ.	She was absent from morning till evening.
انْتَظَرْتُكِ مِنَ الصَّبَاحِ حَتَّى الظَّهِيرَةِ.	I waited for you from morning till noon.
صَامَ مِنْ أَوَّلِ رَمَضَانَ إِلَى آخِرِهِ.	He fasted from the first day of Ramadan to the last day.
لَمْ يَنْتَبِهِ الطَّالِبُ لِلْأُسْتَاذِ مِنْ بِدَايَةِ الْمُحَاضَرَةِ.	The student did not pay attention to the professor from the start of the lecture.
أَمْطَرَتْ أَمْسِ مِنَ الصَّبَاحِ إِلَى اللَّيْلِ.	It rained yesterday from morning till night.

مِنْ can be used to indicate the origin of people or things, as in the following:

هُوَ بِرِيطَانِيٌّ مِنْ أَصْلٍ فِلَسْطِينِيٍّ.	He is British of Palestinian descent.
كَوَّنْتُ ثَرْوَتِي مِنَ التِّجَارَةِ وَالأَعْمَالِ الْحُرَّةِ.	I built up my fortune from trade and entrepreneurship.
صَدِيقَتِي لَيْلَى مِنْ عَائِلَةٍ بُرْجُوازِيَّةٍ مَعْرُوفَةٍ.	My friend Laila is from a well-known, bourgeois family.
تَعَرَّفْتُ عَلَى سَيِّدَةٍ مِنَ الطَّبَقَةِ الرَّاقِيَةِ مِنَ الْمُجْتَمَعِ الْبِرِيطَانِيِّ.	I have met a lady from the upper class of British society.

مِنْ can also be used to indicate or identify a specific part from a whole, as in the following:

كَانَ يَقْبَعُ في زاوِيَةٍ مِنَ الْبَيْتِ.	He crouched motionlessly in a corner of the house.
يَجْلِسُ بَعْضُ الطَّلَبَةِ في الْمَقَاعِدِ الْخَلْفِيَّةِ مِنَ الصَّفِّ.	Some students sit in the back seats of the classroom.
اِلْتَقَيْتُ بِهِ في الطَّابَقِ الْعُلْوِيِّ مِنَ الْبِنَايَةِ.	I met him on the top floor of the building.
احْتَلَّ الْأَعْدَاءُ الْجَانِبَ الْغَرْبِيَّ مِنَ الْمَدِينَةِ وقَطَعُوا الطَّرِيقَ.	The enemies occupied the western side of the city and cut off the road.

مِنْ is used to indicate what something is made of or consists of, as in the following:

تَرْفُضُ ابْنَتِي أَنْ تَلْبِسَ أَيَّ شَيءٍ مَصْنُوعٍ مِنْ جِلْدِ الْحَيَوَانَاتِ.	My daughter refuses to wear anything made of real leather.
اشْتَرَيْتُ ثَوْبًا مِنْ قُطْنٍ.	I bought a cotton dress.
وَضَعْتُ حَوْلَ عُنُقِي كُوفِيَّةً مِنَ الصُّوفِ.	I wrapped a woolen scarf around my neck.
سَكَنْتُ في بِنَايَةٍ مِنْ ثَلَاثَةِ طَوَابِقَ.	I lived in a three-story building.
أَهْدَانِي سَاعَةً مِنَ الْمَاسِ بِمُنَاسَبَةِ عِيدِ مِيلَادِي.	He gave me a diamond watch, as a present, for my birthday.

مِنْ is often found with verbs denoting liberation, escape and freeing oneself from something, as in these cases:

هَرَبَ اللِّصُّ مِنَ السِّجْنِ.	The thief escaped from prison.
تَحَرَّرَ الشَّعْبُ مِنَ الاسْتِعْمَارِ بَعْدَ كِفَاحٍ طَوِيلٍ.	After a long struggle, the people were liberated from colonialism.
عَلَيْنَا أَنْ نَتَخَلَّصَ مِنَ الرَّوَاسِبِ السَّلْبِيَّةِ الَّتِي تُعِيقُنَا عَنِ التَّقَدُّمِ.	We have to rid ourselves of the negative residues that hinder our progress.
يَتَهَرَّبُ بَعْضُ الآبَاءِ مِنْ مَسْؤُولِيَّاتِهِم فِي تَرْبِيَةِ الْأَوْلَادِ.	Some parents shirk their responsibility for bringing their children up.
نَجَوْتُ مِنَ الْمَوْتِ، عِدَّةَ مَرَّاتٍ، بِأُعْجُوبَةٍ.	On several occasions, I have miraculously survived death.

مِنْ is used in a causative sense to indicate the cause of an action or a situation that has taken or will take place, as in the following examples:

هَلَعَ الطِّفْلُ مِنَ الْخَوْفِ بَعْدَ أَنْ شَاهَدَ ذَلِكَ الْفِيلْمَ.	The child panicked out of fear after watching that movie.

Two-letter prepositions 49

نَامَ عَلِيٌّ مِنْ شِدَّةِ الإِرْهاقِ فِي العَمَلِ طَوَالَ النَّهارِ.	Ali slept all day long out of sheer exhaustion from his workload.
نَسِيَتِ المَرْأَةُ مُراقَبَةَ طِفْلِها مِنْ كَثْرَةِ الأَعْمالِ المَنْزِلِيَّةِ.	The woman forgot to keep an eye on her child because of her preoccupation with the household chores.
ذَهَلَتْ عَنْهُ مِنْ شِدَّةِ الانْشِغالِ بِالعَمَلِ.	Being wholeheartedly preoccupied with work, she forgot all about him.

مِنْ is used following numerical expressions and before the plural genitive form of a noun, as in the following:

حَضَرَ اثْنانِ مِنْ أَفْرادِ الشُّرْطَةِ إِلى مَكانِ الحادِثِ.	Two policemen arrived at the scene of the accident.
لَقِيَ خَمْسَةٌ مِنَ الإِرْهابِيِّينَ حَتْفَهُمْ فِي العَمَلِيَّةِ الانْتِحارِيَّةِ.	Five terrorists were killed in the suicide attack.
أَبْدى عَشَرَةٌ مِنَ المُتَطَوِّعِينَ اسْتِعْدادَهُمْ لِتَنْظِيفِ الشّارِعِ.	Ten volunteers expressed their willingness to clean the street.
انْدَلَعَ حَرِيقٌ فِي خَمْسَةٍ مِنْ طَوابِقِ فُنْدُقٍ ضَخْمٍ فِي دُبَي.	A fire broke out in five floors of a big hotel in Dubai.
يُصِرُّ الكاتِبُ أَنْ يُعَرِّفَ نَفْسَهُ بِأَنَّهُ واحِدٌ مِنْ عامَّةِ النّاسِ فِي مَدِينَتِهِ.	The author insists on presenting himself as just one of the ordinary people in his city.

مِنْ also occurs with information on weight and quantity, as in the following:

تُصَدِّرُ مِصْرُ سَنَوِيًّا مِئاتِ الآلافِ مِنَ الأَطْنانِ مِنَ القُطْنِ.	Egypt exports hundreds of thousands of tons of cotton annually.
يُقَدَّرُ احْتِياطِيُّ العِراقِ مِنَ النِّفْطِ الخامِ بِأَكْثَرَ مِنْ عَشَرَةِ مَلايِينَ مِنَ الأَمْتارِ المُكَعَّبَةِ.	Iraq's crude oil reserves are estimated at more than ten million cubic meters.
عَثَرْتُ عَلى مِحْفَظَةٍ نِسائِيَّةٍ مَتْرُوكَةٍ عَلى الرَّصِيفِ، فِيها مَبْلَغٌ مِنَ المالِ.	I found a purse left with a sum of money on the pavement.
طَلَبْتُ مِنْهُ أَنْ يَجْلُبَ كِيلُو مِنَ التُّفّاحِ، وَرَطْلًا مِنْ زَيْتِ الطَّعامِ، وَقِنِّينَةً مِنْ ماءِ الوَرْدِ.	I asked him to bring a kilo of apples, a pound of cooking oil and a bottle of rose water.

مِنْ can be used to specify time, as in the following:

مَرَّتِ الأَيّامُ الأَخِيرَةُ مِنْ رِحْلَتِنا بِسُرْعَةٍ شَدِيدَةٍ.	The last days of our trip passed very quickly.
سَهِرْنا حَتّى السّاعاتِ الأَخِيرَةِ مِنَ اللَّيْلِ.	We stayed up late at night.

وُلِدَ الْكَاتِبُ فِي السَّاعَةِ الْوَاحِدَةِ مِنْ مَسَاءِ يَوْمِ الِاثْنَيْنِ، مِنْ شَهْرِ كَانُونَ الْأَوَّلِ.	The author was born at 1:00 p.m., on a Monday in December.
لَقَدْ كُنْتُ هُنَا مِنَ السَّاعَةِ السَّابِعَةِ صَبَاحًا.	I have been here since seven o'clock in the morning.
لَمْ أَرَهُ مِنْ سَاعَتَيْنِ.	I have not seen him for two hours.

مِنْ is used when stating days of the week or the month, as in the following:

فِي الْأُسْبُوعِ الثَّانِي مِنْ رَمَضَانَ	In the second week of Ramadan.
فِي الْأَيَّامِ الْأَخِيرَةِ مِنْ دِيسَمْبِرِ.	In the last few days of December.

مِنْ can be used to convey the idea of measurement or a distance from one place to another, as in the following:

بَيْتِي أَقْرَبُ إِلَى الْجَامِعَةِ مِنْ بَيْتِكَ.	My house is closer to the university than yours.
كَمِ الْمَسَافَةُ مِنَ الرِّيَاضِ إِلَى مَكَّةَ الْمُكَرَّمَةِ؟	What is the distance from Riyadh to Makka?
تَقَعُ الْجَامِعَةُ عَلَى بُعْدِ عَشَرَةِ كِيلُومِتْرَاتٍ مِنْ مَرْكَزِ الْمَدِينَةِ.	The university is located ten kilometers away from the city center.

مِنْ is used with the particles (دون) and (غير), translated as 'without' or 'devoid of', as in the following:

جَاءَتْ إِلَى الْحَفْلَةِ شِبْهَ عَارِيَةٍ مِنْ غَيْرِ حَيَاءٍ أَوْ حِشْمَةٍ.	She came to the party semi-naked with no shame or modesty.
غَضِبَتْ مِنِّي مِنْ غَيْرِ سَبَبٍ.	She was angry with me for no reason.
لَا يَسْتَطِيعُ الْقِيَامَ بِذَلِكَ مِنْ غَيْرِ إِذْنِي.	He cannot do that without my permission.
ظَهَرَتْ صُورَةٌ فِي بَعْضِ الْمَجَلَّاتِ الْعَرَبِيَّةِ لِعَارِضَةِ أَزْيَاءٍ مِنْ دُونِ مَلَابِسَ.	A photo of a naked fashion model appeared in some of the Arab magazines.

مِنْ can occur in a compound preposition, and in this type of construction, it will always precede the following semi-preposition; see the following cases:

لَا أَعْتَقِدُ أَنَّنَا الْتَقَيْنَا مِنْ قَبْلُ.	I do not think that we have met before.
نَجَا شَخْصَانِ مِنْ تَحْتِ الْأَنْقَاضِ بَعْدَ الزِّلْزَالِ بِثَلَاثَةِ أَيَّامٍ.	Two people have been rescued from under the rubble three days after the quake.
أَلْقَى الشَّابُّ نَظْرَةً عَلَى جَارَتِهِ مِنْ خَلْفِ سِتَارِ النَّافِذَةِ.	The young man had a look at his neighbor from behind the window curtains.
رَمَى نَفْسَهُ مِنْ فَوْقِ الطَّابَقِ الْعُلْوِيِّ لِلْبِنَايَةِ.	He threw himself off the top floor of the building.

Two-letter prepositions 51

مِنْ can also be used for emphasis. This usage is, however, not common in modern-day usage or in the media. In this context, it is redundant. It must be preceded by an indefinite subject noun, the object of a verb, the interrogative particle (هَلْ), a subject of a noun (مُبْتَدَأ) or an absolute object (مَفْعُول مُطْلَقْ), such as in the following examples:

لَيْسَ لِلْخَائِنِ مِنْ صَدِيقٍ.	A traitor has no friend.
مَا مِنْ مُجِيبٍ لِدَعَوَاتِنَا.	No one has ever answered our prayers.

When مِنْ precedes a definite noun, and especially a plural, it denotes an indefinite quantity or number, such as in these examples:

تَبَقَّى الْكَثِيرُ مِنَ الطَّعَامِ بَعْدَ حَفْلَةِ الْعَشَاءِ أَمْسِ.	There is a lot of food left over from yesterday's dinner party.
سَكَبَتْ لَهُ كَأْسًا مِنَ الْعَصِيرِ.	She poured him a glass of juice.
شَرِبْنا مِنَ الْمَاءِ حَتَّى ارْتَوَيْنَا.	We drank water until we quenched our thirst.

مِنْ can include the meanings of other prepositions. However, it is worth pointing out that these uses are not common in the media and other contemporary uses, as in the following:

سَأُسَافِرُ مِنْ أَوَّلِ الأُسْبوعِ.	I will leave at the beginning of the week.	مِنْ is used with the same meaning as (فِي).
اقْتَرَبَ مِنْكَ.	He got close to you.	مِنْ is used with the same meaning as (إِلَى).
أَمْسَكْتُهُ مِنْ يَدِهِ.	I hold him by the hand.	مِنْ is used with the same meaning as (الْبَاء).
لَا تَبْتَعِدْ مِنْ هَذَا الْمَكَانِ.	Do not go far from this place.	مِنْ is used with the same meaning as (عَنْ).
لَعَلَّ اللهَ يُنْصِفُنَا مِنَ الظَّالِمِينَ.	May God save us from injustice.	مِنْ is used with the same meaning as (عَلَى).

مِنْ is also used to express comparative and contrastive relationships between two people or two things, and in this case, it is translated as 'than', as in the following:

مُحَمَّدٌ أَطْوَلُ مِنْ حُسِين.	Mohammad is taller than Hussein.
الْغَرْبُ أَكْثَرُ تَقَدُّمًا مِنَ الشَّرْقِ فِي التِّكْنُولُوجِيا.	The West is more advanced than the East with regard to technology.
الْجَوُّ أَكْثَرُ حَرَارَةً الْيَوْمَ مِنْ أَمْسِ.	The weather today is warmer than yesterday.

مِنْ is used in superlative constructions and is translated as 'one of . . .', as in the following:

تُعْتَبَرُ قَضِيَّةُ فِلَسْطِينَ مِنْ أَهَمِّ القَضَايَا العَرَبِيَّةِ وَالإِسْلامِيَّةِ.	The question of Palestine is one of the most important Arab and Islamic causes.
فِي رَأْيِي، إِنَّ جِبَالَ لُبْنَانَ هِيَ مِنْ أَجْمَلِ الأَمَاكِنِ فِي الشَّرْقِ الأَوْسَطِ.	In my opinion, the mountains of Lebanon are one of the most beautiful places in the Middle East.
أَخْبَرْتُهُ بِأَنَّهُ مِنْ أَذْكَى النَّاسِ الَّذِينَ أَعْرِفُهُمْ.	I told him that he is one of the most intelligent people I have ever known.
زَمِيلَتِي مِنْ أَرَقِّ النِّسَاءِ اللَّوَاتِي تَعَرَّفْتُ عَلَيْهِنَّ.	My colleague is one of the nicest women I've ever met.
فِي السَّبْعِينَاتِ مِنَ القَرْنِ المَاضِي، كَانَ العِرَاقُ مِنْ أَوَّلِ الدُّوَلِ العَرَبِيَّةِ الَّتِي وَضَعَتْ خُطَّةً لِمَحْوِ الأُمِّيَّةِ.	In the 1970s, Iraq was one of the first Arab countries to draw up a literacy plan.

مِنْ is used to differentiate between two contrasting people or things, as in the following:

(وَاللهُ يَعْلَمُ المُفْسِدَ مِنَ المُصْلِحِ) (2: 220)	"God knows well him who works corruption from him who sets aright".
لَا نَسْتَطِيعُ دَائِمًا أَنْ نَعْرِفَ الوَفِيَّ مِنَ الخَائِنِ إِلَّا بَعْدَ أَنْ نَمُرَّ بِظُرُوفٍ صَعْبَةٍ.	We cannot always tell a sincere person from a traitor except when we experience difficult circumstances.
عَلَى الإِنْسَانِ أَنْ يُمَيِّزَ الحَقَّ مِنَ البَاطِلِ.	One has to differentiate between right and wrong.
لَمْ أَعُدْ أَعْرِفُ اللَّيْلَ مِنَ النَّهَارِ.	I can no longer differentiate between night and day.

مِنْ can be used with expressions such as 'some of', 'many of', 'the majority of' or 'a minority of', as in the following cases:

الكَثِيرُ مِنَ القَادَةِ لَا يَسْتَطِيعُونَ مُوَاجَهَةَ هَذِهِ التَّحَدِّيَاتِ.	Many leaders do not measure up to these challenges.
إِنَّهُمْ لَا يُمَثِّلُونَ الغَالِبِيَّةَ مِنَ النَّاسِ.	They do not represent the majority of people.
الأَقَلِّيَّةُ مِنَ الطُّلَّابِ يُدْرِكُونَ أَهَمِّيَّةَ الوَقْتِ.	Few students appreciate the importance of time.

Two-letter prepositions 53

الْعَدِيدُ مِنَ الأَشْخَاصِ يَمِيلُونَ إِلَى قِرَاءَةِ الْجَرَائِدِ فِي الصَّبَاحِ قَبْلَ الْفَطُورِ.	Many people are inclined to read newspapers in the morning before breakfast.

مِنْ is also used with an adjective or particle with the definite article (الـ) followed by either (أَنْ) or (أَنَّ), where the adjective or particle employed determines the use of (أَنْ) or (أَنَّ), as in the following:

لَيْسَ مِنَ الضَّرُورِيِّ أَنْ تَمْلِكَ مَالًا كَثِيرًا كَيْ تَكُونَ سَعِيدًا فِي الْحَيَاةِ.	You do not necessarily need to have much money to be happy in life.
مِنَ الْوَاضِحِ أَنَّهُم لَا يَهْتَمُّونَ بِالأُمُورِ الاِقْتِصَادِيَّةِ.	Obviously, they do not care about economic matters.
مِنَ الْوَاجِبِ عَلَيْنَا أَنْ نَكُونَ قُدْوَةً لِطُلَّابِنَا فِي الإِلْتِزَامِ بِالْمَوَاعِيدِ.	It is our duty to be examples to be followed by our students in keeping to appointments.
مِنَ الْغَرِيبِ أَنَّ الأُسْتَاذَ لَمْ يَكُنْ حَاضِرًا أَثْنَاءَ الدَّرْسِ.	It is strange that the teacher did not show up to class.
مِنَ الصَّعْبِ أَنْ نَعْرِفَ أَسْبَابَ الْخِصَامِ بَيْنَ الصَّدِيقَيْنِ.	It is difficult to know the causes of the discord between the two friends.

مِنْ can be used with verbs meaning to 'take out', 'extract', 'remove' or 'snatch', as in the following:

اِسْتَخْرَجَ الْعُلَمَاءُ الْبِتْرُولَ مِنْ بَاطِنِ الأَرْضِ.	The scientists extracted oil from underground.
أَخْرَجَ الْوَلَدُ يَدَهُ مِنْ جَيْبِهِ.	The boy has got his hand out of his pocket.
اِسْتَوْرَدَ التَّاجِرُ بِضَاعَتَهُ مِنَ الْيَمَنِ.	The trader imported the goods from Yemen.
أَخْرَجَ الْكِيسَ مِنْ جَيْبِهِ.	He took the bag out of his pocket.
نَزَعَ الأَبُ الدُّمْيَةَ مِنْ يَدِّ وَلَدِهِ.	The father snatched the doll from his son's hand.

مِنْ can be used with verbs denoting buying, importing or renting, as in the following:

اِشْتَرَيْتُ الْحَلْوَى مِنَ الْبِقَالَةِ.	I bought candies from the grocery.
اِسْتَأْجَرَ مُحَمَّدٌ الدَّارَ مِنْ عَمْرُو.	Mohammed leased the house from Amr.
اِسْتَوْرَدَتِ الشَّرِكَةُ الْبَضَائِعَ مِنَ الصِّينِ.	The company imported the goods from China.
جَلَبَ الْمَلَابِسَ مِنَ الْخَارِجِ.	He brought the clothes from outside.
اِجْتَلَبَ الْبَضَائِعَ مِنَ الْخَارِجِ.	He imported the goods from abroad.

مِنْ is used with verbs meaning 'waking up' or 'standing up', as the following:

أَيْقَظَهُ الرَّعْدُ مِنْ سُبَاتِهِ العَمِيقِ.	The thunder woke him up from his deep sleep.
قَامَ الطِّفْلُ لَيْلَةَ أَمْسِ مِنْ نَوْمِهِ عِدَّةَ مَرَّاتٍ.	The child woke up several times last night.

مِنْ is also used with verbs employed to express astonishment or complaining, as in the following:

وَاسْتَغْرَبَ أَحْمَدُ مِنْ أَحْوَالِهِم.	Ahmed was astonished at their situation.
شَكَا الشَّابُّ مِنْ قَسْوَتِهَا عَلَى الفُقَرَاءِ.	The young man complained about her cruelty toward poor people.
تَظَلَّمَ مِنْ جَارِهِ لِسُوءِ مُعَامَلَتِهِ.	He grumbled about his neighbor for having treated him badly.

مِنْ can also be used with verbs meaning to ease, lessen or reduce or to be devoid of, as in the following:

قَلَّلَ الرَّجُلُ مِنْ ثِقَلِ الحِمْلِ.	The man reduced the weight of the load.
خَفَّفَ الطَّبِيبُ مِنْ آلَامِ المَرِيضِ.	The doctor eased the patient's pain.
تَجَرَّدَ القَاتِلُ مِنْ كُلِّ مَعَانِي الرَّحْمَةِ.	The murderer is devoid of any sense of mercy.

مِنْ is used with verbs expressing revenge, disdain, detestation or hatred, as in the following:

انْتَقَمْتُ مِنَ القَاتِلِ.	I took revenge on the murderer.
اقْتَصَّ مِنْ عَدُوِّهِ.	He has retaliated against his enemy.
اشْمَأَزَّ الشَّعْبُ مِنَ الحُكَّامِ المُسْتَبِدِّينَ.	People detested the ruling dictators.
نَفَرَ المُشْتَرُونَ مِنْ سُوءِ مُعَامَلَةِ البَائِعِ.	The buyers stayed away because of the trader's mistreatment.

مِنْ is also used with verbs meaning to exercise caution as in the following:

احْتَرَسَ المَارَّةُ مِنْ حُفَرِ الطَّرِيقِ.	The pedestrians were wary of the holes in the road.
اِحْتَمَى بِمِظَلَّتِهِ مِنَ المَطَرِ.	He used his umbrella to protect himself from the rain.
احْتَاطَ سُكَّانُ القَرْيَةِ مِنْ هُجُومِ الأَعْدَاءِ عَلَيْهِم.	The villagers took precautions against any attack by their enemies.

Two-letter prepositions 55

مِنْ can be used with verbs meaning finding out, inquiring or responding, as in the following:

اِسْتَفْهَمَ مِنْ صَدِيقِهِ عَنْ مَوعِدِ الإِجْتِمَاعِ.	He asked his friend about the time of the meeting.
فَهِمَ التِّلْمِيذُ الدَّرسَ مِنَ المُعَلِّمِ.	The student understood the lesson as explained by the teacher.
سَمِعَ الله لِمَنْ حَمِدَهُ.	God listens to those who thank him.

مِنْ can also be used with verbs meaning giving, spending or saving, as in the following cases:

أَنْفَقْتُ مِنْ مَالِي الخَاصِّ.	I spent from my own funds.
قَدَّمَ المَلِكُ مِنَحًا وَعَطَايَا مِنْ مَالِهِ.	The king gave grants and gifts from his own funds.
وَفَّرَ الوالِدُ مِنْ طَعَامِ اليَوْمِ مَا يَكْفِي لِليَوْمَيْنِ المُقْبِلَيْنِ.	The father saved some of today's food for the next two days.
اِدَّخَرَ الطَّالِبُ مِنْ مَصرُوفِهِ اليَومِيِّ.	The student has saved from his allowance.

مِنْ is used with verbs denoting selecting or choosing a person or from a group of people or things as, for example, in the following:

اخْتَارَ الشَّعبُ مُمَثِّلِيهِ مِنَ الأحزَابِ.	People have chosen their representatives from the parties.
اصطَفَى اللهُ الرُّسُلَ مِنْ خِيرَةِ الخَلقِ.	Allah chose prophets from the best of His creation.
اسْتَخْلَصَ الفَلَّاحُ الزُّبدَ مِنَ اللَّبَنِ.	The peasant extracted butter from milk.

مِنْ is used following words meaning nearness and approaching, such as in the following:

سَقَطَتْ قَذِيفَةٌ بِالقُرْبِ مِنْ مَدْرَسَةِ الأطْفَالِ.	A shell fell near a children's school.
أخِيرًا اسْتَأجَرْنَا بَيتًا قَرِيبًا مِنَ النَّادِي؛ عَلَى الأَقَلّ، نَسْتَطِيعُ أَنْ نَتَرَدَّدَ عَلَيهِ، كُلَّ يَومٍ، بِلَا مَشَقَّةٍ.	Finally, we rented a house close to the club so that we could at least go there regularly and easily every day.
اسْتَلْقَى عَلَى الأَرِيكَةِ قَرِيبًا مِنَ التِّلْفَازِ، وَهُوَ يُعَانِي مِنْ مَشَقَّةِ العَمَلِ طَوَالَ النَّهَارِ.	He lay down on the couch close to the television, as he was suffering from the effects of working hard all day long.
إنَّ الفَرِيقَ المِصرِيَّ يَدْنُو مِنْ إنْجَازٍ إفرِيقِيٍّ غَيرِ مَسْبُوقٍ فِي مُبَارَاةِ الدَّورِيِّ الأوَّلِ لِكُرَةِ القَدَمِ فِي إفرِيقيَا.	The Egyptian team is close to an unprecedented achievement in their first match in the CAF Champions League.

Two-letter prepositions

مِنْ can be used with following words meaning a kind of, type of or a touch of, as in the following:

أَصَابَهُ نَوْعٌ مِنَ الجُنُونِ.	He had a kind of madness.
انْتَابَتْهُ نَوْبَةٌ مِنَ الضَّحِكِ وَالْهِسْتِيرِيَا.	He went into a fit of laughter and hysterics.
يَعْتَرِينَا أَحْيَانًا فِي الظَّلَامِ شَيْءٌ مِنَ الرَّهْبَةِ.	We sometimes have a bit of a fright in the darkness.

مِنْ can be used before sentences or phrases that contain two opposing adjectives in juxtaposition, the first denoting a variable state of affairs in contrast with the second. These phrases usually indicate a sweeping generalization to include all members of a class, as the following examples show:

خَرَجَ النَّاسُ مِنْ شُجَاعٍ وَجَبَانٍ لِلْمُظَاهَرَاتِ فِي الشَّارِعِ يُنَدِّدُونَ بِالْإِرْهَابِ.	People both courageous and cowardly went out onto the streets demonstrating against terrorism.
أَخْبَرَنِي بِأَنَّهُ لَا يَخْشَى أَحَدًا فِيهِمْ مِنْ قَوِيِّهِمْ لِضَعِيفِهِمْ.	He told me that he did not fear any one of them, whether strong or weak.
يُهَاجِرُ شَبَابُ الْعَرَبِ مِنْ غَنِيِّهِمْ وَفَقِيرِهِمْ مِنْ بُلْدَانِهِمْ هَرَبًا مِنَ الْإِرْهَابِ وَتَرَدِّي الظُّرُوفِ الْأَمْنِيَّةِ.	Both the rich and the poor amongst the Arab youth are leaving their countries to escape from terrorism and the deteriorating security situation.

مِنْ is used before (بَاب), and it is translated as 'out of', although the word (بَاب) may deleted in certain contexts, as in the following:

كَانَ لِقَاؤُنَا مِنْ بَابِ الصُّدْفَةِ الْمَحْضَةِ.	Our meeting was a mere coincidence.
رَحَّبْتُ بِالْجَمِيعِ وَقُلْتُ لَهُمْ، بِصَوْتٍ خَافِتٍ، كَلِمَاتِ التَّرْحِيبِ، مِنْ بَابِ الْأَدَبِ.	Out of courtesy I welcomed everybody quietly and softly.
نَصَحْتُهُ مِنْ حِرْصِي عَلَيْهِ، وَمِنْ بَابِ الصَّدَاقَةِ.	I advised him out of both concern and friendship.

When مِنْ is used to introduce a verbal clause, the clause must begin with the subjunctive particle (أَنْ) followed by a present-tense verb in subjunctive mode, as in the following:

الْجُنُودُ أَشْجَعُ مِنْ أَنْ يَتَرَاجَعُوا مِنْ سَاحَاتِ الْقِتَالِ.	Soldiers are braver than to retreat from the battlefield.
لَيْسَ هُنَاكَ مِهْنَةٌ أَسْمَى مِنْ أَنْ تُعَلِّمَ الْأَطْفَالَ الْقِرَاءَةَ وَالْكِتَابَةَ.	There is no higher calling than teaching children to read and write.
كُنْتُ مُتَرَدِّدَةً مِنْ أَنْ أُفَاتِحَ مُدِيرَ الشَّرِكَةِ بِمَسْأَلَةِ الْعِلَاوَةِ السَّنَوِيَّةِ.	I was hesitant to ask the company boss about the annual bonus.

Two-letter prepositions

When مِنْ precedes a pronominal clause, it must begin with either the particle (أَنَّ) or (إِنَّ), as in the following:

أَنا وَاثِقَةٌ مِنْ أَنَّكُمْ تَسْتَطيعُونَ حَلَّ الْمَشاكِلِ بِطُرُقٍ وِدِّيَّةٍ، وَلا داعِيَ لِلُّجُوءِ إِلَى الْمَحاكِمِ.	I am confident that you can resolve your disputes amicably with no need to resort to the courts.
تَأَكَّدْ مِنْ أَنَّها فَتاةٌ تُناسِبُكَ قَبْلَ أَنْ تَطْلُبَ يَدَها لِلزَّواجِ.	Make sure she is the girl for you before you ask for her hand in marriage.
لَسْتُ مُنْدَهِشَةً كَثيرًا مِنْ أَنَّهُ رَسَبَ في كُلِّ الْمَساقاتِ لِهَذا الْفَصْلِ لِأَنَّهُ أَهْمَلَ واجِباتِهِ.	I am not too surprised that he failed in all the courses this semester because he was neglecting his assignments.
تَأَكَّدَتِ الشُّرْطَةُ مِنْ أَنَّ السَّجينَ الْهارِبَ لا يَزالُ في الْمَدينَةِ.	The police confirmed that the fugitive was still in the city.

(مِنْ أَجْلِ) may be followed by pronoun suffixes, a noun phrase, iḍāfa or a clause, as in the following cases:

حَضَرْنا الْإِجْتِماعَ مِنْ أَجْلِهِ.	We attended the meeting for his sake.
حَضَرْنا الْإِجْتِماعَ مِنْ أَجْلِ مُديرِ الشَّرِكَةِ.	We attended the meeting for the sake of the company manager.
حَضَرْنا الْإِجْتِماعَ مِنْ أَجْلِ الْمُديرِ الْجَديدِ.	We attended the meeting for the sake of the new manager.
حَضَرْنا الْإِجْتِماعَ مِنْ أَجْلِ الْمُديرِ الَّذي عُيِّنَ قَبْلَ أُسْبوعٍ.	We attended the meeting for the sake of the manager who was appointed a week ago.

(مِنْ طَرَفِ / مِنْ ناحِيَةٍ / مِنْ جانِبِ / مِنْ جِهَةِ / مِنْ قِبَلِ) can be followed by pronoun suffixes, noun phrase, iḍāfa or a clause, as in the following:

(Note that while all of these phrases can in general mean 'on the part of', 'by' or 'from', the exact meaning of each phrase depends on the context.)

عَرَفْنا الْيَوْمَ بِأَنَّ مُعْظَمَ أَعْضاءِ مَجْلِسِ الْبَلَدِيَّةِ مُنْتَخَبُونَ مِنْ طَرَفِ الْأَهالي.	We learned today that most of the members of the municipal council are elected by the people.
أَصْدَرَ الْقائِدُ الْأَعْلَى لِجَيْشِ الْخُلَفاءِ أَمْرًا بِعَدَمِ إِطْلاقِ النَّارِ عَلَى أَهالي الْمَناطِقِ السُّكَّانِيَّةِ حَتَّى لَوْ جاءَتْ طَلَقاتٌ مِنْ جِهَتِهِمْ.	The Supreme Commander of the Allied Army issued an order not to fire on the residents of the populated areas, even if shots came from them.
أُرْتُكِبَتِ الْجَريمَةُ مِنْ قِبَلِ عِصاباتٍ مَحَلِّيَّةٍ.	The crime was committed by local gangs.
تَمَّ تَوْزيعُ الْمُساعَداتِ مِنْ قِبَلِ مُنَظَّماتٍ إِنْسانِيَّةٍ.	The aid was distributed by humanitarian organizations.

Note the use of the passive voice with the phrase (مِنْ قِبَلْ) in the last two examples. مِنْ can precede adjectives on the (أَفْعَل) pattern, as in the following:

لَا يَزَالُ حِفْظُ السَّلَامِ وَاحِدًا مِنْ أَبْرَزِ أَنْشِطَةِ الأُمَمِ الْمُتَّحِدَةِ وَأَكْثَرِها ضَرُورَةً وَحَسْمًا.	Peacekeeping remains one of the most prominent, essential and critical activities of the United Nations.
كَانَ الْفَسَادُ مِنْ أَكْبَرِ الْمُعَوِّقَاتِ لِلتَّنْمِيَةِ.	Corruption has been one of the biggest obstacles to development.
هَذَا الْيَوْمُ مِنْ أَعْظَمِ أَيَّامِ حَيَّاتِي.	This day has been one of the greatest days of my life.
إِنَّهُ وَاحِدٌ مِنْ أَفْضَلِ الأَفْلَامِ الاِسْتِعْرَاضِيَّةِ عَلَى الإِطْلَاقِ.	It's one of the best musicals of all time.

مِنْ can precede a definite plural, as in the following:

الْجَفَافُ وَالْفَيَضَانَاتُ مِنْ أَسْبَابِ ازْدِيَادِ الْهِجْرَةِ.	Droughts and floods are some of the causes of increased migration.
مِنَ الْمُفَارَقَاتِ أَنَّ اخْتِلَافَاتِهِم هِيَ مَا تُقَرِّبُهُم.	Paradoxically, it is their differences that bring them closer together.
وَغَالِبًا مَا تَكُونُ هَذِهِ الْجَمَاعَاتُ مِنْ وَسَائِلِ السَّلَامِ وَالازْدِهَارِ.	Those groups are often instruments of peace as well as prosperity.
هَذَا جُزْءٌ مِنَ الْعَنَاصِرِ الأَسَاسِيَّةِ لِحُقُوقِ الإِنْسَانِ.	This is part of the essential elements of human rights.

مِنْ is used with the expressions (مِنْ جَانِبٍ آخَر، مِنْ جَانِب، مِنْ جِهَة، مِنْ جِهَةٍ أُخْرَى، مِنْ نَاحِيَةٍ، مِنْ نَاحِيَةٍ أُخْرَى), 'on the one hand ... and on the other', as in the following:

جَاءَ لِقَاءُ الرَّئِيسِ بِمَجْلِسِ نِقَابَةِ الصَّحَفِيِّينَ لِيُشَكِّلَ نُقْطَةَ تَحَوُّلٍ أُخْرَى فِي إِدَارَةِ الصِّرَاعِ بَيْنَ الْحُكُومَةِ مِنْ جَانِبٍ، وَالصَّحَفِيِّينَ وَالْمُعَارِضِينَ مِنْ جَانِبٍ آخَرَ.	The president's meeting at the Journalist Union Council was another turning point in managing the conflict between the government, on one hand, and the journalists and the opposition, on the other.
السَّبَبُ فِي هِجْرَةِ الشَّبَابِ هُوَ الْبَطَالَةُ مِنْ جِهَةٍ، وَعَدَمُ الاِسْتِقْرَارِ فِي الْبَلَدِ مِنْ جِهَةٍ أُخْرَى.	The reason for youth migration is unemployment, on the one hand, and instability in the country, on the other.
يُعَانِي الشَّعْبُ مِنَ الْفَقْرِ مِنْ جِهَةٍ، وَمِنْ انْعِدَامِ فُرَصِ الْعَمَلِ مِنْ جِهَةٍ أُخْرَى.	The people are suffering from poverty, on the one hand, and from lack of job opportunities, on the other.
ازْدَادَتِ الْبَطَالَةُ فِي الْبَلَدِ مِنْ جِهَةٍ، وَارْتَفَعَتْ أَسْعَارُ السِّلَعِ الاِسْتِهْلَاكِيَّةِ مِنْ جِهَةٍ أُخْرَى.	Unemployment in the country has gone up. This is one thing, and furthermore, the prices of consumer goods have also increased.

Two-letter prepositions 59

مِنْ is used with the pronoun (ما), 'from what', as in the following:

| مِمَّا قَرَأْتُ مِنْ مَقَالَاتِهِ، تَبَيَّنَ أَنَّهُ صَحَفِيٌّ جَيِّدٌ. | He seems a good journalist from what I have read of his articles. |
| مِمَّا شَاهَدْتُ مِنَ الأَفْلَامِ فِي الْفَتْرَةِ الْأَخِيرَةِ، يَبْدُو أَنَّ السِّينَمَا الْعَرَبِيَّةَ تَتَطَوَّرُ. | Judging from the movies that I have watched recently, it appears that the Arab cinema is progressing. |

Note (مِنْ + ما)

When مِنْ is followed immediately by the relative pronoun (ما), it is written as (مِمَّا).

| ظَنَنْتُمْ أَنَّ اللهَ لَا يَعْلَمُ كَثِيرًا مِمَّا تَعْمَلُونَ | You thought that God would never know much about the things that you were doing. |

مِنْ can occur after the interrogative particle (كَمْ) followed by a plural genitive noun. It is then translated as 'how many', 'how much' or 'how long', as in the following:

كَمْ مِنَ الطُّلَّابِ حَضَرُوا الدَّرْسَ؟	How many students came to the class?
كَمْ مِنَ الدُّولَارَاتِ نَحْتَاجُ؟	How many dollars do we need?
كَمْ مِنَ الْوَقْتِ تَسْتَغْرِقُ رِحْلَتُنَا؟	How long does our trip take?
كَمْ مِنْ كِتَابٍ عِنْدَكَ؟	How many books do you have?

Note that (كَمْ + مِنْ) may also denote a rhetorical question or statement, as in the following:

| كَمْ مِنْ غَنِيٍّ تَعِيسٍ فِي حَيَاتِهِ! | How many rich people are unhappy in their lives! |
| كَمْ مِنْ أَحْلَامٍ لَمْ تَتَحَقَّقْ! | How many dreams have not come true! |

Note

When مِنْ is used following the negation particle (مَا), the combination is translated as 'nobody', 'no one' or 'nothing', as in the following.

مَا مِنْ أَحَدٍ يَتَحَمَّلُهُ.	There is no one who can tolerate him.
مَا مِنْ إِلَهٍ غَيْرُهُ.	There is no God but Him.
مَا مِنْ شَيْءٍ يَقِفُ فِي طَرِيقِ نَجَاحِهِ.	There is nothing that could stand in the way of his success.

Two-letter prepositions

مِنْ can be used following or with the particle (كُلّ) to mean 'both' or 'each of', as in the following cases:

انْضَمَّتِ الْهَيْئَةُ إلَى عُضْوِيَّةِ كُلٍّ مِنَ الاتِّحَادَاتِ وَالْمُؤَسَّسَاتِ الْمَحَلِّيَّةِ.	The commission joined as a member of both the federations and the local institutions.
مَاذَا يَقُودُ كُلٌّ مِنْ مُحَمَّدٍ وَصَلَاحٍ؟	What do Muhammad and Salah each drive?
تَشَكَّلَتِ الْجَمْعِيَّةُ بِعُضْوِيَّةِ كُلٍّ مِنَ السُّودَانِ وَمِصْرَ.	The association was formed with both Sudan and Egypt as members.

When مِنْ is preceded by an indefinite noun and followed by a definite plural of the same noun, this indicates that the identity of a person or a thing is completely indeterminate, as in the following:

أَمِيرٌ مِنَ الأُمَرَاءِ	a certain prince
بَابٌ مِنَ الأَبْوَابِ	a certain door

مِنْ with pronoun suffixes

مِنْ can be followed by a noun or a pronoun. When it joins a pronoun, it becomes a prefix and the pronoun becomes a suffix. The following table shows how different pronouns appear after the مِنْ:

مِنْ + هما	مِنْهُمَا	مِنْ + أنا	مِنِّي*
مِنْ + نحن	مِنَّا*	مِنْ + أنتَ	مِنْكَ
مِنْ + أنتم	مِنْكُمْ	مِنْ + أنتِ	مِنْكِ
مِنْ + أنتن	مِنْكُنَّ	مِنْ + هو	مِنْه
مِنْ + هم	مِنْهُمْ	مِنْ + هي	مِنْهَا
مِنْ + هنّ	مِنْهُنَّ	مِنْ + أنتما	مِنْكُمَا

* The ن of مِنْ is doubled when connected to the suffixes of the first person.

Note the use of مِنْ to express surprise or disbelief indefinite noun مِنْ + pronoun suffix + ل + يا:

يَا لَكَ مِنْ خَبِيثٍ!	How evil you are!
يَا لَهُ مِنْ قَائِدٍ!	What a great leader he is!

Notes on translation

Compare the prepositions in the following Arabic sentences with their corresponding English translations.

Two-letter prepositions

هَزَّ الْإِنْفِجَارُ أَجْزَاءً مِنَ الْعَاصِمَةِ الْعِرَاقِيَّةِ.	The explosion shook parts of the Iraqi capital.
لَا يَجُوزُ لِلطَّيَّارِينَ الطَّيَرَانُ خِلَالَ ثَمَانِي سَاعَاتٍ مِنْ مُعَاقَرَتِهِمُ الْخَمْرَ.	Pilots are not permitted to operate aircraft within eight hours of having consumed alcohol.
يَضُمُّ الْمَبْنَى عَدَدًا مِنَ الْمَكَاتِبِ الْحُكُومِيَّةِ.	The building is home to a number of government offices.
إِنَّ مُوَاجَهَةَ غَلَاءِ الْمَعِيشَةِ أَوْلَوِيَّةٌ مُتَقَدِّمَةٌ مِنْ أَوْلَوِيَّاتِ وِزَارَةِ الِاقْتِصَادِ.	Tackling the high cost of living is one of the top priorities of the Ministry of Economics.
أَفَادَ شَاهِدُ عِيَانٍ بِالْقُرْبِ مِنْ مَوْقِعِ الِانْفِجَارِ بِأَنَّ طِفْلَيْنِ وَأَرْبَعَةَ رِجَالٍ كَانُوا مِنْ بَيْنِ الْمَوْتَى.	An eyewitness close to the site of the explosion reported that two children and four men were among the dead.
إِنَّ الْعَصَبِيَّةَ الْقَبَلِيَّةَ هِيَ مِنْ أَهَمِّ مُرَكَّبَاتِ الثَّقَافَةِ الْبَدَوِيَّةِ.	Tribalism is one of the most important components of Bedouin culture.
دَامَ الزِّلْزَالُ مَا يُقْرُبُ مِنْ عِشْرِينَ ثَانِيَةً.	The earthquake lasted around twenty seconds.
يَعِيشُ مَا يُقْرُبُ مِنْ 34 مِلْيُونَ مَكْسِيكِيٍّ فِي الْوِلَايَاتِ الْمُتَّحِدَةِ.	About 34 million Mexicans live in the United States.
أَهْدَى الرَّئِيسُ السُّودَانِيُّ مِصْرَ 5000 رَأْسٍ مِنَ الْأَبْقَارِ الْحَيَّةِ، هَذَا بِالْإِضَافَةِ إِلَى 2000 رَأْسٍ قَدَّمَهَا مُمَثِّلُو الْقِطَاعِ الْخَاصِّ.	The Sudanese president gave Egypt 5,000 heads of cattle as a gift, in addition to another 2,000 heads (of cattle) given by representatives from the private sector.
يُؤَكِّدُ مِنْ جَدِيدٍ تَطَلُّعَهُ إِلَى أَنْ تُنْهِيَ الْمَحْكَمَةُ أَعْمَالَهَا فِي أَقْرَبِ وَقْتٍ مُمْكِنٍ.	He reiterated his expectation that the court would conclude its deliberations as soon as possible.

Fixed expressions with مِنْ

اِعْتِبَارًا مِنْ	as of/from	سَيَتِمُّ تَطْبِيقُ أَسْعَارِ الصَّرْفِ الْجَدِيدَةِ اِعْتِبَارًا مِنَ الشَّهْرِ الْقَادِمِ.	New exchange rates are to be applied as of the beginning of next month.
بَعْضٌ مِنْ	some of	وَهَذِهِ بَعْضٌ مِنَ الْمَشَاكِلِ الَّتِي تُقْلِقُنَا.	These are some of the problems that concern us.
سِلْسِلَةٌ مِنْ	a series of	تَعَرَّضَتْ تَشِيلِي لِسِلْسِلَةٍ مِنَ الْفَيَضَانَاتِ.	Chile has experienced a series of floods.
سَيْلٌ مِنْ	a spate of	فُوجِئَ رَئِيسُ الْحُكُومَةِ بِسَيْلٍ مِنَ الِانْتِقَادَاتِ فِي صُحُفِ الْمُعَارَضَةِ.	The prime minister was surprised by a spate of criticism in the opposition newspapers.

قَلِيل مِنْ	a bit of / a small amount of	كَانَ عَلَيْهِمْ أَنْ يَعْمَلُوا طَوَالَ اللَّيْلِ لِلْحُصُولِ عَلَى الْقَلِيلِ مِنَ الْمَالِ فَقَطْ.	They had to work the whole night long just to get a bit of cash.
كَثِير مِنْ	plenty of/a lot of	هُنَاكَ الْكَثِيرُ مِنَ الْمَشَارِيعِ الْعِمْلَاقَةِ الَّتِي يَجِبُ الْعَمَلُ عَلَيْهَا.	There are plenty of massive projects to work on.
مَجْمُوعَة مِنْ	a group of/a set of	كُنْتُ مَارًّا مِنْ أَمَامِ الْمُتْحَفِ عِنْدَمَا رَأَيْتُ مَجْمُوعَةً مِنَ التَّلَامِيذِ يَرْسُمُونَ اللَّوْحَاتِ.	I was passing by the museum when I saw a group of students painting.
مِمَّا لَا جَدَلَ فِيهِ أَنَّ	undisputed that	مِمَّا لَا جَدَلَ فِيهِ أَنَّ السَّفَرَ يَزِيدُ مِنْ مَعْرِفَةِ الْإِنْسَانِ بِالثَّقَافَاتِ الْأُخْرَى.	It is undisputed that traveling increases people's knowledge of other cultures.
مِمَّا لَا رَيْبَ فِيهِ أَنَّ	certainly/ undoubtedly	مِمَّا لَا رَيْبَ فِيهِ أَنَّ نَتَائِجَ الْإِنْتِخَابَاتِ الْأَخِيرَةِ كَانَتْ مُتَوَقَّعَةً إِلَى حَدٍّ كَبِيرٍ.	There is no doubt that the results of the last elections were largely predictable.
مِمَّا لَا شَكَّ فِيهِ أَنَّ	undoubtedly/ no doubt	مِمَّا لَا شَكَّ فِيهِ أَنَّ دُوَلَ مِنْطَقَةِ الْخَلِيجِ تَمُرُّ بِمَرْحَلَةِ تَحَرُّرٍ اِقْتِصَادِيٍّ كَبِيرَةٍ.	There is no doubt that the Gulf countries are going through a phase of great economic liberalization.
مِنْ أَجْلِ	for/to/in order to	لَا بُدَّ مِنْ بَذْلِ الْجُهُودِ مِنْ أَجْلِ تَحْقِيقِ السَّلَامِ الشَّامِلِ بَيْنَ الْفِلَسْطِينِيِّينَ وَالْإِسْرَائِيلِيِّينَ.	Efforts must be made in order to achieve comprehensive peace between Palestinians and Israelis.
مِنْ إِجْمَالِي	of the total	يَسْكُنُ هَذِهِ الْمُقَاطَعَةَ عَشَرَةً بِالْمِئَةِ مِنْ إِجْمَالِي عَدَدِ السُّكَّانِ.	Ten percent of the total population lives in this county.
مِنْ أَصْلِ	out of [an original number]	شَارَكَ فِي الْإِنْتِخَابَاتِ أَرْبَعَةُ أَحْزَابٍ مِنْ أَصْلِ عَشَرَةِ أَحْزَابٍ.	Four out of ten parties have participated in the elections.
مِنْ أَعْمَاقِ الْقَلْبِ	from the bottom of the heart	كَانَتْ كَلِمَاتُهَا صَادِقَةً وَتَخْرُجُ مِنْ أَعْمَاقِ الْقَلْبِ.	Her words were candid and came from the bottom of her heart.
مِنَ الْأَدَبِ أَنْ	it's polite to	مِنَ الْأَدَبِ أَنْ تَحْتَرِمَ مَنْ هُوَ أَكْبَرُ مِنْكَ سِنًّا.	It's polite to respect those who are older than you.

Two-letter prepositions 63

It would be better for the economy to create new jobs in the labor market.	مِنَ الْأَفْضَلِ لِلْاِقْتِصَادِ خَلْقُ وَظَائِفَ جَدِيدَةٍ فِي سُوقِ الْعَمَلِ.	be preferable/be better	مِنَ الْأَفْضَلِ
From now on there will be negotiations between the alliance and the council.	مِنَ الْآنَ فَصَاعِدًا سَتَكُونُ هُنَاكَ مُشَاوَرَاتٌ بَيْنَ الْحِلْفِ وَالْمَجْلِسِ.	from now on	مِنَ الْآنَ فَصَاعِدًا
It is quite obvious that our actions alone cannot save us.	مِنَ الْبَدِيهِيِّ أَنَّ أَعْمَالَنَا وَحْدَهَا لَنْ تَكْفِيَ لِإِنْقَاذِنَا.	it goes without saying/it is obvious	مِنَ الْبَدِيهِيِّ
It's cowardly to ask others to present their work while you hide your own.	مِنَ الْجُبْنِ أَنْ تُخْفِي أَعْمَالَكَ وَتَطْلُبَ مِنَ الْآخَرِينَ أَنْ يُقَدِّمُوا أَعْمَالَهُمْ.	it's cowardice/cowardly to	مِنَ الْجُبْنِ أَنْ
It's noteworthy that the excavation is a joint project between the British Museum and the government of Sudan.	وَمِنَ الْجَدِيرِ بِالذِّكْرِ أَنَّ الْحَفْرِيَاتِ مَشْرُوعٌ مُشْتَرَكٌ بَيْنَ الْمُتْحَفِ الْبِرِيطَانِيِّ وَالْحُكُومَةِ السُّودَانِيَّةِ.	it's noteworthy	مِنَ الْجَدِيرِ بِالذِّكْرِ
It became obvious that they were being held as hostages in order to be exchanged.	مِنَ الْجَلِيِّ أَنَّ هَؤُلَاءِ الْأَشْخَاصَ قَدْ أُخِذُوا رَهَائِنَ مِنْ أَجْلِ مُبَادَلَتِهِمْ.	it is obvious/it is clear	مِنَ الْجَلِيِّ
It would be wrong to ignore the problems of the poor and marginalized in society.	مِنَ الْخَطَأِ تَجَاهُلُ مُشْكِلَاتِ الْفُقَرَاءِ وَالْمُهَمَّشِينَ فِي الْمُجْتَمَعِ.	It is wrong/mistake	مِنَ الْخَطَأِ
When my son came home, he was covered in dirt from head to toe.	عِنْدَمَا رَجَعَ ابْنِي إِلَى الْبَيْتِ كَانَ مُغَطًّى بِالطِّينِ مِنَ الرَّأْسِ إِلَى الْقَدَمَيْنِ.	from head to toe	مِنَ الرَّأْسِ إِلَى الْقَدَمِ
It was not easy to accept the presence of the occupation.	لَمْ يَكُنْ تَقَبُّلُ وُجُودِ الْاِحْتِلَالِ مِنَ السُّهُولَةِ بِمَكَانٍ.	easy	مِنَ السُّهُولَةِ بِمَكَانٍ
It's very brave for people to face up to their own fears.	إِنَّهُ مِنَ الشَّجَاعَةِ أَنْ يُوَاجِهَ الْمَرْءُ مَخَاوِفَهُ.	it's courageous to	مِنَ الشَّجَاعَةِ أَنْ
It is normal that the budget should show a shortfall every now and then.	مِنَ الطَّبِيعِيِّ أَنْ يَكُونَ هُنَاكَ عَجْزٌ فِي الْمِيزَانِيَّةِ مِنْ وَقْتٍ لِآخَرَ.	is natural/is normal	مِنَ الطَّبِيعِيِّ

Two-letter prepositions

مِنَ الْغَرَائِبِ	one of the wonders …	سُورُ الصِّينِ الْعَظِيمُ هُوَ وَاحِدٌ مِنَ الْغَرَائِبِ فِي هَذَا الْعَالَمِ.	The Great Wall of China is one the wonders of the world.
مِنَ الْقِمَّةِ إِلَى الْقَاعِ	top-down	هُنَاكَ خُطَّةٌ مِنْ قِبَلِ الْحُكُومَةِ لِلِاسْتِفَادَةِ مِنَ الْكَفَاءَاتِ الْجَيِّدَةِ يَجْرِي حَالِيًّا مُنَاقَشَتُهَا مِنَ الْقِمَّةِ إِلَى الْقَاعِ.	There is a plan on the part of the government to take advantage of the good competencies being discussed from top to bottom.
مِنَ الْكَرَمِ أَنْ	it is generous to	إِنَّهُ لَمِنَ الْكَرَمِ أَنْ تَتَصَدَّقَ عَلَى الْمُحْتَاجِينَ إِذَا اسْتَطَعْتَ.	It is generous to give charity to the needy if you can.
مِنَ اللَّافِتِ لِلنَّظَرِ	is remarkable/ is striking	مِنَ اللَّافِتِ لِلنَّظَرِ حَقًّا أَنَّ عَدَدَ الدُّوَلِ الأَطْرَافِ قَدِ ارْتَفَعَ فِي هَذِهِ الْفَتْرَةِ الْقَصِيرَةِ.	It is indeed remarkable that the number of member states has risen within such a short period of time.
مِنَ الْمُتَعَارَفِ عَلَيهِ	it is well accepted/ recognized	مِنَ الْمُتَعَارَفِ عَلَيهِ الْآنَ أَنَّ الْفِئَاتِ الْمُهَمَّشَةَ دَاخِلَ أَيِّ مُجْتَمَعٍ يَشْتَدُّ تَعَرُّضُهَا لِخَطَرِ الْإِصَابَةِ بِفَيرُوسِ نَقْصِ الْمَنَاعَةِ الْمُكْتَسَبَةِ.	It is now widely recognized that marginalized groups within any society face a heightened vulnerability to infection with HIV.
مِنَ الْمُتَوَقَّعِ	it is anticipated/it is foreseen	مِنَ الْمُتَوَقَّعِ أَنْ يَكُونَ تَنْفِيذُ الْمَشْرُوعِ بَطِيئًا.	It is anticipated that the implementation of the project will be slow.
مِنَ الْمُثِيرِ لِلْإِنْتِباهِ	it is striking	مِنَ الْمُثِيرِ لِلْإِنْتِباهِ أَنَّ اللَّاجِئِينَ يَتَمَتَّعُونَ إِلَى حَدٍّ مَا بِأَحْوَالٍ مَعِيشِيَّةٍ أَفْضَلَ مِمَّا يَتَمَتَّعُ بِهِ الْأَشْخَاصُ الْمُشَرَّدُونَ.	It is a striking thought that in some ways, refugees enjoy better living conditions than homeless people.
مِنَ الْمُثِيرِ لِلشَّفَقَةِ	it's pathetic	مِنَ الْمُثِيرِ لِلشَّفَقَةِ عَدَمُ عِلْمِهِمْ بِمَا سَيَحْصَلُ لَاحِقًا.	It's pathetic that they didn't anticipate what was coming next.
مِنَ الْمُحْتَمَلِ	it is possible/ it is likely	مِنَ الْمُحْتَمَلِ أَنْ يَكُونَ هَذَا الْعَامُ مُحَدَّداً لِمَصِيرِ الْقَارَّةِ.	This year is likely to be decisive for the fate of the continent.
مِنَ الْمُرَجَّحِ	is likely that	مِنَ الْمُرَجَّحِ أَنْ تَكُونَ الْحُكُومَةُ قَدِ اتَّخَذَتْ قَرَارًا بِإِلْغَاءِ الرُّسُومِ.	It is likely that the government has decided to abolish fees.

Two-letter prepositions 65

It's a chivalrous act to help a stranger without charge.	مِنَ الْمُرُوءَةِ أَنْ تُسَاعِدَ غَرِيبًا دُونَ مُقَابِلَ.	it's a chivalrous act/an act of chivalry to …	مِنَ الْمُرُوءَةِ أَنْ
The lawyer concluded that it is unlikely that the authorities had knowledge of the complainant's recent activities.	اِسْتَنْتَجَ الْمُحَامِي أَنَّهُ مِنَ الْمُسْتَبْعَدِ أَنْ تَكُونَ السُّلُطَاتُ عَلَى دِرَايَةٍ بِأَنْشِطَةِ صَاحِبَةِ الشَّكْوَى الْأَخِيرَةِ.	it is unlikely/ out of the question	مِنَ الْمُسْتَبْعَدِ
It is not surprising that they are once again making an unsuccessful attempt to mislead the international community.	لَيْسَ مِنَ الْمُسْتَغْرَبِ قِيَامُهُمْ مَرَّةً أُخْرَى بِمُحَاوَلَةٍ فَاشِلَةٍ لِتَضْلِيلِ الْمُجْتَمَعِ الدُّوَلِيِّ.	surprisingly	مِنَ الْمُسْتَغْرَبِ
The benefits of investing in this sector are known to be lucrative.	مِنَ الْمَعْرُوفِ أَنَّ الاِسْتِثْمَارَ فِي هَذَا الْقِطَاعِ يَعُودُ بِمَنَافِعَ كَبِيرَةٍ.	is known	مِنَ الْمَعْرُوفِ
It is well known that good education is a main tool for bringing about change.	مِنَ الْمَعْلُومِ أَنَّ التَّعْلِيمَ الْجَيِّدَ هُوَ أَحَدُ الْأَدَوَاتِ الرَّئِيسَةِ لِإِحْدَاثِ التَّغْيِيرِ.	it is well known	مِنَ الْمَعْلُومِ
It would be worthwhile for the government to gain knowledge about those positive programs.	وَقَدْ يَكُونُ مِنَ الْمُفِيدِ أَنْ تَطَّلِعَ الْحُكُومَةُ عَلَى تِلْكَ الْبَرَامِجِ الْإِيجَابِيَّةِ.	worthwhile/ helpful	مِنَ الْمُفِيدِ
The opening of economic negotiations was scheduled to take place in the middle of this month.	كَانَ مِنَ الْمُقَرَّرِ بَدْءُ الْمُفَاوَضَاتِ الاِقْتِصَادِيَّةِ فِي مُنْتَصَفِ الشَّهْرِ.	is scheduled/ is planned	مِنَ الْمُقَرَّرِ
Therefore, it is possible to prohibit such activities.	وَلِذَلِكَ مَنِ الْمُمْكِنِ حَظْرُ أَنْشِطَةٍ كَهَذِهِ.	it is possible	مَنِ الْمُمْكِنِ
Education should be seen as a continuous process from cradle to grave.	يَنْبَغِي النَّظَرُ إِلَى التَّعْلِيمِ بِاعْتِبَارِهِ عَمَلِيَّةً مُتَوَاصِلَةً مِنَ الْمَهْدِ إِلَى اللَّحْدِ.	from cradle to grave	مِنَ الْمَهْدِ إِلَى اللَّحْدِ
It is a pity you can't come tonight.	مِنَ الْمُؤْسِفِ أَنَّكَ لَنْ تَسْتَطِيعَ الْحُضُورَ اللَّيْلَةَ.	it is a pity/it is unfortunate	مِنَ الْمُؤْسِفِ
The answer will definitely vary between different parties.	مِنَ الْمُؤَكَّدِ أَنَّ الْإِجَابَةَ سَتَخْتَلِفُ بَيْنَ رَأْيٍ وَآخَرَ.	definitely/ certainly	مِنَ الْمُؤَكَّدِ

Two-letter prepositions

English example	Arabic example	Meaning	Preposition
It is rare for a visitor to China not to want to visit Beijing.	مِنَ النَّادِرِ أَنْ تَجِدَ زَائِرًا إِلَى الصِّينِ لَا يَرْغَبُ فِي زِيَارَةِ مَدِينَةِ بِكِين.	it is rare/ rarely	مِنَ النَّادِرِ
It is still imperative to address the various legal and logistical challenges.	وَلَا يُزَالُ مِنَ الْوَاجِبِ التَّصَدِّي لِعَدَدٍ مِنَ التَّحَدِّيَاتِ الْقَانُونِيَّةِ وَاللُّوجِسْتِيَّةِ	must be/is imperative	مِنَ الْوَاجِبِ
Obviously this is a very sensitive issue for many people.	مِنَ الْوَاضِحِ أَنَّهَا قَضِيَّةٌ حَسَّاسَةٌ بِالنِّسْبَةِ لِلْعَدِيدِ مِنَ الْأَشْخَاصِ.	obviously/ apparently/ clearly	مِنَ الْوَاضِحِ
The visit of the European official to the region was a matter of courtesy.	جَاءَتْ زِيَارَةُ الْمَسْؤُولِ الْأُورُوبِّيِّ إِلَى الْمِنْطَقَةِ مِنْ بَابِ الْمُجَامَلَةِ.	a matter of / to do with ...	مِنْ بَابِ
Foreign capital flight is amongst the reasons for economic recession.	مِنْ بَيْنِ أَسْبَابِ الرُّكُودِ الْاِقْتِصَادِيِّ هُرُوبُ رَأْسِ الْمَالِ الْأَجْنَبِيِّ.	among	مِنْ بَيْنِ
Oil prices have fallen in domestic markets for a period of one month but have since started to rise once again.	انْخَفَضَتْ أَسْعَارُ النَّفْطِ فِي الْأَسْوَاقِ الْمَحَلِّيَّةِ لِمُدَّةِ شَهْرٍ وَمِنْ ثَمَّ عَاوَدَتِ الْارْتِفَاعَ.	and then/ have since	مِنْ ثَمَّ
On the other hand, some of these reforms have had adverse effects on the poor.	مِنْ جَانِبٍ آخَرَ أَحْدَثَتْ بَعْضُ هَذِهِ الْإِصْلَاحَاتِ آثَارًا سَلْبِيَّةً بِالنِّسْبَةِ لِلْفُقَرَاءِ.	on the other hand	مِنْ جَانِبٍ آخَرَ
The World Bank expectations have raised concerns once again over the performance of the region's economies.	أَثَارَتْ تَوَقُّعَاتُ الْبَنْكِ الدُّوَلِيِّ الْمَخَاوِفَ مِنْ جَدِيدٍ حَوْلَ أَدَاءِ اقْتِصَادَاتِ الْمِنْطَقَةِ.	again/once again	مِنْ جَدِيدٍ
Two police officers were killed, and some civilians were injured due to the explosion.	قُتِلَ شُرْطِيَّانِ وَأُصِيبَ مَدَنِيُّونَ آخَرُونَ مِنْ جَرَّاءِ الْانْفِجَارِ.	as a result of/owing to/ due to	مِنْ جَرَّاءِ
Construction workers represent 60% of the total population.	يُمَثِّلُ عُمَّالُ الْبِنَاءِ 60% مِنْ جُمْلَةِ السُّكَّانِ.	of the total	مِنْ جُمْلَةِ
On the other hand, the judges have taken measures to expedite proceedings.	قَامَ الْقُضَاةُ مِنْ جِهَةٍ أُخْرَى بِاتِّخَاذِ التَّدَابِيرِ اللَّازِمَةِ لِلتَّعْجِيلِ بِالْإِجْرَاءَاتِ.	on the other hand	مِنْ جِهَةٍ أُخْرَى

Two-letter prepositions

Luckily the governments have agreed the terms of the convention.	مِنْ حُسْنِ الْحَظِّ أَنَّ الْحُكُومَاتِ وَافَقَتْ عَلَى بُنُودِ الاِتِّفَاقِيَّةِ.	luckily/it is fortunate	مِنْ حُسْنِ الْحَظِّ
It is good manners not to interfere in other people's affairs.	مِنْ حُسْنِ الْخُلُقِ أَلَّا نَتَدَخَّلَ فِي أُمُورِ الْآخَرِينَ.	it's good manners to	مِنْ حُسْنِ الْخُلُقِ
People have the right to object to government policies.	مِنْ حَقِّ الشَّعْبِ الاِعْتِرَاضُ عَلَى سِيَاسِيَّاتِ الْحُكُومَةِ.	right to	مِنْ حَقِّ
Our bank was ranked first among all the Arab banks in terms of the volume of customers' deposits.	اِحْتَلَّ مَصْرِفُنَا الْمَرْتَبَةَ الْأُولَى مِنْ بَيْنِ الْمَصَارِفِ الْعَرَبِيَّةِ مِنْ حَيْثُ حَجْمِ وَدَائِعِ الْعُمَلَاءِ.	in terms of/ as regards	مِنْ حَيْثُ
Through my stay in the West I have come to notice the difference in customer service in our country and over there.	مِنْ خِلَالِ إِقَامَتِي فِي الْغَرْبِ لَاحَظْتُ الْفَرْقَ بَيْنَ أُسْلُوبِ خِدْمَةِ الْعُمَلَاءِ فِي بِلَادِنَا وَهُنَاكَ.	through	مِنْ خِلَالِ
The opposition has conducted a dialogue with the government behind the scenes.	أَجْرَتِ الْمُعَارَضَةُ الْحِوَارَ مَعَ الْحُكُومَةِ مِنْ خَلْفِ السِّتَارِ.	behind	مِنْ خَلْفِ
It's a cause for concern that the danger of nuclear weapons has not yet been eliminated.	مِنْ دَوَاعِي الْقَلَقِ أَنَّهُ لَمْ يَتِمَّ حَتَّى الْآنَ إِزَالَةُ خَطَرِ الْأَسْلِحَةِ النَّوَوِيَّةِ.	cause for concern	مِنْ دَوَاعِي الْقَلَقِ
It is my pleasure to welcome you to this meeting.	إِنَّهُ مِنْ دَوَاعِي سُرُورِي أَنْ أُرَحِّبَ بِكُمْ فِي هَذَا الاِجْتِمَاعِ.	my pleasure to	مِنْ دَوَاعِي سُرُورِي
The budget has been adopted without debating all the articles in parliament.	تَمَّ اِعْتِمَادُ الْمُوَازَنَةِ مِنْ دُونِ مُنَاقَشَةِ جَمِيعِ الْبُنُودِ فِي الْبَرْلَمَانِ.	without	مِنْ دُونِ
The case has not been handled from a religious or moral perspective.	لَمْ يَتِمَّ التَّعَامُلُ مَعَ الْقَضِيَّةِ مِنْ زَاوِيَةٍ دِينِيَّةٍ أَوْ أَخْلَاقِيَّةٍ.	from the perspective/ angle of	مِنْ زَاوِيَةٍ
It's bad manners to make fun of others.	إِنَّهُ لَمِنْ سُوءِ الْخُلُقِ أَنْ تَعِيبَ عَلَى الْآخَرِينَ.	it's bad manners to	مِنْ سُوءِ الْخُلُقِ
The Hanging Gardens of Babylon are one of the wonders of the ancient world.	حَدَائِقُ بَابِلَ الْمُعَلَّقَةُ هِيَ وَاحِدَةٌ مِنْ عَجَائِبِ وَغَرَائِبِ الْعَالَمِ الْقَدِيمِ.	one of the wonders . . .	مِنْ عَجَائِبِ

Two-letter prepositions

English	Arabic example	Gloss	Preposition
The Queen Alia Bridge was inaugurated by King Faisal II in 1956.	تَمَّ اِفْتِتَاحُ جِسْرِ "الْمَلِكَةِ عَالِيَةَ" سَنَةَ 1956 مِنْ قِبَلِ الْمَلِكِ فَيْصَلٍ الثَّانِي.	by	مِنْ قِبَلِ
He apologized for his racist comment and alleged that he'd meant it as a joke.	اِعْتَذَرَ عَنِ التَّعْلِيقِ الْعُنْصُرِيِّ وَقَالَ إِنَّهُ قَالَهُ مِنْ قَبِيلِ الْمِزَاحِ.	by way of.../as a sort of...	مِنْ قَبِيلِ
We are hearing good news from every direction.	تَأْتِينَا الْأَخْبَارُ الْجَيِّدَةُ مِنْ كُلِّ اِتِّجَاهٍ.	from every direction/on all sides	مِنْ كُلِّ اِتِّجَاهٍ
Foreign goods from all over have swamped Middle Eastern markets.	اِمْتَلَأَتْ أَسْوَاقُ الشَّرْقِ الْأَوْسَطِ بِالْبَضَائِعِ الْأَجْنَبِيَّةِ مِنْ كُلِّ حَدَبٍ وَصَوْبٍ.	from far and wide/from all over	مِنْ كُلِّ حَدَبٍ وَصَوْبٍ
It is in the interest of the new government to engage in discussions with neighboring states.	مِنْ مَصْلَحَةِ الْحُكُومَةِ الْجَدِيدَةِ أَنْ تَبْدَأَ التَّحَاوُرَ مَعَ دُوَلِ الْجِوَارِ.	in the interest of	مِنْ مَصْلَحَةِ
Out of a desire to strengthen bilateral relations, the two states have signed several trade agreements.	مِنْ مُنْطَلَقِ تَعْزِيزِ الْعَلَاقَاتِ الثُّنَائِيَّةِ، وَقَّعَ الْبَلَدَانِ عِدَّةَ اِتِّفَاقَاتٍ تِجَارِيَّةٍ.	out of a desire to.../with the basic aim of...	مِنْ مُنْطَلَقِ
The new law should be discussed from the human rights standpoint.	يَجِبُ مُنَاقَشَةُ الْقَانُونِ الْجَدِيدِ مِنْ مَنْظُورِ حُقُوقِ الْإِنْسَانِ.	from the standpoint of/from the perspective of	مِنْ مَنْظُورِ
On the other hand, the collapse in the currency purchasing power has contributed to increasing social tensions.	مِنْ نَاحِيَةٍ أُخْرَى، سَاهَمَ اِنْهِيَارُ الْقُوَّةِ الشِّرَائِيَّةِ لِلْعُمْلَةِ فِي زِيَادَةِ التَّوَتُّرَاتِ الِاجْتِمَاعِيَّةِ.	on the other hand	مِنْ نَاحِيَةٍ أُخْرَى
There are a lot of social problems of this kind.	هُنَاكَ الْعَدِيدُ مِنَ الْمَشَاكِلِ الِاجْتِمَاعِيَّةِ مِنْ هَذَا الْقَبِيلِ.	of this kind	مِنْ هَذَا الْقَبِيلِ
Most of Jerusalem's Christian population have emigrated. It would therefore be wrong to focus only on Islamic sacred places.	هَاجَرَ مُعْظَمُ سُكَّانِ الْقُدْسِ مِنَ الْمَسِيحِيِّينَ. وَمِنْ هُنَا فَإِنَّهُ مِنَ الْخَطَأِ التَّرْكِيزُ عَلَى الْمُقَدَّسَاتِ الْإِسْلَامِيَّةِ وَحْدَهَا.	therefore/accordingly	مِنْ هُنَا
All that you need is to paint a few sections here and there for this wall to be as it was before.	طِلَاءُ بَعْضِ الْأَجْزَاءِ مِنْ هُنَا وَهُنَاكَ هُوَ كُلُّ مَا تَحْتَاجُ إِلَيْهِ لِتُعِيدَ هَذَا الْجِدَارَ كَمَا كَانَ.	here and there	مِنْ هُنَا وَهُنَاكَ

Two-letter prepositions

English	Arabic example	Meaning	Preposition
It is the duty of the government to allow political participation for everyone.	مِنْ وَاجِبِ الْحُكُومَةِ إِفْسَاحُ الْمَجَالِ لِلْجَمِيعِ لِلْمُشَارَكَةِ السِّيَاسِيَّةِ.	duty of	مِنْ وَاجِبِ
The show will try to provide images that reflect reality in our communities.	سَيُحَاوِلُ الْبَرْنَامَجُ تَقْدِيمَ صُوَرٍ حَيَّةٍ مِنْ وَاقِعِ مُجْتَمَعَاتِنَا.	from reality	مِنْ وَاقِعِ
The ruling party was running the presidential elections from behind the scenes.	كَانَ الْحِزْبُ الْحَاكِمُ يُدِيرُ الْاِنْتِخَابَاتِ الرِّئَاسِيَّةَ مِنْ وَرَاءِ الْكَوَالِيسِ.	from behind	مِنْ وَرَاءِ
From time to time, armed groups direct their attacks against the regular forces.	تُوَجِّهُ الْجَمَاعَاتُ الْمُسَلَّحَةُ هَجَمَاتٍ عَلَى الْقُوَّاتِ النِّظَامِيَّةِ مِنْ وَقْتٍ لِآخَرَ.	occasionally/ from time to time	مِنْ وَقْتٍ لِآخَرَ
The political activist was arrested a month ago and since then nothing has been known about him.	تَمَّ اعْتِقَالُ النَّاشِطِ السِّيَاسِيِّ مِنْ شَهْرٍ، وَمِنْ يَوْمِهَا لَمْ تَخْرُجْ أَيَّةُ أَخْبَارٍ عَنْهُ.	since then	مِنْ يَوْمِهَا
It is unfortunate for the citizens that the government didn't intervene to reduce prices.	مِنْ سُوءِ حَظِّ الْمُوَاطِنِينَ أَنَّ الْحُكُومَةَ لَمْ تَتَدَخَّلْ لِخَفْضِ الْأَسْعَارِ.	it is unfortunate/ unluckily for ...	مِنْ سُوءِ حَظٍّ
In the nineties, Egypt faced a wave of attacks on tourists.	شَهِدَتْ مِصْرُ فِي التِّسْعِينَاتِ مَوْجَةً مِنَ الْاِعْتِدَاءَاتِ عَلَى السَّائِحِينَ.	wave of	مَوْجَةٌ مِنَ

عَنْ

عَنْ is used to serve at least nine functions. Like many other prepositions, عَنْ includes the functions of other prepositions. It is considered to be a 'true preposition'.

عَنْ *in context*

أَعْرَبَ مَنْدُوبُ الْأُمَمِ الْمُتَّحِدَةِ عَنْ قَلَقِهِ مِنَ الْوَضْعِ فِي سُورِيَا، كَمَا تَحَدَّثَ عَنِ الْأَوْضَاعِ الْمُتَرَدِّيَةِ لِلْمَدَنِيِّينَ وَعَجْزِهِمْ مِنَ الْخُرُوجِ عَنْ مَنَازِلِهِمْ، وَتَأَخُّرِ الْمَعُونَاتِ الْإِنْسَانِيَّةِ عَنِ الْوُصُولِ إِلَى الْمَدَنِيِّينَ. وَطَلَبَ مِنَ الْأَطْرَافِ الْمُتَنَازِعَةِ الْاِبْتِعَادَ عَنِ الْأَمَاكِنِ الْآهِلَةِ بِالسُّكَّانِ، كَمَا دَعَا إِلَى عُدُولِ الْجَمِيعِ عَنْ حَمْلِ السِّلَاحِ وَالرُّجُوعِ

70 *Two-letter prepositions*

> إِلَى طَاوِلَةِ الْمُحَادَثَاتِ لِحَلِّ الْأَزْمَةِ. وَفِي نِهَايَةِ حَدِيثِهِ قَالَ بِأَنَّهُ سَيَتَحَدَّثُ عَمَّا قَرِيبٍ مَعَ الْأَمِينِ الْعَامِّ لِلْأُمَمِ الْمُتَّحِدَةِ عَنِ الْوَضْعِ الْحَالِيِّ فِي سُورِيَا.
>
> The United Nations delegate expressed concern regarding the situation in Syria and talked about the deteriorating circumstances of civilians, their inability to leave their homes and the delay in providing them with humanitarian aid. He called upon the warring parties to keep away from populated areas. He also called for everyone to lay down their arms and to return to the negotiating table so as to resolve the crisis. At the end of his speech, he said he would soon be talking to the UN Secretary-General about the current situation in Syria.

Notes on عَنْ *in context*

In the preceding paragraph, عَنْ is used in several places as an integral part of different verbs that collocate with this preposition, as in (أَعْرَبَ عَنْ، تَحَدَّثَ عَنْ، عَجَزَ عَنْ، تَأَخَّرَ عَنْ). It may or may not always follow the verbs immediately, as in (أَعْرَبَ عَنْ). In (بِالْابْتِعَادِ عَنِ), the preposition is used as part of a collocation with a verbal noun. The word (عَمَّا) in (عَمَّا قَرِيبٍ) is a combination of (مَا + عَنْ). Note that the (نْ) at the end of عَنْ is deleted, and shadda is added to مَا.

Functions of عَنْ

عَنْ is used to denote a departure away from, or distance from, something or someone, although it is worth noting that the Basra grammar school sanctioned only particular functions of عن. This departure or distance can be with reference to places or people, as in the following:

نَصَحْتُ صَدِيقِي أَنْ يَبْتَعِدَ عَنْ أَصْدِقَاءِ السُّوءِ.	I advised my friend to distance himself from bad crowds.
سَافَرْتُ عَنِ الْبَلَدِ.	I traveled out of the country.
يَغِيبُ وَلَدُكَ دَوْمًا عَنْ صَلَاةِ الْجُمُعَةِ.	Your son often misses Friday prayers.
يَتَرَفَّعُ الْمُؤْمِنُ عَنِ الْفَسَادِ خَوْفًا مِنَ اللهِ.	A believer avoids corruption for fear of God.

عَنْ may be used to provide a reason for or account of an action, as in the following:

لَمْ أَذْهَبْ إِلَى بَيْتِهِ إِلَّا عَنْ طَلَبٍ مِنْهُ.	I only went to his house because he asked me to.
لَمْ أُحَارِبْهُ إِلَّا دِفَاعًا عَنِ الْحَقِّ.	I only fought him to defend the truth.
نَصِيحَتِي لَهَا كَانَتْ عَنْ مَحَبَّةٍ.	My advice to her was out of love.
قُمْتُ بِالْأَعْمَالِ الْخَيْرِيَّةِ عَنْ قَنَاعَةٍ.	I engaged in charity work out of conviction.

Two-letter prepositions

عَنْ is used as a causative and with verbs meaning 'to result from', as in the following:

الْهِجْرَةُ الْمُتَزَايِدَةُ لِلشَّبَابِ الْعَرَبِ إِلَى الْغَرْبِ نَاجِمَةٌ عَنْ عَدَمِ الْاِسْتِقْرَارِ فِي بُلْدَانِهِمْ.	The increase in Arab youth migration to the West is due to instability in their countries.
تَجَنَّبَ رَجُلُ الْأَعْمَالِ الْاِسْتِثْمَارَ فِي الشَّرِكَةِ عَنْ دِرَايَةٍ بِخَسَائِرِهَا.	The businessman avoided investing in the company in view of his knowledge of its losses.
إِنَّ الْفَسَادَ الْمُتَفَشِّي فِي الْكَثِيرِ مِنْ دَوَائِرِ الدَّوْلَةِ نَاتِجٌ عَنِ إِهْمَالِ الْحُكُومَةِ لِمُحَاسَبَةِ الْمَسْؤُولِينَ.	The widespread corruption in many state departments is the result of the government's neglect in holding officials accountable.
كَافَأَنِي الْمُدِيرُ عَنْ خَدَمَاتِي.	The manager rewarded me for my services.

عَنْ can be used to denote 'with', 'by means of' or 'with the aid of', as in the following examples:

رَمَيْتُ عَنِ الْقَوْسِ.	I fired (the arrow) with the bow.
ضَرَبْتُ الْخَائِنَ عَنِ السَّيْفِ.	I struck the traitor with the sword.
سَافَرْتُ عَنْ طَرِيقِ الْبَحْرِ.	I traveled by sea.

عَنْ may be used to denote 'in lieu of', 'instead of' or 'rather than', as in the following:

حَجَّ مُحَمَّدٌ عَنْ أَبِيهِ.	Mohammad went to pilgrimage on his father's behalf.
لَا تَعْتَمِدْ عَلَى الْفَرَضِيَّاتِ بَدَلًا عَنِ الْحَقَائِقِ.	Don't rely on assumptions instead of facts.
أُفَضِّلُ دَفْعَ الْغَرَامَةِ عَنْ دُخُولِ السِّجْنِ.	I prefer to pay a fine rather than go to jail.
تَوَلَّى الْمُوَظَّفُ إِدَارَةَ الْاِجْتِمَاعِ بَدَلًا عَنْ مُدِيرِ الشَّرِكَةِ.	The meeting was chaired by an employee rather than by the chairman of the company.

عَنْ is also used with verbs indicating denegation, stopping, discontinuing or abandoning, as in the following cases:

طَلَبَتِ الْحُكُومَةُ مِنَ الْمُتَظَاهِرِينَ أَنْ يَتَخَلَّوْا عَنِ الْمَبَانِي الَّتِي اسْتَوْلُوا عَلَيْهَا.	The government asked the protestors to give up the buildings they had seized.
فَشِلَتِ الْجُهُودُ الدُّوَلِيَّةُ فِي إِقْنَاعِ إِسْرَائِيلَ بِالْعُدُولِ عَنْ قَرَارِهَا بِبِنَاءِ مُسْتَوْطَنَاتٍ جَدِيدَةٍ.	International efforts have failed to convince Israel to abandon its decision to build new settlements.

يَعْجِزُ الإِنْسَانُ الخَجُولُ عَنِ التَّحَدُّثِ أَمَامَ النَّاسِ أَحْيَانًا.	A shy person is sometimes unable to talk in public.
تَوَقَّفَ شَقِيقِي عَنِ التَّدْخِينِ بَعْدَ مُحَاوَلَاتٍ عَدِيدَةٍ.	My brother gave up smoking after numerous attempts.

عَنْ is also used to denote origin, basis, source or foundation, as in the following:

أَخَذَ الْعِلْمَ عَنْ أَسَاتِذَةٍ كِبَارٍ.	He acquired his knowledge from great teachers.
قَدْ يَتَوَارَثُ الأَطْفَالُ عَنْ آبَائِهِمْ صِفَاتٍ خُلُقِيَّةً.	Children may inherit their moral values from their parents.
هَلْ يَجُوزُ أَخْذُ الْعِلْمِ عَنْ رِجَالِ الدِّينِ؟	Is it right to get knowledge from religious scholars?

عَنْ can be used with verbs meaning to reveal, remove or uncover, as in the following:

كَشَفَتِ الْوَثِيقَةُ عَنْ عَمَلِيَّاتِ تَزْوِيرٍ عَلَى أَعْلَى الْمُسْتَوَيَاتِ.	The document revealed fraud at the highest levels.
تُحَاوِلُ الْمُجْتَمَعَاتُ الْعَرَبِيَّةُ نَزْعَ الْقُيُودِ عَنِ الْمَرْأَةِ الَّتِي تَمْنَعُهَا عَنْ مُشَارَكَتِهَا فِي الْمُجْتَمَعِ.	Arab societies endeavor to remove restrictions that prevent women from playing their role in society.
رَفَعَ عَنْ وَجْهِهَا الْحِجَابَ.	He removed the veil from her face.
أَكَّدَ وَزِيرُ الْخَارِجِيَّةِ الأَمْرِيكِيُّ أَمْسِ مُجَدَّدًا أَنَّهُ مِنْ غَيْرِ الْمُمْكِنِ التَّفْكِيرُ فِي رَفْعِ الْعُقُوبَاتِ عَنْ إِيرَانَ حَالِيًّا.	The US secretary of state reiterated yesterday that it was impossible to contemplate lifting the sanctions on Iran at present.

عَنْ is also used with verbs meaning 'to stop', 'to cease' or 'to move away/from':

هُنَاكَ شَرِكَاتٌ تُقَامُ وَأُخْرَى تَتَوَقَّفُ عَنِ الْعَمَلِ أَوْ يُعْلَنُ إِفْلَاسُهَا.	There are companies that become established and others that stop working or declare bankruptcy.
مَرَّتْ بِضْعُ دَقَائِقَ قَبْلَ أَنْ يَعْتَدِلَ وَاقِفًا وَيَتَنَحَّى عَنِ الْفِرَاشِ.	It was few minutes before he got up and left the bed.

عَنْ may be used with verbs expressing distraction or perplexity, negligence, delay, slow performance, lagging behind or carelessness, as in these cases:

تَشَاغَلَ الطَّالِبُ عَنْ وَاجِبَاتِهِ الْمَدْرَسِيَّةِ بِاللَّهْوِ مَعَ أَصْحَابِهِ.	The student was too busy playing with his friends to do his homework.

Two-letter prepositions

سَهَا عَدْنَانُ عَنْ صَلَاةِ الظُّهْرِ.	Adnan inadvertently forgot the midday prayer.
يَتَقَاعَسُ بَعْضُ الطُّلَّابِ عَنْ أَدَاءِ وَاجِبِهِمْ.	Some students neglect to do their homework.
لَمْ يَتَوَانَ مَحْمُودٌ عَنْ تَحْقِيقِ حُلْمِهِ، بِالرَّغْمِ مِنْ بَتْرِ قَدَمَيْهِ.	Mahmoud was not impeded from realizing his dreams, in spite of his amputated feet.
تَأَخَّرَ القِطَارُ عَنْ مَوْعِدِ وُصُولِهِ المُقَرَّرِ.	The train was late arriving than its scheduled time.

عَنْ can also be used with verbs expressing separation from or isolation; see the following examples:

افْتَرَقَ الحُلَفَاءُ عَنْ بَعْضِهِمْ بَعْضًا بَعدَ انْتِهَاءِ الحَرْبِ.	The allies went their separate ways after the end of the war.
بَعدَ المُفَاوَضَاتِ، انْشَقَّ الإِقْلِيمُ عَنِ الدَّوْلَةِ وَأَعْلَنَ اسْتِقْلَالَهُ.	The province broke away from the country and declared its independence after the negotiations.
انْعَزَلَ أَحْمَدُ عَنْ أَصْحَابِهِ.	Ahmed has isolated himself from his friends
شَرَدَ البَعِيرُ عَنِ القَطِيعِ.	The camel strayed too far from the herd.
يَحْتَاجُ الإِعْلَامُ أَنْ يَنْزِعَ عَنْ نَفْسِهِ هَذِهِ الصُّورَةَ النَّمَطِيَّةَ.	Media outlets need to get rid of these stereotypes.

عَنْ is also used with verbs expressing forgiveness, overlooking or excusing, as in the following:

تَجَاوَزْتُ عَنْ أَخْطَاءِ أَوْلَادِي لِصِغَرِ سِنِّهِمْ.	I disregarded my children's mistakes, because of how young they were.
صَفَحَ صَدِيقِي عِمَادُ عَنْ كُلِّ مَنْ أَسَاءَ إِلَيْهِ.	My friend Imad forgave all those who had offended him.
تَغَاضَى عَنْ أَفْعَالِهِ وَلَمْ يُعِرْهُ اهْتِمَامًا.	He ignored his acts and didn't pay any attention to him.
حَاوِلْ أَنْ تَتَغَاضَى عَنْ أَفْعَالِ زُمَلَائِكَ وَلَا تُعِرْ لَهُمْ اهْتِمَامًا.	Try to disregard your colleagues' actions and do not pay attention to them.

عَنْ is used with verbs expressing 'holding back', 'slowing down', 'failing' or 'impeding', as in the following:

كَانَ يَعْتَمِدُ عَلَى نُصْرَةِ زُمَلَائِهِ وَلَكِنَّهُمْ لِلْأَسَفِ تَخَلَّوْا عَنْهُ.	He was relying on his colleagues' support, but unfortunately, they let him down.

أَخَّرَ دَفْعَ دُيُونِهِ عَنْ مَوْعِدِ السَّدَادِ.	He has fallen behind the due date for paying off his debts.
قَرَّرَ وَالِدِي أَنْ يَصْرِفَ النَّظَرَ عَنْ رِحْلَتِهِ إِلَى أُورُوبَا.	My father has decided to change his mind on his trip to Europe.

عَنْ can include the meanings of other prepositions. However, it is worth pointing out that these uses are not common in the media and other contemporary fields.

- عَنْ is used with the same meaning as (بعد):

(لَتَرْكَبُنَّ طَبَقًا عَنْ طَبَقٍ) (84:19)	"You shall surely ride stage after stage"

- عَنْ is used with the same meaning as (على):

(وَمَنْ يَبْخَلْ فَإِنَّمَا يَبْخَلُ عَنْ نَفْسِهِ) (47:38)	"Whose is niggardly is niggardly only to his own soul"

- عَنْ is used with the same meaning as (في):

لَا أَتَأَخَّرُ عَنِ الدِّفَاعِ عَنْ وَطَنِي.	I will not hold back from defending my country.

- عَنْ is used with the same meaning as (من):

(وَهُوَ الَّذِي يَقْبَلُ التَّوْبَةَ عَنْ عِبَادِهِ) (42:25)	"He who accepts repentance from His servants"

- عَنْ is used with the same meaning as (الباء):

(ما ضَلَّ صَاحِبُكُمْ وَمَا غَوَى وما ينطِقُ عَنِ الهَوَى) (53:2)	"Your comrade is not astray, neither errs, nor speaks he out of caprice"

عَنْ can be used in the place of the particle (بَعْدُ), 'after', as in the following:

عَنْ قَرِيبٍ سَتَظْهَرُ نَتَائِجُ الِامْتِحَانِ.	The exam results will be issued shortly.
عَمَّا قَلِيلٍ سَيَحْضُرُ أَهْلُهُ.	His relatives will come soon.

عَمَّا is a compound word that consists of the two elements (عَنَ + مَا), as in the examples that follow:

سَأَلَنِي الطَّالِبُ عَمَّا شَرَحْتُهُ فِي الْمُحَاضَرَةِ.	The student asked me about what I explained in the lecture.
عَمَّا قَرِيبٍ سَتَظْهَرُ نَتَائِجُ الِامْتِحَانَاتِ.	The exam result will come out soon.
سَأَعُودُ عَمَّا قَلِيلٍ.	I will come back shortly.

Two-letter prepositions 75

عَنْ *with pronouns*

عَنْهُمَا	عَنْ + هما		عَنِّي	عَنْ + أنا
عَنَّا	عَنْ + نحن		عَنْكَ	عَنْ + أنتَ
عَنْكُم	عَنْ + أنتم		عَنْكِ	عَنْ + أنتِ
عَنْكُنَّ	عَنْ + أنتن		عَنْهُ	عَنْ + هو
عَنْهُمْ	عَنْ + هم		عَنْهَا	عَنْ + هي
عَنْهُنَّ	عَنْ + هنّ		عَنْكُمَا	عَنْ + أنتما

اِبْتَعَدَ عَنْكَ.	He stayed away from you.
خَرَجَ الطِّفْلُ عِنْدَمَا غَفَلَتْ وَالِدَتُهُ عَنْهُ.	The boy left when his mother became distracted from him.
سَأَلْتُ عَنْكُمْ أَصِدِقَاءَكُمْ.	I asked your friends about you.

Notes on translation

Compare عَنْ in the Arabic sentences that follow with the corresponding English translations.

تَحَدَّثَتْ عَنِ التَّحَدِّيَاتِ الَّتِي يُوَاجِهُهَا الرُّؤَسَاءُ التَّنْفِيذِيُّون.	She has discussed the challenges faced by company CEOs.
طَلَبَت الْحُكومَةُ مِنَ الْمُجْتَمَعِ الدُّوَلي دَعْمَ الْمَشْرُوعِ عَنْ طَرِيقِ تَوفِيرِ التَّمْوِيلِ المَطْلُوبِ.	The government asked the international community to support the project by providing the necessary funds.
يُرْجَى تَقْدِيمُ مَعْلُومَاتٍ عَنِ المُحْتَاجِينَ وعَنِ اللَّاجِئِينَ.	Please provide information on people in need and refugees.
سَيُعْرَضُ التَّقْرِيرُ كُلَّ ثَلَاثَةِ سِنينَ عِوَضًا عَنْ عَرْضِهِ سَنَوِيًّا.	The report will be presented every three years rather than annually.
اِبْقَ بَعِيدًا عَنْ هَذَا الْمَكَانِ.	Stay away from this place.
كَانَ هُوَ الْمَسْؤُولَ عَنْ إِبْعَادِكَ عَنْ هَذِهِ الصَّفْقَةِ.	He was the reason behind cutting you out of the deal.
يَجْرِي جَمْعُ هَذِهِ المَعْلُومَاتِ بِالنِّيَابَةِ عَنْ خَالِدٍ.	The information is being collected on behalf of Khalid.

Fixed expressions with عَنْ

English	Arabic example	Meaning	Expression
As regards the commercial agreements, the private sector has won most of them.	أَمَّا عَنِ الاِتِّفَاقِيَّاتِ التِّجَارِيَّةِ، فَقَدْ حَازَ فِيهَا القِطَاعُ الخَاصُّ بِحِصَّةِ الأَسَدِ.	regarding/as to/as regards	أَمَّا عَنْ

بَدِيلًا عَنْ	as a substitute for	قَرَّرَتِ الحُكُومَةُ اسْتِيرَادَ النَّفْطِ العِرَاقِيِّ بَدِيلًا عَنِ النَّفْطِ السَّعُودِيِّ.	The government decided to import Iraqi oil as a substitute for Saudi oil.
بِصَرْفِ النَّظَرِ عَنْ	regardless of	تَمَّ قُبُولُ جَمِيعِ طَلَبَاتِ المُتَقَدِّمِينَ بِصَرْفِ النَّظَرِ عَنْ مُؤَهِّلَاتِهِمْ وَأَعْمَارِهِمْ.	All the applications were accepted regardless of the qualifications and ages of the applicants.
بَعِيدٌ عَنْ	far from	تَسْعَى الشُّعُوبُ العَرَبِيَّةُ لِتَأْسِيسِ نُظُمِ حُكْمٍ دِيمُوقْرَاطِيَّةٍ بَعِيدَةٍ عَنِ الدِّكْتَاتُورِيَّةِ.	Arab people are trying to establish democratic governance systems that are far from dictatorship.
بِغَضِّ النَّظَرِ عَنْ	regardless of	كُلَّمَا زَادَتِ الحَمَلَاتُ الإِعْلَانِيَّةُ، زَادَتِ المَبِيعَاتُ بِغَضِّ النَّظَرِ عَنْ جَوْدَةِ المُنْتَجِ.	As advertising campaigns increase, so the sales increase regardless of the quality of the product.
بِمَعْزِلٍ عَنْ	independently of/apart from	قَامَتِ الحُكُومَةُ بِإِصْدَارِ القَرَارَاتِ الأَخِيرَةِ بِمَعْزِلٍ عَنْ رَأْيِ الجَمَاهِيرِ.	The government has issued its latest resolutions quite apart from public opinion.
تُوُفِّيَ عَنْ عُمْرٍ	he died at the age of	تُوُفِّيَ الشَّابُّ عَنْ عُمْرٍ يَبْلُغُ الثَّلَاثِينَ عَامًا.	The young man died at the age of thirty.
خَارِجٌ عَنْ	beyond/out of/outside of	الوَضْعُ فِي جَنُوبِ البِلَادِ خَارِجٌ عَنْ سَيْطَرَةِ الحُكُومَةِ بِسَبَبِ نَشَاطَاتِ الجَمَاعَاتِ المُسَلَّحَةِ.	The situation in the south of the country is out of the government's control because of the activities of armed groups.
الخُرُوجُ عَنِ المَأْلُوفِ	out of the ordinary/anomalous	لَيْسَ الخُرُوجُ عَنِ المَأْلُوفِ سَيِّئًا فِي كُلِّ الظُّرُوفِ.	Doing things out of the ordinary isn't always a bad thing, in all circumstances.
رَضِيَ الله عَنْهُ	may God bless him	أَرْسَلَ الخَلِيفَةُ الثَّالِثُ عُثْمَانُ بْنُ عَفَّانَ رَضِيَ الله عَنْهُ دُعَاةً إِلَى الصِّينِ.	The third Caliph Othman Bin Affan (may God bless him) sent proselytizers to China.
رَغْمًا عَنْ	in spite of (oneself)/unwillingly	بَقِيَ السُّكَّانُ فِي المَدِينَةِ المُحَاصَرَةِ رَغْمًا عَنْ أُنُوفِهِمْ.	The citizens stayed in the besieged city against their own will.

Two-letter prepositions 77

زَائِد عَن حَدِّهِ	over the top/ exceeds the limit	أَدَّى تَدَخُّلُ الجَيْشِ الزَّائِدُ عَنْ حَدِّهِ فِي الاقْتِصَادِ إِلَى تَرَاجُعِ الأَدَاءِ الاقْتِصَادِيِّ.	The army's excessive intervention in the economy resulted in an economic recession.
زِيَادَةً عَن	more than/an increase over	حَقَّقَتْ أَرْبَاحُ الشَّرِكَةِ زِيَادَةً كَبِيرَةً عَنِ العَامِ السَّابِقِ.	The company's profits showed an increase over the previous year.
عَاجِز عَن	unable to	النَّجَاحُ الاقْتِصَادِيُّ الَّذِي حَقَّقَتْهُ الحُكُومَةُ الجَدِيدَةُ مَا زَالَ عَاجِزًا عَنْ حَلِّ مُشْكِلَاتِ البَطَالَةِ وَتَدَنِّي مُسْتَوَى الخِدْمَاتِ الأَسَاسِيَّةِ.	The economic success which the new government has achieved is still unable to solve the unemployment problems and the poor level of essential services.
عَدا عَن	other than/ except for	شَارَكَ جَمِيعُ اللَّاعِبِينَ فِي المُبَارَاةِ النِّهَائِيَّةِ عَدَا عَنِ اللَّاعِبِ المُصَابِ.	All the players played in the final match except the injured player.
عَمَّا قَرِيبٍ	soon/shortly	سَتَتَحَوَّلُ الرِّوَايَةُ عَمَّا قَرِيبٍ إِلَى فِيلْمٍ سِينِمَائِيٍّ.	The novel will soon be a movie.
عَن آخِرِهِ	completely/ entirely/to the brim	مُخَيَّمَاتُ اللَّاجِئِينَ الفِلَسْطِينِيِّينَ فِي لُبْنَانَ مُكْتَظَّةٌ بِالسُّكَّانِ عَنْ آخِرِهَا.	Palestinians refugee camps in Lebanon are full to the brim with people living in them.
عَن جَدَارَةٍ	rightfully/ deservedly	فَازَ الفَرِيقُ بِالكَأْسِ عَنْ جَدَارَةٍ.	The team has deservedly won the cup.
عَن حُسْنِ نِيَّةٍ	in good faith	اعْتَرَفَ الرَّجُلُ بِالمُخَالَفَةِ وَلَكِنَّهُ أَصَرَّ بِأَنَّهَا كَانَتْ عَنْ حُسْنِ نِيَّةٍ وَجَهْلٍ بِالقَوَانِينِ.	The man admitted that he broke the law, but he insisted that he had done so in good faith and in ignorance of the laws.
عَنْ سَبْقِ الإِصْرَارِ وَالتَّرَصُّدِ	premeditated	تَمَّ اتِّهَامُ السُّلُطَاتِ بِانْتِهَاكِ حُقُوقِ الإِنْسَانِ عَنْ سَبْقِ الإِصْرَارِ وَالتَّرَصُّدِ.	The authorities were accused of a premeditated violation of human rights.
عَن سَطْحِ البَحْرِ	above sea level	يَقَعُ المُنْتَجَعُ عَلَى قِمَّةِ مُرْتَفَعٍ يَعْلُو 700 مِتْرٍ عَنْ سَطْحِ البَحْرِ.	The resort is 700 meters above sea level.
عَنْ سَهْوٍ/ عَنْ خَطَأٍ	by mistake/in error	تَمَّ نَشْرُ الخَبَرِ مَرَّتَيْنِ عَنْ خَطَأٍ.	The news was published twice by mistake.

عَنْ طَرِيقٍ	by/through/via	وَصَلَ مُعْظَمُ الحُجَّاجِ إِلَى المَمْلَكَةِ عَنْ طَرِيقِ مَطَارِ جِدَّةِ.	Most pilgrims have reached the kingdom through Jeddah Airport.
عَنْ طَرِيقِ الخَطَأِ	by mistake/by accident	أَصَابَ الشُّرْطِيُّ زَوْجَتَهُ عَنْ طَرِيقِ الخَطَأِ أَثْنَاءَ تَنْظِيفِ سِلَاحِهِ.	The police officer shot his wife by accident while he was cleaning his weapon.
عَنْ طِيبِ خَاطِرٍ	willingly/readily	تَطَوَّعْنَا لِمُسَاعَدَةِ المَرْضَى عَنْ طِيبِ خَاطِرٍ.	We willingly volunteered to help the patients.
عَنْ ظَهْرِ قَلْبٍ	by heart	يَحْفَظُ الشَّاعِرُ جَمِيعَ قَصَائِدِهِ عَنْ ظَهْرِ قَلْبٍ.	The poet memorizes all his poems by heart.
عَنْ عِلْمٍ	knowingly	تَحَدَّثَ الكَثِيرُ مِنَ النَّاسِ عَنْ أَسْبَابِ المُشْكِلَةِ عَنْ عِلْمٍ أَوْ عَنْ غَيْرِ عِلْمٍ.	Many people knowingly or unknowingly talked about the reasons behind this problem.
عَنْ قَرِيبٍ	soon	سَيَرْحَلُ عَنِ المَدِينَةِ عَنْ قَرِيبٍ وَسَيَعُودُ إِلَى قَرْيَتِهِ.	He will soon leave the city and go back to his village.
عَنْ قَنَاعَةٍ	convinced	اِعْتَنَقَ الرَّجُلُ الإِسْلَامَ عَنْ قَنَاعَةٍ وَطِيبِ خَاطِرٍ.	The man was convinced and freely willing to embrace Islam.
عَنْ كَثَبٍ / عَنْ قُرْبٍ	closely	تُرَاقِبُ الحُكُومَةُ الأَدَاءَ الاِقْتِصَادِيَّ عَنْ كَثَبٍ.	The government is closely watching the economic performance.
عِوَضًا عَنْ	in lieu of	تَسْعَى الحُكُومَةُ إِلَى تَشْجِيعِ الاِسْتِثْمَارَاتِ الأَجْنَبِيَّةِ طَوِيلَةِ الأَجَلِ عِوَضًا عَنِ الاِسْتِثْمَارَاتِ العَرَبِيَّةِ قَصِيرَةِ الأَجَلِ.	The government is attempting to encourage long-term foreign investments in lieu of short-term Arab investments.
غَائِبٌ عَنِ الوَعْيِ	unconscious	بَقِيَ المُصَابُ فِي المُسْتَشْفَى لِمُدَّةِ أُسْبُوعٍ بَعْدَ الحَادِثِ وَهُوَ غَائِبٌ عَنِ الوَعْيِ.	After the accident, the injured man stayed unconscious in the hospital for a week.
غَنِيٌّ عَنِ القَوْلِ	needless to say/it goes without saying that	غَنِيٌّ عَنِ القَوْلِ أَنَّ الأَدَاءَ الحُكُومِيَّ لَمْ يَتَحَسَّنْ فِي ظِلِّ الحُكْمِ العَسْكَرِيِّ.	It goes without saying that the performance of the government didn't improve under the military regime.

Two-letter prepositions 79

In addition to the British Airways' daily flights to Cairo, there are other flights to Hurghada.	فَضْلًا عَنِ الرِّحْلَاتِ اليَوْمِيَّةِ لِلْخُطُوطِ البَرِيطانِيَّةِ لِلقاهِرَةِ، هُناكَ رِحْلاتٌ أُخْرَى إلى الغَرْدَقَةِ.	moreover/in addition to	فَضْلًا عَنْ
The United States considers peace as an irreversible strategic choice to bring stability to the region.	تَعْتَبِرُ أَمْرِيكا أَنَّ السَّلامَ خِيارٌ إسْتَراتِيجِيٌّ لا رَجْعَةَ عَنْهُ لِتَحْقِيقِ الإسْتِقْرارِ في المِنْطَقَةِ.	no going back	لا رَجْعَةَ عَنْهُ
The American diet is different from the Egyptian diet.	النِّظامُ الغِذائِيُّ الأَمْرِيكِيّ مُخْتَلِفٌ عَنْ نَظِيرِهِ المِصْرِيِّ.	different from	مُخْتَلِفٌ عَنْ
The occupation army is responsible for many crimes against civilians.	جَيْشُ الإحْتِلالِ مَسْؤُولٌ عَنِ الكَثِيرِ مِنَ الجَرائِمِ ضِدَّ المَدَنِيِّينَ.	responsible for	مَسْؤُول عَنْ
A representative of the International Red Crescent attended the meeting.	حَضَرَ الإجْتِماعَ مُمَثِّلٌ عَنِ الصَّلِيبِ الأَحْمَرِ الدُّوَلِيِّ.	representative of/representing	مُمَثِّل عَنْ
The president must reconcile between the interests of the government, the opposition and the army, not to mention the interests of the masses.	يَجِبُ عَلَى الرَّئِيسِ التَّوْفِيقُ بَيْنَ مَصالِحِ الحُكُومَةِ والمُعارَضَةِ والجَيْشِ، ناهِيكَ عَنْ مَصالِحِ الجَماهِيرِ.	not to mention	ناهِيكَ عَنْ
The ambassador signed the agreement on behalf of the president.	وَقَّعَ السَّفِيرُ الإتِّفاقِيَّةَ نِيابَةً عَنِ الرَّئِيسِ.	on behalf of	نِيابَةً عَنْ

فِي

The preposition فِي is equivalent to 'in', 'at' and 'on' in English and is mainly used to indicate location and time, in addition to other functions.

فِي *in context*

أَفادَ مُراسِلُنا فِي بَغْدادَ بِأَنَّهُ شاهَدَ فِي طَرِيقِهِ إلى العَمَلِ مُظاهَرَةً كَبِيرَةً، وَقَدِ احْتَشَدَ النّاسُ فِي الصَّباحِ أَمامَ المَحْكَمَةِ العُلْيا الَّتِي تَقَعُ فِي ساحَةِ الشُّهَداءِ فِي وَسَطِ العاصِمَةِ، حَيْثُ إنَّ المَحْكَمَةَ تَتَخَصَّصُ فِي الفَصْلِ فِي النِّزاعاتِ الدُّسْتُورِيَّةِ

80 *Two-letter prepositions*

لِلْمُطَالَبَةِ بِمُساءَلَةِ المَسؤُولِينَ فِي المَنَاصِبِ الْعُلْيَا فِي جَمِيعِ أَنحَاءِ الْعِرَاقِ. اِتَّهَمَ المُحْتَشِدُونَ المَسؤُولِينَ الَّذِينَ أَهْمَلُوا مَسْؤُولِيَّةِ الْحِفَاظِ عَلَى الْاِسْتِقْرَارِ وَالنَّزَاهَةِ فِي الْبِلَادِ. قَالَ أَحَدُ المُتَظَاهِرِينَ بِأَنَّ وَاجِبَ السُّلُطَاتِ أَنْ تَنْظُرَ فِي أَمْرِ الْفَسَادِ المُتَفَشِّي فِي الْعِرَاقِ وَالَّذِي يَسْرِي كَالنَّارِ فِي الْهَشِيمِ بَيْنَ المَسؤُولِينَ.

> Our correspondent in Baghdad reported that he witnessed a large demonstration on his way to work. People gathered in the morning in front of the Supreme Court, which is located at Martyrs Square in the capital. This is where the court specializes in resolving constitutional disputes and seeks accountability for senior officials in all parts of Iraq. They accused the officials who ignored their responsibility to maintain stability and integrity in the country. One of the demonstrators said that it was the duty of the authorities to look into the rampant corruption among officials in Iraq, which has spread like a wildfire.

Notes on فِي in context

In the preceding passage, فِي is used to denote the physical location of people or the location where the incident took place, as in (فِي بَغْدَادَ، فِي طَرِيقِهِ، فِي سَاحَةِ الشُّهَدَاءِ،). فِي is also used to refer to the status and occupation of people in the phrase (فِي المَنَاصِبِ الْعُلْيَا). It also used in the passage with verbs (تَتَخَصَّصُ فِي، تَنْظُرَ فِي).

Functions of فِي

فِي is used to designate locations such as places, spaces, cities and countries, as in the following examples:

كُنْتُ فِي الْبَيْتِ طَوَالَ الْيَوْمِ.	I was at home all day.
أَعِيشُ فِي دُبَي مُنْذُ سَنَةِ 2005.	I have been living in Dubai since 2005.
جَرَى سِبَاقُ الْخَيْلِ فِي الْمَيْدَانِ.	The horse race took place in the field.
تَسْقُطُ الثُّلُوجُ بِغَزَارَةٍ فِي الدُّوَلِ الإسكندنافِيَّةِ.	Snow falls heavily in Scandinavian countries.
وَجَدْنَا فَأْرًا فِي الصُّنْدُوقِ.	We found a rat in the box.

فِي is also used to designate the point in time, as in the following:

اِسْتَيْقَظْتُ فِي السَّاعَةِ السَّابِعَةِ صَبَاحًا.	I woke up at 7:00 a.m.
كَانَتِ الْمُحَاضَرَةُ مُمِلَّةً فِي الْبِدَايَةِ.	The lecture was boring at the beginning.
غَادَرْنَا فِي الْمَسَاءِ.	We left in the evening.
أَرَاكَ فِي شَهْرِ يَنَايِرَ.	I'll see you in January.
مَاتَ عَدَدٌ كَبِيرٌ مِنَ الأَطْفَالِ فِي حَرْبِ الْعِرَاقِ.	A lot of children died during the Iraq War.

Two-letter prepositions 81

فِي may be used to designate duration, as in the following:

سَأَقُومُ بِقِرَاءَةِ الْعَدِيدِ مِنَ الْكُتُبِ فِي هَذَا الْعَامِ.	I will read a lot of books this year.
كُنْتُ فِي شَبَابِيَ مُغْرَمةً بِصَوْتِ عَبْدِ الْحَلِيمِ حافِظَ.	I was in my youth smitten by Abdel Halim Hafez's voice.
سَيُعْقَدُ الْمُؤْتَمَرُ فِي مُنْتَصَفِ أَغُسْطُسَ.	The conference will be held in mid-August.
لَمْ أَرَ أَحَدًا مِنْ أَصْدِقائِيَ فِي الْأَيَّامِ الْأَخِيرَةِ.	I have not seen any of my friends in recent days.
سَتُقَامُ الْإِحْتِفالَاتُ فِي الْأَيَّامِ الْقَلِيلَةِ الْمُقْبِلَةِ.	The celebrations will take place during the next few days.

فِي can also be used in a locative figurative sense with nouns and noun phrases, as in the following:

قَرَأْتُ بَعْضَ الْمَعْلُومَاتِ الْهَامَّةِ فِي الْكِتَابِ.	I read some important information in the book.
(لَقَدْ كَانَ لَكُمْ فِي رَسُولِ الله أُسْوَةٌ حَسَنَةٌ) (33:21)	"You have had a good role model in God's Messenger"
أَخْبَرَنِي وَالِدِي بِأَنَّهُ سَيَنْظُرُ فِي أَمْرِ سَفَرِي لِلدِّرَاسَةِ إِلَى فَرَنْسا.	My father told me that he will look into the issue of my study trip to France.
(وَلَكُمْ فِي الْقِصَاصِ حَيَاةٌ) (2:179)	"In retaliation there is a life for you"

فِي may also be used to designate a relationship between a cause and its effect, as in the following:

مَاتَ فِي حادِثِ سَيَّارَةٍ.	He died in a car accident.
سُجِنَ عَلِيٌّ فِي ذَنْبٍ لَمْ يَقْتَرِفْهُ.	Ali was imprisoned for an offence he did not commit.
"دَخَلَتِ امْرَأَةٌ النَّارَ فِي هِرَّةٍ".	"A woman entered (Hell) Fire because of a cat." [Note: This is Prophet Mohammad's saying, when the Prophet told the story of a woman who did not feed her cat and did not treat her well and so entered Hell because of this behavior.]

فِي is used with verbs expressing the idea of excelling and being distinguished, as in the following:

نَبَغَ عَنْتَرَةَ فِي كِتَابَةِ الشِّعرِ.	Antara excelled in composing poetry.
ضَلُعَ الطَّالِبُ فِي عُلُومِ الْحَاسِبِ.	The student was skilled in computer sciences.

بَرَعَ الإِمَامُ فِي الْعُلُومِ الدِّينِيَّةِ.	The Imam excelled in religious science.
طَلَبْتُ مِنْ اِبْنَتِي أَنْ تَتَأَنَّقَ فِي اِخْتِيَارِ أَلْفَاظِهَا.	I asked my daughter to choose her words eloquently.

فِي is also used with verbs expressing negligence and carelessness, as in the following:

قَصَّرَ الْمُوَظَّفُ فِي عَمَلِهِ.	The employee was careless about his job.
تَهَاوَنَ بَعْضُ الْمُوَظَّفِينَ فِي أَدَاءِ وَاجِبَاتِهِمْ.	Some employees were complacent about fulfilling their duties.
فَشَلَ الْقَائِدُ فِي إِنْجَازِ الْمُهِمَّةِ.	The leader failed to complete the mission.
أَهْمَلَ فِي عَمَلِهِ.	He neglected his work.

فِي may be used with verbs meaning to elaborate and speak at length on some subject, as in the following:

أَطْنَبَ فِي الْوَصْفِ.	He has given an exaggerated description.
أَفَاضَ الْقَوْمُ فِي الْحَدِيثِ عَنِ الأَمْرِ.	The people have talked extensively about the issue.
اِسْتَرْسَلَ الرَّئِيسُ فِي حَدِيثِهِ.	The president talked at length.

فِي can be used as well with verbs about summarizing or being brief or restrained, such as the following:

اُخْتُصِرَ الْكِتَابُ فِي مُقَدِّمَتِهِ.	The introduction summarizes the whole book.
اِقْتَصَدَ الْوَالِدُ فِي الإِنْفَاقِ عَلَى أُسْرَتِهِ.	The father was frugal with money when spending on his family.
أَوْجَزَ فِي الْكَلَامِ عَنْ حَالَتِهِ الْمَادِّيَّةِ.	He was brief in talking about his financial situation.

فِي is also used to denote the idea of 'regarding' or 'about', as in the following:

لَا فَائِدَةَ مِنَ التَّفْكِيرِ فِي الْمَوْتِ مَا دُمْنَا لَا نَسْتَطِيعُ رَدْعَهُ.	There is no point in thinking about death because we cannot prevent it.
يَتَحَدَّثُ بَعْضُ أَصْدِقَائِي اللُّبْنَانِيِّينَ فِي الأُمُورِ السِّيَاسِيَّةِ كَثِيرًا.	Some of my Lebanese friends talk a lot about politics.
كَانَ جَمَالُ الدِّينِ الأَفْغَانِيُّ يَنْشُرُ أَفْكَارَهُ فِي الدِّينِ وَالِاجْتِمَاعِ وَالسِّيَاسَةِ عَلَى مَدَى ثَمَانِيَةِ أَعْوَامٍ هِيَ فَتْرَةُ إِقَامَتِهِ بِمِصْرَ.	During his eight-year stay in Egypt, Jamal al-Din al-Afghani was spreading his ideas about religion, society and politics.
أَصْبَحَ حَقُّ الإِنْسَانِ فِي السَّفَرِ وَالِانْتِقَالِ بَيْنَ الدُّوَلِ مِثْلُ حَقِّهِ فِي الْمَاءِ وَالْهَوَاءِ.	The right of a person to travel and move between countries has become like his right to water and fresh air.

Two-letter prepositions 83

فِي can also be used with verbs expressing ideas of forgiveness and tolerance, as in the following:

هُنَاكَ تَسَاهُلٌ فِي الْقَوَانِينِ وَالْإِجْرَاءَاتِ الَّتِي تُتَّخَذُ بِحَقِّ مُرْتَكِبِي جَرَائِمِ الشَّرَفِ فِي بَعْضِ الدُّوَلِ الآسِيَوِيَّةِ.	Leniency is shown in the laws and actions taken against perpetrators of honor crimes in some Asian countries.
أَكَّدَ الرَّئِيسُ بِأَنَّهُ لَا تَهَاوُنَ فِي مُكَافَحَةِ الْفَسَادِ وَاجْتِثَاثِ جُذُورِهِ.	The president stressed that there would be no laxity in fighting corruption and rooting it out.
عَلَى الْآبَاءِ غَرْسُ التَّسَامُحِ فِي عَقْلِ وَقَلْبِ أَوْلَادِهِمْ كَيْ نَتَمَكَّنَ مِنْ نَبْذِ التَّعَصُّبِ وَالْعُنْفِ فِي مُجْتَمَعَاتِنَا.	Parents must instill tolerance in the minds and hearts of their children so that we can renounce intolerance and violence in our societies.

فِي may also be used with such reflexive phrases as (فِي أَعْمَاقِي، فِي قَرَارَةِ نَفْسِي، فِي سِرِّي، فِي نَفْسِي), meaning 'in myself' or 'deep down', as in the following cases:

اسْتَغْرَبَ فِي قَرَارَةِ نَفْسِهِ الصَّدَى الَّذِي تَرَكَتْهُ مُحَاضَرَتُهُ عَنِ السَّلَامِ فِي الشَّرْقِ الْأَوْسَطِ.	He was surprised deep down at the reaction to his lecture on peace in the Middle East.
تَمَنَّيْتُ فِي سِرِّي أَنْ يَعْدِلَ أَخِي عَنْ زَوَاجِهِ مِنْ لَيْلَى.	Secretly, I wished that my brother would change his mind about his marriage to Laila.
كَانَ فِي أَعْمَاقِي شَيْءٌ يُخْبِرُنِي بِأَنَّهُ سَيَرْجِعُ لِي فِي الْأَخِيرِ.	There was something deep inside me that told me he would eventually come back to me.
أَقْدَمَ زَمِيلِي عَلَى هَذَا الْعَمَلِ لِشَيْءٍ فِي نَفْسِ يَعْقُوبَ.	My colleague did this with an ulterior motive.

فِي is used with verbs expressing the idea of becoming lost (literally or in thought), as in the following:

تَاهَ فِي أَزِقَّةِ حَيٍّ قَدِيمٍ.	He got lost in the alleys of an old neighborhood.
مَوَاشِيهِمْ لَا تَسْرَحُ فِي الْمَرَاعِي الْبَعِيدَةِ.	Their cattle are not grazing freely in the distant pastures.
شَرَدَ الْجَمَلُ فِي الصَّحْرَاءِ.	The camel strayed into the desert.

فِي is also used with verbs meaning to comfort and pay respects, as in the following:

زَارَنِي أَصْدِقَائِي فِي الْبَيْتِ لِيُعَزُّونِي فِي وَفَاةِ وَالِدِي رَحِمَهُ اللهُ.	My friends visited me at home to pay their respect for the death of my father, may God have mercy on him.

حَاوَلْتُ أَنْ أُصَبِّرَ زَمِيلِي الْعِرَاقِيَّ فِي مَأْسَاةِ غَرَقِ الْعَبَّارَةِ فِي نَهْرِ دِجْلَةَ فِي بَغْدَادَ.	I tried to comfort my Iraqi colleague over the tragedy of the ferry that sank in the Tigris River in Baghdad.
شَكَرَ عَلِيٌّ مَنْ وَاسَاهُ فِي وَفَاةِ عَمِّهِ.	Ali thanked those who paid their respects for the passing of his uncle.

فِي can also be used to establish or point to the relationships between two elements, as in the following:

مَاتَ ابْنُ صَدِيقِي فِي حَادِثِ سَيَّارَةٍ.	My friend's son died in a car accident.
ابْتَسَمَ الْوَلَدُ فِي فَرَحٍ.	The boy smiled in joy.
أَغْلَقَتِ الْمَرْأَةُ الْبَابَ فِي عَصَبِيَّةٍ.	The woman closed the door in anger.
تَنَفَّسَ الْمُوَظَّفُ فِي ارْتِيَاحٍ عِنْدَمَا سَمِعَ بِخَبَرِ تَرْقِيَتِهِ.	The employee breathed a sigh of relief when he heard the news of his promotion.

فِي is used to designate the subject or a theme of a conversation or discussion, as in the following:

أَبْدَى مُحَمَّدٌ رَأْيَهُ فِي شَأْنِ اللَّاجِئِينَ.	Mohammed expressed his opinion about the refugees.
لَا أُحِبُّ الْحَدِيثَ فِي أُمُورِ الدِّينِ كَثِيرًا.	I do not like to talk much about religion.
تَعَمَّقَ الْكَاتِبُ فِي مَسْأَلَةِ فِلَسْطِينَ فِي الْمَقَالَةِ لِكَوْنِهِ مُتَخَصِّصًا فِي هَذَا الْمَوْضُوعِ.	The author gave an insight into the question of Palestine in the article because he is specialized in this subject.
كَتَبَ أُسْتَاذِي عِدَّةَ مَقَالَاتٍ فِي مَوْضُوعِ الْفَلْسَفَةِ الْإِسْلَامِيَّةِ.	My professor wrote several articles on the subject of Islamic philosophy.

فِي is also used with various adverbial expressions to indicate the state or condition of someone or something, as in these cases:

يَجِبُ أَنْ يَكُونَ فِي أَفْضَلِ شَكْلٍ مُمْكِنٍ.	It has to be in the best way possible.
يَحْصُلُ الطَّلَاقُ حَتَّى فِي أَحْسَنِ الْعَائِلَاتِ.	Divorce occurs even in the best of families.
الْأَهْلِيُّ هَذَا الْمَوْسِمَ لَيْسَ فِي أَفْضَلِ حَالَاتِهِ.	The Alahli team this season is not at its best.
ظَهَرَتِ الْعَرُوسُ فِي أَجْمَلِ صُورَةٍ يَوْمَ عُرْسِهَا.	The bride looked her very best on her wedding day.

فِي can also be used to denote the term 'per', as in the following:

يَجِبُ أَنْ تَتَنَاوَلَ ثَلَاثَ وَجَبَاتٍ فِي الْيَوْمِ.	You must have three meals per day.

Two-letter prepositions 85

لَا يَزِيدُ مُعَدَّلُ دَخْلِ الْعَائِلَةِ عَلَى ثَلَاثَةِ آلَافِ جُنَيْهٍ فِي الشَّهْرِ.	Average family income does not exceed three thousand pounds per month.
الْحَدُّ الْأَقْصَى لِلسُّرْعَةِ هُوَ مِئَةُ كِيلُومِتْرٍ فِي السَّاعَةِ.	The speed limit is 100 kilometers per hour.
يَزُورُنِي صَدِيقِي الْهُوْلَنْدِيُّ فِي السَّنَةِ مَرَّتَيْنِ.	My Dutch friend visits me twice a year.

فِي is also used to designate desire or aspiration as, for example, in the following:

أَرْغَبُ فِي السَّفَرِ إِلَى الصِّينِ.	I want to travel to China.
لَا تَطْمَعْ فِي أَمْوَالِ النَّاسِ.	Don't covet other people's money.
يَأْمُلُ إِبْرَاهِيمُ فِي الْحُصُولِ عَلَى مِنْحَةٍ لِدِرَاسَةِ الْمَاجِسْتِيرِ.	Ibrahim hopes to get a scholarship to study for a master's degree.

فِي can include the meanings of other prepositions. However, it is worth pointing out that these uses are not common in the media and other contemporary areas. Examples include the following:

فِي is used with the same meaning as (إِلَى):

(وَلَوْ شِئْنَا لَبَعَثْنَا فِي كُلِّ قَرْيَةٍ نَذِيرًا) (25:51)	"If We had willed, We would have raised up in every city a warner"

فِي is used with the same meaning as (مِن).

تَخَرَّجَ وَالِدِي فِي كُلِّيَّةِ الْحُقُوقِ.	My father graduated from the Faculty of Law.

فِي is used with the same meaning as (عَلَى).

(وَلَأُصَلِّبَنَّكُمْ فِي جُذُوعِ النَّخْلِ) (20:71)	"I shall crucify you upon the trunks of palm-trees"

فِي can also mean 'with' (مَع) in some cases, such as in the following:

كُنَّا فِي خَمْسَةِ نِسَاءٍ.	We were with five women.
عَبَرُوا الْبَحْرَ فِي سِتِّينَ أَلْفًا.	He crossed the sea with 60,000 men.

فِي is also used to designate proportion, as in the following:

طُولُهَا 30 مِتْرًا فِي 80 مِتْرًا.	It is 30 meters in length by 80 meters in breadth.
اِضْرِبْ 10 فِي 5.	Multiply 10 by 5.
حَجْمُ غُرْفَةِ نَوْمِي لَا يَزِيدُ عَنْ أَرْبَعَةِ أَمْتَارٍ فِي مِتْرَيْنِ وَنِصْفٍ.	The size of the bedroom is not more than four meters by two-and-a-half meters.

Two-letter prepositions

فِي can be used with the indefinite relative pronoun (مَا) to form the compound (فِيمَا), as in the following:

فِيمَا يَبْدُو أَنَّ حَمْلَةً دِبْلُومَاسِيَّةً مُكَثَّفَةً تَقُومُ بِهَا إِسْرَائِيلُ عَلَى الصَّعِيدِ الْخَارِجِيِّ.	It seems that there is an intensive diplomatic campaign abroad pursued by Israel.
تَسَرَّبَتْ أَخْبَارٌ عَنِ انْشِقَاقٍ فِي مَوْقِفِ الْقِيَادَةِ الرُّوسِيَّةِ حَوْلَ الشِّيشَانِ فِيمَا يَظْهَرُ.	News leaked about the split in the position of the Russian leadership on Chechnya, as it appears.
أَتَسَاءَلُ أَحْيَاناً فِيمَا إِذَا كَانَتِ الْوُعُودُ الْحُكُومِيَّةُ بِضَمَانِ نَزَاهَةِ الْإِنْتِخَابَاتِ وَشَفَافِيَّتِهَا تَكْفِي لِمَحْوِ الْفَسَادِ.	I wonder if the repeated promises by the government to ensure the fairness and transparency of the elections are enough to eliminate the corruption.
تُحَاوِلُ الدُّوَلُ الْعَرَبِيَّةُ حَلَّ الْمَشَاكِلِ فِيمَا بَيْنَهَا عَنْ طَرِيقِ الْحِوَارِ.	Arab states are trying to solve their problems through dialogue.

فِي is also used with the interrogative (مَا) to form the compound (فِيمَ), meaning 'what' or 'what is ... for' or 'why', where half of the interrogative (مَا) is deleted, as in the following:

فِيمَ تُفَكِّرُ؟	What are you thinking of?
فِيمَ الصِّرَاعُ بَيْنَ الْأَصْدِقَاءِ؟	What is conflict between friends for?
فِيمَ هَذَا الْغَضَبُ؟	What is this anger for?

فِي with pronouns

When فِي joins a pronoun, it becomes a prefix and the pronoun becomes a suffix. The following table shows how different pronouns appear after the preposition:

فِيهِمَا	فِي + هما	فِيَّ	فِي + أنا
فِينَا	فِي + نحن	فِيكَ	فِي + أنتَ
فِيكُمْ	فِي + أنتم	فِيكِ	فِي + أنتِ
فِيكُنَّ	فِي + أنتن	فِيهِ	فِي + هو
فِيهِمْ	فِي + هم	فِيهَا	فِي + هي
فِيهِنَّ	فِي + هن	فِيكُمَا	فِي + أنتما

رَغْمَ انْفِصَالِهِمَا، مَا زَالَتْ تُفَكِّرُ فِيهِ.	Despite their break up, she still thinks of him.
أَخْبَرَنِي بِأَنَّ الْعَيْبَ فِيَّ.	He told me that the fault is in me.
لَا أَثِقُ فِيهِمْ.	I don't trust them.

Notes on translation

Compare the translation of فِي in the following Arabic passages in the corresponding English sentences:

اِنْعَقَدَ الْمُؤْتَمَرُ فِي 6 مَارِسٍ فِي اِحْتِفَالٍ عُقِدَ فِي دُبَي.	The conference was held on 6 March in a ceremony held at Dubai.
سَتَنْظُرُ اللَّجْنَةُ فِي دَوْرَتِهَا الرَّابِعَةِ فِي هَذِهِ التَّقَارِيرِ.	The commission will examine these reports at its fourth session.
الرُّدُودُ يَجْرِي أَخْذُهَا فِي عَيْنِ الْاِعْتِبَارِ.	The responses are being taken into account.
أَشَارَ الرَّئِيسُ الْأَمْرِيكِيُّ، فِي كَلِمَةٍ أَلْقَاهَا فِي طُوكِيُو إِلَى أَهَمِيَّةِ تَوْحِيدِ الْجُهُودِ لِإِحْلَالِ السَّلَامِ الْعَالَمِيّ.	The American president has pointed out during a speech he delivered in Tokyo the importance of uniting efforts to bring world peace.
أَرْغَبُ فِي الْعَوْدَةِ إِلَى الْوَطَنِ.	I would like to go back home.

Useful expressions

English	Arabic example	Meaning	Expression
Antigovernment protests spread across the country.	اِنْتَشَرَتِ التَّظَاهُرَاتُ الْمُنَاهِضَةُ لِلْحُكُومَةِ فِي أَرْجَاءِ الْبِلَادِ.	across	فِي أَرْجَاءِ
An official settlement was achieved within the framework of a negotiation process.	تَمَّ التَّوَصُّلُ إِلَى تَسْوِيَةٍ رَسْمِيَّةٍ فِي إِطَارِ عَمَلِيَّةٍ تَفَاوُضِيَّةٍ.	within the framework of	فِي إِطَارِ
The security forces were deployed across the city in the aftermath of the explosion.	وَفِي أَعْقَابِ التَّفْجِيرِ اِنْتَشَرَتْ قُوَّاتُ الْأَمْنِ فِي الْمَدِينَةِ.	in the aftermath of	فِي أَعْقَابِ
Basically, any improvement in conditions needs radical solutions.	تَحْسِينُ الْأَوْضَاعِ يَتَطَلَّبُ فِي الْأَسَاسِ حُلُولًا جَذْرِيَّةً.	basically	فِي الْأَسَاسِ
The number of deaths in prisons has increased in recent years.	زَادَتْ أَعْدَادُ الْوَفَيَاتِ فِي السُّجُونِ فِي الْأَعْوَامِ الْأَخِيرَةِ.	in recent years	فِي الْأَعْوَامِ الْأَخِيرَةِ
The activities of the group were at first directed against the occupation.	كَانَتْ أَنْشِطَةُ الْجَمَاعَةِ فِي الْبِدَايَةِ مُوَجَّهَةً ضِدَّ الْاِحْتِلَالِ.	at first	فِي الْبِدَايَةِ

Two-letter prepositions

English sentence	Arabic sentence	English phrase	Arabic phrase
The army's weapons were deployed on land and at sea in preparation for the battle against the enemies.	تَمَّ نَشْرُ أَسْلِحَةِ الجَيْشِ فِي البَرِّ وَالبَحْرِ اسْتِعْدَادًا لِلْمَعْرَكَةِ مَعَ الأَعْدَاءِ.	on land and at sea	فِي البَرِّ وَالبَحْرِ
As a matter of fact, the laws are not being enforced fairly on all citizens.	فِي الحَقِيقَةِ لَا يَتِمُّ تَطْبِيقُ القَوَانِينِ عَلَى جَمِيعِ المُوَاطِنِينَ بِعَدَالَةٍ وَشَفَافِيَّةٍ.	as a matter of fact	فِي الحَقِيقَةِ
A lot of young Arabs are striving to work or study abroad.	يَسْعَى الكَثِيرُ مِنَ الشَّبَابِ العَرَبِ لِلْعَمَلِ أَوِ الدِّرَاسَةِ فِي الخَارِجِ.	abroad	فِي الخَارِجِ
The government announced the eradication of domestic terrorism.	أَعْلَنَتِ الحُكُومَةُ القَضَاءَ عَلَى الإِرْهَابِ فِي الدَّاخِلِ.	internally	فِي الدَّاخِلِ
The union is striving to make a significant impact in the international arena.	يَسْعَى الاتِّحَادُ إِلَى إِحْدَاثِ تَأْثِيرٍ كَبِيرٍ فِي السَّاحَةِ الدَّوَلِيَّةِ.	in the arena	فِي السَّاحَةِ
Some government officials receive bribes secretly.	يَتَلَقَّى بَعْضُ المَسْؤُولِينَ الحُكُومِيِّينَ الرَّشَاوَى فِي الخَفَاءِ.	secretly	فِي السِّرِّ / فِي الخَفَاءِ
As for small importing companies, the focus is most probably on food and beverages.	بِالنِّسْبَةِ لِشَرِكَاتِ الاسْتِيرَادِ الصَّغِيرَةِ، يَتِمُّ التَّرْكِيزُ فِي الغَالِبِ عَلَى المَوَادِّ الغِذَائِيَّةِ وَالمَشْرُوبَاتِ.	most probably	فِي الغَالِبِ
An agreement will be signed between Morocco and the European Union in the near future.	سَيَتِمُّ التَّوْقِيعُ عَلَى اتِّفَاقِ الشَّرَاكَةِ بَيْنَ المَغْرِبِ وَالاتِّحَادِ الأُورُوبِّيِّ فِي القَرِيبِ العَاجِلِ.	in the near future/very soon	فِي القَرِيبِ العَاجِلِ
The firefighter saved the man's life at the last moment before the explosion.	أَنْقَذَ الإِطْفَائِيُّ حَيَاةَ الرَّجُلِ فِي اللَّحْظَةِ الأَخِيرَةِ قَبْلَ الانْفِجَارِ.	at the moment	فِي اللَّحْظَةِ
Inflation will not exceed 7 percent.	نِسْبَةُ التَّضَخُّمِ لَنْ تَتَجَاوَزَ السَّبْعَةَ فِي المِائَةِ.	percent	فِي المِائَةِ
Cooperation in the military sphere between the two countries increased.	زَادَ التَّعَاوُنُ بَيْنَ البَلَدَيْنِ فِي المَجَالِ العَسْكَرِيِّ.	in the field/in the sphere	فِي المَجَالِ

Two-letter prepositions

English sentence	Arabic example	Meaning	Phrase
Better luck next time.	حَظٌّ أَفْضَلُ فِي المَرَّةِ القَادِمَةِ.	in time/occasion	فِي المَرَّةِ
Other protests will not happen in the future.	لَنْ تَخْرُجَ تَظَاهُرَاتٌ أُخْرَى فِي المُسْتَقْبَلِ.	in the future	فِي المُسْتَقْبَلِ
The government aims in the first place to attract foreign investment and to get capital.	تَهْدُفُ الحُكُومَةُ فِي المَقَامِ الأَوَّلِ إِلَى جَذْبِ الاِسْتِثْمَارِ الأَجْنَبِيِّ وَالحُصُولِ عَلَى رُؤُوسِ الأَمْوَالِ.	in the first place	فِي المَقَامِ الأَوَّلِ
Eventually, the police officers arrested all the gang members.	فِي النِّهَايَةِ تَمَكَّنَ رِجَالُ الشُّرْطَةِ مِنَ القَبْضِ عَلَى جَمِيعِ أَفْرَادِ العِصَابَةِ.	eventually	فِي النِّهَايَةِ
The party is indeed facing serious financial problems.	يُعَانِي الحِزْبُ فِي الوَاقِعِ مِنْ مُشْكِلَاتٍ مَالِيَّةٍ ضَخْمَةٍ.	indeed	فِي الوَاقِعِ
Waiting for the elections, the candidates mobilize voters.	فِي اِنْتِظَارِ مَوْعِدِ الاِنْتِخَابَاتِ يَلْجَأُ المُرَشَّحُونَ إِلَى حَشْدِ النَّاخِبِينَ.	waiting for	فِي اِنْتِظَارِ
Initially, the contracts will be signed, and the necessary funds will be secured.	فِي بَادِئِ الأَمْرِ سَيَتِمُّ تَوْقِيعُ العُقُودِ وَتَأْمِينُ التَّمْوِيلِ اللَّازِمِ.	initially/in the first place	فِي بَادِئِ الأَمْرِ
In the estimation of the World Bank, the world has witnessed mass displacements in the past decade.	فِي تَقْدِيرِ البَنْكِ الدُّوَلِيِّ شَهِدَ العَالَمُ مَوْجَاتِ نُزُوحٍ جَمَاعِيَّةٍ فِي العَقْدِ الأَخِيرِ.	in the estimation	فِي تَقْدِيرِ
The report, under all circumstances, shall be forwarded to the chief executive.	يَجِبُ أَنْ يُرْفَعَ التَّقْرِيرُ، فِي جَمِيعِ الأَحْوَالِ، إِلَى الرَّئِيسِ التَّنْفِيذِيِّ.	in any case/in all circumstances	فِي جَمِيعِ الأَحْوَالِ
After the earthquake, the country was in need of money to help in reconstruction.	كَانَ البَلَدُ فِي حَاجَةٍ إِلَى الأَمْوَالِ لِلمُسَاعَدَةِ عَلَى تَمْوِيلِ إِعَادَةِ الإِعْمَارِ بَعْدَ الزِّلْزَالِ.	in need of	فِي حَاجَةٍ
In case of loss, this will be borne by the investor.	فِي حَالَةِ حُدُوثِ خَسَارَةٍ فَسَيَتَحَمَّلُهَا المُسْتَثْمِرُ.	in the case of/in the event of	فِي حَالَةِ

The launch of the space station was in itself an extraordinary event.	كَانَ إِطْلَاقُ المَحَطَّةِ الفَضَائِيَّةِ فِي حَدِّ ذَاتِهِ حَدَثًا اسْتِثْنَائِيًّا.	on its own	فِي حَدِّ ذَاتِهِ
The purpose of the convention is to establish a free-trade area between the two countries by 2020.	يَرْمِي الاتِّفَاقُ إِلَى إِنْشَاءِ مِنْطَقَةٍ لِلتَّبَادُلِ الحُرِّ بَيْنَ البَلَدَيْنِ فِي حُدُودِ عَامِ 2020.	within/by [a certain time]	فِي حُدُودِ
While contacts between the leaders of the two countries are going on, the attacks on the borders are continuing.	فِي حِينٍ تَسْتَمِرُّ الاتِّصَالَاتُ مَعَ قِيَادَتَيْ البَلَدَيْنِ، تَتَوَاصَلُ الهَجَمَاتُ عَلَى الحُدُودِ.	while	فِي حِينٍ
At the closure of the conference, recommendations were announced.	فِي خِتَامِ المُؤْتَمَرِ، تَمَّ إِعْلَانُ التَّوْصِيَاتِ.	at the closure of/end of	فِي خِتَامِ
Historical sites in the city are in danger as a result of war.	وَضْعُ الأَمَاكِنِ التَّارِيخِيَّةِ فِي المَدِينَةِ أَصْبَحَ فِي خَطَرٍ نَتِيجَةَ الحَرْبِ.	in danger	فِي خَطَرٍ
The children looked at the magician in amazement and fascination.	نَظَرَ الأَطْفَالُ إِلَى السَّاحِرِ فِي دَهْشَةٍ وَانْبِهَارٍ.	in amazement/ astonishment	فِي دَهْشَةٍ / ذُهُولٍ
According to some observers, all Arabs must improve democracy in the region.	فِي رَأْيِ بَعْضِ المُرَاقِبِينَ، يَجِبُ عَلَى كُلِّ العَرَبِ تَحْسِينُ وَضْعِ الدِّيمُوقْرَاطِيَّةِ فِي المِنْطَقَةِ.	according to	فِي رَأْيِ
He got used to spending Ramadan in the vastness of the Great Mosque.	تَعَوَّدَ عَلَى قَضَاءِ شَهْرِ رَمَضَانَ فِي رِحَابِ المَسْجِدِ الحَرَامِ.	in the wings of/in the vastness of	فِي رِحَابِ
Her husband died at the prime of his life in war.	تُوُفِّيَ زَوْجُهَا فِي الحَرْبِ وَهُوَ فِي رَيْعَانِ الشَّبَابِ.	prime of	فِي رَيْعَانِ الشَّبَابِ
In the context of finding solutions to the water crisis, the government will work on ground water extraction.	فِي سِيَاقِ البَحْثِ عَنْ حُلُولٍ لِأَزْمَةِ المِيَاهِ، سَتَعْمَلُ الحُكُومَةُ عَلَى اسْتِخْرَاجِ المِيَاهِ الجَوْفِيَّةِ.	in the context of	فِي سِيَاقِ

Two-letter prepositions 91

Concerning the amendment to the Investment Act, the Parliament will hold serious discussions.	فِي شَأْنِ تَعْدِيلِ قَانُونِ الاسْتِثْمَارِ، سَيُجْرِي البَرْلَمَانُ مُنَاقَشَاتٍ جَادَّةً.	concerning	فِي شَأْنِ
The political crisis has been an investment serving the interest(s) of external parties.	تَمَّ اسْتِثْمَارُ الأَزْمَةِ السِّيَاسِيَّةِ فِي صَالِحِ جِهَاتٍ خَارِجِيَّةٍ.	in the interest(s) of	فِي صَالِحِ
The government is in the process of establishing industrial firms and agricultural enterprises.	الحُكُومَةُ فِي صَدَدِ إِنْشَاءِ شَرِكَاتٍ صِنَاعِيَّةٍ وَمَشْرُوعَاتٍ زِرَاعِيَّةٍ.	in the process of	فِي صَدَدِ
The agreement has been drafted in a way that satisfies all parties.	تَمَّتْ صِيَاغَةُ الاتِّفَاقِ فِي صُورَةٍ تُرْضِي جَمِيعَ الأَطْرَافِ.	in a way/in a form of	فِي صُورَةِ / شَكْلِ
In the light of the economic crisis, social problems have been exacerbated.	تَفَاقَمَتِ المُشْكِلَاتُ الاجْتِمَاعِيَّةُ فِي ظِلِّ الأَزْمَةِ الاقْتِصَادِيَّةِ.	in the light of	فِي ظِلِّ
In the time of the current president, all the economic indicators deteriorated.	فِي عَهْدِ الرَّئِيسِ الحَالِيِّ تَدَهْوَرَتْ جَمِيعُ المُؤَشِّرَاتِ الاقْتِصَادِيَّةِ.	in the time/ era of	فِي عَهْدِ
The negotiations between the two parties were extremely difficult.	كَانَتِ المُفَاوَضَاتُ بَيْنَ الجَانِبَيْنِ فِي غَايَةِ الصُّعُوبَةِ.	extremely	فِي غَايَةِ
In the absence of an effective police, crime rates have increased.	فِي غِيَابِ الشُّرْطَةِ الفَعَّالَةِ، زَادَتْ مُعَدَّلَاتُ الجَرِيمَةِ.	in the absence of	فِي غِيَابِ
The parties found themselves in the middle of a political storm.	وَجَدَتِ الأَحْزَابُ نَفْسَهَا فِي قَلْبِ عَاصِفَةٍ سِيَاسِيَّةٍ.	in the middle of	فِي قَلْبِ
In the game, the player was at the peak of his fitness.	ظَهَرَ اللَّاعِبُ فِي المُبَارَاةِ فِي قِمَّةِ لِيَاقَتِهِ.	the peak of	فِي قِمَّةِ

Countries in Africa score badly in the field of human rights.	لَا تُحَقِّقُ البُلْدَانُ الإِفْرِيقِيَّةُ مَرَاكِزَ جَيِّدَةً فِي مَجَالِ حُقُوقِ الإِنْسَانِ.	in the area of/ in the field of	فِي مَجَالِ
In an attempt to put an end to monopolization, the government will enact new laws.	سَتَسُنُّ الحُكُومَةُ قَوَانِينَ جَدِيدَةً فِي مُحَاوَلَةٍ لِوَضْعِ حَدٍّ لِعَمَلِيَّاتِ الِاحْتِكَارِ.	in an attempt to	فِي مُحَاوَلَةٍ
Security forces deployed along the perimeter of the explosion area.	انْتَشَرَتْ قُوَّاتُ الأَمْنِ فِي مُحِيطِ مِنْطَقَةِ الِانْفِجَارِ.	the perimeter of	فِي مُحِيطِ
The region entered a new stage of modernization.	دَخَلَتِ المِنْطَقَةُ فِي مَرْحَلَةٍ جَدِيدَةٍ مِنْ مَرَاحِلِ التَّحْدِيثِ.	in the stage of	فِي مَرْحَلَةٍ
In response to solidarity between women, solidarity between men has increased.	فِي مُقَابِلِ التَّضَامُنِ بَيْنَ النِّسَاءِ، زَادَ التَّضَامُنُ بَيْنَ الرِّجَالِ.	in exchange for/in response to	فِي مُقَابِلِ
At a young age, the little girl took on the responsibility of taking care of her family.	تَحَمَّلَتِ الفَتَاةُ مَسْؤُولِيَّةَ رِعَايَةِ الأُسْرَةِ وَهِيَ فِي مُقْتَبَلِ الْعُمَرِ.	At a young age	فِي مُقْتَبَلِ الْعُمَرِ
Members of the government are foremost among those people who will be brought to face justice.	قَدْ يَكُونُ أَعْضَاءُ الحُكُومَةِ فِي مُقَدِّمَةِ مَنْ تَطَالُهُمْ يَدُ العَدَالَةِ.	at the forefront of/ foremost among	فِي مُقَدِّمَةٍ
In Europe, in the middle of the last century, feminists' voices were raised.	فِي مُنْتَصَفِ القَرْنِ المَاضِي تَعَالَتْ أَصْوَاتُ النِّسْوِيَّاتِ فِي أُورُوبَا.	in the middle of	فِي مُنْتَصَفِ
In the eyes of policy makers in Washington, D.C., the situation in the region is calm.	فِي نَظَرِ صَانِعِي القَرَارِ فِي وَاشِنْطُنَ فَإِنَّ الوَضْعَ فِي المِنْطَقَةِ هَادِئٌ.	in the eyes of	فِي نَظَرِ
Young people claimed their right to have a good education, and at the same time to work and enjoy health care.	طَالَبَ الشَّبَابُ بِحَقِّهِمْ فِي التَّعْلِيمِ الجَيِّدِ وَفِي نَفْسِ الوَقْتِ بِحَقِّهِمْ فِي العَمَلِ وَالرِّعَايَةِ الصِّحِّيَّةِ.	at the same time	فِي نَفْسِ الوَقْتِ

Two-letter prepositions 93

The president is in trouble because of the protests.	وَجَدَ الرَّئِيسُ نَفْسَهُ فِي وَرْطَةٍ بِسَبَبِ الإِحْتِجَاجَاتِ.	in trouble	فِي وَرْطَةٍ
Opposition parties are now tools in the hands of the army.	أَصْبَحَتْ أَحْزَابُ المُعَارَضَةِ أَدَاةً فِي يَدِ الجَيْشِ.	in the hands of	فِي يَدِ
The United Nations wondered whether displaced people would go back home or not.	تَسَاءَلَتِ الأُمَمُ المُتَّحِدَةُ فِيمَا إِذَا سَيَعُودُ النَّازِحُونَ إِلَى دِيَارِهِمْ أَمْ لَا.	whether	فِيمَا إِذَا
The minister had previously served as a senior expert in the International Monetary Fund.	كَانَ الوَزِيرُ فِيمَا سَبَقَ يَشْغَلُ مَنْصِبَ كَبِيرِ خُبَرَاءَ بِصُنْدُوقِ النَّقْدِ الدُّوَلِيِّ.	previously	فِيمَا سَبَقَ
In the past, the US administration was keen to find a two-state solution.	فِيمَا مَضَى كَانَتِ الإِدَارَةُ الأَمْرِيكِيَّةُ حَرِيصَةً عَلَى حَلِّ الدَّوْلَتَيْنِ.	in the past	فِيمَا مَضَى
With regard to unemployment, females' unemployment rate was higher than the males'.	وَفِيمَا يَخُصُّ البَطَالَةَ، كَانَتْ نِسْبَةُ البَطَالَةِ فِي الإِنَاثِ أَعْلَى مِنْهَا فِي الذُّكُورِ.	with regard to	فِيمَا يَخُصُّ

كَي

The particle كَي is similar to two other particles in Arabic, (لِ) and (حَتَّى). These are considered to be prepositions when followed by an implicit noun or (المَصْدَر المُؤَوَّل), i.e. an implicit verbal noun that consists of a suppressed particle أَنْ + a verb. However, when these particles are followed by an accusative-marked present-tense verb, they become subjunctive particles, and the verbs will be in the subjunctive mood.

كَي is rarely used as a preposition in Modern Standard Arabic. It is used primarily as a subjunctive particle to designate the intention of someone and the object acted on. It is translated as 'in order to'.

In (جِئْتُ كَيْ أَتَعَلَّمَ), the combination of (أَنْ) followed by the present-tense verb (أَتَعَلَّمَ) is considered to be the implicit object of the preposition كي.

Note

If كَيْ is followed by the particle أَنْ and a verb, or if the particle أَنْ is suppressed but assumed after كَيْ, then كَيْ is considered to be a preposition in both cases, as in the following two sentences:

| جِئْتُ كَيْ أَنْ أَتَعَلَّمَ. | I came to learn. |
| مَارِسْ الرِّيَاضَةَ كَيْ يَطُولَ عُمْرُكَ. | Do sports so as to live longer. |

In the second sentence above it is assumed that there is أَنْ after كَيْ as (كَيْ أَنْ يَطُولَ).

The prepositional كَيْ can be followed by the interrogative particle ما, and it becomes (كَيْمَا or كَيْمَه), and it has the same meaning as 'why', as in these cases:

كَيْمَا سَافَرْتَ إِلَى بَغْدَادَ؟	Why did you travel to Baghdad?
كَيْمَا فَعَلْتَ هَذَا؟	Why did you do that?
كَيْمَا قَتَلُوهُ؟	Why did they kill him?

كَيْ as a subjunctive particle is used in the sense of 'in order to', as in the following:

| دَرَسْتُ كَيْ أَنْجَحَ فِي الْإِمْتِحَانِ. | I studied in order to pass the exam. |
| عُدْتُ إِلَى الْمَنْزِلِ كَيْ أُسَاعِدَ أُمِّي. | I went back home to/in order to help my mom. |

Note

When كَيْ is preceded by the particle (لِ) in the sense of 'in order to', كَيْ will be considered to be a subjunctive particle and not a preposition, such as in the following cases:

| سَأَلَ الْكَثِيرَ مِنَ الْأَسْئِلَةِ لِكَيْ يَكْشِفَ الْحَقِيقَةَ. | He asked a lot of questions in order to unveil the truth. |
| ذَهَبَا إِلَى السُّوقِ لِكَيْ يَشْتَرِيَا الْحَلْوَى. | They went to market to buy candy. |

Note

If (لَا) is added to كَيْ it will become (كَيْلَا), which means 'in order not to', as shown in the following:

| هَرَبَ كَيْلَا يَعْتَرِفَ بِالْحَقِيقَةِ. | He ran away in order not to tell the truth. |
| سَافَرْنَا كَيْلَا نَشْعُرَ بِالْمَلَلِ فِي الْعُطْلَةِ. | We traveled so that we wouldn't get bored during the holiday. |

Two-letter prepositions 95

The particle (لِ) can be added to (كَيْلا = لِكَيْلا), but it will not change the meaning, as in the following:

لا تُخبِرهُ عَمَّا حَدَثَ لِكَيْلا يَشْعُرَ بِالْحُزْنِ.   Don't tell him what happened so that he won't feel sad.

شَرِبْتُ الْقَهْوَةَ لِكَيْلا أَشْعُرَ بِالنُّعاسِ.   I drank coffee so as not to feel sleepy.

Note

When (كي + ما) come together to make a statement, they become (كَيْمَا), which is used in the sense of 'so that', as in the following:

جِئْتُ كَيْمَا أَتَحَدَّثَ مَعَ الطَّبِيبِ.   I came to speak with the doctor.

Exercises

I What is the function of (مِن – عَن – في) in the sentences below?

1 اشْتَرى الرَّجُلُ طَفَّايَةَ سَجائِرَ مِنَ الرُّخامِ الذَّهَبِيِّ.
2 تَحَرَّرَ الْبَلَدُ مِنَ الْإِسْتِعْمارِ.
3 حادَ السّائِقُ عَنْ طَريقِهِ.
4 ما جِئْتُكَ إِلّا عَنْ حاجَةٍ مُلِحَّةٍ.
5 عاقَبَ الْمُديرُ الْمُوَظَّفَ في غَضَبٍ.
6 سِرْتُ مِنْ عَجْمانَ إِلى الشّارِقَةِ.
7 تَقابَلْنا في الْحَرَمِ الْجامِعِيِّ.
8 كَمْ تَتَقاضى في السّاعَةِ الْواحِدَةِ؟
9 قَضَيْنا عُطْلَةَ الصَّيْفِ في مِصْرَ.
10 غَفَلَ عَنْ صَلاتِهِ.

II Complete the sentences below with the appropriate pronoun suffixes:

1 تَحَدَّثَ الْمُحاضِرُ عَنْ أُصولِ الْعائِلاتِ التي جاءَ مِنْ ــــ هؤُلاءِ الوافِدونَ.
2 هُناكَ الْعَديدُ مِنَ الْمُؤَشِّراتِ لِلتَّراجُعِ الاقْتِصادِيِّ مِنْ ــــ الْعَجْزُ الغِذائي الْمُتَزايِد.
3 كانَ مِنْ ــــ مَنْ هاجَمَ الْحَرَكَةَ بِدَعْوى أَنَّها حَرَكَةٌ مُتَّفِقَةٌ مَعَ الْمَصالِحِ الْخارِجِيَّةِ.
4 أَنا اعْتَمِدُ على كُلِّ واحِدٍ مِنْ ــــ فيما يَخُصّ هذا الشَّأن.
5 يَحْتاجُ الإعْلامُ أَنْ يَنْزِعَ عَنْ ــــ هذِهِ الصّورَةَ النَّمَطِيَّةَ.
6 الْعَصَبِيَّةُ والْعُنصُرِيَّةُ والتَّفرِقَةُ بِكُلِّ أَلوانِها، لِنَفصِلَ الحَديثَ عَنْ ــــ كُلٌّ على حِدَةٍ.
7 لَقَدْ تَفاجَأْتُ بِثَقافَةٍ أُخْرى تَماماً لا نَعْرِفُ عَنْ ــــ شَيْئاً.
8 تَرْجَمَ زَميلي كِتاباً عن شكسبير وجَمَعَ مَعْلوماتٍ كَثيرةً عَنْ ــــ.
9 أُريدُ أَنْ أُخْبِرَهُم كُلَّ شَيءٍ عَنْ ــــ، يا سَيِّدَ أَحْمَد.
10 شارَكْتُ في نَدْوَةٍ ثَقافِيَّةٍ طُرِحَ مَوضوعُ الازْدِواجِيَّةِ في ــــ.

Two-letter prepositions

III Choose the correct preposition to complete the sentences.

1. عادَ بَعدَ سَنَواتٍ طَويلَةٍ (كي – عن – في) الغُربَةِ إلى بِلادِه.
2. تَسْتَوردُ مُعظَمُ البُلدانِ العَرَبيّةِ مَواداً غِذائيّةً (مِنْ – عن – في) أجلِ سَدّ حاجاتِ السُّكان.
3. تَلَقَّيْنا دَعْوَةً (مِنْ – عن – في) ابنِ أخي لِكي نَحضُرَ حَفْلَ زِفافِه.
4. طَرحَ زَميلي اقتِراحًا لِصاحِبِ الشَّركَةِ لَمْ يُناقَشْ (مِنْ – عن – في) قَبْلُ.
5. لَمْ يَتَحدَّثْ النَّائِبُ (مِنْ – عن – في) رُدودِ الأفعالِ الشَّعْبِيّةِ الأخيرة.
6. إنّ الاستِمراريّةَ المَعْنِيةَ (في- مِن- عَن) مَفهومِ التَّنميةِ تُشيرُ إلى الامتِدادِ والرّوابِطِ بَيْنَ الأجْيالِ.
7. تَمّ ذَلِكَ مُقابِلَ رُؤْيةٍ واضِحَةٍ (في- مِن- عَن) دُولِ شَرقِ آسيا المَذْكورة.
8. كانَ ذَلِكَ مِقياساً تركيبياً مستخلصاً (في - مِن - عَن) مَجموعَةِ مُعطَياتٍ إحْصائيّةٍ واقعيةٍ للمُجْتَمَع.
9. يُعَبّر هذا الكِتابُ (في- مِن- عَن) الثّقافةِ المَحَلّيّة.
10. أعْرَبَ الرَّئِيسُ (في-ِ مِن – عَن) امْتِنانِهِ للدّعمِ الذي قَدّمَهُ مَجلِسُ الوُزَراء لَه.

IV Fill in the gaps with a suitable preposition from the following (مِن – عن – في).

1. كانَ ذَلِكَ نَتيجَةَ المُواجَهةِ الشَّرِسَةِ ـــــــ قِبَلِ الأنظِمةِ القائِمةِ.
2. هذِهِ المُشاوَراتُ أتَت ـــــــ الوَقتِ الذي كُنا في أمسِّ الحاجَةِ إلَيها.
3. تَعمَلُ الحُكومَةُ على تَمويلِ بَرامِجِ التَّدريبِ ـــــــ طَريقِ المَعهدِ البِريطانيِ.
4. وُلِدَ الكاتِبُ في قَرْيةٍ صَغيرةٍ ـــــــ جُنوبِ لبُنان لِأسْرَةٍ مَيسورةِ الحَال.
5. يَسْعى مَجلِسُ الأمْنِ ـــــــ جانِبِه إلى العَمَلِ على تَسْريعِ عَمَليَّةِ السّلامِ في المَنْطِقة.
6. يَجوزُ للأولادِ أنْ يَحجُّوا نِيابَةً ـــــــ آبائِهم وأُمَّهاتِهم المُتَوفّقين.
7. حَظِيَ الحِزبُ الحاكِمُ بدَعْمِ الأغْلَبيّةِ ـــــــ الأنْتِخَاباتِ البَرْلَمانيةِ.

V Make sensible sentences with the phrases in the columns below.

1	عَلينا أنْ نَضعَ خُططًا استِراتيجيَّةً	A	مِن أهلِ العِلمِ والفِكرِ.
2	تَتَمَيَّزُ هذِهِ الأنشِطةُ بالشُّموليِّةِ كَما تَتَمَيَّزُ بالاستِمْرارِيَّةِ	B	لِكي نَتَمَكَّنَ مِنَ التَّقليلِ مِنَ الأوْقاتِ العَصيبةِ التي نَتَعَرَّضُ لها.
3	تُنادي الأُمَمُ المُتَّحِدةُ بِتَسويةٍ نِهائيّةٍ لِمُشْكِلةِ السَّلامِ	C	حَتّى يَتِمَّ تَحْقيقُ أهدافِها.
4	أُسِّسَ المُنتَدى بِهَدَفِ إيجادِ مُلْتَقى يَجتَمِعُ فيهِ المُفَكِّرونَ والباحِثونَ	D	في عِدّةِ اتِّجاهاتٍ
5	هُناكَ جُهودٌ عَرَبيّةٌ جَماعيّةٌ هائِلةٌ	E	في الشَّرقِ الأوْسَطِ.

VI Translate the following sentences in Arabic.

1. My friend visited me with a dish of Omani sweets.
2. The university is located ten kilometers away from the city center.
3. The current financial crisis forced many companies to sacrifice long-term investments.
4. The train was delayed by half an hour from its scheduled time.
5. We spent the summer vacation in Egypt.

VII Translate the following sentences into English.

1. تَقَابَلْنَا فِي الْحَرَمِ الْجَامِعِيِّ.
2. تَخَلَّفَ عَنْ حُضُورِ الْحَفْلِ لِأَسْبَابٍ عَائِلِيةٍ.
3. يَحْتَاجُ الْإِعْلَامُ أَنْ يَنْزِعَ عَنْ نَفْسِهِ هَذِهِ الصُّورَةَ النَّمَطِيَّةَ.
4. مَاتَ عَدَدٌ كَبِيرٌ مِنَ الْأَطْفَالِ فِي حَرْبِ الْعِرَاقِ.
5. سَتُقَامُ الْاِحْتِفَالَاتُ فِي الْأَيَّامِ الْقَلِيلَةِ الْمُقْبِلَةِ.

4 Three-letter prepositions

This chapter covers the three-letter prepositions (رُبَّ / مُنْذُ / عَدَا / خَلَا / عَلَى / إِلَى). It discusses the main functions and usage of each preposition and includes selected contextual examples that illustrate their different functions.

إِلَى

إِلَى is mainly used in the sense of 'in the direction of' or 'toward' and is commonly translated as 'to', 'for' or 'toward'. According to *A Frequency Dictionary of Arabic* (2011), it is the ninth-most commonly used word in Arabic. It can be used in spatial and temporal contexts, and it implies movement toward a certain point in place or time. In some contexts, it is synonymous with (اللَّام) or (حَتَّى).

إِلَى in context

> - مِنْ فَضْلِكَ، إِلَى أَيْنَ يَتَّجِهُ هَذَا القِطَارُ؟
> = هَذَا القِطَارُ يَتَّجِهُ إِلَى الإِسْكَنْدَرِيَّةِ.
> - كُنْتُ أَظُنُّ أَنَّهُ القِطَارُ المُتَّجِهُ إِلَى بُورسَعِيد.
> = لَقَدْ تَمَّ نَقْلُ قِطَارِ بُورسَعِيد إِلَى الرَّصِيفِ المُجَاوِرِ.
> - الرَّصِيفُ المُجَاوِرُ إِلَى اليَمِينِ؟
> = نَعَم.
>
> - Excuse me please! Where is this train heading to?
> = This train is heading to Alexandria.
> - I thought that it was the train heading to Port Said.
> = The Port Said train was transferred to the adjacent platform.
> - The adjacent platform to the right?
> = Yes.

Notes on the usage of إِلَى in context

The preposition إِلَى is used mainly to indicate movement in a certain direction, such as in (تَمَّ نَقْلُ قِطَارِ بُورسَعِيد إِلَى الرَّصِيفِ المُجَاوِرِ) and (يَتَّجِهُ إِلَى الإِسْكَنْدَرِيَّةِ), and it expresses locality, for example, (الرَّصِيفُ المُجَاوِرُ إِلَى اليَمِينِ).

Functions of إِلَى

إِلَى is used to indicate movement toward a place, a goal or an end, as in the following examples:

تَسْعَى الْحُكُومَةُ الْمِصْرِيَّةُ إِلَى إِنْشَاءِ مَشَارِيعَ جَدِيدَةٍ.	The Egyptian government seeks to establish new projects.
تَهْدِفُ الْخُطَّةُ إِلَى زِيَادَةِ الدَّخْلِ الْقَومِيِّ مِنَ الْعُمْلَاتِ الأَجْنَبِيَّةِ.	The plan aims to increase the national income of foreign currency.
هُنَاكَ أَسْبَابٌ خَفِيَّةٌ تَدْفَعُ أَعْدَادًا مُتَزَايِدَةً إِلَى الهِجْرَةِ.	There are hidden causes that are driving increasing numbers of people to immigrate.
سَيَقُومُ أُنْبُوبُ الْغَازِ بِنَقْلِ الْغَازِ الْجَزَائِرِيّ إِلَى إِسْبَانِيَا عَبْرَ الْمَغْرِبِ.	The gas pipeline will transport Algerian gas to Spain via Morocco.
يَتَوَجَّهُ الْمُوَاطِنُونَ الْيَوْمَ إِلَى صَنَادِيقِ الاِقْتِرَاعِ لاِخْتِيَارِ مُمَثِّلِيهِم فِي الْبَرْلَمَانِ.	Citizens are heading to the polls today to choose their representatives in the parliament.

إِلَى is used to indicate the destination of movement, as in the following cases:

وَصَلَ وَفْدٌ لِيبِيٌّ إِلَى الْقَاهِرَةِ أَمْسِ.	A Libyan delegation arrived in Cairo yesterday.
ذَهَبْتُ إِلَى دِمَشْقَ فِي طَرِيقِي إِلَى اللَّاذِقِيَّةِ.	I went to Damascus on my way to Latakia.
مِنَ الْمُتَوَقَّعِ أَنْ يَرْتَفِعَ الْمَعْرُوضُ النَّفْطِيُّ فِي الْعَامِ الْمُقْبِلِ إِلَى 20 مِلْيُونَ بِرْمِيلٍ فِي الْيَوْمِ.	Oil supply is expected to rise next year to 20 million barrels per day.
يَقُولُ الْمُفَوَّضُ الأُورُوبِي إِنَّ التَّوَصُّلَ إِلَى اتِفَاقٍ لَنْ يَكُونَ سَهْلًا.	The European Commissioner says that reaching an agreement will not be easy.
مِنَ الْمُتَوَقَّعِ أَنْ تَصِلَ أَسْعَارُ الْفَائِدَةِ الأَمْرِيكِيَّةِ إِلَى سِتَّةٍ فِي الْمِئَةِ.	Interest rates in the US are expected to reach 6 per cent.

إِلَى is used with a temporal function to express the time for which something lasts or continues, in the sense of 'to' or 'until', as in the following:

عَاشَ فِي مَنْفَاهُ الإِجْبَارِيّ إِلَى 1950.	He lived in compulsory exile until 1950.
يَعُودُ أَقْدَمُ الْمَخْطُوطَاتِ إِلَى الْقَرْنِ التَّاسِعِ الْمِيلَادِيّ.	The earliest manuscripts date back to the ninth century AD.
اِسْتَمَرَّتِ الْحَرْبُ بَيْنَ الْعِرَاقِ وَإِيرَانَ مِنْ عَامِ 1980 إِلَى عَامِ 1988.	The war between Iraq and Iran lasted from 1980 to 1988.
سَيْطَرَ الْهُكْسُوسُ عَلَى حُكْمِ مِصْرَ مِنْ مُنْتَصَفِ الْقَرْنِ 17 إِلَى مُنْتَصَفِ الْقَرْنِ 16 ق.م.	The Hyksos ruled Egypt between the mid-17th and the mid-16th centuries BC.
قَرَّرَتِ النِّقَابَةُ تَأْجِيلَ الإِضْرَابِ إِلَى مَوْعِدٍ غَيْرِ مُحَدَّدٍ.	The union decided to postpone the strike until an unspecified date.

> **Note**
> Relevant to this usage are some expressions that indicate saying, 'Goodbye', or 'See you', as in (إِلَى اللِّقَاءَ) 'see you'; (إِلَى الغَدِ), 'until tomorrow'; and the expression 'forever', (إِلَى الأَبَدِ).

إلى is used to indicate locality, as in the following:

جَلَسْنَا إِلَى المَائِدَةِ لِتَنَاوُلِ العَشَاءِ.	We sat at the table to have dinner.
يَقَعُ الفُنْدُقُ إِلَى شَمَالِ الشَّاطِئِ.	The hotel is located to the north of the beach.
يَقَعُ الإِقْلِيمُ إِلَى الغَرْبِ مِنَ الحُدُودِ الشَّمَالِيَّةِ.	The province is located west of the northern borders.
جَلَسَتِ العَرُوسُ إِلَى اليَمِينِ وَالعَرِيسُ إِلَى اليَسَارِ.	The bride sat to the right and the groom to the left.
تَقَعُ مَدِينَةُ بِئْرِ العَبْدِ الَّتِي تَشْتَهِرُ بِآثَارِهَا القَدِيمَةِ إِلَى الشَّرْقِ مِنَ العَرِيشِ.	Bir al-Abed, which is famous for its ancient ruins, is located to the east of Arish.

إلى is used to indicate the person to whom an action is directed, as in the following:

نَقَلَ المُفَوَّضُ الأُورُوبِّيُّ رِسَالَةً إِلَى أَعْضَاءِ الكُونغرِس الأَمْرِيكِي.	The European Commissioner conveyed a message to members of the US Congress.
الإِسَاءَةُ إِلَى الآخَرِينَ غَيْرُ مَقْبُولَةٍ تَحْتَ أَيِّ ظَرْفٍ.	Abuse of others is unacceptable under any circumstances.
سَتُسَلَّمُ مُتَعَلَّقَاتُ الضَّحَايَا إِلَى أَقَارِبِهِم.	The victims' belongings will be handed over to their relatives.
قَامَتْ الفَائِزَةُ بِإِهْدَاءِ مِيدَالِيَّتِهَا إِلَى جَلَالَةِ المَلِكِ.	The winner dedicated her medal to His Majesty, the King.
سَيُقَدِّمُ السَّفِيرُ طَلَبًا رَسْمِيًّا إِلَى الرَّئِيسِ.	The ambassador will submit a formal request to the president.

إلى is also used to indicate proximity in expressions such as (إِلَى جَانِبِ) and (إِلَى جِوَارِ), as in the following:

اِجْلِسْ إِلَى جِوَارِي.	Sit next to me.
تَقَعُ المَكْتَبَةُ إِلَى جَانِبِ المَطْعَمِ.	The library is located next to the restaurant.
سَيَتِمُّ إِنْشَاءُ شُقَقٍ سَكَنِيَّةٍ فَاخِرَةٍ إِلَى جِوَارِ الفُنْدُقِ.	Luxury apartments will be built next to the hotel.

Three-letter prepositions 101

سَأَضَعُ الكُتُبَ الجَدِيدَةَ إِلَى جَانِبِ الكُتُبِ القَدِيمَةِ عَلَى الرَّفِ.	I will put the new books alongside the old books on the shelf.
يَحْرِصُ الزُّوَّارُ الأَجَانِبُ عَلَى الْتِقَاطِ صُوَرٍ تَذْكَارِيَّةٍ إِلَى جِوَارِ الآثَارِ.	Foreign visitors are keen to take photos next to the monuments.

إِلَى can be used with some adverbs expressing direction of movement, as in the cases that follow:

اِرْجِعْ إِلَى الخَلْفِ لَوْ سَمَحْتَ.	Go back, please.
خَرَجَ إِلَى الشُّرْفَةِ وَنَظَرَ إِلَى الأَسْفَلِ.	He went out to the balcony and looked down.
اِرْتَفَعَتْ أَسْهُمُ بُورْصَةِ دُبَيٍّ إِلَى أَعْلَى مُسْتَوَيَاتِهَا.	Shares in the Dubai stock exchange rose to their highest levels.

Notes on usage

إِلَى can be used with some verbs to give the sense of 'inclined to', as in the following:

تَمِيلُ الحُكُومَاتُ الدِّكْتَاتُورِيَّةُ إِلَى حَجْبِ المَعْلُومَاتِ عَنِ الشُّعُوبِ.	Dictatorships tend to withhold information from people.
لَوْنُ شَعْرِهَا يَمِيلُ إِلَى السَّوَادِ.	The color of her hair tends toward black.
العَلَاقَاتُ بَيْنَ البَلَدَيْنِ مُتَوَتِّرَةٌ وَلَا تُوجَدُ مُؤَشِّرَاتٌ أَنَّ هَذَا التَّوَتُّرَ إِلَى زَوَالٍ.	The relations between the two countries are tense, and there are no signs that this tension will tend to go away.

إِلَى can be used with some verbs to give the sense of 'to join' or 'to add to', as in the following:

ضَمَّ الأَبُ ابْنَهُ إِلَيْهِ.	The father took his son to live with him.
لَا تَضُمَّ مَالَهُ إِلَى مَالِكَ.	Do not include his money in yours.
سَتَنْضَمُّ بَعْضُ دُوَلِ أُورُوبَا الشَّرْقِيَّةِ إِلَى حِلْفِ النَّاتُو.	Some Eastern European countries will join NATO.
أَضَفْتُ بَعْضَ العُمْلَاتِ الأَجْنَبِيَّةِ إِلَى مَجْمُوعَتِي.	I added some foreign coins to my collection.

إِلَى can be used to indicate preference, as in the following:

الاِبْنُ أَحَبُّ إِلَى أُمِّهِ مِنْ أَبِيهِ.	The mother loves the son more than the father.
بِالنِّسْبَةِ إِلَيْهِ، هَذَا العَمَلُ مُمِلٌّ جِدًّا.	In his opinion (literally 'for him'), this job is very boring.

أَيُّ أَنْوَاعِ الأَدَبِ أَحَبُّ إِلَى الشَّبَابِ؟	What types of literature do young people prefer?
لَيْسَ هُنَاكَ مَا هُوَ أَحَبُّ إِلَى قَلْبِ المَرْءِ مِنْ بَنِيهِ.	There is nothing that one loves more than one's children.

إِلَى can be used with some verbs that indicate saying, as in the following cases:

أَشَارَ رَئِيسُ الوُزَرَاءِ إِلَى أَنَّ الحُكُومَةَ تُؤْمِنُ بِدَوْرِ القِطَاعِ الخَاصِّ كَشَرِيكٍ أَسَاسِيٍّ فِي عَمَلِيَّةِ التَّنْمِيَةِ الاِقْتِصَادِيَّةِ.	The prime minister noted that the government believes in the role of the private sector as a key partner in economic development.
نَوَّهَ تَقْرِيرٌ أَمْرِيكِيٌّ إِلَى أَنَّ التَّنَبُّؤَ بِمُسْتَقْبَلِ الدِّيْمُقْرَاطِيَّةِ فِي الشَّرْقِ الأَوْسَطِ صَعْبٌ.	A US report noted that predicting the future of democracy in the Middle East is difficult.
سَيَكُونُ لِزَامًا عَلَى المَبْعُوثِ الأُمَمِيِّ أَنْ يَتَحَدَّثَ إِلَى كَافَّةِ الأَطْرَافِ.	The UN envoy will have to speak to all parties.
دَعَتْ مُنَظَّمَاتُ المُجْتَمَعِ المَدَنِيِّ إِلَى اِحْتِرَامِ حَقِّ الشَّعْبِ فِي التَّظَاهُرِ السِّلْمِيِّ.	Civil society organizations called for respect for the right of the people to demonstrate peacefully.

إِلَى can be used with some verbs that indicate listening, as in the following:

أَصْغَى الجُمْهُورُ إِلَى فَيْرُوزَ بِاهْتِمَامٍ.	The audience listened to Fayrouz attentively.
اِسْتَمَعَ الوَفْدُ إِلَى شَرْحٍ مُفَصَّلٍ عَنِ الفُرَصِ الاِسْتِثْمَارِيَّةِ فِي البَلَدِ.	The delegation listened to a detailed explanation of investment opportunities in the country.
أَنْصَتَ السِّيَاسِيُّ إِلَى آرَاءِ النَّازِحِينَ.	The politician listened to the views of the refugees.

إِلَى is used in a number of expressions that mean 'in addition', as in the following:

بِالإِضَافَةِ إِلَى ذَلِكَ	In addition to this
وَإِلَى ذَلِكَ	In addition
إِلَى جَانِبِ ذَلِكَ	Besides

إِلَى can also be used with expressions such as 'et cetera', as in the following:

إِلَى آخِرِهِ	Et cetera
إِلَى غَيْرِ ذَلِكَ	And so on

An old usage of إِلَى is in fixed expressions that mean 'get away from me':

إِلَيْكَ عَنِّي!	Get away from me!

Notes

In many contexts, the uses of (إِلَى) and (لِ) are confused with each other, particularly due to interference from colloquial Arabic, where (إِلَى) is often replaced with (لِ).

Although (اِحْتَاجَ إِلَى) is more idiomatic than (اِحْتَاجَ لِ), the latter has been used so often that it has become accepted as a correct usage. Another common error is to use this verb with a direct object. The verb (اِحْتَاجَ) can only refer to its object via the preposition (إِلَى).

So it is not idiomatic to say (اِحْتَاجَ لِلْمَالِ) or (اِحْتَاجَ المَالَ), but instead, it should be (اِحْتَاجَ إِلَى المَالِ).

Notes on translation

إِلَى serves several functions, and therefore it can be translated into English in different ways as 'in', 'at', 'by' or 'for', among others. Moreover, in some contexts it does not appear directly in the translation. The following examples illustrate some of these possible translations:

وَصَلَتِ الإِحْتِجَاجَاتُ إِلَى ذُرْوَتِهَا خِلَالَ الشَّهْرِ الأَخِيرِ.	Protests reached their peak during last month.
نَظَرَ الأَطْفَالُ إِلَى الهَدَايَا بِسَعَادَةٍ بَالِغَةٍ.	The children looked at the gifts with great joy.
إِلَى جَانِبِ المَشَاكِلِ السِّيَاسِيَّةِ، تُعَانِي البِلَادُ مِنْ مُشْكِلَاتٍ اِقْتِصَادِيَّةٍ.	In addition to political problems, the country suffers from economic problems.
دَفَعَتِ الثَّوْرَةُ الحُكُومَاتِ إِلَى التَّفْكِيرِ بِصُورَةٍ جِدِّيَّةٍ فِي رَفْعِ مُسْتَوَى مَعِيشَةِ المُوَاطِنِينَ.	The revolution prompted governments to think seriously about raising the standard of living of citizens.
أَدَّتِ الأَزْمَةُ الإِقْتِصَادِيَّةُ العَالَمِيَّةُ إِلَى حُدُوثِ كَسَادٍ فِي الأَسْوَاقِ.	The global economic crisis led to a recession in the markets.
تَصِلُ الأَنْهَارُ وَالجَدَاوِلُ إِلَى جَمِيعِ الوِدْيَانِ.	Rivers and streams reach all valleys.
يَتَطَلَّعُ الطُّلَابُ إِلَى اِنْتِهَاءِ فَتْرَةِ الإِمْتِحَانَاتِ.	Students look forward to the end of the examination period.
سَيَتَوَجَّهُ وَزِيرُ الدِّفَاعِ إِلَى وَاشِنْطُن.	The minister of defense will head to Washington.
عَمَلِيَّاتُ الإِصْلَاحِ تَحْتَاجُ إِلَى وَقْتٍ.	Reforms need time.
دَعَتْ مِصْرُ إِلَى عَقْدِ اِجْتِمَاعٍ طَارِئٍ لِمَجْلِسِ الأَمْنِ الدَّوْلِيِّ.	Egypt called for an emergency meeting of the UN Security Council.

The talks between the two presidents will address issues of common concern.	المُبَاحَثَاتُ بَيْنَ الرَّئِيسَيْنِ سَوْفَ تَتَطَرَّقُ إِلَى القَضَايَا ذَاتِ الاِهْتِمَامِ المُشْتَرَكِ.
There is a French initiative in the Security Council, along with a Canadian initiative.	هُنَاكَ مُبَادَرَةٌ فَرَنْسِيَّةٌ فِي مَجْلِسِ الأَمْنِ إِلَى جَانِبِ مُبَادَرَةٍ كَنَدِيَّةٍ.
The region could turn into a zone of global conflict.	قَدْ تَتَحَوَّلُ المِنْطَقَةُ إِلَى مِنْطَقَةِ صِرَاعٍ شَامِلٍ.
The United States seeks to extend its hegemony to important regions of the world.	تَسْعَى الوِلَايَاتُ المُتَّحِدَةُ إِلَى مَدِّ هَيْمَنَتِهَا إِلَى المَنَاطِقِ المُهِمَّةِ فِي العَالَمِ.
The statement pointed out that three army officers were killed on the border.	أَشَارَ البَيَانُ إِلَى أَنَّ ثَلَاثَةً مِنْ ضُبَّاطِ الجَيْشِ قُتِلُوا عَلَى الحُدُودِ.

إِلَى *with pronoun suffixes*

When إِلَى is followed by a pronoun suffix, it becomes إِلَي. The following table shows how different pronouns appear after the preposition.

إِلَيْهِما	إِلَى + هُمَا		إِلَيَّ	إِلَى + أَنَا
إِلَيْنَا	إِلَى + نَحْنُ		إِلَيْكَ	إِلَى + أَنْتَ
إِلَيْكُم	إِلَى + أَنْتُم		إِلَيْكِ	إِلَى + أَنْتِ
إِلَيْكُنَّ	إِلَى + أَنْتُنَّ		إِلَيْهِ	إِلَى + هُوَ
إِلَيْهِم	إِلَى + هُم		إِلَيْها	إِلَى + هِيَ
إِلَيْهِنَّ	إِلَى + هُنَّ		إِلَيْكُما	إِلَى + أَنْتُمَا

It seems to me that we met before.	يُخَيَّلُ إِلَيَّ أَنَّنَا تَقَابَلْنَا مِنْ قَبْلُ.
I would like to talk to you on an important subject.	أَوَدُّ أَنْ أَتَحَدَّثَ إِلَيْكَ فِي مَوْضُوعٍ هَامٍّ.
I extend to you my warmest congratulations on the wedding.	أَتَقَدَّمُ إِلَيْكُم بِأَحَرِّ التَّهَانِي بِمُنَاسَبَةِ الزَّوَاجِ.
This seminar is very important, and I was looking forward to it.	هَذِهِ النَّدْوَةُ مُهِمَّةٌ لِلْغَايَةِ وَكُنْتُ أَتَطَلَّعُ إِلَيْهَا.
My parents live in a nearby town, and I go to see them every week.	يَعِيشُ وَالِدَايَ فِي مَدِينَةٍ قَرِيبَةٍ وَأَذْهَبُ إِلَيْهِمَا كُلَّ أُسْبُوعٍ.
They were charged with murder.	وُجِّهَتْ إِلَيْهِم تُهْمَةُ القَتْلِ العَمْدِ.

Three-letter prepositions

إلَى with interrogatives and conjunctions

إلَى with interrogatives

إلَى + مَاذَا = إلَامَ

إلَامَ تُشِيرُ هَذِهِ النَّتَائِجُ؟	What do these results indicate?
إلَامَ تَرْمُزُ أَلْوَانُ اللَّوْحَةِ؟	What do the colors of the painting symbolize?
إلَامَ نَعْزُو مَوْجَاتِ العُنْفِ فِي المُجْتَمَعِ؟	To what do we attribute waves of violence in society?

إلَى + مَنْ = إلَى مَنْ

إلَى مَنْ هَذِهِ الرِسَالَةُ؟	To whom is this letter addressed?
إلَى مَنْ نَشْكُو؟	To who do we complain?
إلَى مَنْ سَتُوَجَّهُ الدَّعَوَاتُ؟	To whom will invitations be sent?

إلَى + مَتَى = إلَى مَتَى

إلَى مَتَى سَتَغِيبُ؟	How long will you be gone?
إلَى مَتَى سَتَبْقَى المَرْأَةُ عُرْضَةً لِلتَّمْيِيزِ فِي مُجْتَمَعِنَا؟	How long will women remain subject to discrimination in our society?
إلَى مَتَى يُمْكِنُ أَنْ تَسْتَمِرَّ هَذِهِ المُشْكِلَةُ؟	How long can this problem continue?

إلَى + أَيْنَ = إلَى أَيْنَ

إلَى أَيْنَ سَتُسَافِرُ؟	Where will you travel?
إلَى أَيْنَ يَتَّجِهُ النَّاسُ لِلحُصُولِ عَلَى حُقُوقِهِم؟	Where do people go to get their rights?
إلَى أَيْنَ سَتَصِلُ مُبَاحَثَاتُ السَّلَامِ؟	What will the peace talks achieve?

إلَى with conjunctions

إلَى + مَا = إلَى مَا

أَشَارَ إلَى مَا يَنْبَغِي الِاهْتِمَامُ بِهِ.	He indicated what should be given attention.
لَا أَسْتَمِعُ إلَى مَا يَقُولُونَهُ.	I do not listen to what they say.
اِنْخَفَضَتْ دَرَجَاتُ الحَرَارَةِ إلَى مَا تَحْتِ الصِّفْرِ.	Temperatures dropped below zero.

Three-letter prepositions

إِلَى + مَن = إِلَى مَنْ

To whom it may concern	إِلَى مَنْ يُهِمُّهُ الأَمْرُ	
We listened to those who talk about the problems of Arab societies.	اِسْتَمَعْنَا إِلَى مَنْ يَتَحَدَّثُ عَنْ مُشْكِلَاتِ المُجْتَمَعَاتِ العَرَبِيَّةِ.	
Compensation has been paid to those who deserve it.	تَمَّ دَفْعُ التَّعْوِيضَاتِ إِلَى مَنْ يَسْتَحِقُّهَا.	

إِلَى *in fixed expressions*

English	Arabic example	Meaning	Expression
Employers exploit workers to the maximum extent.	يَسْتَغِلُّ أَرْبَابُ العَمَلِ العُمَّالَ إِلَى أَقْصَى حَدٍّ.	to the maximum	إِلَى أَقْصَى حَدٍّ
The project started two years ago but has not finished yet.	بَدَأَ تَنْفِيذُ المَشْرُوعِ مُنْذُ سَنَتَيْنِ وَلَكِنَّهُ لَمْ يَتِمَّ إِلَى الآنَ.	yet/until now	إِلَى الآنَ
Syrian refugees continue to suffer in neighboring countries to this day.	تَسْتَمِرُّ مُعَانَاةُ اللَّاجِئِينَ السُّورِيِّينَ فِي دُوَلِ الجِوَارِ إِلَى اليَوْمِ.	to this day	إِلَى اليَوْمِ
I will continue to work until I achieve my goal.	سَأَظَلُّ أَعْمَلُ إِلَى أَنْ أُحَقِّقَ هَدَفِي.	until	إِلَى أَنْ
To what extent did government activities contribute to attracting tourists to the country?	إِلَى أَيِّ حَدٍّ سَاهَمَتْ أَنْشِطَةُ الحُكُومَةِ فِي اِسْتِقْطَابِ السَّائِحِينَ إِلَى البِلَادِ؟	to what extent	إِلَى أَيِّ حَدٍّ
To what extent is the work of non-governmental organizations influenced by freedom of expression?	إِلَى أَيِّ مَدَى يَتَأَثَّرُ عَمَلُ المُنَظَّمَاتِ غَيْرِ الحُكُومِيَّةِ بِحُرِّيَّةِ التَّعْبِيرِ؟	to what extent	إِلَى أَيِّ مَدَى
In addition to novels, Taha Hussein wrote many literary studies.	إِلَى جَانِبِ الرِّوَايَاتِ، كَتَبَ طَهَ حُسَيْنْ العَدِيدَ مِنَ الدِّرَاسَاتِ الأَدَبِيَّةِ.	in addition	إِلَى جَانِبِ
The United States has largely succeeded in exploiting the policies of Arab governments to strengthen its influence in the region.	نَجَحَتِ الوِلَايَاتُ المُتَّحِدَةُ إِلَى حَدٍّ كَبِيرٍ فِي اِسْتِثْمَارِ سِيَاسَاتِ الحُكُومَاتِ العَرَبِيَّةِ لِتَعْزِيزِ نُفُوذِهَا فِي المِنْطَقَةِ.	to a large extent	إِلَى حَدٍّ كَبِيرٍ

Three-letter prepositions 107

The movement calmed down somewhat in the hotel after the conference ended.	هَدَأَتِ الْحَرَكَةُ إِلَى حَدٍّ مَا فِي الْفُنْدُقِ بَعْدَ اِنْتِهَاءِ الْمُؤْتَمَرِ.	to some extent	إِلَى حَدٍّ مَا
The judge requested that the verdict not be announced for a while.	طَلَبَ الْقَاضِي عَدَمَ إِعْلَانِ الْحُكْمِ إِلَى حِينٍ.	for a while	إِلَى حِينٍ
The presidents will not meet until the summit.	لَنْ يَتَقَابَلَ الرُّؤَسَاءُ إِلَى حِينِ اِنْعِقَادِ الْقِمَّةِ.	until	إِلَى حِينٍ
The problem of the depletion of water resources in Jordan is exacerbated to the extent that it has become one of the most important environmental problems in the country.	تَتَفَاقَمُ مُشْكِلَةُ نُضُوبِ الْمَوَارِدِ الْمَائِيَّةِ فِي الْأُرْدُنِّ، إِلَى دَرَجَةِ أَنَّهَا أَصْبَحَتْ وَاحِدَةً مِنْ أَهَمِّ الْمَشَاكِلِ الْبِيئِيَّةِ فِي الْبِلَادِ.	to the extent that	إِلَى دَرَجَةِ أَنَّ
We will travel after we get the visas, and until then, we will continue to wait.	سَنُسَافِرُ بَعْدَ الْحُصُولِ عَلَى تَأْشِيرَاتِ الدُّخُولِ، وَإِلَى ذَلِكَ الْحِينِ سَنَظَلُّ مُنْتَظِرِينَ.	until then	إِلَى ذَلِكَ الْحِينِ
It is strange that the problem of soaring prices is aggravated to this extent.	مِنَ الْغَرِيبِ أَنْ تَتَفَاقَمَ مُشْكِلَةُ اِرْتِفَاعِ الْأَسْعَارِ إِلَى هَذَا الْحَدِّ الْخَطِيرِ.	to this extent	إِلَى هَذَا الْحَدِّ
The cultural and scientific exchange between the two countries continues to this day at the highest level.	يَتَوَاصَلُ التَّبَادُلُ الثَّقَافِيُّ وَالْعِلْمِيُّ بَيْنَ الْبَلَدَيْنِ إِلَى يَوْمِنَا هَذَا عَلَى أَعْلَى الْمُسْتَوَيَاتِ.	to this day	إِلَى يَوْمِنَا هَذَا

عَلَى

عَلَى is mainly used to indicate higher elevation in the sense of '*over*' or '*above*' and is commonly translated as 'on'. عَلَى is closely related to the root (ع ل و), which means 'to rise'. According to *A Frequency Dictionary of Arabic* (2011), عَلَى is the seventh-most commonly used word in Arabic. It can be used in spatial and temporal contexts.

عَلَى in context

- أَيْنَ المَجَلَّاتُ الَّتِي تَرَكْتُهَا عَلَى الطَّاوِلَةِ؟
= وَضَعْتُهَا فِي غُرْفَتِي عَلَى المَكْتَبِ.
- إِذًا، عَلَيْكَ أَنْ تُعِيدَهَا إِلَى مَكَانِهَا لِأَنَّنِي لَمْ أَقْرَأْهَا بَعْدُ.
= عَلَى رَأْسِي! آسِف عَلَى الإِزْعَاج لِأَنَّنِي نَقَلْتُها مِن دُونِ إِذْنٍ.
- لَا تَتَعَجَّلْ فِي إِرْجَاعِهَا، فَأَنَا عَلَى مَوْعِدٍ مَعَ الطَّبِيبِ بَعْدَ قَلِيلٍ.
= شُكْرًا عَلَى تَفَهُّمِكَ!
- عَفْوًا!

- Where are the magazines that I left on the table?
= I put them in my room on the desk.
- So, you have to take them back because I have not read them yet.
= With pleasure! Sorry for the inconvenience because I moved them without permission.
- Do not rush returning them, as I have an appointment with the doctor shortly.
= Thanks for your understanding!
- You are welcome!

Notes on the usage of عَلَى in context

The preposition عَلَى is used in the sense of *on* or *above*, for example, in (عَلَى الطَّاوِلَةِ) and (عَلَى المَكْتَبِ), and it expresses necessity, such as in (عَلَيْكَ أَنْ تُعِيدَهَا). It is also used in a temporal sense, for example, (عَلَى مَوْعِدٍ). In addition, it can used in some idiomatic expressions, as in (عَلَى رَأْسِي), which means 'with pleasure'.

Functions of عَلَى

عَلَى is used to indicate the meaning of 'on' or 'above', as in the following:

وَضَعْتُ الكُتُبَ عَلَى الرَّفِّ.	I put the books on the shelf.
أَرْتَدِي قُبَّعَةً عَلَى رَأْسِي.	I wear a hat on my head.
حَمَلَ ابْنَهُ عَلَى كَتِفِهِ.	He carried his son on his shoulder.
عَلَى جُدْرَانِ بَيْتِنَا صُوَرٌ لِأَبِي.	There are pictures of my father on the walls of our house.

عَلَى is used to indicate locality, as in the following:

وَقَفَ الجُنُودُ عَلَى جَبْهَةِ القِتَالِ.	Soldiers stood at the front.
تَقَعُ المَدِينَةُ عَلَى بُعْدِ سَبْعَةِ أَمْيَالٍ.	The city is seven miles away.
كَانَ هُنَاكَ شَخْصَانِ عَلَى مَقْرُبَةٍ مِنَ الرَّئِيسِ.	There were two people close to the president.
تَقَعُ مَدِينَةُ ذَهَب عَلَى البَحْرِ الأَحْمَرِ.	Dahab is located on the Red Sea.

عَلَى is used figuratively to indicate difficulty, as in the following:

تَقَعُ مَسْؤُولِيَّةُ اتِّخَاذِ القَرَارِ عَلَى عَاتِقِي.	I should take responsibility for decision making.
أَصْبَحَ هَذَا العَمَلُ عِبْئًا عَلَيْنَا.	This job has become a burden to us.
يَقَعُ عَلَى عَاتِقِ الشَّرِكَاتِ الصِّنَاعِيَّةِ دَعْمُ التَّبَادُلِ التِّجَارِيِّ مَعَ العَالَمِ.	Industrial companies have the burden of supporting trade exchange with the world.
طَالَبَتِ النِّيَابَةُ بِتَوْقِيعِ أَقْصَى العُقُوبَةِ عَلَى المُدَّعَى عَلَيْهِم.	The prosecution demanded that the maximum sentence be imposed on the defendants.
اسْتِمْرَارُ العُقُوبَاتِ عَلَى لِيبِيَا لَنْ يُؤَدِّي إِلَى حَلِّ الأَزْمَةِ.	Continued sanctions on Libya will not solve the crisis.

عَلَى is also used in the sense of 'against', as in the following:

تَغَلَّبُوا عَلَيْنَا فِي المُبَارَاةِ.	They beat us in the match.
أَدَّتْ هَيْمَنَةُ الجَيْشِ عَلَى مَقَالِيدِ السُّلْطَةِ إِلَى مُشْكِلَاتٍ اقْتِصَادِيَّةٍ.	The army's dominance led to economic problems.
أَجْبَرَهُ التَّمْيِيزُ العِرْقِيُّ عَلَى الهَرَبِ مِنْ بَلَدِهِ.	Ethnic discrimination forced him to flee his country.
أَرْغَمَتِ الحُكُومَةُ السُّكَّانَ عَلَى تَرْكِ مَنَازِلِهِم لِإِقَامَةِ المَشْرُوعِ.	The government forced residents to leave their homes in order to establish the project.

عَلَى is used to express necessity or obligation, as in the following:

عَلَيَّ أَنْ أَنْتَهِيَ مِنَ الوَاجِبَاتِ قَبْلَ الصَّبَاحِ.	I have to finish all assignments before morning.
عَلَيْكَ أَنْ تَذْهَبَ إِلَى عَمَلِكَ كُلَّ صَبَاحٍ.	You have to go to your workplace every morning.
يَجِبُ عَلَيْنَا أَنْ نُرَاجِعَ السِّيَاسَةَ الَّتِي نَتَّبِعُهَا عِنْدَ مُوَاجَهَةِ أَزْمَةٍ مِنَ الأَزَمَاتِ.	We must review the policy we follow when facing a crisis.
عَلَى العَرَبِ أَنْ يُحَرِّرُوا اقْتِصَادَاتِهِم لِاجْتِذَابِ الاسْتِثْمَارَاتِ الأَجْنَبِيَّةِ.	Arabs should liberalize their economies to attract foreign investment.
عَلَى الأُمَمِ المُتَّحِدَةِ اتِّخَاذُ كُلِّ الخُطُوَاتِ الدِّبْلُومَاسِيَّةِ لِإِقْنَاعِ الدُّوَلِ الأَعْضَاءِ بِتَنْفِيذِ القَرَارَاتِ الدَّوْلِيَّةِ.	The United Nations should take all diplomatic steps necessary to persuade member states to implement international resolutions.

عَلَى is used with a temporal meaning to express the time of an event, as in the following:

اِسْتَيْقَظْتُ عَلَى نُورِ الصَّبَاحِ.	I woke up at the morning light.
اِفْتَرَقْنَا عَلَى وَعْدٍ بِاللِّقَاءِ.	We parted, but we promised to meet again.
أَوْدَتْ حَوَادِثُ السَّيَّارَاتِ بِحَيَاةِ خَمْسَةِ أَشْخَاصٍ عَلَى فَتَرَاتٍ مُتَبَاعِدَةٍ.	Car accidents killed five people intermittently.
المُصَارَعَةُ هِيَ رِيَاضَةٌ قَدِيمَةٌ عُرِفَتْ عَلَى زَمَنِ الرُّومَانِ.	Wrestling is an old sport known at the time of the Romans.

عَلَى is used with verbs such as (مَضَى) and (مَرَّ) to indicate the passage of time since an event, as in the following:

مَرَّ أَرْبَعُونَ عَامًا عَلَى اِنْتِهَاءِ الحَرْبِ.	Forty years have passed since the war ended.
مَضَى عَلَى الحَادِثِ عَامَانِ.	Two years have passed since the accident.
مَرَّتْ أَعْوَامٌ عَلَى الأَزْمَةِ وَلَمْ يَتَحَسَّنِ الوَضْعُ.	Years have passed since the crisis, yet the situation has not improved.
مَرَّتْ سَنَةٌ عَلَى الحَادِثَةِ.	A year passed after the accident.
مَضَى عَلَى تَقَاعُدِ الأُسْتَاذِ رُبْعُ قَرْنٍ مِنَ الزَّمَنِ.	The professor retired a quarter of a century ago.

Notes on the usage of عَلَى

عَلَى is used in constructions that mean 'on the basis of', as in the following:

يَقُومُ العَقْدُ عَلَى المُسَاوَاةِ فِي الحُقُوقِ وَالوَاجِبَاتِ.	The contract is based on equality in rights and duties.
قَبِلْتُ الصُّلْحَ عَلَى شَرْطَيْنِ.	I accepted reconciliation on two conditions.
وُضِعَتْ خُطَّةُ المُوَازَنَةِ عَلَى أَسَاسِ المُشَارَكَةِ بَيْنَ القِطَاعَيْنِ العَامِ وَالخَاصِّ.	The budget plan was set on the basis of partnership between the public and private sectors.
فَازَ المُرَشَّحُ فِي الاِنْتِخَابَاتِ عَلَى أَسَاسِ وُعُودِهِ بِأَنْ يَجْعَلَ البَطَالَةَ فِي أَوْلَوِيَّةِ اِهْتِمَامَاتِهِ.	The candidate won elections on the basis of his promises to make unemployment a priority.

عَلَى can be followed by (أَنَّ) and a nominal clause. In this sense, it can mean 'however', as in the following cases:

عَلَى أَنَّ نُشُوبَ الأَزْمَةِ لَمْ يَكُنْ مِنْ دُونِ مُقَدِّمَاتٍ.	However, the outbreak of the crisis was not without warning.

Three-letter prepositions 111

عَلَى أَنَّ أَهَمَّ مَا تُرَاهِنُ عَلَيْهِ الصِّينُ اليَوْمَ هُوَ أَنْ تَسْتَفِيدَ مِنْ هُونْغ كُونْغ اِسْتِفَادَةً اِقْتِصَادِيَّةً كَامِلَةً.	However, the most important thing that China is betting on today is to reap the full benefit from Hong Kong economically.
حَقَّقَتِ الحُكُومَةُ مَكَاسِبَ كَبِيرَةً، عَلَى أَنَّ ذَلِكَ لَمْ يَمْنَعْهَا مِنْ فَرْضِ المَزِيدِ مِنَ الضَّرَائِبِ.	The government has achieved great gains; however, this did not prevent it from imposing more taxes.
عَلَى أَنَّ هَذَا التَّقَدُّمَ نَحْوَ التَّعَدُّدِيَّةِ لَنْ يَمُرَّ مِنْ دُونِ مُقَاوَمَةٍ.	However, this progress toward pluralism will not occur without resistance.
عَلَى أَنَّ الحَرْبَ غَيَّرَتِ الهَيْكَلَ الاِجْتِمَاعِيَّ إِلَى حَدٍّ كَبِيرٍ.	The war has changed the social structure to a large extent.

عَلَى can be followed by (أَنْ) and a present-tense verb. In this sense, it indicates terms and conditions, as in the following cases:

شَمِلَ الاِتِّفَاقُ 250 دَائِرَةً عَلَى أَنْ يَحْصُلَ الحِزْبُ الحَاكِمُ عَلَى 170 مِقْعَدًا فِي مُقَابِلِ 80 لِلْمُعَارَضَةِ.	The agreement included 250 constituencies, with the ruling party gaining 170 seats and the opposition gaining 80 seats.
يَسْتَمِرُّ المَشْرُوعُ خَمْسَةَ أَعْوَامٍ عَلَى أَنْ يُشَارِكَ القِطَاعُ الخَاصُّ بِنِسْبَةِ 45 فِي المِئَةِ.	The project will continue for five years and the private sector will contribute 45 percent.
مِنَ المُقَرَّرِ أَنْ يَبْدَأَ بِنَاءُ البَيْتِ فِي أَوَاخِرِ هَذَا العَامِ عَلَى أَنْ يَنْتَهِيَ العَمَلُ فِيهِ فِي أَوَاخِرِ العَامِ القَادِمِ.	The construction of the house is due to start late this year and will be completed by the end of next year.
يَقْضِي الاِتِّفَاقُ بِاسْتِيرَادِ 6 مَلَايِينَ حَاسُوبٍ هَذَا العَامَ عَلَى أَنْ يَرْتَفِعَ العَدَدُ فِي السَّنَوَاتِ المُقْبِلَةِ.	Under the agreement, 6 million computers will be imported this year, and the number will increase in the coming years.
سَتَنْسَحِبُ إِسْرَائِيلُ عَلَى أَنْ يَنْتَشِرَ الجَيْشُ اللُّبْنَانِيُّ عَلَى جَانِبِهِ مِنَ الحُدُودِ الدَّوْلِيَّةِ.	Israel will withdraw, provided that the Lebanese army is deployed on its side of the international border.

عَلَى can be followed by (هَذَا) or (ذَلِكَ). In this sense, it can mean 'thus', as in following:

عَلَى ذَلِكَ فَإِنَّ التَّحَالُفَاتِ القَبَلِيَّةَ تَصُبُّ فِي مَصْلَحَةِ القَاعِدَةِ فِي اليَمَنِ.	Thus, tribal alliances are in the interest of al-Qaeda in Yemen.
وَعَلَى ذَلِكَ تُصْبِحُ سَاحَةُ التَّنَافُسِ الدَّوْلِيَّةِ مَفْتُوحَةً أَمَامَ الجَمِيعِ.	Thus, international competition is open to all.
وَعَلَى هَذَا، قَدْ يَتَدَنَّى سِعْرُ بِرْمِيلِ النَّفْطِ بِحُلُولِ العَامِ المُقْبِلِ.	Thus, the price of a barrel of oil could fall by next year.

وَعَلَى هَذَا يَكُونُ صُنْدُوقُ النَّقْدِ الدَّوْلِيِّ قَدِ اسْتَرَدَّ مُعْظَمَ القَرْضِ.	Thus, the IMF has recovered most of the loan.
وَعَلَى ذَلِكَ تَمَّ تَنْظِيمُ حَمْلَةٍ تَطَوُّعِيَّةٍ لِجَمْعِ التَّبَرُّعَاتِ لِصَالِحِ ضَحَايَا الزِّلْزَالِ.	Thus, a voluntary fundraising campaign was organized for earthquake victims.

عَلَى is used with some verbs to indicate emphasis or insistence, as in the following:

أَكَّدَ السِّيَاسِيُّونَ عَلَى أَهَمِّيَّةِ انْخِرَاطِ المُوَاطِنِينَ فِي العَمَلِ السِّيَاسِيِّ.	Politicians stressed the importance of citizens' involvement in political work.
شَدَّدَ الوَزِيرُ عَلَى ضَرُورَةِ إِجْرَاءِ مُرَاجَعَةٍ شَامِلَةٍ لِلتَّعْلِيمِ العَالِي.	The minister stressed the need for a comprehensive review of higher education.
أَصَرَّ النِّظَامُ عَلَى رَفْضِ الحِوَارِ وَمُبَادَرَاتِ السَّلَامِ.	The regime insisted on rejecting dialogue and peace initiatives.
نَحْنُ مُصَمِّمُونَ عَلَى أَنْ نُنْجِزَ مَهَمَّتَنَا.	We are determined to accomplish our mission.

عَلَى is used with some verbs indicating dominance and control, as in the following:

أَدْرَكَ سُكَّانُ العِرَاقِ أَهَمِّيَّةَ السَّيْطَرَةِ عَلَى المِيَاهِ عَنْ طَرِيقِ إِقَامَةِ السُّدُودِ وَمَدِّ القَنَوَاتِ.	The people of Iraq realized the importance of controlling water by building dams and extending canals.
ذَكَرَتِ الصَّحِيفَةُ أَنَّ السِّيَادَةَ عَلَى دَارْفُور مَا تَزَالُ لِلسُّودَانِ.	The newspaper mentioned that sovereignty over Darfur still lies with Sudan.
تُهَيْمِنُ الإنكِلِيزِيَّةُ حَالِيًّا عَلَى الإِنْتَرْنِت، وَهَذَا يَفْرِضُ عَلَى المُسْتَخْدِمِينَ التَّعَامُلَ بِهَا.	English currently dominates the internet, which requires users to deal with it.
تُسَيْطِرُ السُّلُطَاتُ العَسْكَرِيَّةُ عَلَى مَقَالِيدِ الحُكْمِ فِي العَدِيدِ مِنْ بُلْدَانِ الشَّرْقِ الأَوْسَطِ.	The military authorities control many countries in the Middle East.

عَلَى is used with some verbs that mean 'to contain', as in the following:

يَشْتَمِلُ المَرْكَزُ الإِسْلَامِيُّ عَلَى فُصُولٍ دِرَاسِيَّةٍ وَمَكْتَبَةٍ وَقَاعَةٍ لِلاِجْتِمَاعِ وَسَكَنٍ لِلطَّلَبَةِ.	The Islamic center includes classrooms, a library, a meeting room and student accommodations.
اِحْتَوَى البَيْتُ الدِّمَشْقِيُّ عَلَى كُلِّ أَسْبَابِ الرَّاحَةِ.	The Damascus house contained all the comforts.
يَشْتَمِلُ المُتْحَفُ عَلَى مُقْتَنَيَاتٍ مِنْ مُخْتَلَفِ عُصُورِ التَّارِيخِ الإِسْلَامِيِّ.	The museum contains collections from different eras of Islamic history.
يَحْتَوِي المَرْكَزُ التِّجَارِيُّ الجَدِيدُ عَلَى أَكْبَرِ نِظَامٍ مُتَخَصِّصٍ لِلكُمْبيوتَر فِي المِنْطَقَةِ.	The new mall has the largest specialized computer system in the region.

Three-letter prepositions

عَلَى is used with some verbs that mean 'to exceed', as in the following:

الجَالِيَةُ الهِنْدِيَّةُ فِي البَلَدِ يَرْبُو عَدَدُهَا عَلَى 300 أَلْفِ نَسَمَةٍ.	The Indian community in the country includes more than 300,000 people.
يَرْبُو عَدَدُ الفَنَادِقِ فِي المَمْلَكَةِ عَلَى 1000 فُنْدُقٍ.	The number of hotels in the Kingdom is more than 1,000.
أَصْبَحَ عَدَدُ المَرْكَبَاتِ فِي المَدِينَةِ يَزِيدُ عَلَى مِلْيُونٍ.	The number of vehicles in the city has exceeded one million.
زَادَ حَجْمُ التَّدَاوُلِ النَّقْدِيِّ فِي السُّوقِ عَلَى عَشْرَةِ بَلَايِينَ دِينَارٍ.	The volume of cash trading in the market exceeded ten billion dinars.

عَلَى can be used in expressions that indicate preference, as in the following:

لَا فَضْلَ لِشَخْصٍ عَلَى آخَرَ.	No one is better than the other.
يُفَضِّلُ مُعْظَمُ النَّاسِ الهُرُوبَ مِنَ المَشَاكِلِ عَلَى مُوَاجَهَتِهَا.	Most people prefer to escape problems rather than face them.
الأَبُ يُحِبُّ ابْنَهُ وَيُؤْثِرُهُ عَلَى نَفْسِهِ.	The father loves his son and favors him over himself.
أَنْتُمْ تُفَضِّلُونَ الِاسْتِقْرَارَ عَلَى التَّغْيِيرِ.	You prefer stability over change.

عَلَى can be used in expressions that indicate a state or condition, as in the following:

اسْتَمَرَّتِ الأَزْمَةُ الِاقْتِصَادِيَّةُ عَلَى حَالِهَا رَغْمَ جُهُودِ الحُكُومَةِ لِحَلِّهَا.	The economic crisis continued in the same way despite the government's efforts to resolve it.
هَذِهِ الزِّيَارَةُ مُفَاجِئَةٌ وَلَمْ أَكُنْ عَلَى عِلْمٍ بِهَا.	This visit was a surprise, and I was not expecting it.
كَانَ المُفَاوِضُونَ عَلَى دِرَايَةٍ بِمَوْقِفِ الطَّرَفِ الآخَرِ.	The negotiators were aware of the position of the other side.
الحُكُومَاتُ العَرَبِيَّةُ عَلَى عَلَاقَةٍ جَيِّدَةٍ مَعَ الغَرْبِ.	The Arab governments have good relations with the West.

عَلَى is used in some expressions that mean 'over a period of', such as the following:

عَلَى مَدَى العَقْدَيْنِ الأَخِيرَيْنِ أَخَذَتِ الأَفْكَارُ الغَرْبِيَّةُ تُهَيْمِنُ عَلَى السَّاحَةِ الثَّقَافِيَّةِ.	Over the past two decades, Western ideas have dominated the cultural scene.
عَلَى مَدَى خَمْسِ دَقَائِقَ لَمْ يَتَمَكَّنْ أَيٌّ مِنَ المُصَارِعَيْنِ مِنْ تَسْجِيلِ نُقْطَةٍ ضِدَّ خَصْمِهِ.	After 5 minutes, no wrestler was able to score a point against the opponent.
سَيَتَوَاصَلُ التَّعَاوُنُ بَيْنَ البَلَدَيْنِ عَلَى المَدَى الطَّوِيلِ.	Cooperation between the two countries will continue in the long run.
عَلَى مَرِّ السَّنَوَاتِ، تَطَوَّرَ المَشْرُوعُ وَزَادَتْ نَجَاحَاتُهُ.	Over the years, the project has evolved and its successes have increased.

114 *Three-letter prepositions*

Notes on translation

عَلَى can be translated in different ways, as 'on', 'at', 'by', 'upon', 'over' and 'against', among others. It can also disappear in the English translation.

جَلَسْنَا عَلَى المَائِدَةِ لِلْعَشَاءِ.	We sat at the table for dinner.
وَقَفَ صَدِيقِي عَلَى النَّهْرِ وَتَذَكَّرَ المَاضِي.	My friend stood by the river and remembered the past.
قَعَدَ الجَدُّ عَلَى بَابِ دَارِهِ.	The grandfather sat at the door of his house.
السَّلَامُ عَلَيْكُمْ!	Peace be upon you!
وَضَعَتْ وَالِدَتِي الأَطْبَاقَ عَلَى المَائِدَةِ.	My mother placed the plates on the table.
كَانَ مُحَمَّدُ عَلِيٍّ وَالِيًا عَلَى مِصْرَ.	Mohammed Ali was a ruler of Egypt.
قَرَأَ الوَلَدُ الرِّسَالَةَ عَلَى وَالِدَيْهِ.	The boy read the letter to his parents.
رَتَّبْتُ كُتُبِي عَلَى الرَّفِّ.	I arranged my books on the shelf.
اِنْقَلَبَ الجَيْشُ عَلَى الرَّئِيسِ المَدَنِيِّ.	The army turned against the civilian president.
أَلْقَيْتُ نَظْرَةً عَلَى الغُرْفَةِ قَبْلَ مُغَادَرَتِهَا.	I had a look at the room before leaving.
اِنْتَصَرَ الجَيْشُ عَلَى المُتَمَرِّدِينَ.	The army defeated the rebels.
المَدِينَةُ جَدِيدَةٌ عَلَيَّ.	The city is new for me.
عَمِلَ عَلَى زِيَادَةِ دَخْلِ أُسْرَتِهِ.	He worked to increase the income of his family.
يَسِيرُ الشَّابُّ عَلَى خُطَى مُعَلِّمِهِ.	The young man follows in the footsteps of his teacher.

عَلَى *with pronoun suffixes*

When عَلَى is followed by a pronoun suffix, it becomes عَلَي. The following table shows how different pronouns appear after the preposition.

عَلَى + هُمَا = عَلَيْهِمَا		عَلَى + أَنَا = عَلَيَّ	
عَلَى + نَحْنُ = عَلَيْنَا		عَلَى + أَنْتَ = عَلَيْكَ	
عَلَى + أَنْتُمْ = عَلَيْكُمْ		عَلَى + أَنْتِ = عَلَيْكِ	
عَلَى + أَنْتُنَّ = عَلَيْكُنَّ		عَلَى + هُوَ = عَلَيْهِ	
عَلَى + هُمْ = عَلَيْهِمْ		عَلَى + هِيَ = عَلَيْهَا	
عَلَى + هُنَّ = عَلَيْهِنَّ		عَلَى + أَنْتُمَا = عَلَيْكُمَا	

Three-letter prepositions 115

عَلَيْكَ مُرَاجَعَةُ الإِدَارَةِ العَامَّةِ لِلهِجْرَةِ لِاسْتِلَامِ جَوَازِ سَفَرِكَ.	You should check with the Immigration Department to get your passport.
عَلَيْكُمْ أَنْ تُفَرِّقُوا بَيْنَ النِّظَامِ الحَاكِمِ وَالشَّعْبِ.	You have to differentiate between the ruling regime and the people.
لَا نَعْتَبُ عَلَيْكُمْ فِي شَيْءٍ.	We don't blame you for anything.
تَسْتَطِيعُونَ الاعْتِمَادَ عَلَيْنَا لِإِكْمَالِ مَهَمَّتِكُمْ.	You can rely on us to complete your mission.
لِلكَنِيسَةِ بَابٌ أَثَرِيٌّ عَلَيهِ كِتَابَاتٌ بِالعَرَبِيَّةِ وَالقِبْطِيَّةِ.	The church has an old door with writings in Arabic and Coptic.
تَمَكَّنَ الجُنُودُ مِنَ التَّغَلُّبِ عَلَيهِمْ.	The soldiers managed to defeat them.

عَلَى with interrogatives and conjunctions

عَلَى with interrogatives

عَلَى + مَا/مَاذَا = عَلَامَ

عَلَامَ اللَّوْمُ؟	What's the blame for?
عَلَامَ تَضْحَكُ؟	What are you laughing at?
عَلَامَ هَذِهِ الضَّجَّةُ؟	What is the noise for?

عَلَى + مَنْ = عَلَى مَنْ

عَلَى مَنْ نَعْتَبُ؟	Who do we blame?
عَلَى مَنْ تَقَعُ مَسْؤُولِيَّةُ اتِّخَاذِ القَرَارَاتِ فِي الوِزَارَةِ؟	Who is responsible for making decisions in the ministry?
عَلَى مَنِ انْقَلَبَ الحِزْبُ؟	Who did the party turn against?

عَلَى with conjunctions

عَلَى + مَا = عَلَى مَا

عَلَى مَا يَبْدُو فَإِنَّ مَا خَطَّطَتْ لَهُ الحُكُومَةُ الجَدِيدَةُ يَجْرِي تَنْفِيذُهُ.	It seems that what the new government has planned is being implemented.
سَتَبْقَى الأَوْضَاعُ عَلَى مَا هِيَ عَلَيْهِ.	The situation will remain the same.
اتَّفَقَتِ الحُكُومَةُ وَالمُعَارَضَةُ عَلَى مَا يَجِبُ القِيَامُ بِهِ.	The government and the opposition agreed on what to do.

عَلَى in fixed expressions

عَلَى العُمُومِ	generally	جَاءَتْ نَتِيجَةُ التَّجْرِبَةِ إِيْجَابِيَّةً عَلَى العُمُومِ.	The result of the experience was generally positive.
عَلَى جَانِبٍ آخَرَ	on the other hand	عَلَى جَانِبٍ آخَرَ قَالَ بَعْضُ مُمَثِّلِي الشَّرِكَاتِ إِنَّ تَكْلِفَةَ المَشْرُوعِ ضَخْمَةٌ.	On the other hand, some representatives of companies said that cost of the project is huge.
عَلَى الجَانِبِ الآخَرِ	on the other hand	عَلَى الجَانِبِ الآخَرِ، يُجَادِلُ البَعْضُ بِأَنَّ مُعْظَمَ الصُّحُفِ الأَمْرِيكِيَّةِ لَا تَعْرِضُ دَائِمًا وِجْهَةَ النَّظَرِ العَرَبِيَّةَ.	On the other hand, some argue that most American newspapers do not always publish Arab points of view.
عَلَى أَرْضِ الوَاقِعِ	on the ground	عَلَى أَرْضِ الوَاقِعِ، تَتَمَثَّلُ المُشْكِلَةُ الحَقِيقِيَّةُ فِي أَدَاءِ الحُكُومَةِ الَّذِي لَا يَرْقَى لِتَطَلُّعَاتِ الشَّعْبِ.	On the ground, the real problem is that the performance of the government does not meet the aspirations of the people.
عَلَى أَسَاسٍ	on the basis	سَتَصِلُ وَارِدَاتُ الذَّهَبِ الصِّينِيَّةُ إِلَى حَوَالَي 250 طُنًّا عَلَى أَسَاسٍ سَنَوِيٍّ.	Chinese gold imports will reach about 250 tons on an annual basis.
عَلَى الإِطْلَاقِ	never	إِنَّ أَفْضَلَ طَرِيقَةٍ لِحِمَايَةِ الأَطْفَالِ مِنْ أَضْرَارِ التَّدْخِينِ هِيَ عَدَمُ التَّدْخِينِ بِالقُرْبِ مِنْهُمْ عَلَى الإِطْلَاقِ.	The best way to protect children from the effects of smoking is to never smoke near them.
عَلَى الأَغْلَبِ	likely	سَتُمَثِّلُ السَّنَوَاتُ القَلِيلَةُ القَادِمَةُ عَلَى الأَغْلَبِ مَرْحَلَةً حَاسِمَةً مِنْ تَارِيخِ الشَّرْقِ الأَوْسَطِ.	It is likely that the next few years will mark a crucial stage in the history of the Middle East.
عَلَى الأَقَلّ	at least	عَلَى الأَقَلّ 60% مِن سُكَّانِ العَالَمِ لَا يُحَقِّقُونَ الحَدَّ الأَدْنَى المُوَصَّى بِهِ لِمُمَارَسَةِ النَّشَاطِ البَدَنِيِّ، وَهُوَ 30 دَقِيقَةً فِي اليَوْمِ.	At least 60% of the world's population does not meet the recommended minimum for physical activity of 30 minutes a day.

Three-letter prepositions 117

The project will be completed after two months at most.	سَيَتِمُّ الإِنْتِهَاءُ مِنْ تَنْفِيذِ المَشْرُوعِ بَعْدَ شَهْرَيْنِ عَلَى الأَكْثَرِ.	at most	عَلَى الأَكْثَرِ
Food prices are up for the tenth month in a row.	تُسَجِّلُ أَسْعَارُ المَوَادِّ الغِذَائِيَّةِ ارْتِفَاعاً لِلشَّهْرِ العَاشِرِ عَلَى التَّوَالِي.	in a row	عَلَى التَّوَالِي
China has always been a large and vast empire.	كَانَتِ الصِّينُ عَلَى الدَّوَامِ اِمْبِرَاطُورِيَّةً شَاسِعَةً بَالِغَةَ الاِتِّسَاعِ.	always	عَلَى الدَّوَامِ
Although Egypt was the first Arab country to conclude a peace treaty with Israel, this peace has been described as cold.	عَلَى الرَّغْمِ مِنْ أَنَّ مِصْرَ كَانَتْ أَوَّلَ دَوْلَةٍ عَرَبِيَّةٍ تَعْقِدُ مُعَاهَدَةً لِلسَّلَامِ مَعَ إِسْرَائِيلَ، فَقَدْ ظَلَّ هَذَا السَّلَامُ يُوصَفُ بِأَنَّهُ بَارِدٌ.	despite/ although	عَلَى الرَّغْمِ مِنْ
The government wants to play a bigger role in the international arena.	تَرْغَبُ الحُكُومَةُ فِي لَعِبِ دَوْرٍ أَكْبَرَ عَلَى السَّاحَةِ الدَّوْلِيَّةِ.	in the arena	عَلَى السَّاحَةِ
The year has witnessed many important developments on the political front.	شَهِدَ العَامُ العَدِيدَ مِنَ التَّطَوُّرَاتِ الهَامَّةِ عَلَى الصَّعِيدِ السِّيَاسِيِّ.	on the — front	عَلَى الصَّعِيدِ
We now have on the table all the elements that may lead to a positive solution.	لَدَيْنَا الآنَ عَلَى الطَّاوِلَةِ كُلُّ العَنَاصِرِ الَّتِي قَدْ تُؤَدِّي إِلَى حَلٍّ إِيجَابِيٍّ.	on the table	عَلَى الطَّاوِلَةِ
The rich people in society are getting richer, but on the contrary, the economic conditions of large segments of society are deteriorating.	يَزْدَادُ الأَغْنِيَاءُ فِي المُجْتَمَعِ غِنًى، وَلَكِنْ عَلَى العَكْسِ فَإِنَّ الأَوْضَاعَ الاِقْتِصَادِيَّةَ لِشَرَائِحَ وَاسِعَةٍ مِنَ المُجْتَمَعِ تَتَدَهْوَرُ.	on the contrary	عَلَى العَكْسِ
The pressure on telephone networks increased immediately in the crisis zone.	زَادَ الضَّغْطُ عَلَى شَبَكَاتِ الهَاتِفِ فِي مِنْطَقَةِ الكَارِثَةِ عَلَى الفَوْرِ.	immediately	عَلَى الفَوْرِ
The credibility of the government is at stake now.	مِصْدَاقِيَّةُ الحُكُومَةِ عَلَى المِحَكِّ الآنَ.	at stake	عَلَى المِحَكِّ

عَلَى مَدَى	over	عَلَى مَدَى سَنَوَاتٍ عَمِلَتِ الحُكُومَاتُ المُتَعَاقِبَةُ عَلَى مُحَارَبَةِ الفَقْرِ.	Over the years, successive governments have worked to fight poverty.
عَلَى المَدَى (البَعِيدِ/ القَرِيبِ)	in the (long-/short-)term/run	هُنَاكَ ضَرُورَةٌ مُلِحَّةٌ لِتَغْيِيرٍ شَامِلٍ لِلنِّظَامِ التَّعْلِيمِيِّ عَلَى المَدَى البَعِيدِ.	There is an urgent need for a comprehensive change in the educational system in the long run.
عَلَى النَّقِيضِ/ عَلَى العَكْسِ	by contrast	نَجَحَتِ الأَحْزَابُ المُوَالِيَةُ لِلحُكُومَةِ فِي السَّيْطَرَةِ عَلَى البَرْلَمَانِ، وعَلَى النَّقِيضِ مِنْ ذَلِكَ، فَشِلَتْ أَحْزَابُ المُعَارَضَةِ فِي إِحْرَازِ أَيِّ نَجَاحٍ.	Pro-government parties succeeded in controlling Parliament; by contrast, opposition parties failed to achieve any success.
عَلَى أَنَّ	however	مَا زَالَتِ الشَّرِكَةُ تَعْمَلُ فِي السُّوقِ، عَلَى أَنَّ انْتِعَاشَ الأَرْبَاحِ مَا زَالَ بِعِيدَ المَنَالِ.	The company is still operating in the market; however, profit recovery is still far from being achieved.
عَلَى ثِقَةٍ	confident	نَحْنُ عَلَى ثِقَةٍ كَبِيرَةٍ بِنَجَاحِ عَمَلِيَّةِ الإِصْلَاحِ السِّيَاسِيِّ فِي البِلَادِ.	We are very confident in the success of the political reform process in the country.
عَلَى حَدِّ قَوْلِ	according to	عَلَى حَدِّ قَوْلِ الوَزِيرِ، فَإِنَّ المُسْتَثْمِرِينَ تَضَرَّرُوا مِنْ ارْتِفَاعِ أَسْعَارِ مَوَادِّ البِنَاءِ.	According to the minister, investors have been affected by the increase of the prices of building materials.
عَلَى حَسَبِ	according to	تُطْرَحُ الأَسْئِلَةُ عَلَى حَسَبِ الفِئَاتِ العُمْرِيَّةِ.	Questions are asked according to age groups.
عَلَى خَلْفِيَّةِ	against a backdrop of	انْدَلَعَتْ احْتِجَاجَاتٌ فِي البِلَادِ عَلَى خَلْفِيَّةِ ارْتِفَاعِ أَسْعَارِ المَعِيشَةِ، وَخَاصَّةً الخُبْزِ.	Protests broke out in the country against a backdrop of rising prices, especially of bread.

Three-letter prepositions 119

عَلَى رَأْسِ	at the top of	جَرَتِ الِانْتِخَابَاتُ عَلَى الرَّغْمِ مِنَ الظُّرُوفِ الصَّعْبَةِ. وَعَلَى رَأْسِ هَذِهِ الظُّرُوفِ كَانَ الْمُنَاخُ غَيْرُ الْمُنَاسِبِ؛ حَيْثُ كَانَتْ دَرَجَاتُ الْحَرَارَةِ تَحْتَ الصِّفْرِ.	The elections were conducted despite the difficult circumstances. At the top of the list of these conditions was the harsh weather, as temperatures were below zero.
عَلَى سَبِيلِ الْمِثَالِ	for example	شَهِدَتِ اسْتِثْمَارَاتُ رِجَالِ الْأَعْمَالِ الْعَرَبِ ارْتِفَاعًا مَلْحُوظًا، فَعَلَى سَبِيلِ الْمِثَالِ: سَيَقُومُ رِجَالُ أَعْمَالٍ سَعُودِيِّينَ بِاسْتِثْمَارِ مَا يَزِيدُ عَلَى 1.5 مِلْيَارِ دُولَارٍ.	The investments of Arab businessmen have increased significantly. For example, Saudi businessmen will invest more than $1.5 billion.
عَلَى صَعِيدِ	at the level	عَلَى صَعِيدِ الْعَلَاقَاتِ الثُّنَائِيَّةِ، يَتَمَتَّعُ الْبَلَدَانِ بِعَلَاقَاتٍ قَوِيَّةٍ.	At the level of bilateral relationships, the countries enjoy strong relationships.
عَلَى مُسْتَوَى	at the level	عَلَى مُسْتَوَى الِاقْتِصَادِ، رَكَّزَتِ الْمُوَازَنَةُ عَلَى مُعَالَجَةِ مُشْكِلَةِ الدُّيُونِ الْخَارِجِيَّةِ.	At the economic level, the budget focused on addressing the external debt problem.
عَلَى ضَوْءِ	in light of	عَلَى ضَوْءِ الِانْسِحَابِ الْأَمْرِيكِيِّ الْوَشِيكِ، تَسْعَى الْقُوَى الْإِقْلِيمِيَّةُ إِلَى إِعَادَةِ تَقْيِيمِ مَصَالِحِهَا وَأَهْدَافِهَا فِي الْمِنْطَقَةِ.	In light of the impending US withdrawal, regional powers are seeking to reassess their interests and objectives in the region.
عَلَى عَاتِقٍ	take upon oneself	أَخَذَ طَهَ حُسَيْن عَلَى عَاتِقِهِ مَهَمَّةَ تَحْدِيثِ التَّعْلِيمِ.	Taha Hussein took upon himself the task of modernizing education.
عَلَى عَجَلٍ	rapidly	تَمَّ اسْتِدْعَاءُ وَزِيرِ الدِّفَاعِ عَلَى عَجَلٍ لِتَدَارُسِ الْأَزْمَةِ.	The defense minister was rapidly summoned to discuss the crisis.

Most Arab countries have a good relationship with Washington.	مُعْظَمُ الدُّوَلِ العَرَبِيَّةِ عَلَى عَلَاقَةٍ جَيِّدَةٍ مَعَ وَاشِنْطُن.	have a relationship	عَلَى عَلَاقَةٍ
A museum in Abu Dhabi like the Louvre has recently been opened.	تَمَّ مُؤَخَّرًا اِفْتِتَاحُ مُتْحَفٍ فِي أَبُو ظَبِي عَلَى غِرَارِ مُتْحَفِ اللُّوفَرِ.	like	عَلَى غِرَارِ
Work on this project continued in full swing.	اِسْتَمَرَّ العَمَلُ عَلَى قَدَمٍ وَسَاقٍ فِي هَذَا المَشْرُوعِ.	in full swing	عَلَى قَدَمٍ وَسَاقٍ
The government has neglected the countryside anyway and has only taken care of the cities.	أَهْمَلَتِ الحُكُومَةُ الرِّيفَ عَلَى كُلِّ حَالٍ، وَلَمْ تَهْتَمَّ إِلَّا بِالمُدُنِ.	anyway	عَلَى كُلِّ حَالٍ
Anyhow, those rifts have now ended and become history.	عَلَى أَيِّ حَالٍ، لَقَدِ انْتَهَتْ تِلْكَ الإِنْقِسَامَاتُ الآنَ وَأَصْبَحَتْ مِنَ التَّارِيخِ.	anyhow	عَلَى أَيِّ حَالٍ
It seems that the opposition benefited from the successive political crises.	عَلَى مَا يَبْدُو اسْتَفَادَتِ المُعَارَضَةُ مِنَ الأَزَمَاتِ السِّيَاسِيَّةِ المُتَلَاحِقَةِ.	it seems	عَلَى مَا يَبْدُو
Before the match the players were not physically and mentally well.	قَبْلَ المُبَارَاةِ لَمْ يَكُنْ اللَّاعِبُونَ عَلَى مَا يُرَامُ بَدَنِيًّا وَذِهْنِيًّا.	well	عَلَى مَا يُرَامُ
NASA has conducted hands-on experiments aboard the International Space Station.	قَامَتْ "نَاسَا" بِإِجْرَاءِ تَجَارِبَ عَمَلِيَّةٍ عَلَى مَتْنِ المَحَطَّةِ الدَّوْلِيَّةِ.	on board	عَلَى مَتْنِ
Prices rose over the first seven months.	اِرْتَفَعَتِ الأَسْعَارُ عَلَى مَدَارِ الأَشْهُرِ السَّبْعَةِ الأُولَى.	over	عَلَى مَدَارِ
Over time, financial institutions have become more specialized.	عَلَى مَدَى الزَّمَنِ، أَصْبَحَتِ المُؤَسَّسَاتُ المَالِيَّةُ أَكْثَرَ تَخَصُّصًا.	over time/ throughout	عَلَى مَدَى
At the political level, both sides agreed to strengthen their cooperation.	عَلَى المُسْتَوَى السِّيَاسِيِّ، اِتَّفَقَ الطَّرَفَانِ عَلَى تَعْزِيزِ التَّعَاوُنِ بَيْنَهُمَا.	at the — level	عَلَى المُسْتَوَى

Three-letter prepositions 121

عَلَى نَحْوِ	in a — way	أَثَّرَتِ الأَحْدَاثُ التَّارِيخِيَّةُ فِي أَدَبِ الرِّحْلَةِ عَلَى نَحْوٍ وَاضِحٍ.	Historical events have clearly influenced travel literature.
عَلَى نَفْسِ	in the same	إِذَا اسْتَمَرَّتْ اتِّجَاهَاتُ الإِسْتِهْلَاكِ الحَالِيَّةِ عَلَى نَفْسِ المِنْوَالِ فَإِنَّ مَلَايِينَ الأَشْخَاصِ سَيَقْتُلُهُمُ التَّبْغُ.	If current consumption trends continue in the same way, millions of people will be killed by tobacco.
عَلَى هَامِشِ	on the sidelines of	أُقِيمَ عَلَى هَامِشِ المُؤْتَمَرِ مَعْرِضٌ لِلْكُتُبِ.	A book fair was held on the sidelines of the conference.
عَلَى يَدِ	by	تَأَسَّسَ مَعْهَدُ الدِّرَاسَاتِ الشَّرْقِيَّةِ فِي إِرْلَانْغِن عَلَى يَدِ المُسْتَشْرِقِ رُوكِرت.	The Institute for Oriental Studies in Erlangen was founded by the orientalist Rückert.
وَعَلَيْهِ	thus	زَادَتِ الأَعْبَاءُ الاقْتِصَادِيَّةُ عَلَى الأُسَرِ، وَعَلَيْهِ فَإِنَّ مُسَاهَمَةَ المَرْأَةِ ارْتَفَعَتْ بِأَكْثَرَ مِنْ ضِعْفَيْنِ.	The economic burdens on families increased. Thus, the contribution of women has more than doubled.

خَلَا / عَدَا

Both (عَدَا) and (خَلَا) are mainly used to express exception (الإِسْتِثْنَاء). They belong to a category of particles called exceptive particles (أَدَوَات الإِسْتِثْنَاء), which include (إِلَّا, خَلَا, عَدَا, غَيْر, سِوَى) and (حَاشَا). Only three of these particles are classified as prepositions: (عَدَا, خَلَا) and (حَاشَا). In fact, they can be used both as verbs or prepositions.

> **Note**
>
> خَلَا is more commonly used as a verb to mean 'to be empty', and in far fewer instances, it is used as a preposition.

Functions of خَلَا / عَدَا

خَلَا is used to express exception as, for example, in the following cases:

نَحْنُ نُلْقِي بِقِمَامَتِنَا فِي الطَّبِيعَةِ كَأَنَّ أَيَّ مَكَانٍ خَلَا بَيْتِنَا مَزْبَلَةٌ لَنَا.	We dump our rubbish in nature, as if any place except our house was a dustbin for us.
اِسْتَقَرَّ السُّكَّانُ فِي المُدُنِ وَفِي الرِّيفِ خَلَا بَعْضِ المَنَاطِقِ الصَّحْرَاوِيَّةِ.	People settled in cities and in the countryside, except for some desert areas.
مُعْظَمُ المُوَاطِنِينَ، خَلَا المُوَظَّفِينَ، لَا يُسَدِّدُونَ ضَرَائِبَ مُبَاشِرَةً عَلَى الدَّخْلِ.	Most citizens, excluding employees, do not pay direct taxes on income.
يَقْضِي الرَّجُلُ حَيَاتَهُ كُلَّهَا فِي العَمَلِ، خَلَا سَاعَاتٍ قَلِيلَةٍ فِي الأُسْبُوعِ.	The man spends his entire life working, except for a few hours a week.

عَدَا is also used to express exception, as in the following cases:

قَاطَعَتْ أَحْزَابُ المُعَارَضَةِ الاِنْتِخَابَاتِ عَدَا حِزْبٍ صَغِيرٍ.	Opposition parties boycotted the elections except for one small party.
اِنْسَحَبَتِ الدَّوْلَةُ مِنْ تَأْدِيَةِ أَدْوَارِهَا فِيمَا عَدَا الدَّوْرِ الأَمْنِيِّ.	The state withdrew from performing its roles except for that of security.
سَافَرَ أَعْضَاءُ الوَفْدِ عَدَا وَزِيرِ الاِقْتِصَادِ الَّذِي أَصَابَهُ المَرَضُ.	The members of the delegation traveled, except the minister of the economy, who fell ill.
شَارَكَتْ جَمِيعُ الدُّوَلِ العَرَبِيَّةِ فِي القِمَّةِ عَدَا المَغْرِبِ.	All Arab countries participated in the summit except for Morocco.

Note

خَلَا / عَدَا can be used both as verbs and as prepositions, as in the following:

رَأَيْتُ أَصْدِقَائِي عَدَا صَدِيقًا.
رَأَيْتُ أَصْدِقَائِي عَدَا صَدِيقٍ.

In the first sentence, (عَدَا) functions as a verb, and it is followed by an accusative noun as its object, while in the second sentence, it functions as a preposition and is followed by a genitive noun. (خَلَا) is used in the same way, as in the following:

رَأَيْتُ أَصْدِقَائِي خَلَا صَدِيقًا.
رَأَيْتُ أَصْدِقَائِي خَلَا صَدِيقٍ.

Three-letter prepositions 123

عَدَا is often preceded by (مَا) to make the construction (مَا عَدَا), which means exactly the same as (عَدَا). It is used more often, and it is followed by an accusative noun:

طَالَبَتِ النِّقَابَةُ الأَطِبَّاءَ بِالتَّوَقُّفِ عَنِ العَمَلِ فِي كَافَّةِ المُسْتَشْفَيَاتِ مَا عَدَا أَقْسَامَ الطَّوَارِئِ.	The union demanded that doctors stop working in all hospitals except for emergency departments.
وَاصَلَتْ أَسْعَارُ جَمِيعِ السِّلَعِ الصُّعُودَ مَا عَدَا الخُبْزَ.	Prices of all commodities continued to rise except for that of bread.
يُقَامُ الحَفْلُ المُوسِيقِيُّ كُلَّ لَيْلَةٍ مَا عَدَا الجُمْعَةِ.	The concert is held every night except Fridays.

عَدَا can be followed by (أَنَّ) to make the construction (عَدَا أَنَّ), which means 'except that' or 'however', and it is followed by a nominal sentence:

يَتَمَتَّعُ لُبْنَانُ بِسُمْعَةٍ طَيِّبَةٍ كَبَلَدِ حُرِّيَّاتٍ، عَدَا أَنَّ الرَّقَابَةَ تُسِيءُ إِلَى هَذِهِ الصُّورَةِ.	Lebanon enjoys a good reputation as a country of freedom, except that censorship harms this image.
المُسْتَهْلِكُ لَا يَثِقُ بِالسِّلَعِ المَحَلِّيَّةِ، عَدَا أَنَّ أَسْعَارَهَا مُنْخَفِضَةٌ مُقَارَنَةً بِالسِّلَعِ المُسْتَوْرَدَةِ.	Consumers do not trust domestic commodities, except that their prices are low compared to imported goods.
مَا يَحْصُلُ الآنَ لَا يَخْتَلِفُ عَمَّا كَانَتْ تَقُومُ بِهِ الحُكُومَةُ فِي المَاضِي، عَدَا أَنَّ التَّرْكِيزَ أَصْبَحَ عَلَى المَشَاكِلِ الخَارِجِيَّةِ.	What is happening now is no different from what the government was doing in the past, except that the focus has shifted to foreign problems.

عَدَا can be used in the construction (فِيمَا عَدَا ذَلِكَ), meaning 'otherwise':

مَنَحَ الدُّسْتُورُ النِّسَاءَ 25% مِنْ مَقَاعِدِ البَرْلَمَانِ، لَكِنَّهُ فِيمَا عَدَا ذَلِكَ لَمْ يُحَسِّنْ وَضْعَ المَرْأَةِ فِي المُجْتَمَعِ.	The constitution gave women 25% of the seats in parliament; otherwise, it did not improve women's position in society.
يُمْكِنُ اعْتِبَارُ أَنَّ الحَرْبَ فِي العِرَاقِ هِيَ فَصْلٌ مِنْ فُصُولِ الحَرْبِ عَلَى الإِرْهَابِ، فِيمَا عَدَا ذَلِكَ فَالمَفْرُوضُ أَنَّ الحَرْبَ قَدْ أَنْجَزَتْ مَهَمَّتَهَا.	The war in Iraq can be seen as a chapter of the war on terror. Otherwise, the war is supposed to have been completed.

عَدَا can be used in the construction (عَدَا عَنْ), which means 'apart from':

عَدَا عَنِ المُدَرِّسِينَ لَمْ يَسْتَطِعِ المِصْرِيُّونَ مُمَارَسَةَ نَشَاطَاتٍ اِقْتِصَادِيَّةٍ فِي البَلَدِ.	Apart from teachers, Egyptians have not been able to engage in economic activities in the country.

124 Three-letter prepositions

	Apart from the Turks and the Kurds, there are large numbers of Arabs, Armenians and Greeks.
عَدَا عَنِ الأَتْرَاكِ والأَكْرَادِ، هُنَاكَ أَعْدَادٌ كَبِيرَةٌ مِنَ العَرَبِ والأَرْمَنِ واليُونَانِ.	
عَدَا عَنِ التَّارِيخِ، نَجَحَ ابْنُكَ في جَمِيعِ المَوَادِّ.	Apart from history, your son passed all his exams.

عَدَا with pronoun suffixes

The following table shows how different pronouns appear after the preposition.

عَدَاهُمَا	عَدَا + هُمَا		عَدَايَ	عَدَا + أَنَا
عَدَانَا	عَدَا + نَحْنُ		عَدَاكَ	عَدَا + أَنْتَ
عَدَاهُمَا	عَدَا + هُمَا		عَدَاكِ	عَدَا + أَنْتِ
عَدَاكُمْ	عَدَا + أَنْتُمْ		عَدَاهُ	عَدَا + هُوَ
عَدَاكُنَّ	عَدَا + أَنْتُنَّ		عَدَاها	عَدَا + هِيَ
عَدَاهُمْ	عَدَا + هُمْ		عَدَاكُما	عَدَا + أَنْتُمَا

	All prisoners were released, except for those two.
خَرَجَ جَمِيعُ السُّجَنَاءِ عَدَاهُمَا.	
حَضَرَ الحَفْلَ جَمِيعُ أَفْرَادِ العَائِلَةِ عَدَاكُمْ.	The ceremony was attended by all the family members except you.
حَكَمَ القَاضِي بِحَبْسِ جَمِيعِ المُتَّهَمِينَ عَدَاهَا.	The judge sentenced all the defendants to imprisonment except her.

خَلَا is not used with pronoun suffixes.

مُنْذُ

مُنْذُ was originally made up of two elements, the preposition (مِنْ) and the adverbial particle (ذُ), which mean 'from that time'. The same construction still appears in the fixed expression (مِنْ ذِي قَبْلُ). It can be contracted into another preposition (مُذْ), which has the same meaning but is used less often.

مُنْذُ and مُذْ are used in temporal contexts only, and they can be translated as 'since', 'for' and 'ago'. They cannot be used with pronoun suffixes.

> **Note**
>
> In medieval Arabic, مُذْ/مُنْذُ were considered to be nouns, and therefore they could be followed by a nominative, but over time, they were established as prepositions. In modern usage, they cannot be followed by a nominative noun.
>
> Wright (1896) argues that, theoretically, the nominative noun was used to indicate speaking about a time which has expired, such as (مُنْذُ يَوْمَانِ); that is,

Three-letter prepositions 125

> the action finished two days ago. Meanwhile, the genitive was used to speak about an unexpired time, for example, (مُنْذُ يَوْمَيْنِ), where the action started two days ago and is still ongoing. However, the genitive construction prevailed, and the nominative is no longer used.

مُنْذُ can function as a preposition (followed by a noun) or as an adverb (followed by a verb), as in the following cases:

لَمْ يَخْرُجْ مِنْ بَيْتِهِ مُنْذُ أُسْبُوعَيْنِ.	He has not left his house for two weeks.
لَمْ يَخْرُجْ مِنْ بَيْتِهِ مُنْذُ مَاتَتْ زَوْجَتُهُ.	He has not left his house since his wife died.

Functions of مُنْذُ

مُنْذُ is used to indicate the time since an action has started, and in this sense, it is translated as 'since' or 'for', as in the following:

مُنْذُ بِدَايَةِ العَامِ ارْتَفَعَ الدُّولَارُ بِنَحْوِ عَشَرَةٍ فِي المِئَةِ مِنْ قِيمَتِهِ.	Since the beginning of the year, the dollar's value has increased by around ten percent.
مُنْذُ فَتْرَةٍ طَوِيلَةٍ، يَتَبَنَّى البَلَدُ سِيَاسَاتٍ تَحَرُّرِيَّةً.	For a long time, the country has adopted liberal policies.
مُنْذُ سَنَوَاتٍ طَوِيلَةٍ وَقِطَاعُ الشَّحْنِ نَاشِطٌ وَمُزْدَهِرٌ جِدًّا.	For many years, the cargo sector has been active and very prosperous.
مُنْذُ عَامَيْنِ وَنِصْفٍ بَدَأْنَا التَّرْكِيزَ عَلَى السِّيَاحَةِ لِزِيَادَةِ الدَّخْلِ مِنَ العُمْلَاتِ الأَجْنَبِيَّةِ.	Two-and-a-half years ago, we began to focus on tourism to increase income in foreign currencies.

مُنْذُ is used to indicate the time that has passed since an event took place in the past, as in the following cases:

مُنْذُ عَامِ 1993 وَصَلَ عَدَدٌ مِنَ الشَّرِكَاتِ الكَنَدِيَّةِ إِلَى دُوَلِ غَرْبِ إِفْرِيقِيَا لِلْبَحْثِ عَنِ الذَّهَبِ.	Since 1993, a number of major Canadian companies arrived in West African countries to search for gold.
مُنْذُ تَأْسِيسِهَا فِي العَامِ المَاضِي حَقَّقَتِ الشَّرِكَةُ عَوَائِدَ مِقْدَارُها 200 مَلْيُونِ دُولَارٍ.	Since its establishment last year, the company has made $200 million in revenue.
تَحَوَّلَ المَهْرَجَانُ المُوسِيقِيُّ مُنْذُ عِدَّةِ أَعْوَامٍ إِلَى مَعْلَمٍ سِيَاحِيٍّ.	For several years, the music festival has been transformed into a tourist attraction.

مُنْذُ عَامِ 1996 حَذَّرَتِ الأُمَمُ المُتَّحِدَةُ مِنْ أَخْطَارِ التَّصَحُّرِ.	Since 1996, the United Nations has warned of the dangers of desertification.
مُنْذُ بِدَايَةِ العَامِ الجَارِي، تَعِيشُ المِنْطَقَةُ اضْطِرَابَاتٍ كُبْرَى.	Since the beginning of this year, the region has been experiencing major unrest.

مُنْذُ can be followed by (أَنْ) and a verbal clause, as in the following:

مُنْذُ أَنْ بَدَأَتِ اللَّجْنَةُ أَعْمَالَهَا قَامَتْ بِالعَدِيدِ مِنَ الإِنْجَازَاتِ.	Since the committee started its work, it has made many achievements.
مُنْذُ أَنْ وَصَلَ الحِزْبُ الدِّيمُقْرَاطِيُّ لِلبَيْتِ الأَبْيَضِ، سَعَى لِقِيَامِ دَوْلَةٍ فِلَسْطِينِيَّةٍ إِلَى جَانِبِ إِسْرَائِيلَ.	Since the Democratic Party arrived in the White House, it has sought to establish a Palestinian state alongside Israel.
مُنْذُ أَنْ بَدَأَ التَّعَامُلُ بِالنُّقُودِ الرَّسمِيَّةِ، تَوَسَّعَتِ التِّجَارَةُ بِشَكْلٍ غَيْرِ مَسْبُوقٍ.	Since the introduction of official money, trade has been expanded in an unprecedented way.
تَصَاعَدَ التَّوَتُّرُ بَيْنَ البَلَدَيْنِ مُنْذُ أَنْ سَقَطَ صَارُوخٌ عَلَى مِنْطَقَةٍ حُدُودِيَّةٍ.	Tensions between the two countries have escalated since a missile fell in a border area.

مُنْذُ can be followed by (مَا) and a verbal clause or (قَبْلَ/بَعْدَ), as in the following:

مُنْذُ مَا يَقْرُبُ مِنْ نِصْفِ قَرْنٍ، تَطَوَّرَتِ العَلَاقَاتُ بَيْنَ البَلَدَيْنِ.	Nearly half a century ago, relationships between the two countries evolved.
عِنْدَمَا قَدِمَتِ الشَّرِكَةُ إِلَى الأَسْوَاقِ مُنْذُ مَا يَزِيدُ عَلَى عَشَرَةِ أَعْوَامٍ قَدَّمَتْ عَدَدًا كَبِيرًا مِنَ المُنْتَجَاتِ.	When the company came to the market more than ten years ago, it presented a large number of products.
يُعْتَبَرُ شَمَالُ البَلَدِ خَارِجَ سَيْطَرَةِ الحُكُومَةِ المَرْكَزِيَّةِ مُنْذُ مَا بَعْدَ الحَرْبِ.	The north of the country has been outside the control of the central government since the end of the war.
هُنَاكَ أَزْمَةٌ اقْتِصَادِيَّةٌ تَعْصِفُ بِالبِلَادِ مُنْذُ مَا يَقْرُبُ مِنْ سِتِّ سَنَوَاتٍ.	There has been an economic crisis that has ravaged the country for nearly six years.

رُبَّ

رُبَّ is a quasi-redundant preposition (حَرْفُ جَرٍّ شَبِيهٍ بِالزَّائِدِ). It is used in limited contexts and in a restricted number of constructions. رُبَّ should be followed by an indefinite noun in the genitive case; then, it should have an adjective or a noun in the nominative case or a verb that functions as the subject of the sentence.

Three-letter prepositions 127

Functions of رُبَّ

رُبَّ is generally used to indicate probability, as in the following cases:

رُبَّ ضَارَّةٍ نَافِعَةٌ.	A harmful thing could have a benefit.
رُبَّ صَدِيقٍ لَكَ تُحِبُّهُ كَأَخٍ.	You could have a friend whom you love like a brother.
رُبَّ مَرِيضٍ اليَوْمَ يَشْفَى غَدًا.	Perhaps the person sick today will recover tomorrow.

رُبَّ can be used with (مَا) as (رُبَّمَا). In this case, مَا is redundant, and (رُبَّمَا) should be followed by a verb, as in the following:

رُبَّمَا يَبْقَى المَعْرِضُ مَفْتُوحًا يَوْمَيْنِ أَوْ ثَلَاثَةً.	The exhibition may remain open for two or three days.
لَا أَسْتَطِيعُ أَنْ أَتَّصِلَ بِصَدِيقِي، رُبَّمَا سَافَرَ.	I cannot contact my friend; he may have traveled.
تَأَخَّرَ الأُسْتَاذُ عَن المُحَاضَرَةِ رُبَّمَا لَنْ يَحْضُرَ اليَوْمَ.	The professor was late for the lecture; he may not come today.

Exercises

I What is the function of the prepositions underlined in the following sentences?

1 مُعْظَمُ الدُّوَلِ العَرَبِيَّةِ <u>عَدَا</u> القَلِيلِ مِنْهَا قَاطَعَ المُؤْتَمَرَ.
2 الجَيْشُ، <u>مُنْذُ</u> اسْتِقْلَالِ الجَزَائِرِ، هُوَ المُتَحَكِّمُ فِي زِمَامِ الأُمُورِ.
3 <u>عَلَى</u> الأَحْزَابِ أَنْ تُسْهِمَ فِي العَمَلِيَّةِ الدِّيمُقْرَاطِيَّةِ.
4 قَطَعَتِ البُلْدَانُ أَشْوَاطًا وَاسِعَةً فِي مَجَالِ التَّعَاوُنِ <u>عَلَى</u> الصَّعِيدِ الاقْتِصَادِيِّ.
5 بَعَثْتُ بِرِسَالَةٍ <u>إِلَى</u> صَدِيقَتِي أَدْعُوهَا إِلَى حَفْلِ تَخَرُّجِي.
6 هَذَا القِطَارُ يَتَّجِهُ <u>إِلَى</u> أَسْوَانَ.
7 سَاهَمَ السَّدُّ فِي الحَدِّ مِنْ أَخْطَارِ فَيَضَانِ النَّهْرِ <u>مُنْذُ</u> إِنْشَائِهِ.
8 <u>رُبَّ</u> أَخٍ لَكَ لَمْ تَلِدْهُ أُمُّكَ.
9 تَمَّ بَيْعُ جَمِيعِ لَوْحَاتِ المَعْرِضِ <u>خَلَا</u> لَوْحَتَيْنِ.
10 قَامَ الجَيْشُ بِإِخْلَاءِ المَنَاطِقِ القَرِيبَةِ مِنَ البُرْكَانِ <u>عَدَا</u> جَزِيرَةٍ نَائِيَةٍ.

II Choose the correct preposition to complete these sentences.

1 قَامَ الاتِّحَادُ الأُورُوبِّيُّ بِدَعْوَةِ اثْنَتَيْ عَشْرَةَ دَوْلَةً مَا (عَدَا - إِلَى - عَلَى) لِيبِيَا إِلَى مُبَادَرَةٍ جَدِيدَةٍ.
2 حَصَلَ (مُنْذُ - إِلَى - عَلَى) لِيسَانْس عُلُومٍ سِيَاسِيَّةٍ وَاقْتِصَادٍ مِنْ جَامِعَةِ الكُوَيْتِ.
3 يَتَّسِمُ القَادَةُ السِّيَاسِيُّونَ بِقَدْرٍ هَائِلٍ مِنَ التَّطَلُّعِ (عَدَا - إِلَى - عَلَى) المُسْتَقْبَلِ.
4 شَهِدَتِ الحَيَاةُ السِّيَاسِيَّةُ انْتِعَاشًا مَلْحُوظًا (مُنْذُ - إِلَى - عَلَى) الانْتِخَابَاتِ الدِّيمُوقْرَاطِيَّةِ.

128 *Three-letter prepositions*

5 كلينتون هُوَ الرَّئِيسُ الثَّانِي والأربَعُون (مُنْذُ - إِلَى - عَلَى) إِنْشَاءِ الوِلَايَاتِ المُتَّحِدَةِ.
6 (مُنْذُ - إِلَى - عَلَى) جَمِيعِ الرُّكَّابِ رَبْطُ أَحْزِمَةِ الأَمَانِ اسْتِعْدَادًا لِبَدْءِ الرِّحْلَةِ.
7 تَمَّ تَوْصِيلُ المُسَاعَدَاتِ لِجَمِيعِ المُتَضَرِّرِينَ (مُنْذُ - إِلَى - عَدَا) سُكَّانِ الجِبَالِ.
8 حِينَ وَصَلَ الطَّالِبُ (مُنْذُ - إِلَى - عَلَى) المَدِينَةِ اسْتَقَرَّ مَعَ شَقِيقِهِ فِي بَيْتٍ صَغِيرٍ.
9 تَرَدَّى وَضْعُ الِاقْتِصَادِ السُّودَانِيِّ (مُنْذُ - إِلَى - عَلَى) انْتِهَاءِ الصَّيْفِ المَاضِي.
10 تَجَنَّبَ الكَاتِبُ ذِكْرَ أَسْمَاءِ الأَشْخَاصِ الحَقِيقِيِّينَ (مُنْذُ - إِلَى - عَدَا) مَنْ سَاعَدُوهُ فِي تَحْقِيقِ هَدَفِهِ.

III Fill in the gaps with a suitable preposition from the following (مُنْذُ – عَدَا – عَلَى – إِلَى – رُبَّ).

1 كُلُّ أَفْرَادِ الأُسْرَةِ مَوْجُودُونَ فِي البَيْتِ ـــــــ ابْنِي فَهُوَ فِي الجَامِعَةِ.
2 عَقَدَتْ تُرْكِيَا مُعَاهَدَةَ وَحْدَةٍ جُمْرُكِيَّةٍ مَعَ الِاتِّحَادِ الأُورُوبِّيِّ ـــــــ عِدَّةِ سَنَوَاتٍ.
3 الِاعْتِمَادُ ـــــــ مَصْدَرٍ وَحِيدٍ لِلْغَازِ هُوَ انْعِكَاسٌ لِسُوءِ التَّخْطِيطِ.
4 تَتَمَيَّزُ المَدِينَةُ بِجَمَالِ شَوَاطِئِهَا الَّتِي تُزَيِّنُهَا أَشْجَارُ النَّخِيلِ المُنْتَشِرَةِ ـــــــ الشَّاطِئِ.
5 تَمِيلُ بَعْضُ الدُّوَلِ فِي المِنْطَقَةِ ـــــــ التَّصَالُحِ الرَّسْمِيِّ مَعَ إِسْرَائِيلَ.
6 قَامَ بِتَرْجَمَةِ الكِتَابِ ـــــــ اللُّغَةِ الفَارِسِيَّةِ.
7 طَبَعَ السِّيَاسِيُّ كِتَابًا يَتَحَدَّثُ عَنْ تَجْرِبَتِهِ ـــــــ بِدَايَةِ عَمَلِهِ.
8 تَمْتَدُّ شَبَكَةُ الطُّرُقِ فِي كُلِّ أَنْحَاءِ البِلَادِ ـــــــ المَنَاطِقِ الجَبَلِيَّةِ فِي الغَرْبِ.
9 ـــــــ ضَرَّةٍ نَافِعَةٍ.
10 دَعَوْتُ جَمِيعَ أَقَارِبِي لِلْحَفْلِ ـــــــ المُسَافِرِينَ مِنْهُمْ.

IV Make sensible sentences with the phrases in the columns.

1 لَمْ يَحْصُلِ الرَّئِيسُ .... A مُنْذُ سُقُوطِ المُلْكِيَّةِ وَخُرُوجِ الِاسْتِعْمَارِ.
2 شَهِدَ اليَمَنُ حُرُوبًا عَدِيدَةً عَلَى أَرْضِهِ .... B عَلَى غَالِبِيَّةٍ كَبِيرَةٍ فِي الِانْتِخَابَاتِ المَاضِيَةِ.
3 لَا يُمْكِنُ تَنَاوُلُ الوَضْعِ الدَّاخِلِيِّ فِي البَلَدِ .... C عَدَا القَبَائِلِ الَّتِي تَسْكُنُ فِي الصَّحْرَاءِ.
4 وَافَقَ الجَمِيعُ عَلَى إِنْشَاءِ خَطِّ الأَنَابِيبِ .... D عَلَى الِاسْتِقْرَارِ وَعَلَى الأَنْشِطَةِ الزِّرَاعِيَّةِ.
5 المُنَاخُ المُعْتَدِلُ فِي المِنْطَقَةِ شَجَّعَ .... E إِلَى العَدَالَةِ الِاجْتِمَاعِيَّةِ.
                                                              دُونَ الإِشَارَةِ

V Translate the following sentences into English.

1 سَتُقَامُ المُبَارَيَاتُ خِلَالَ الفَتْرَةِ مِنْ 16 إِلَى 24 أُغُسْطُسَ.
2 يُسَيْطِرُ الجُمْهُورِيُّونَ عَلَى الكُونْغِرِسِ.
3 عَلَى مَرِّ الزَّمَنِ أَثْبَتَتِ الصَّحَافَةُ اسْتِقْلَالِيَّتَهَا عَنِ الحُكُومَاتِ فِي البُلْدَانِ الدِّيمُوقْرَاطِيَّةِ.
4 تَنْوِي الحُكُومَةُ رَفْعَ أَسْعَارِ الكَهْرُبَاءِ لِلِاسْتِهْلَاكِ المَنْزِلِيِّ الَّذِي يَزِيدُ عَلَى 500 كِيلُو وَاط شَهْرِيًّا.
5 مُنْذُ عَامَيْنِ سُمِحَ لِلْوِلَايَاتِ المُتَّحِدَةِ بِتَصْدِيرِ المَنْسُوجَاتِ إِلَى مِصْرَ.

VI Translate the following sentences into Arabic.

1. We must take the practical steps required to involve marginalized groups.
2. My brother sat on my left.
3. We saw boats sailing on the lake.
4. Since the pre-Islam era, Arab tribes were in conflict with each other.
5. The truce was accepted on the condition of the release of prisoners from both sides.

5 Four-letter prepositions

This category includes the two prepositions, which are made up of four letters, i.e. حَتَّى and حَاشَا.

حَتَّى

حَتَّى can be translated as 'until', 'up to', 'as far as', 'including', 'even', or 'in order to'. It is a multifunctional word, with different semantic and syntactic meanings determined by its function in the sentence. Traditional grammarians differ in their classifications of حَتَّى, some categorizing it as a preposition and others as a noun or verb depending on its function.

حَتَّى in context

أَوَصَلْتُ أَمْس شَقِيقَتِي مِنْ بَيْتِنَا حَتَّى بَاب الْجَامِعَة الَّتِي تَدْرُسُ فِيهَا، ثُمَّ زُرْتُ صَدِيقِي فِي الْمَسَاءِ، وَسَهِرْتُ مَعَهُ حَتَّى سَاعَاتٍ مُتَأَخِّرَةٍ مِنَ اللَّيْلِ. وَفِي الْعَشَاء أَكَلْنَا حَتَّى شَبِعْنَا. كُنَّا طَوَالَ اللَّيْلِ نَتَحَدَّثُ عَن مَوَاضِيعَ كَثِيرَةٍ، وَعَن ذِكْرَيَاتِ الطُّفُولَةِ، حَتَّى دَاهَمَنِي النُّعَاسُ، فَرَجَعْتُ إِلَى الْبَيتِ، حَيْثُ كَانَ الْجَمِيعُ مُسْتَغْرِقِينَ فِي نَوْمٍ عَمِيقٍ، حَتَّى وَالِدِي الَّذِي اعْتَادَ أَنْ يَسْهَرَ حَتَّى أَذَانِ الفَجْرِ.

> Yesterday I took my sister from our house to the gate of the university where she is studying. Then I visited my friend in the evening and stayed with him until late at night. At dinner, we ate until we were full. We talked all night long about many subjects and memories of childhood until I was sleepy. I went home, where everyone was in deep sleep, even my father, who used to stay up for the dawn prayer call.

Notes on the usage of حَتَّى in context

حَتَّى in the preceding paragraph is used to designate the arrival point of a destination (حَتَّى بَاب الْجَامِعَة). It is also used to designate a spatial point of time: حتى أَذَانِ الْفَجْرِ، حَتَّى سَاعَاتٍ مُتَأَخِّرَةٍ). In these examples, حَتَّى is followed by explicit nouns, while in (حَتَّى شَبِعْنَا) and (حَتَّى دَاهَمَنِي النُّعَاسُ), it is followed in both cases by verbs and (أَنِ الْمُضْمَرَة) 'the suppressed أَنْ'. The combination of the so-called suppressed (أَنْ), and the verb is (مَصْدَر مُؤَوَّل) 'implicit verbal noun'. حَتَّى is considered to be a preposition in all of these cases.

The difference between حَتَّى and إِلَى

حَتَّى and إِلَى can be used interchangeably. However, حَتَّى indicates motion toward a destination or toward an object and, at the same time, the arrival at an object. For حَتَّى to be considered as a preposition, the motion toward the object must indicate the attainment of the extreme or near extreme of the limits of the object in question, as in (سَهِرْنَا لَيْلَةَ الْأَمْسِ حَتَّى الْفَجْرِ); on the other hand, إِلَى indicates motion toward an object regardless of whether the arrival actually takes place or not, as in (سَافَرَ عَلِيٌّ إِلَى بَغْدَادَ) 'Ali traveled to Baghdad' (Wright, 1896: 146).

Additionally, unlike إِلَى, حَتَّى does not take pronouns so that the words following the prepositional حَتَّى must be explicit nouns or verbs and (أَنْ الْمُضْمَرَة) 'the suppressed أَنْ'. Meanwhile إِلَى can be followed by explicit nouns or pronouns.

The difference between حَتَّى as a preposition and as an adverb

Arab grammarians have often used the following example to differentiate between حَتَّى as a preposition and as an adverb: (أَكَلْتُ السَّمَكَةَ حَتَّى رَأْسِها), 'I ate the fish up to its head'.

حَتَّى in the preceding sentence is considered to be a preposition, and the noun after it is in the genitive. The action of eating in here may include the head of the fish or until the extreme limit of it. However, in the sentence (أَكَلْتُ السَّمَكَةَ حَتَّى رَأْسَها), 'I ate the fish, including the head', the head is included in the eating, and so therefore, حَتَّى is not a preposition but an adverb that is referred to as (عَاطِفَة), 'conjunctive'.

Functions of حتى

The prepositional حَتَّى is followed by a noun in the genitive like other prepositions and translated in this function as 'up to', 'until', 'till', or 'as far as'.

The temporal use of حَتَّى followed by explicit nouns can be seen in the following:

يَسْتَمِرُّ عَرْضُ الْمَسْرَحِيَّةِ عَلَى خَشَبَةِ مَسْرَحِ دَارِ الْأُوبِرَا حَتَّى يَوْمِ الْخَمِيسِ.	The play will run until Thursday at the Opera House theater.
كَانَتْ تُرْكِيَا مَرْكَزًا لِلْحُكْمِ الْعُثْمَانِيِّ حَتَّى عَامِ 1922.	Turkey was the center of Ottoman rule until 1922.
دَرَسْتُ لَيْلَةَ الْأَمْسِ حَتَّى الْفَجْرِ.	Last night, I studied until dawn.
الْغَرِيبُ أَنَّ الْأَبَوِيَّةَ مَا زَالَتْ حَاضِرَةً فِي وَسَائِلِ الْإِعْلَامِ حَتَّى يَوْمِنَا هَذَا.	It is strange that a patriarchal attitude is still present in the media until this very day.
لَقَدْ بَقِيتُ مُسْتَيْقِظًا حَتَّى السَّاعَةِ 3 صَبَاحًا.	I was up until 3 a.m.

The spatial use of حَتَّى followed by explicit nouns is shown in these examples:

سَافَرْنَا بِالسَّيَّارَةِ حَتَّى جَدَّةَ.	We traveled by car until we reached Jeddah.
رَافَقْتُ صَدِيقِي حَتَّى بَابِ الشَّرِكَةِ.	I accompanied my friend as far as the company gate.
مَشَيْتُ مِنَ الْبَيْتِ حَتَّى الْجَامِعَةِ.	I walked from my home to the university.

حَتَّى can also be used figuratively as shown in these examples:

دَافَعَ الْجُنْدِيُّ عَن وَطَنِهِ حَتَّى آخِرِ رَمَقٍ.	The soldier defended his country to his last breath.
بَذَلْتُ مَالِي حَتَّى آخِرِ دِرْهَمٍ عَنْدِي.	I spent all my money down to the last penny.
أُحِبُّهَا مِنْ رَأْسِهَا حَتَّى أَخْمَصِ قَدَمَيْهَا.	He loved her from head to toe.
سَأُدَافِعُ عَن الْحَقِّ حَتَّى آخِرِ لَحْظَةٍ مِنْ عُمْرِي.	I will defend the truth until the last moment of my life.

The prepositional حَتَّى can also be followed by verbs and (أَنْ الْمُضْمَرَة) 'the suppressed أَنْ', as in the following cases:

سَأَبْقَى هُنَا حَتَّى نَسْتَنْفِدَ الْوَقُودَ.	I'll stay here till we run short of fuel.
لَنْ أَتْرُكَكَ حَتَّى تُعْطِيَنِي حَقِّي.	I will not leave you until you give me my right.
ابْقَ فِي مَكَانِكَ حَتَّى يَصِلَ وَالِدُكَ.	Stay where you are until your father arrives.
سَنَبْقَى فِي النَّادِي حَتَّى يَحُلَّ الظَّلَامُ.	We will stay in the club till it's dark.

حَتَّى *can function as an adverb* (عَاطِفَة), *translated as 'even' or 'including'*

In this function, حَتَّى has no impact on the following nouns or noun phrases. As an adverb, the conjoined noun after حَتَّى must be part of the preceding noun in the sentence, as shown in the following cases:

أَعْجَبَتْنِي الْفَتَاةُ حَتَّى ابْتِسَامَتُهَا.	I liked the young lady, including her smile.
مَاتَ النَّاسُ حَتَّى الْأَنْبِيَاءُ.	The people died, even the prophets.
حَضَرَ الْأَسَاتِذَةُ الِاجْتِمَاعَ حَتَّى الدُّكْتُورُ عَلِيٌّ.	The teachers attended the meeting, even Dr Ali.

Four-letter prepositions 133

إِذَا كَانَتِ الْوَثِيقَةُ صَادِرَةً مِنْ جِهَةٍ رَسْمِيَّةٍ فَإِنَّهَا تُقْبَلُ فِي أَيِّ مَكَانٍ حَتَّى فِي الدُّوَلِ وَالْمُؤَسَّسَاتِ الْأَجْنَبِيَةِ.	If the document is issued by a governmental authority, it will be accepted anywhere, even in foreign countries and organizations.
عَلَيْكَ أَنْ تُرْسِلَ الرِّسَالَةَ حَتَّى إِنْ لَمْ يَتَسَلَّمْهَا أَحَدٌ.	You should send the letter even if no one receives it.
مُهِمَّتِي فِي الصُّلْحِ بَيْنَ الصَّدِيقَيْنِ صَعْبَةٌ جِدًّا، حَتَّى إِنَّهَا قَدْ تَكُونُ مُسْتَحِيلَةً.	My mission to mediate between my two friends is a very difficult one, and it may even be impossible.
لِلْأَسَفِ، لَا يُمَيِّزُ بَعْضُ طُلَّابِ الْجَامِعَةِ حَتَّى بَيْنَ الِاسْمِ وَالصِّفَةِ.	Sadly, some university students do not differentiate even between adjectives and adverbs.
يَبْدُو أَنَّ سُؤَالِي كَانَ مُحْرِجًا لِلْغَايَةِ حَتَّى إِنَّهُمْ لَمْ يَرُدُّوا عَلَيْهِ.	It seems that my question was extremely embarrassing, so much so that they did not even answer it.

When حَتَّى is followed by (الْآنَ), it has no influence on (الْآنَ), which remains invariable, as in the following:

كُلُّ مَا قُمْتَ بِهِ صَحِيحٌ، حَتَّى الْآنَ.	Everything you have done is right, so far.
إِنَّ الْجُهُودَ الَّتِي بَذَلَتْهَا بَعْضُ الْمُؤَسَّسَاتِ الْخَيْرِيَّةِ حَتَّى الْآنَ مُشَجِّعَةٌ.	Efforts made so far by philanthropic organizations are encouraging.
كَانَ هَذَا أَفْضَلَ طَبَقٍ قَامَ زَوْجِي بِإِعْدَادِهِ حَتَّى الْآنَ.	This has been the best dish prepared by my husband so far.
لَمْ تُعَالِجِ الْأُمَمُ الْمُتَّحِدَةُ بِشَكْلٍ حَاسِمٍ قَضِيَّةَ السَّلَامِ فِي الشَّرْقِ الْأَوْسَطِ، حَتَّى الْآنَ.	The United Nations has not hitherto dealt decisively with the question of peace in the Middle East.
أَعْتَقِدُ أَنَّ كُلَّ قَرَارَاتِكَ فِي هَذَا الْأَمْرِ صَائِبَةٌ حَتَّى الْآنَ.	I think all your decision-making regarding this matter has been appropriate so far.

حَاشَا

حَاشَا is one of the so-called (حُرُوفِ الِاسْتِثْنَاءِ), exception particles. It mainly indicates exceptions. Other exception particles include (حَاشَا and إِلَّا, خَلَا, عَدَا, غَيْر, سِوَى).

Only (خَلَا، عَدَا and حَاشَا) are considered to be prepositions. Further discussion of خَلَا and عَدَا can be found in Chapter 4.

حَاشَا is both a preposition and a verb. When it acts as a preposition, the noun after it is governed by حَاشَا, while as a verb, the noun will be its object.

حَاشَا in context

حَضَرَ جَمِيعُ الطُّلَّابِ الْمُحَاضَرَةَ أَمْسِ حَاشَا مُحَمَّدٍ، شَرَحْتُ لَهُمُ الدَّرْسَ، ثُمَّ طَلَبْتُ مِنْهُمْ تَسْلِيمَ الْوَاجِبِ، وَلَكِنَّنِي فُوجِئْتُ بِأَنَّهُمْ لَمْ يَعْمَلُوا الْوَاجِبَ، حَاشَا عَلِيٍّ؛ فَانْتَقَدْتُهُمْ عَلَى الْإِهْمَالِ، ثُمَّ قُلْتُ حَاشَاكَ يَا عَلِيُّ مِنَ الْإِهْمَالِ، فَأَنْتَ طَالِبٌ تَسْتَحِقُّ التَّشْجِيعَ.

Yesterday all the students attended the lecture, except for Muhammad. I explained the lesson to them. I then asked them to hand in their assignments, but I was surprised that – with the exception of Ali – they had not done the assignments. I rebuked them for their negligence. But then I told Ali that he was exempt from this charge of negligence since he was a student who deserved encouragement.

Notes on the usage of حَاشَا in context

حَاشَا in the preceding passage is used as a preposition in (حَاشَا مُحَمَّدٍ) and (حَاشَا عَلِيٍّ), while it functions as a verb in (حَاشَاكَ يَا عَلِيُّ).

In the following examples, حَاشَا is used as a preposition, and the nouns are therefore in the genitive case:

حَضَرَ الطُّلَّابُ حَاشَا وَاحِدٍ مِنْهُمْ.	The students came, except one.
أُحِبُّ كُلَّ النَّاسِ حَاشَا الْخَادِعِينَ.	I like all people, apart from those who cheat.
مَنْ أَرَادَ - حَاشَا عُمَرَ - تَدْرِيسَ الْعَرَبِيَّةِ فَقَدْ أَخْطَأَ.	Anyone other than Omar who wants to teach Arabic is mistaken.
قَابَلَ مُدِيرُ الشَّرِكَةِ الْمُوَظَّفِينَ حَاشَا مُحَمَّدٍ.	The company director met the employees, except for Mohammad.
فَاطِمَةُ أَحَبُّ النَّاسِ إِلَيَّ حَاشَا عَلِيٍّ.	Fatima is the person I love best, apart from Ali.

Note

The phrases (حَاشَا لله / حَاشَا الله) are often used to express ideas such as 'far be it from . . . / God forbid . . .'.

In the following examples, حَاشَا is used as a verb:

مَنِ ادَّعَى - حَاشَا امْرِئِ الْقَيْسِ - رِيَادَةَ الشِّعْرِ فَقَدْ جَهِلَ.	Whoever claims that anyone other than Imru'-l-Qays is the pioneer of poetry doesn't know what he's talking about!
لَا فَخْرَ - حَاشَا حَاتِمِ الطَّائِي - لِأَحَدٍ بِالْكَرَمِ.	No one other than Hatim al-Tayy' can claim that he is generous.

Exercises

I Make sensible sentences with the phrases in the columns.

A	حَتَّى وَصَلَتْ أَبُوظَبِيٍّ.		كُنْتُ رَفِيقَتَهُ	1
B	حَتَّى الْمَطْعَمِ.		سَهِرْنَا لَيْلَةَ أَمْسِ	2
C	حَتَّى تَغْرُبَ الشَّمْسُ.		سَافَرْتُ بِالسَّيَّارَةِ	3
D	حَتَّى الصَّبَاحِ.		لَا أَعُودُ مِنَ الْعَمَلِ	4
E	حَتَّى فَارَقَ الْحَيَاةَ.		سِرْتُ مِنَ الْعَمَلِ	5

II Translate the following sentence into Arabic.

1. I studied Arabic grammar until morning.
2. We ate the chicken until we were full.
3. Ali read the book until the final page.
4. I waited for him until six o'clock in the evening.
5. We stayed in front of the house until Hind came.

III Translate the following sentence into English.

1. قَاتَلَ الْجُنُودُ حَتَّى النَّصْرِ.
2. اِسْتَمَعْتُ لِلْقَاضِي حَتَّى اِنْتَهَى مَنِ الْحُكْمِ.
3. جَاءَ الضُّيُوفُ حَاشَا سَارَّةٍ.
4. حَاشَا لله أَنْ أَغْدِرَ بِشَرِيكِي فِي الْعَمَلِ.
5. شَاهَدَتُ الْفِيلْمَ حَتَّى نِهَايَتِهِ.

6 Locative adverbs

Locative adverbs (الظُرُوف) or adverbs of time and place (ظُرُوف الزَمَانِ والمَكَانِ) are nouns that indicate the time and/or place of an event. In Arabic, the word (ظَرْف) means 'container' or 'circumstance', as locative adverbs indicate the circumstances surrounding a certain event, particularly its time and place. Arab grammarians also use the term (المَفْعُول فِيهِ), or 'adverbial object', to refer to the same category of words.

There is not a specific category in English which corresponds to the Arabic locative adverbs; therefore, some English grammarians do not distinguish between prepositions and locative adverbs. In her thesis about Arabic prepositions, Ryding-Lentzner (1977) calls (الظُرُوف) 'locative adverbs', and in her grammar book (2005), she calls certain locative adverbs 'semi-prepositions' to acknowledge the fact that they share some characteristics with prepositions, although they are not technically prepositions. It is worth noting that many native speakers of Arabic also consider several locative adverbs as prepositions, particularly (مع), 'with'; (عند), 'at'; and (بين), 'between'. Locative adverbs can be classified into three categories: adverbs of time (ظُرُوف الزَمَانِ), adverbs of place (ظُرُوف المَكَانِ) and adverbs of time and place (ظُرُوف الزَمَانِ والمَكَانِ). Grammatically, locative adverbs are accusative in case.

> **Note**
>
> What distinguishes locative adverbs from other nouns that indicate time and place is that they have the meaning of فِي implied in them, as in the following:
>
> قَابَلْتُهَا مَسَاءً. = فِي المَسَاءِ
>
> اِنْتَظَرْتُكَ يَمِينَ المَكْتَبَةِ. = فِي جِهَةِ اليَمِينِ

Adverbs of time (ظُرُوف الزَمَانِ) answer the question, 'When?', as in the following:

مَتَى تَسْتَيقِظُ؟

When do you wake up?

أَسْتَيْقِظُ مُبَكِّرًا.

I wake up early.

أَسْتَيْقِظُ عِنْدَ الفَجْرِ.

I wake up at dawn.

Adverbs of place (ظروف المكان) answer the question, 'Where?', as in the following:

أَيْنَ تَسْكُنُ؟

Where do you live?

أَسْكُنُ قَرِيبًا مِنَ الجَامِعَةِ.

I live close to university.

أَسْكُنُ قُرْبَ الجَامِعَةِ.

I live close to university.

Locative adverbs can be further classified as either specific (مُحَدَّد) or vague (مُبْهَم). Specific locative adverbs refer to a specific time or place, for example, (صَبَاحًا، مَسَاءً), and vague locative adverbs refer to a nonspecific time or place, for example, (قَبْلَ، عِنْدَ، حِيْنَ).

Examples of specific locative adverbs include the following:

وَصَلْتُ إِلَى وِجْهَتِي صَبَاحًا.

I reached my destination in the morning.

Examples of vague locative adverbs include the following:

اِتَّصِلْ بِي عِنْدَ الوُصُولِ.

Call me when you arrive.

اِنْتَظِرْنِي حَيْثُ أَنْتَ.

Wait for me where you are.

Certain locative adverbs, for example, (قَبْلَ، بَعْدَ، بَيْنَ، عِنْدَ، مَعَ، قُرْبَ، خِلَالَ), can be used for both time and place depending on the context, as in the following:

قَضَيْتُ اليَوْمَ عِنْدَ خَالَتِي.

I spent the day at my aunt's.

نَزَلَ عِنْدَ المَسَاءِ.

He left in the evening.

غَادَرَ القِطَارُ قَبْلَ الفَجْرِ.

The train left before dawn.

نَزَلْتُ قَبْلَ المَحَطَّةِ الأَخِيرَةِ.

I disembarked before the last stop.

Most locative adverbs are declinable; that is, they show endings that denote their case, for example, صَبَاحًا، شَمَالًا. However, there are others that are indeclinable or fixed, for example, (فَوْقَ، بَيْنَ، عِنْدَ). Some indeclinable locative adverbs behave like prepositions, as they are always followed by a genitive noun (مَجْرُور), but unlike prepositions, they function as the first word in an iḍāfa construction, since they are classified as nouns not particles. Ryding (2011) calls this category of words 'semi-prepositions', for example:

بَعْدَ الظُّهْرِ
قَبْلَ النَّوْمِ

In the following section, the most important indeclinable locative adverbs that are classified as semi-prepositions are discussed.

بَيْنَ

بَيْنَ means 'between' or 'among'. It can be followed by a dual or plural noun, or by singular nouns, a noun and a pronoun or two pronoun suffix joined by (و). When two nouns are used, there is no need to repeat بَيْنَ; however, if a pronoun is used, it has to be repeated. بين can collocate with verbs indicating unity, for example, (فَصَلَ بَيْنَ، قَسَّمَ بَيْنَ، وَحَّدَ بَيْنَ، جَمَعَ بَيْنَ، زَاوَجَ بَيْنَ، قَرَنَ بَيْنَ); division, for example, (قَارَنَ بَيْنَ، وَازَنَ بَيْنَ، سَاوَى بَيْنَ، فَاضَلَ بَيْنَ); or comparison, for example, (فَرَّقَ بَيْنَ).

جَلَسْنَا فِي المَطْعَمِ بَيْنَ المُحَاضَرَتَيْنِ.	We sat in the restaurant between the two lectures.
بَيْنَ المَشَارِيعِ الجَدِيدَةِ هُنَاكَ خَمْسَةُ مَصَانِعَ لِلمَوَادِ الغِذَائِيَّةِ.	There are five food factories among the new projects.
ظَهَرَتْ بَوَادِرُ أَزْمَةٍ دِبْلُومَاسِيَّةٍ بَيْنَ المَغْرِبِ ومِصْرَ.	A diplomatic crisis has emerged between Morocco and Egypt.
ظَلَّ هَذَا الأَمْرُ سِرًّا بَيْنِي وَبَيْنَ زَوْجَتِي لِسَنَوَاتٍ طَوِيلَةٍ.	This matter was a secret between me and my wife for many years.
هُنَاكَ خِلَافَاتٌ عَمِيقَةٌ بَيْنَنَا وَبَيْنَهُم وَمِنَ الصَّعْبِ تَجَاوُزُهَا.	There are deep disagreements between us and them, and it is difficult to overcome them.

بَيْنَ can be preceded by (مَا) or (فِيمَا), as in the following:

مَا بَيْنَ حَرْبِ الخَلِيجِ الأُولَى والثَّانِيَةِ، عَانَى المُوَاطِنُ العِرَاقِيُّ عَلَى جَمِيعِ الأَصْعِدَةِ.	Between the first and second Gulf War, the Iraqi people suffered at all levels.
تَتَنَافَسُ الفِرَقُ المُشَارِكَةُ فِيمَا بَيْنَهَا لِلفَوْزِ بِالكَأْسِ.	The teams compete among each other to win the cup.
أَتَنَاوَلُ الكَثِيرَ مِنَ القَهْوَةِ بَيْنَ الفُطُورِ والغَدَاءِ.	I drink a lot of coffee between breakfast and lunch.
مَا بَيْنَ 60% و70% مِنَ التِّجَارَةِ الخَارِجِيَّةِ لِلبَلَدِ مُسَعَّرَةٌ بِالدُّولَارِ.	Between 60% and 70% of the country's foreign trade is pegged to the dollar.

Locative adverbs 139

تَعْمَلُ أَحْزَابُ المُعَارَضَةِ فِيمَا بَيْنَهَا لِمُوَاجَهَةِ الحِزْبِ الحَاكِمِ فِي الإِنْتِخَابَاتِ النِّيَابِيَّةِ.	Opposition parties are working together to confront the ruling party in the parliamentary elections.

بَيْنَ can be preceded by (مِنْ), and in this case, it will be a genitive noun, as in the following:

كَانَتْ أُسْتَاذَتِي مِنْ بَيْنِ الأَسَاتِذَةِ الَّذِينَ تُكَرِّمُهُمُ الجَامِعَةُ هَذَا العَامَ.	My teacher was among the professors whom the university honors this year.
مِنْ بَيْنِ المَوَاضِيعِ الَّتِي تَمَّتْ مُنَاقَشَتُها فِي النَّدْوَةِ سُبُلُ تَعْزِيزِ الوِحْدَةِ بَيْنَ دُوَلِ المِنْطَقَةِ.	Among the topics discussed at the symposium were ways to strengthen unity among the countries of the region.
مِنْ بَيْنِ مَزَايَا أَشْجَارِ البُنِّ أَنَّ ثِمَارَهَا تَنْضُجُ مَرَّاتٍ عِدَّةً عَلَى مَدَارِ السَّنَةِ.	Among the advantages of coffee trees is that their fruit ripens several times in the year.
كَانَتْ شَرِكَةُ عَمِّي مِنْ بَيْنِ الشَّرِكَاتِ الرَّاعِيَةِ لِلْبُطُولَةِ.	My uncle's company was one of the sponsors of the championship.

بَيْنَ can appear as part of two expressions (بَيْنَا) and (بَيْنَمَا), which mean 'while'. (بَيْنَا) is rarely found in current usage, but (بَيْنَمَا) is used often, and it is mainly used in the sense of 'as', 'while' and 'whereas', as in the following:

بَيْنَمَا نَحْنُ نَسِيرُ إِلَى المَقْهَى، إِذْ حَاوَلَ لِصٌّ سَرِقَةَ نُقُودِنَا.	As we walked to the cafe, a thief tried to steal our money.
بَيْنَمَا كَانَتِ الطَّائِرَةُ تُحَاوِلُ الهُبُوطَ، اضْطُرَّ الطَّيَّارُ لِلتَّحْلِيقِ مُجَدَّدًا لِسُوءِ الأَحْوَالِ الجَوِّيَّةِ.	While the plane was trying to land, the pilot had to fly again due to the bad weather.
انْخَفَضَتْ أَسْهُمُ شَرِكَاتِ الإِتِّصَالَاتِ، بَيْنَمَا ارْتَفَعَتْ أَسْهُمُ شَرِكَاتِ النَّفْطِ.	Telecommunications stocks fell, while oil stocks rose.
يَبْلُغُ دَخْلُ البِلَادِ مِنَ العُمْلَاتِ الأَجْنَبِيَّةِ خَمْسَةَ مِلْيَارَاتِ دُولَارٍ، بَيْنَمَا البِلَادُ تَحْتَاجُ ضِعْفَ ذَلِكَ.	The country's foreign exchange income is five billion dollars, while the country needs twice as much.

بين *in fixed expressions*

The positions of the parties were indecisive; therefore, the talks failed and the agreement was not signed.	كَانَتْ مَوَاقِفُ الأَطْرَافِ بَيْنَ بَيْنٍ وَلِذَلِكَ فَشِلَتِ المُحَادَثَاتُ وَلَمْ يَتِمَّ تَوْقِيعُ الإِتِّفَاقِ.	undecisive	بَيْنَ بَيْنٍ

After armed conflict broke out between government forces and rebels, the civilians found themselves caught in the middle.	بَعْدَ انْدِلَاعِ الصِّرَاعِ المُسَلَّحِ بَيْنَ القُوَّاتِ الحُكُومِيَّةِ وَالمُتَمَرِّدِينَ، وَجَدَ المَدَنِيُّونَ أَنْفُسَهُمْ بَيْنَ شِقَّيِ الرَّحَى.	caught in the middle	بَيْنَ شِقَّيِ الرَّحَى
From the American occupation to sectarian governments, the Iraqi people suffered between a rock and a hard place.	مِنَ الاحْتِلَالِ الأَمْرِيكِيِّ إِلَى الحُكُومَاتِ الطَّائِفِيَّةِ عَانَى الشَّعْبُ العِرَاقِيُّ بَيْنَ المِطْرَقَةِ وَالسِّنْدَانِ.	between a rock and a hard place	بَيْنَ المِطْرَقَةِ وَالسِّنْدَانِ
Government officials stressed that border problems cannot be solved overnight.	أَكَّدَ المَسْؤُولُونَ الحُكُومِيُّونَ أَنَّ المَشَاكِلَ الحُدُودِيَّةَ لَا يُمْكِنُ أَنْ تُحَلَّ بَيْنَ عَشِيَّةٍ وَضُحَاهَا.	overnight	بَيْنَ عَشِيَّةٍ وَضُحَاهَا
The Sahel region suffers from food crises from time to time.	تُعَانِي مِنْطَقَةُ السَّاحِلِ الإِفْرِيقِيِّ مِنْ أَزَمَاتٍ غِذَائِيَّةٍ بَيْنَ حِينٍ وَآخَرَ.	from time to time	بَيْنَ حِينٍ وَآخَرَ

بَيْنَ can join pronoun suffixes as follows:

بَيْنَهُمَا	بَيْنَ + هُمَا	بَيْنِي	بَيْنَ + أَنَا
بَيْنَنَا	بَيْنَ + نَحْنُ	بَيْنَكَ	بَيْنَ + أَنْتَ
بَيْنَكُمْ	بَيْنَ + أَنْتُمْ	بَيْنَكِ	بَيْنَ + أَنْتِ
بَيْنَكُنَّ	بَيْنَ + أَنْتُنَّ	بَيْنَهُ	بَيْنَ + هُوَ
بَيْنَهُمْ	بَيْنَ + هُمْ	بَيْنَهَا	بَيْنَ + هِيَ
بَيْنَهُنَّ	بَيْنَ + هُنَّ	بَيْنَكُمَا	بَيْنَ + أَنْتُمَا

عِنْدَ

عِنْدَ is a common locative adverb in Arabic. Its basic function is to express existence or proximity. It is often translated as 'at', 'in' and 'by', among others. It has to be used in conjunction with a noun or a pronoun suffix. It can be used to express proximity in spatial or temporal contexts, and it can be used figuratively as well, as in the following:

أَسْكُنُ عِنْدَ صَدِيقِي مُنْذُ وُصُولِي لِلْجَامِعَةِ.	I have stayed at my friend's since I arrived at the university.
اِجْتَمَعَ الزَّائِرُونَ عِنْدَ بَابِ المُتْحَفِ فِي اِنْتِظَارِ المُرْشِدِ السِّيَاحِيِّ.	Visitors gathered at the museum door waiting for the tour guide.

Locative adverbs 141

تَوَقَّفَ القِطَارُ عِنْدَ رَصِيفِ المَحَطَّةِ ثُمَّ بَدَأَ الرُّكَّابُ بِالنُّزُولِ.	The train stopped at the station, and the passengers began to disembark.
عِنْدَمَا أَزُورُ قَرْيَتَنَا، أَسْكُنُ عِنْدَ أَهْلِي فِي بَيْتِ العَائِلَةِ.	When I visit our village, I live with my family at the family home.
مِنَ الضَّرُورِيِّ أَنْ نَتَوَقَّفَ عِنْدَ هَذِهِ الإِحْصَاءَاتِ وَنُحَلِّلَهَا.	It is necessary to stop at these statistics and analyze them.

عِنْدَ can be used to express proximity in temporal contexts, as in the following:

سَيَكُونُ مَوْعِدُ الاجْتِمَاعِ عِنْدَ الحَادِيَةَ عَشْرَةَ صَبَاحًا.	The meeting will be at 11 a.m.
نَصْحُو عِنْدَ الفَجْرِ وَنَنَامُ عِنْدَ مُنْتَصَفِ اللَّيْلِ.	We wake up at dawn and sleep at midnight.
سَنَعْرِفُ نَتِيجَةَ الاجْتِمَاعِ عِنْدَ الصَّبَاحِ.	We will know the outcome of the meeting in the morning.
عِنْدَ وُصُولِ الرَّئِيسِ إِلَى القَاعَةِ، يَجِبُ أَنْ يَقِفَ جَمِيعُ الحَاضِرِينَ.	When the president arrives in the hall, all those present must stand.
اِنْخَفَضَتْ أَسْعَارُ الأَسْهُمِ عِنْدَ إِغْلَاقِ البُورْصَةِ.	Stock prices fell at the close of the stock market.

Sometimes when عَنْدَ is used in temporal contexts, it is translated as 'when', especially when it is followed by a verbal noun (مَصْدَر), as in the following:

عِنْدَ عَوْدَتِهِ مِنْ رُومَا، الْتَقَى الوَزِيرُ بِالرَّئِيسِ لِإِطْلَاعِهِ عَلَى نَتِيجَةِ المُحَادَثَاتِ.	When the minister returned from Rome, he met with the president to brief him on the outcome of the talks.
عِنْدَ اسْتِعْمَالِ هَاتِفِكَ فِي مَكَانٍ عَامٍّ، كُنْ حَرِيصًا قَبْلَ إِعْطَاءِ بَيَانَاتِكَ الشَّخْصِيَّةِ لِأَيِّ شَخْصٍ.	When using your phone in a public place, be careful before giving your personal data to anyone.
عِنْدَ وُصُولِي إِلَى لَنْدَن، تَعَرَّفْتُ عَلَى الكَثِيرِ مِنَ العَرَبِ المُغْتَرِبِينَ.	When I arrived in London, I met a lot of Arab expatriates.
عِنْدَ اعْتِقَالِ اللِّصِّ، لَمْ تَكُنْ لَدَيْهِ أَيَّةُ وَثَائِقَ ثُبُوتِيَّةٍ.	When the thief was arrested, he did not have any identity documents.
عِنْدَ دُخُولِي إِلَى الجَامِعَةِ، كَانَتِ الحَرَكَةُ الإِسْلَامِيَّةُ فِي أَوْجِهَا.	When I joined university, the Islamic movement was at its height.

Locative adverbs

عِنْدَ can be used to indicate possession. When it is used to express possession, it is usually translated as 'have' in English, as in the following:

هَلْ عِنْدَكَ بَيْتٌ فِي هَذِهِ المَدِينَةِ؟	Do you have a house in this city?
لَيْسَ عِنْدِي وَقْتٌ لِمُنَاقَشَةِ هَذَا المَوْضُوعِ الآنَ.	I do not have time to discuss this now.
عِنْدِي شَكٌّ فِي مِصْدَاقِيَّةِ هَذَا الخَبَرِ.	I have doubts about the credibility of this news.
عِنْدَنَا الكَثِيرُ مِنَ المَوَارِدِ الطَّبِيعِيَّةِ فِي بَلَدِنَا.	We have a lot of natural resources in our country.

عِنْدَ can be used to express opinion or judgment, and in this sense, it can be translated as 'for', as in the following:

عِنْدَ هِيجِل، الدَّوْلَةُ هِيَ جُزْءٌ مِنَ المُجْتَمَعِ.	For Hegel, the state is part of society.
القُضَاةُ عِنْدَ المِصْرِيِّينَ يَحْظَوْنَ بِتَقْدِيرٍ وَاسِعٍ مِنْ مُخْتَلَفِ الأَوْسَاطِ الشَّعْبِيَّةِ وَالرَّسْمِيَّةِ.	For the Egyptians, judges are highly appreciated by various popular and official circles.
مِصْرُ عِنْدَ جَمَال حَمْدَان هِيَ قَلْبُ العَالَمِ العَرَبِيِّ والإِسْلَامِيِّ.	Egypt, for Gamal Ḥamdan, is the heart of the Arab and Islamic world.
يَسُودُ عِنْدَ مُعْظَمِ الغَرْبِيِّينَ انْطِبَاعٌ بِأَنَّ العَالَمَ العَرَبِيَّ لَا يَصْلُحُ لِلدِّيمُوقْرَاطِيَّةِ.	For most Westerners, the Arab world is considered not suitable for democracy.

عِنْدَ can be followed by (مَا) to make (عِنْدَمَا), which means 'when' or 'whenever', as in the following:

عِنْدَمَا تَتَجَوَّلُ فِي المَدِينَةِ تَجِدُ الكَثِيرَ مِنَ الأَمَاكِنِ التَّارِيخِيَّةِ وَسْطَ المَنَاطِقِ السَّكَنِيَّةِ وَالتِّجَارِيَّةِ.	When you walk around the city you find lots of historical places amid residential and commercial areas.
عِنْدَمَا يُفَكِّرُ أَيُّ شَخْصٍ فِي السَّفَرِ، يَنْبَغِي عَلَيْهِ التَّخْطِيطُ لِرِحْلَتِهِ جَيِّدًا.	When anyone thinks about traveling, they should plan their trip well.
عِنْدَمَا حَصَلَتْ سُورِيَّةُ عَلَى اسْتِقْلَالِهَا عَنْ فَرَنْسَا عَامَ 1946 كَانَ اقْتِصَادُهَا ذَا طَابَعٍ زِرَاعِيٍّ.	When Syria gained its independence from France in 1946, its economy was agricultural.
عِنْدَمَا وَصَلْنَا إِلَى مَقَرِّ الصَّحِيفَةِ، وَجَدْنَا رَئِيسَ التَّحْرِيرِ فِي انْتِظَارِنَا.	When we arrived at the newspaper headquarters, we found the editor waiting for us.
عِنْدَمَا تَتَدَخَّلُ السِّيَاسَةُ فِي الفَنِّ، يَنْحَدِرُ مُسْتَوَى الإِبْدَاعِ.	When politics interferes with art, the level of creativity declines.

Locative adverbs 143

عِنْدَ can be preceded by (مِنْ) to make (مِنْ عِنْدِ) which usually translates as 'from', as in the following:

حَصَلْتُ عَلَى الدَّوَاءِ مِنْ عِنْدِ الصَّيْدَلِيِّ.	I got the medicine from the pharmacist.
هَذِهِ المُشْكِلَةُ لَمْ تَبْدَأْ مِنْ عِنْدِنَا.	This problem did not start from us.
جَمِيعُ تَفَاصِيلِ هَذِهِ القِصَّةِ مِنْ عِنْدِ المُؤَلِّفِ وَلَا تَمُتُّ لِلْوَاقِعِ بِصِلَةٍ.	All the details of this story are from the author, and they do not relate to reality in any way.
الصِّحَّةُ نِعْمَةٌ مِنْ عِنْدِ اللهِ.	Health is a blessing from God.
لَا أَعْرِفُ كَيْفَ أَصِلُ مِنْ عِنْدِي إِلَى عِنْدِكُمْ.	I do not know how to get from my place to yours.

عِنْدَ can be followed by (إِذْ) to make (عِنْدَئِذٍ), which means 'then' or 'at that time', as in the following:

سَنَنْتَصِرُ عَلَى الأَعْدَاءِ، وَعِنْدَئِذٍ سَيَفْرَحُ الشَّعْبُ وَيَحْتَفِلُ بِالْإِنْتِصَارِ.	We will triumph over the enemies, and then the people will be happy and celebrate victory.
وَافَقَ الرَّئِيسُ عَلَى مَطَالِبِ المُحْتَجِّينَ، وَعِنْدَئِذٍ قَرَّرَ المُتَظَاهِرُونَ فَضَّ الإِعْتِصَامِ.	The president accepted the protesters' demands, and then demonstrators decided to break the sit-in.
وَاجَهَتْهُ الشُّرْطَةُ بِجَمِيعِ الأَدِلَّةِ، وَعِنْدَئِذٍ إِنْهَارَ وَاعْتَرَفَ بَالجَرِيمَةِ.	The police confronted him with all the evidence, and then he collapsed and admitted the crime.
سَيَصِلُ الوَفْدُ الرَّسْمِيُّ بَعْدَ سَاعَتَيْنِ وَعِنْدَئِذٍ سَيَكُونُ الجَمِيعُ فِي اسْتِقْبَالِهِ.	The official delegation will arrive after two hours, and then everyone will be welcoming them.
سَأَلْتُهُ عَنْ سَبَبِ تَأَخُّرِهِ عَنِ المَوْعِدِ، وَعِنْدَئِذٍ اعْتَذَرَ.	I asked him why he was late, and then he apologized.

عِنْدَ can join pronoun suffixes as follows:

عِنْدَهُمَا	عِنْدَ + هُمَا		عِنْدِي	عِنْدَ + أَنَا
عِنْدَنَا	عِنْدَ + نَحْنُ		عِنْدَكَ	عِنْدَ + أَنْتَ
عِنْدَكُمْ	عِنْدَ + أَنْتُمْ		عِنْدَكِ	عِنْدَ + أَنْتِ
عِنْدَكُنَّ	عِنْدَ + أَنْتُنَّ		عِنْدَهُ	عِنْدَ + هُوَ
عِنْدَهُمْ	عِنْدَ + هُمْ		عِنْدَهَا	عِنْدَ + هِيَ
عِنْدَهُنَّ	عِنْدَ + هُنَّ		عِنْدَكُمَا	عِنْدَ + أَنْتُمَا

مَعَ

(مَعَ) is a very commonly used locative adverb, which is often confused as a preposition. It means 'with'; thus, it indicates accompaniment or association, and it can be used literally to mean physically accompanying or figuratively to mean 'with' in the sense of supporting, as in the following:

خَرَجْتُ لِلْعَشَاءِ مَعَ زَوْجَتِي لِلِاحْتِفَالِ بِعِيدِ زَوَاجِنَا.	I went out for dinner with my wife to celebrate our wedding anniversary.
أُحِبُّ أَنْ أَجْلِسَ فِي هُدُوءٍ مَعَ كِتَابٍ وَفِنْجَانِ قَهْوَةٍ.	I like to sit quietly with a book and a cup of coffee.
فِي الْهِنْدِ يُفَضِّلُونَ أَنْ يَأْكُلُوا الدَّجَاجَ مَعَ الْكَارِي.	In India they prefer to eat chicken with curry.
هَلْ أَنْتُمْ مَعِي أَمْ ضِدِّي؟	Are you with me or against me?
نَحْنُ نَقِفُ مَعَ الْحَقِّ وَمَعَ الْمَظْلُومِينَ.	We stand with what is right and with the oppressed.

As an adverb of time, مَعَ means 'at' or 'with', as in the following:

وَصَلْنَا مَعَ فَجْرِ الْيَوْمِ.	We arrived at the dawn of the day.
تَوَسَّعَتِ الْقَرْيَةُ وَزَادَتْ مَسَاحَتُهَا مَعَ مُرُورِ السَّنَوَاتِ.	The village expanded and expanded over the years.
مَعَ بِدَايَةِ الصَّيْفِ بَدَأَتِ الْفَنَادِقُ تَزْدَحِمُ فِي أَرْجَاءِ الْمَدِينَةِ السِّيَاحِيَّةِ.	With the start of summer, hotels around the tourist city began to get crowded.

مَعَ can be used to indicate possession. When it is used to express possession, it is usually translated as 'have' in English, and it indicates having something at the time of speaking, as in the following:

هَلْ مَعَكَ نُقُودٌ؟	Do you have money?
جِئْتُ إِلَى الْمُحَاضَرَةِ وَمَعِي كُلُّ الْكُتُبِ.	I came to the lecture with all the books.
مَعَكَ حَقِيبَةٌ كَبِيرَةٌ جِدًّا. هَلْ أَنْتَ مُسَافِرٌ؟	You have a very large bag. Are you traveling?
لَيْسَ مَعَنَا أَيَّةُ أَغْرَاضٍ نَدْفَعُ عَلَيْهَا جَمَارِكَ.	We have no belonging for which we pay customs.

مَعَ can also be used as an adverbial object (مَعًا), and in this case, it means 'together', as in the following:

وَصَلَ أَقَارِبِي إِلَى الْحَفْلِ مَعًا.	My relatives arrived at the party together.
عَمِلْنَا مَعًا لِسَنَوَاتٍ طَوِيلَةٍ وَزَادَتْ بَيْنَنَا الثِّقَةُ.	We worked together for many years and our mutual trust increased.

Locative adverbs 145

قَضَيْنَا مَعًا أَيَّامًا جَمِيلَةً فِي رِحْلَةِ المَصِيفِ.	We spent happy days together on the summer resort trip.
يَجِبُ عَلَى الدُّوَلِ الأَعْضَاءِ أَنْ تَتَعَاوَنَ مَعًا لِتَحْقِيقِ السَّلَامِ والرَّخَاءِ لِشُعُوبِهَا.	Member states must cooperate with each other to achieve peace and prosperity for their peoples.

مَعَ can be followed by (هَذَا) or (ذَلِكَ) to express contrast, in the sense of 'yet' or 'nevertheless', as in the following:

نَشَأَ صَدِيقِي فِي عَائِلَةٍ دِبْلُومَاسِيَّةٍ، وَمَعَ هَذَا فَقَدْ رَفَضَ العَمَلَ فِي السِّلْكِ الدِّبْلُومَاسِيِّ وَقَرَّرَ أَنْ يَعْمَلَ فِي التِّجَارَةِ.	My friend grew up in a diplomatic family, yet he refused to work in the diplomatic corps and decided to work in commerce.
عَانَى البَلَدُ مِنْ وَيْلَاتِ الحَرْبِ الأَهْلِيَّةِ، وَمَعَ ذَلِكَ فَقَدْ تَحَسَّنَ الإِقْتِصَادُ وعَادَتِ السِّيَاحَةُ فِي غُضُونِ سَنَوَاتٍ قَلِيلَةٍ.	The country suffered from the scourge of civil war, yet its economy improved and tourism returned in a few years.
فَرَضَتِ الحُكُومَةُ حَظْرَ التَّجَوُّلِ فِي المَدِينَةِ، وَمَعَ ذَلِكَ فَقَدِ اسْتَمَرَّتْ التَّظَاهُرَاتُ طَوَالَ اللَّيْلِ وَالنَّهَارِ.	The government imposed a curfew in the city, nevertheless demonstrations continued all night and all day.
هُنَاكَ فَوَائِدُ كَثِيرَةٌ لِلاِتِّفَاقِ، وَمَعَ هَذَا فَقَدْ رَفَضَتِ الدَّوْلَتَانِ التَّوْقِيعَ عَلَيهِ.	There are many benefits to the agreement, yet the two countries refused to sign it.

مَعَ can be followed by (أَنَّ) to express contrast, in the sense of 'although', as in the following:

مَعَ أَنَّ الأَجْهِزَةَ الجَدِيدَةَ أَحْدَثُ وَأَغْلَى، فَإِنَّ الأَجْهِزَةَ القَدِيمَةَ كَانَتْ أَسْرَعَ وَأَكْثَرَ كَفَاءَةً.	Although the new equipment is more advanced and more expensive, older devices were faster and more efficient.
مَعَ أَنَّهُ تَخَرَّجَ مُنْذُ خَمْسِ سَنَوَاتٍ، فَإِنَّهُ لَمْ يَجِدْ وَظِيفَةً مُنَاسِبَةً حَتَّى الآنَ.	Although he graduated five years ago, he has not found a suitable job yet.
مَعَ أَنَّ الإِسْلَامِ سَاوَى بَيْنَ الرَّجُلِ وَالمَرْأَةِ، فَإِنَّ الكَثِيرَ مِنَ البُلْدَانِ الإِسْلَامِيَّةِ لَدَيْهَا قَوَانِينُ تُمَيِّزُ بَيْنَ الجِنْسَيْنِ.	Although Islam made men and women equal, many Muslim countries have gender-discriminatory laws.
مَعَ أَنَّهَا كَانَتِ الضَّحِيَّةَ، فَقَدِ احْتَجَزَتْهَا الشُّرْطَةُ لِلتَّحْقِيقِ مَعَهَا.	Although she was the victim, the police detained her for questioning.

مع *in fixed expressions*

مَعَ السَّلَامَةِ	good-bye	فِي نِهَايَةِ الرِّحْلَةِ سَلَّمَتْ عَلَيْنَا، وَهَتَفَتْ: "مَعَ السَّلَامَةِ!"	At the end of the trip, she greeted us and shouted, "Good-bye!"

Locative adverbs

مَعَ الأَسَفِ	unfortunately	
مَعَ الأَسَفِ، حَالَتُهُ الصِّحِّيَّةُ مُتَدَهْوِرَةٌ وَلَا أَمَلَ في شِفَائِهِ مِن دُونِ جِرَاحَةٍ.	Unfortunately, his health is deteriorating, and there is no hope of recovery without surgery.	
مَعَ الوَقْتِ	over time	
تَزَايَدَتْ أَهَمِّيَّةُ التَّوَاصُلِ الإِجْتِمَاعِيِّ مَعَ الوَقْتِ.	Social media has become increasingly important over time.	
وَبِخَاصَّةٍ مَعَ	especially with	
زَادَتْ مُعَانَاةُ المُوَاطِنِ البَسِيطِ، وَبِخَاصَّةٍ مَعَ الإِرْتِفَاعِ المُسْتَمِرِّ فِي أَسْعَارِ المَحْرُوقَاتِ.	The suffering of ordinary citizens has increased, especially with the continuous rise in fuel prices.	

مَعَ can join pronoun suffixes as follows:

مَعَهُمَا	مَعَ + هُمَا		مَعِي	مَعَ + أَنَا
مَعَنَا	مَعَ + نَحْنُ		مَعَكَ	مَعَ + أَنْتَ
مَعَكُمْ	مَعَ + أَنْتُمْ		مَعَكِ	مَعَ + أَنْتِ
مَعَكُنَّ	مَعَ + أَنْتُنَّ		مَعَهُ	مَعَ + هُوَ
مَعَهُمْ	مَعَ + هُمْ		مَعَهَا	مَعَ + هِيَ
مَعَهُنَّ	مَعَ + هُنَّ		مَعَكُمَا	مَعَ + أَنْتُمَا

لَدَى

لَدَى is used in a very similar way as (عِنْدَ), so it indicates existence or proximity, and it is used in spatial and temporal contexts, as in the following:

قَضَيْتُ اللَّيْلَ لَدَى صَدِيقِي.	I spent the night at my friend.
وَصَلْنَا العَاصِمَةَ لَدَى طُلُوعِ الشَّمْسِ.	We reached the capital at sunrise.
يَعْمَلُ بَاحِثًا لَدَى مُؤَسَّسَةِ كَارْنِيجِي لِلسَّلَامِ.	He is a researcher at the Carnegie Endowment for Peace.
كَانَ زَوْجُهَا سَفِيرًا لِلسُّعُودِيَّةِ لَدَى الوِلَايَاتِ المُتَّحِدَةِ الأَمْرِيكِيَّةِ.	Her husband was an ambassador of Saudi Arabia to the United States of America.

In temporal contexts, لَدَى is often used in the sense of 'upon' or 'at', such as in the following:

لَدَى وُصُولِنَا إِلَى قَاعَةِ المُؤْتَمَرِ، بَدَأَتِ الكَلِمَةُ الإِفْتِتَاحِيَّةُ.	Upon our arrival at the conference hall, the opening speech began.
تَحَدَّثَ الرَّئِيسُ مَعَ الصَّحَفِيِّينَ لَدَى عَوْدَتِهِ مِنَ القِمَّةِ العَرَبِيَّةِ.	The president spoke to journalists on his return from the Arab summit.

Locative adverbs 147

لَدَى اِفْتِتَاحِ المَرْكَزِ التِّجَارِيِّ الجَدِيدِ، أَعْلَنَ صَاحِبُهُ عَنْ تَخْفِيضَاتٍ كَبِيرَةٍ فِي الأَسْعَارِ.	At the opening of the new mall, the owner announced significant price reductions.
لَدَى إِعْلَانِ نَتِيجَةِ المُسَابَقَةِ، هَنَّأَ الوَزِيرُ الفَائِزِينَ.	Upon announcing the outcome of the competition, the minister congratulated the winners.

لَدَى is also used to express possession in the same way as (عِنْدَ), as in the following:

لَدَيْنَا الكَثِيرُ مِنَ الوَاجِبَاتِ هَذَا الأُسْبُوعَ.	We have a lot of homework this week.
لَدَى الشَّرِكَةِ فُرُوعٌ فِي جَمِيعِ بُلْدَانِ الشَّرْقِ الأَوْسَطِ.	The company has branches in all countries of the Middle East.
لَيْسَ لَدَى الحُكومَةِ الجَدِيدَةِ بَرَامِجُ فَعَّالَةٌ لِمُوَاجَهَةِ الفَقْرِ وَالبَطَالَةِ.	The new government does not have effective programs to tackle poverty and unemployment.
كَانَ لَدَى الحَاكِمِ العَسْكَرِيِّ سُلُطَاتٌ مُطْلَقَةٌ فِي البِلَادِ.	The military ruler had absolute powers in the country.

Note

We can find (لَدَى) in formal expressions, such as titles of formal positions, for example:

السَّفِيرُ الأَمْرِيكِيُّ لَدَى القَاهِرَةِ

The American ambassador to Cairo.

مُرَاسِلُ الصَّحِيفَةِ لَدَى الأُمَمِ المُتَّحِدَةِ

The newspaper correspondent to the UN.

لَدَى can join pronoun suffixes, and in this case, it becomes (لَدَيْ):

لَدَيْهِمَا	لَدَى + هُمَا	لَدَيَّ	لَدَى + أَنَا
لَدَيْنَا	لَدَى + نَحْنُ	لَدَيْكَ	لَدَى + أَنْتَ
لَدَيْكُمْ	لَدَى + أَنْتُمْ	لَدَيْكِ	لَدَى + أَنْتِ
لَدَيْكُنَّ	لَدَى + أَنْتُنَّ	لَدَيْهِ	لَدَى + هُوَ
لَدَيْهِمْ	لَدَى + هُمْ	لَدَيْهَا	لَدَى + هِيَ
لَدَيْهِنَّ	لَدَى + هُنَّ	لَدَيْكُمَا	لَدَى + أَنْتُمَا

Locative adverbs

لَدُنْ is a highly formal variation of (لَدَى). It is found in some Qur'anic verses, and it can also be found in highly formal texts, for example, some UN documents, but not much in media texts. It is often preceded by the preposition (مِنْ), and it means 'from' or 'by', as in the following:

حَظِيَ القَرَارُ بِتَأْيِيدٍ كَبِيرٍ مِنْ لَدُنْ جَمِيعِ الدُّوَلِ الأَعْضَاءِ فِي الأُمَمِ المُتَّحِدَةِ.	The resolution has received considerable support from all UN member states.
يَجِبُ أَنْ يَتِمَّ التَّصْدِيقُ عَلَى القَانُونِ مِنْ لَدُنِ المَلِكِ.	The law must be ratified by the king.
أَثَارَتِ الهَجَمَاتُ الإِرْهَابِيَّةُ اسْتِنْكَارًا شَدِيدًا مِنْ لَدُنِ الحُكُومَةِ وَالهَيْئَاتِ الدَّوْلِيَّةِ.	The terrorist attacks have aroused strong condemnation from the government and international bodies.
تَحْظَى المَنَاطِقُ الأَثَرِيَّةُ وَالتَّارِيخِيَّةُ بِالرِّعَايَةِ وَالاهْتِمَامِ مِنْ لَدُنِ اليُونِسْكُو.	Archaeological and historical sites are given the care and attention of UNESCO.

(لَدُنْ) does not come with pronoun suffixes.

بَعْدَ / قَبْلَ

بَعْدَ means 'after', and it has temporal or spatial functions, depending on the context, as in the following:

هَلْ يُمْكِنُكَ مُقَابَلَتِي بَعْدَ بَابِ مَحَطَّةِ القِطَارِ؟	Can you meet me past the train station gate?
يَنْوِي الرَّئِيسُ الفَرَنْسِيُّ زِيَارَةَ الإِمَارَاتِ العَرَبِيَّةِ المُتَّحِدَةِ بَعْدَ السُّعُودِيَّةِ.	The French president plans to visit the United Arab Emirates after Saudi Arabia.
سَارَ الجُنُودُ فِي صَفٍّ بَعْدَ القَائِدِ.	The soldiers walked in line after the commander.
بَعْدَ تَوَقُّفِ صُدُورِ المَجَلَّةِ انْتَقَلَ الصَّحَفِيُّ إِلَى صَحِيفَةِ الأَخْبَارِ.	After the publication of the magazine stopped, the journalist moved to *Al-Akhbar* newspaper.

قَبْلَ means 'before', and it has temporal or spatial functions, depending on the context:

بَدَأَتْ قَبْلَ أُسْبُوعَيْنِ الإِجْرَاءَاتُ التَّنْفِيذِيَّةُ لِدَمْجِ الشَّرِكَتَيْنِ.	The executive procedures for merging the two companies began two weeks ago.
يَجِبُ أَنْ تَصِلَ المَطَارَ قَبْلَ مَوْعِدِ المُغَادَرَةِ بِسَاعَتَيْنِ.	You must arrive at the airport two hours before departure time.
تَوَقَّفَتْ جَمِيعُ السَّيَّارَاتِ قَبْلَ نُقْطَةِ التَّفْتِيشِ.	All cars stopped before the checkpoint.

Locative adverbs 149

قَبْلَ/بَعْدَ can be used for ordering items:

جَاءَتْ شَرِكَةُ سَامسُونج بَعْدَ مَايكرُوسُوفْت فِي المَبِيعَاتِ.	Samsung came after Microsoft in sales.
فَازَتْ فَرَنْسَا بِكَأْسِ العَالَمِ فِي كُرَةِ القَدَمِ، وَبَعْدَهَا جَاءَتْ كُرْوَاتِيا فِي المَرْكَزِ الثَّانِي.	France won the World Cup in football, followed by Croatia in second place.
دَخَلْتُ إِلَى قَاعَةِ المُحَاضَرَةِ وَدَخَلَ بَعْدِي الأُسْتَاذُ، ثُمَّ أُغْلِقَ البَابُ وَلَمْ يَدْخُلْ أَحَدٌ.	I entered the lecture hall, and the professor followed me; then the door closed, and no one entered.
فِي المَرْكَزِ الأَوَّلِ لِلْمُسَابَقَةِ جَاءَ العَدَّاءُ المَغْرِبِيُّ وَبَعْدَهُ جَاءَ العَدَّاءُ السُودَانِيُّ.	In the first place of the competition came the Moroccan runner, and after him came the Sudanese runner.

بَعْدُ can be used in the sense of 'yet', and in this context, it has to be preceded by a negative statement:

الشَّرِكَةُ لَدَيْهَا طَلَبِيَّاتٌ لَمْ تُلَبَّ بَعْدُ.	The company has orders that have not been met yet.
هَذَا القَانُونُ لَمْ يُعْرَضْ عَلَى البَرْلَمَانِ بَعْدُ.	This law has not yet been submitted to Parliament yet.
لَمْ تَتَحَقَّقْ أَيَّةُ نَتَائِجَ عَلَى الأرْضِ بَعْدُ.	No results have been achieved on the ground yet.
لَمْ يَتِمَّ الإِعْلَانُ عَنْ مَوْعِدِ زِيَارَةِ الرَّئِيسِ الأَمْرِيكِيِّ لِلْمِنْطَقَةِ بَعْدُ.	The date of the US president's visit to the region has not been announced yet.

قَبْلَ/بَعْدَ can be followed by a noun or a clause consisting of (أَنْ) and a verb:

بَعْدَ أَنْ اسْتَقَلَّ القِطَارَ أَدْرَكَ أَنَّهُ نَسِيَ حَقِيبَتَهُ.	After taking the train, he realized that he had forgotten his bag.
اتَّصِلْ بِي بَعْدَ أَنْ تَرْجِعَ مِنَ السَّفَرِ.	Call me after you return from your trip.
بَعْدَ أَنْ هَدَأَتِ الأَزْمَةُ الدِّبْلُومَاسِيَّةُ، بَدَأَتْ مُحَاوَلَاتُ إِعَادَةِ الإِتِّصَالِ بَيْنَ البَلَدَيْنِ.	After the diplomatic crisis subsided, attempts to reconnect between the two countries began.
لَا يُمْكِنُكَ مُغَادَرَةُ المَشْفَى قَبْلَ أَنْ تَتَحَسَّنَ صِحَّتُكَ.	You cannot leave the hospital before your health improves.

قَبْلَ/بَعْدَ can be preceded by (مَا) to make the expressions (مَا قَبْلَ) and (مَا بَعْدَ), which literally mean 'what come before' and 'what comes after'; sometimes this translates as the prefixes pre- and post-:

تَمَّ اكْتِشَافُ كَهْفٍ يَعُودُ تَارِيخُهُ إِلَى مَا قَبْلِ التَّارِيخِ.	A prehistoric cave was discovered.

كَانَتْ هُنَاكَ اِمْبِراطُورِيَّتَانِ كَبيرَتَانِ تُسَيْطِرَانِ عَلَى العَالَمِ في عَصْرِ مَا قَبْلِ الإِسْلَامِ.	There were two great empires that controlled the world in the pre-Islamic era.
يُمْكِنُ الحَدِيثُ عَنْ تَارِيخِ القَضِيَّةِ الفِلَسْطِينِيَّةِ مَا بَعْدَ مفاوضَاتِ السَّلامِ.	We can talk about the history of the Palestinian issue after the peace negotiations.
تَمَّ إِنْتَاجُ الكَثِيرِ مِنَ السِّلَعِ الجَدِيدَةِ في مَرْحَلَةِ مَا بَعْدَ الثَّوْرَةِ الصِّنَاعِيَّةِ.	Many new goods were produced in the post-Industrial Revolution era.

قَبْلَ/بَعْدَ can be followed by (ذَلِكَ) to make the expressions (بَعْدَ ذَلِكَ) and (قَبْلَ ذَلِكَ), which literally mean 'before that' and 'after that':

تَمَّ تَوْحِيدُ مَمَالِكِ اليُونَانِ تَحْتَ قِيَادَةِ المَلِكِ فيليب وَبَعْدَ ذَلِكَ بَدَأَ المَلِكُ المَقْدُونِيُّ يُخَطِّطُ لِمُوَاجَهَةِ الفُرْسِ في آسيَا الصُّغْرَى.	The kingdoms of Greece were united under the leadership of King Philip; then the Macedonian king began planning to confront the Persians in Asia Minor.
أَقَامَ الوَزِيرُ المِصرِيُّ مَأْدُبَةَ غَدَاءٍ لِلْوَفْدِ العُمَانِي، وَأَجْرَى بَعْدَ ذَلِكَ سِلْسِلَةَ لِقَاءَاتٍ حَوْلَ التَّعَاوُنِ الثُّنَائِيِّ بَيْنَ البَلَدَيْنِ.	The Egyptian minister held a lunch banquet for the Omani delegation and then held a series of meetings on bilateral cooperation between the two countries.
كَانَ رَئِيسُ التَّحْرِيرِ الجَدِيدِ قَبْلَ ذَلِكَ يَتَوَلَّى مَنْصِبَ نَائِبِ رَئِيسِ التَّحْرِيرِ.	The new editor-in-chief was previously a deputy editor-in-chief.
سَيَجْتَمِعُ مَجْلِسُ الأَمْنِ لِمُنَاقَشَةِ القَضِيَّةِ نِهَايَةَ الشَّهْرِ القَادِمِ، وَسَتُقَدِّمُ اللَّجْنَةُ الأُمَمِيَّةُ تَوْصِيَاتِهَا إِلَى الأَمِينِ العَامِ قَبْلَ ذَلِكَ المَوْعِدِ.	The Security Council will meet to discuss the issue at the end of next month, and the UN Committee will submit its recommendations to the Secretary-General before that date.

Note

قَبْلَ/بَعْدَ have diminutive forms (قُبَيْلَ/بُعَيْدَ), which mean 'shortly after' and 'shortly before'. (قُبَيْلَ) is used more often than (بُعَيْدَ):

قُبَيْلَ نِهَايَةِ المُبَارَاةِ، أَحْرَزَ اللَّاعِبُ الجَزَائِرِيُّ هَدَفَ الفَوْزِ لِفَرِيقِهِ.
Toward the end of the match, the Algerian player scored the winning goal for his team.

اِسْتَيْقَظْتُ مِنْ نَوْمِي قُبَيْلَ شُرُوقِ الشَّمْسِ.
I awoke just before sunrise.

Locative adverbs 151

بَعْدَ / قَبْلَ *in fixed expressions*

English	Arabic	Meaning	Expression
The book fair will begin after tomorrow.	سَتَبْدَأُ فَعَالِيَّاتُ مَعْرِضِ الكُتُبِ بَعْدَ غَدٍ.	after tomorrow	بَعْدَ غَدٍ
Errors no longer allowed.	الخَطَأُ لَمْ يَعُدْ مَسْمُوحًا بَعْدَ الآنَ.	no longer	بَعْدَ الآنَ
After their separation, she decided not to see him anymore.	بَعْدَ انْفِصَالِهِمَا، قَرَّرَتْ أَلَّا تَرَاهُ بَعْدَ اليَوْمَ.	anymore	بَعْدَ اليَوْمِ
I will go out with my sister in the afternoon to shop.	سَأَخْرُجُ مَعَ أُخْتِي بَعْدَ الظُّهْرِ لِلتَّسَوُّقِ.	afternoon	بَعْدَ الظُّهْرِ
The global food crisis is worsening day by day.	تَتَفَاقَمُ أَزْمَةُ الغِذَاءِ العَالَمِيَّةُ يَوْمًا بَعْدَ يَوْمٍ.	day by day	يَوْمًا بَعْدَ يَوْمٍ
The ruling party succeeded in the parliamentary elections and later formed the government.	نَجَحَ الحِزْبُ الحَاكِمُ فِي الإنْتِخَابَاتِ البَرْلَمَانِيَّةِ، وَفِيمَا بَعْدُ قَامَ بِتَشْكِيلِ الحُكُومَةِ.	later	فِيمَا بَعْدُ
Finally, after a long wait, Egypt obtained a loan from the International Monetary Fund.	أَخِيرًا وبَعْدَ طُولِ انْتِظَارٍ، حَصَلَتْ مِصْرُ عَلَى قَرْضٍ مِنْ صُنْدُوقِ النَّقْدِ الدَّوْلِيِّ.	after a long wait	بَعْدَ طُولِ انْتِظَارٍ

بَعْدَ can join pronoun suffixes as follows:

بَعْدَهُمَا	بَعْدَ + هُمَا		بَعْدِي	بَعْدَ + أَنَا
بَعْدَنَا	بَعْدَ + نَحْنُ		بَعْدَكَ	بَعْدَ + أَنْتَ
بَعْدَكُمْ	بَعْدَ + أَنْتُمْ		بَعْدَكِ	بَعْدَ + أَنْتِ
بَعْدَكُنَّ	بَعْدَ + أَنْتُنَّ		بَعْدَهُ	بَعْدَ + هُوَ
بَعْدَهُمْ	بَعْدَ + هُمْ		بَعْدَهَا	بَعْدَ + هِيَ
بَعْدَهُنَّ	بَعْدَ + هُنَّ		بَعْدَكُمَا	بَعْدَ + أَنْتُمَا

قَبْلَ can join pronoun suffixes as follows:

قَبْلَهُمَا	قَبْلَ + هُمَا		قَبْلِي	قَبْلَ + أَنَا
قَبْلَنَا	قَبْلَ + نَحْنُ		قَبْلَكَ	قَبْلَ + أَنْتَ
قَبْلَكُمْ	قَبْلَ + أَنْتُمْ		قَبْلَكِ	قَبْلَ + أَنْتِ
قَبْلَكُنَّ	قَبْلَ + أَنْتُنَّ		قَبْلَهُ	قَبْلَ + هُوَ
قَبْلَهُمْ	قَبْلَ + هُمْ		قَبْلَهَا	قَبْلَ + هِيَ
قَبْلَهُنَّ	قَبْلَ + هُنَّ		قَبْلَكُمَا	قَبْلَ + أَنْتُمَا

خِلَالَ

خِلَالَ means 'within' or 'during' when it is used as an adverb of time, and it means 'through' when it is used as an adverb of place:

خِلَالَ الإِجْتِمَاعِ، اتَّفَقَ الرَّئِيسَانِ عَلَى عَدَدٍ مِنَ المَشْرُوعَاتِ المُشْتَرَكَةِ.	During the meeting, the presidents agreed on a number of joint projects.
خِلَالَ الحَرْبِ العَالَمِيَّةِ الثَّانِيَةِ أَلْقَى الأَمْرِيكِيُّونَ قُنْبُلَتَيْنِ ذَرِّيَّتَيْنِ عَلَى مَدِينَتَيّ هِيرُوشِيمَا وَنَجَازَاكِي.	During the Second World War, the Americans dropped two atomic bombs on the cities of Hiroshima and Nagasaki.
تَمَّ القَبْضُ عَلَى المُجْرِمِ خِلَالَ مُحَاوَلَةِ الهَرَبِ مِنَ الشُّرْطَةِ.	The criminal was arrested during an attempt to escape from the police.
تَوَغَّلَ السَّائِحُونَ خِلَالَ غَابَاتِ الأَمَازُون الكَثِيفَةِ.	Tourists ventured through the dense Amazon forests.

خِلَالَ can be preceded by (مِنْ) to make the expressions (مِنْ خِلَالِ), which means 'through', 'via' or 'by means of':

تُخَطِّطُ الحُكُومَةُ لِدَعْمِ المَصَانِعِ صَغِيرَةِ الحَجْمِ مِنْ خِلَالِ إِقَامَةِ مَعَارِضَ دَوْلِيَّةٍ تُسَاعِدُهَا عَلَى تَسْوِيقِ مُنْتَجَاتِهَا فِي الخَارِجِ.	The government plans to support small-scale factories by setting up international exhibitions to help market their products abroad.
يُرِيدُ الشَّعْبُ تَغْيِيرَ الرَّئِيسِ مِنْ خِلَالِ صَنَادِيقِ الاِقْتِرَاعِ.	The people want to change the president through the ballot box.
تَمَّ تَشْدِيدُ الضَّغْطِ الأَمْرِيكِيِّ عَلَى الحُكُومَةِ الإِيرَانِيَّةِ مِنْ خِلَالِ فَرْضِ عُقُوبَاتٍ اِقْتِصَادِيَّةٍ جَدِيدَةٍ.	US pressure on the Iranian government has been tightened by new economic sanctions.
تَسْعَى لِيبْيَا إِلَى تَطْوِيرِ صِنَاعَةِ الغَازِ مِنْ خِلَالِ إِبْرَامِ عُقُودٍ مَعَ شَرِكَاتٍ عَالَمِيَّةٍ لِرَفْعِ مُعَدَّلِ الإِنْتَاجِ وَالتَّصْدِيرِ.	Libya seeks to develop the gas industry through the conclusion of contracts with international companies to raise the rate of production and export.

خِلَالَ can be preceded by (فِي) to make the expressions (فِي خِلَالِ), which means 'during' or 'within':

اِرْتَفَعَ مُعَدَّلُ التَّضَخُّمِ بِشَكْلٍ كَبِيرٍ فِي خِلَالِ العَامِ المَاضِي.	The rate of inflation rose significantly during the past year.
تَمَّتْ كِتَابَةُ التَّقْرِيرِ فِي خِلَالِ يَوْمَيْنِ كَمَا طَلَبَ المُدِيرُ.	The report was written within two days as requested by the manager.

Locative adverbs 153

خِلالَ can join pronoun suffixes, as follows:

خِلالَهُمَا	خِلالَ + هُمَا		خِلالِي	خِلالَ + أَنَا
خِلالَنَا	خِلالَ + نَحْنُ		خِلالَكَ	خِلالَ + أَنْتَ
خِلالَكُمْ	خِلالَ + أَنْتُمْ		خِلالَكِ	خِلالَ + أَنْتِ
خِلالَكُنَّ	خِلالَ + أَنْتُنَّ		خِلالَهُ	خِلالَ + هُوَ
خِلالَهُمْ	خِلالَ + هُمْ		خِلالَهَا	خِلالَ + هِيَ
خِلالَهُنَّ	خِلالَ + هُنَّ		خِلالَكُمَا	خِلالَ + أَنْتُمَا

قُرْبَ

قُرْبَ means 'near' or 'close to', and it can be used in both spatial and temporal contexts:

تَمَرْكَزَتْ قُوَّاتُ الأَمْنِ قُرْبَ المَطَارِ وَالأَمَاكِنِ الحَيَوِيَّةِ الأُخْرَى فِي العَاصِمَةِ.	Security forces are stationed near the airport and other vital locations in the capital.
تَزْخَرُ الأَسْوَاقُ بِالمَوَادِ الغِذَائِيَّةِ قُرْبَ حُلُولِ شَهْرِ رَمَضَانَ المُبَارَكِ.	The markets are full of food as Ramadan approaches.
سَقَطَتْ عِدَّةُ قَذَائِفَ قُرْبَ قَاعِدَةٍ أَمرِيكِيَّةٍ فِي العِرَاقِ، مِمَّا رَفَعَ مُسْتَوَى التَّأَهُّبِ لَدَى القُوَّاتِ.	Several shells landed near an American base in Iraq, raising the alert level of the troops.
تَمَّ الإِعْلَانُ عَنْ كَثِيرٍ مِنَ الحَفَلَاتِ وَالأَنْشِطَةِ التَّرْفِيهِيَّةِ قُرْبَ انْتِهَاءِ العَامِ.	Many concerts and entertainment activities were announced close to the end of the year.

قُرْبَ can be preceded by (مَعَ) to make (مَعَ قُرْبِ), which means 'with the approach of' or 'with the advent of'. This structure is used in temporal contexts, and it is often followed by a certain event:

مَعَ قُرْبِ الإِنْتِخَابَاتِ البَرْلَمَانِيَّةِ يَتَصَاعَدُ الحِرَاكُ فِي صُفُوفِ المُعَارَضَةِ.	With parliamentary elections nearing, opposition activities are rising.
مَعَ قُرْبِ حُلُولِ الأَعْيَادِ، قَرَّرَتِ الحُكُومَةُ صَرْفَ زِيَادَةٍ عَلَى الرَّوَاتِبِ.	With holidays nearing, the government decided to give a raise on salaries.
مَعَ قُرْبِ انْطِلَاقِ مَهْرَجَانِ الجُونَةِ السِّينَمَائِيِّ، تَوَافَدَ السِّينَمَائِيُونَ وَالصَّحَفِيُّونَ إِلَى المَدِينَةِ السَّاحِلِيَّةِ الجَمِيلَةِ.	With the imminent launch of the El Gouna Film Festival, filmmakers and journalists flock to the beautiful coastal city.
مَعَ قُرْبِ زِيَارَةِ الوَزِيرِ، اجْتَمَعَ المُدَرَاءُ لِإِكْمَالِ التَّحْضِيرَاتِ.	With the minister's looming visit, directors met to complete preparations.

154 Locative adverbs

قُرْبَ can be preceded by (عَنْ) to make (عَنْ قُرْبٍ), which means 'closely'. This structure is used in spatial contexts:

تَابَعَ مُعْظَمُ المِصْرِيِّينَ أَحْدَاثَ الثَّوْرَةِ عَنْ قُرْبٍ.	Most Egyptians followed the events of the revolution closely.
السِّيَاسِيُّ النَّاجِحُ هُوَ الَّذِي يَعْرِفُ شَعْبَهُ عَنْ قُرْبٍ.	It is the successful politician who knows his people closely.
مَطْلُوبٌ مِنَ البَاحِثِ أَنْ يَعْرِفَ الظَّاهِرَةَ الَّتِي يَدْرُسُهَا عَنْ قُرْبٍ.	The researcher is required to know the phenomenon that he is studying closely.
تَدَرَّبَ المُجَنَّدُونَ الجُدُدُ عَلَى إِطْلَاقِ النَّارِ عَنْ قُرْبٍ.	New recruits were trained to shoot from a near distance.

قُرْبَ is used in the construction (بِالقُرْبِ مِنْ), which means 'near' or 'in the vicinity of'. This structure is used in spatial contexts:

تَمَّ الكَشْفُ عَنْ مَقْبَرَةٍ فِرْعَوْنِيَّةٍ بِالقُرْبِ مِنْ مِنْطَقَةِ أَهْرَامَاتِ الجِيزَةِ.	A pharaonic tomb was discovered near the pyramids of Giza.
سُمِعَ دَوِيُّ انْفِجَارٍ فِي وَسَطِ العَاصِمَةِ كَابُول بِالقُرْبِ مِنْ وَزَارَةِ الاتِّصَالَاتِ الأَفْغَانِيَّةِ.	An explosion was heard in the center of Kabul near the Afghan Ministry of Communications.
تَجَمَّعَ المُتَظَاهِرُونَ بِالقُرْبِ مِنْ مَقَرِّ قِيَادَةِ الجَيْشِ.	Demonstrators gathered near the army's headquarters.
تَقَعُ القَرْيَةُ بِعُمْقِ الجِبَالِ وَبِالقُرْبِ مِنْ الحُدُودِ الجَنُوبِيَّةِ.	The village lies deep in the mountains near the southern borders.

قُرْبَ can join pronoun suffixes, as follows:

قُرْبَهُمَا	قُرْبَ + هُمَا		قُرْبِي	قُرْبَ + أَنَا
قُرْبَنَا	قُرْبَ + نَحْنُ		قُرْبَكَ	قُرْبَ + أَنْتَ
قُرْبَكُمْ	قُرْبَ + أَنْتُمْ		قُرْبَكِ	قُرْبَ + أَنْتِ
قُرْبَكُنَّ	قُرْبَ + أَنْتُنَّ		قُرْبَهُ	قُرْبَ + هُوَ
قُرْبَهُمْ	قُرْبَ + هُمْ		قُرْبَهَا	قُرْبَ + هِيَ
قُرْبَهُنَّ	قُرْبَ + هُنَّ		قُرْبَكُمَا	قُرْبَ + أَنْتُمَا

نَحْوَ

نَحْوَ means 'around' in temporal contexts and 'toward' in spatial contexts, and it can be used figuratively:

Locative adverbs

تَسْعى جَميعُ الأطْرافِ لإحْرازِ تَقَدُّم نَحْوَ السَّلامِ العادِلِ والشَّامِلِ في المِنْطَقَةِ.	All parties seek to make progress toward just and comprehensive peace in the region.
يَبْدُو أَنَّ الجَميعَ سائِرُونَ نَحْوَ الهَدَفِ بِشَكْلٍ دَقيقٍ وَفَعّالٍ.	It seems that everyone is moving toward the goal accurately and effectively.
أَبْحَرَتِ السَّفينَةُ نَحْوَ الشَّواطِئِ الصّومالِيَّةِ مُحَمَّلَةً بِالمُساعَداتِ الإنْسانِيَّةِ.	The ship sailed toward the Somali shores laden with humanitarian aid.

نَحْوَ means 'toward' in spatial contexts, and it can be used figuratively in contexts of expressing attitudes:

لا يُمْكِنُني أَنْ أَتَجاهَلَ شُعُوري نَحْوَ هذِهِ المُشْكِلَةِ.	I cannot ignore my feelings about this problem.
تَوَجَّهَ الحُجّاجُ نَحْوَ عَرَفاتٍ.	The pilgrims went to Arafat.
تَتَوَجَّهُ سِياساتُ الصّينِ الإقْتِصادِيَّةُ نَحْوَ إفريقيا.	China's economic policies are geared toward Africa.
تَتَطَلَّعُ الشُّعُوبُ المَقْمُوعَةُ نَحْوَ الدّيمُوقْراطِيَّةِ وَالتَّغييرِ.	Repressed peoples look forward to democracy and change.

نَحْوَ can be preceded by several prepositions and other locative adverbs:

اِسْتَمَرَّتِ المُقابَلَةُ لِنَحْوِ ساعَتَيْنِ.	The interview lasted around two hours.
قَبْلَ نَحْوِ أُسْبُوعَيْنِ، أَجْرَتِ الوُفُودُ مُحادَثاتٍ سِرِّيَّةً فِي بْرُوكْسِل.	About two weeks ago, delegations held secret talks in Brussels.
تَمَّ الإعْدادُ لِعَرْضِ المَسْرَحِيَّةِ في لُبْنانَ مُنْذُ نَحْوِ شَهْرَيْنِ.	The play was planned in Lebanon about two months ago.
تَمَّ اِنْتِخابُ رَئيسٍ لِلْحُكومَةِ بَعْدَ نَحْوِ سَنَتَيْنِ مِنَ الأَزْمَةِ السِّياسِيَّةِ.	A prime minister was elected after nearly two years of political crisis.

Note

نَحْوَ is commonly used in the sense of 'around' or 'approximately':

شَهَدَ الحَفْلُ نَحْوَ أَلْفِ شَخْصٍ.

The party was witnessed by about a thousand people.

لِلأديبِ نَحْوَ عِشْرينَ رِوايَةً وَتِسْعينَ قِصَّةً قَصيرَةً.

The author has about 20 novels and ninety short stories.

Note

نَحْوَ is also commonly used in the sense of 'in a way':

اِنْطَلَقَتِ التَّظَاهُرَاتُ عَلَى نَحْوٍ مُفَاجِئٍ.
Demonstrations began suddenly.

تَتَصَاعَدُ الرُّوحُ الوَطَنِيَّةُ عَلَى نَحْوٍ كَبِيرٍ فِي الأَزَمَاتِ.
The national spirit largely intensifies in crisis.

نَحْوَ can join pronoun suffixes as follows:

نَحْوَهُمَا	نَحْوَ + هُمَا		نَحْوِي	نَحْوَ + أَنَا
نَحْوَنَا	نَحْوَ + نَحْنُ		نَحْوَكَ	نَحْوَ + أَنْتَ
نَحْوَكُمْ	نَحْوَ + أَنْتُمْ		نَحْوَكِ	نَحْوَ + أَنْتِ
نَحْوَكُنَّ	نَحْوَ + أَنْتُنَّ		نَحْوَهُ	نَحْوَ + هُوَ
نَحْوَهُمْ	نَحْوَ + هُمْ		نَحْوَهَا	نَحْوَ + هِيَ
نَحْوَهُنَّ	نَحْوَ + هُنَّ		نَحْوَكُمَا	نَحْوَ + أَنْتُمَا

Adverbs of time

As stated earlier, adverbs of time (ظُرُوفُ الزَّمَانِ) answer the question, 'When?', and they can be classified into specific and vague. Adverbs of time can also be classified into inflected (مُعْرَب), and in this case, they will always be in the accusative case (مَنْصُوب) and uninflected (مَبْنِي), and in this case, they will have fixed final vowel. Inflected adverbs of time (ظُرُوفُ الزَّمَانِ المُعْرَبَةُ) are based on nouns that refer to time, for example, days of the week, months, seasons, periods of time and so on (سَاعَةً، الرَّبِيعَ، الخَرِيفَ).

اِنْتَظَرْتُكَ سَاعَةً.	I waited for you for an hour.
تَزْدَهِرُ الحَدِيقَةُ رَبِيعًا وَتَتَسَاقَطُ أَوْرَاقُ الأَشْجَارِ خَرِيفًا.	The garden blooms in Spring and the leaves fall in Autumn.

Uninflected adverbs of time (ظُرُوفُ الزَّمَانِ المَبْنِيَّةُ) have fixed voweling, for example, (أَبَدًا، إِذَا، الآنَ، أَمْسِ، أَيَّانَ، بَيْنَا، بَيْنَمَا، حِينَ، رَيْثَ، عَوْضُ، قَطَّ، لَمَّا، مَتَى).

In this section, the most important adverbs of time that function as semi-prepositions are explained.

إِبَّانَ

إِبَّانَ is an adverb of time that means 'while', and it is often followed by an event:

تَزِيدُ مَوْجَاتُ النُّزُوحِ إِبَّانَ الحُرُوبِ.	Waves of displacement increase during wars.

Locative adverbs 157

هَاجَرَ الشَّاعِرُ مِنْ بَلَدِهِ إبَّانَ الحَرْبِ الأَهْلِيَّةِ.	The poet emigrated from his country during the civil war.
أَبْحَرَتِ السَّفِينَةُ إبَّانَ العَاصِفَةِ.	The ship sailed during the storm.
تَحْدُثُ اِعْتِقَالَاتٌ كَثِيرَةٌ إبَّانَ الاِنْقِلَابَاتِ العَسْكَرِيَّةِ.	Many arrests happen during military coups.

أَبَدَ

أَبَدَ is an adverb of time that means 'eternity'. It is originally a noun, but it can be used as an adverb of time when it comes as the first word of iḍāfa, and the second word of iḍāfa is usually a noun that refers to a long period.

تَبْدُو المَعَابِدُ الفِرْعَونِيَّةُ كَأَنَّهَا سَتَبْقَى أَبَدَ الدَّهْرِ.	Pharaonic temples look as if they would last forever.
سَنَبْقَى فِي أَوْطَانِنَا أَبَدَ الآبِدِينَ.	We will remain in our home forever and ever.
سَنَظَلُّ أَبَدَ الدَّهْرِ أَوْفِيَاءَ لِعُهُودِنَا.	We will forever be faithful to our promises.
يَذْكُرُ النَّاسُ العُظَمَاءَ وَالزُّعَمَاءَ إلَى أَبَدِ الآبِدِينَ.	People will remember great people and leaders for ever and ever.

أَثْنَاءَ

أَثْنَاءَ means 'while' and 'during'. It is used in the same way as (خِلَالَ), except that it is not used as an adverb of place:

قَاطَعَتْنِي عِدَّةَ مَرَّاتٍ أَثْنَاءَ إلْقَاءِ مُحَاضَرَتِي.	She interrupted me several times during my lecture.
لَا يُمْكِنُكَ الخُرُوجُ مِنَ المَسْرَحِ أَثْنَاءَ العَرْضِ.	You cannot get out of the theater during the show.
أَثْنَاءَ الحَرْبِ الأَهْلِيَّةِ فَقَدَ الآلَافُ أَرْوَاحَهُمْ وَمُمْتَلَكَاتِهِمْ.	During the civil war, thousands lost their lives and property.
ضَلَّ المُغَامِرُونَ طَرِيقَهُمْ أَثْنَاءَ صُعُودِ الجَبَلِ وَتَمَّ إنْقَاذُهُم بِاسْتِخْدَامِ المِرْوَحِيَّاتِ.	The adventurers lost their way as they climbed the mountain and were rescued by helicopters.

أَثْنَاءَ can be followed by (ذَلِكَ) to make (أَثْنَاءَ ذَلِكَ), which means 'during this' or 'meanwhile':

حَكَمَ الرَّئِيسُ لِمُدَّةِ ثَلَاثِينَ سَنَةً وَأَثْنَاءَ ذَلِكَ تَدَهْوَرَ الوَضْعُ الاِقْتِصَادِيُّ وَالسِّيَاسِيُّ.	The president ruled for thirty years, and during that time the economic and political situation deteriorated.

عِشْتُ فِي الغَرْبِ سَنَوَاتٍ طَوِيلَةً وَأَثْنَاءَ ذَلِكَ تَغَيَّرَ وَطَنِي إِلَى حَدٍّ كَبِيرٍ.	I lived in the West for many years, and during that time my homeland changed a lot.
كَانَ سَائِرًا مَعَ صَدِيقِهِ عَلَى حَافَّةِ النَّهْرِ فَتَعَثَّرَ أَثْنَاءَ ذَلِكَ وَكَادَ أَنْ يَسْقُطَ.	He was walking with his friend on the river bank, and he stumbled during that and almost fell.
اسْتَمَرَّتِ الخِلَافَاتُ بَيْنَ البَلَدَيْنِ لِسَنَوَاتٍ طَوِيلَةٍ وَأَثْنَاءَ ذَلِكَ نَشَبَتْ بَيْنَهُمَا عِدَّةُ نِزَاعَاتٍ وَحُرُوبٍ.	Disagreements between the two countries have continued for many years, during which many disputes and wars broke out between them.

إِثْرَ

إِثْرَ is an adverb of time that means 'after' or 'following'. It can be followed by a noun indicating an event or an action or a verb:

انْتَقَلَ إِلَى أَمْرِيكَا إِثْرَ نُشُوبِ الحَرْبِ فِي بِلَادِهِ.	He moved to the US after the outbreak of war in his country.
تَمَّ إِعْلَانُ قِيَامِ الجُمْهُورِيَّةِ فِي مِصْرَ إِثْرَ قِيَامِ ثَوْرَةِ عَامِ 1952.	The republic was proclaimed in Egypt following the revolution of 1952.
إِثْرَ لِقَائِهِمْ بِالأَمِينِ العَامِ لِلْأُمَمِ المُتَّحِدَةِ، تَعَهَّدَ القَادَةُ بِزِيَادَةِ التَّبَرُّعَاتِ لِتَحْسِينِ أَوْضَاعِ اللَّاجِئِينَ فِي المِنْطَقَةِ.	Following their meeting with the UN Secretary-General, leaders pledged to increase donations to improve the situation of refugees in the region.
إِثْرَ الحَرْبِ ارْتَفَعَتْ أَسْعَارُ النَّفْطِ فِي السُّوقِ العَالَمِيَّةِ.	After the war, oil prices rose in the international market.

آنَاءَ

آنَاءَ means 'while' and 'during'. It literally means 'hours', and it usually collocates with the noun (اللَّيْلِ). It is used in the same way as (خِلَالَ), except that it is not used as an adverb of place.

تَوَاصَلَ القَصْفُ عَلَى القَرْيَةِ آنَاءَ اللَّيْلِ وَأَطْرَافَ النَّهَارِ.	The shelling continues on the village, night and day.
أُحِبُّ السَّهَرَ آنَاءَ اللَّيْلِ لِلْقِرَاءَةِ وَالكِتَابَةِ.	I love to spend the night reading and writing.

غَدَاةَ

غَدَاةَ means 'in the early morning' and 'tomorrow'. It is used to refer to the day after a certain event. It is also used to mean 'after' or 'following':

عَقَدَ الرُّؤَسَاءُ اجْتِمَاعًا سِرِّيًّا غَدَاةَ افْتِتَاحِ القِمَّةِ.	The presidents held a secret meeting after the opening of the summit.

اِسْتَقَالَ رَئِيسُ المَجْلِسِ العَسْكَرِيِّ غَدَاةَ الِاحْتِجَاجَاتِ الشَّعْبِيَّةِ الوَاسِعَةِ.	The head of the military council resigned following mass popular protests.
تَمَّ سَحْبُ جَمِيعِ القُوَّاتِ العَسْكَرِيَّةِ الأَجْنَبِيَّةِ مِنَ العِرَاقِ غَدَاةَ اِنْتِهَاءِ مَهَامِهَا هُنَاكَ.	All foreign military forces were withdrawn from Iraq after their duties ended.
تَمَّ إِعْلَانُ تَأْسِيسِ الجُمْهُورِيَّةِ الإِسْلَامِيَّةِ فِي إِيرَانَ غَدَاةَ سُقُوطِ الشَّاهِ.	The establishment of the Islamic Republic in Iran was declared after the fall of the shah.

It should be noted here that these are not all the adverbs of time in Arabic. There are many adverbs of time that have not been included here, for example, (قَطُّ، أَيَّانَ، إِذْ، أَنَّى، مَتَى، أَمْسِ، ثَمَّ، غَدَاً، لَمَّا،), among others, as they do not function as semi-prepositions, and therefore, they fall outside the scope of this publication.

Adverbs of place

Adverbs of place (ظُرُوفُ المَكَانِ) answer the question, 'Where?', and they can be classified into specific and vague. Adverbs of place can also be classified into inflected (مُعْرَب), and in this case, they will always be in the accusative case (مَنْصُوب) and uninflected (مَبْنِيّ), and in this case, they will have fixed final vowel. Inflected adverbs of place (ظُرُوفُ المَكَانِ المُعْرَبَة) are based on nouns that refer to places, for example, directions, names of places and so on.

سَنُسَافِرُ جَنُوبًا فِي عُطْلَةِ الشِّتَاءِ.	We will travel south in the winter break.
مَشَيْتُ مَيْلًا.	I walked for a mile.

Uninflected adverbs of time (ظُرُوفُ المَكَانِ المَبْنِيَّة) have fixed voweling, for example, (أَمَامَ، فَوْقَ، تَحْتَ، وَرَاءَ، دُونَ، عَبْرَ).

In this section, the most important adverbs of place that function as semi-prepositions are explained.

أَمَامَ / قُدَّامَ

أَمَامَ and قُدَّامَ are synonyms, and they are both adverbs of place that mean 'in front of' or 'before':

تَحَدَّثَ رَئِيسُ الوُزَرَاءِ أَمَامَ الصَّحَفِيِّينَ.	The prime minister spoke to reporters.
قَابَلْتُ أَصْدِقَائِي أَمَامَ المَكْتَبَةِ المَرْكَزِيَّةِ.	I met my friends in front of the central library.
وَجَدْتُ قُدَّامِي بَابًا يُوصِلُ إِلَى مَمَرٍّ سِرِّيٍّ.	I found a door in front of me, and it was connected to a secret passage.

Locative adverbs

تَجَمَّعَ المُتَظاهِرُونَ أَمامَ السَّفارَةِ العِراقِيَّةِ فِي لَنْدَن.	Demonstrators gathered outside the Iraqi Embassy in London.

أَمامَ and قُدّامَ can be used figuratively:

هذَا الشّابُ الطَّمُوحُ أَمامَهُ مُسْتَقْبَلٌ باهِرٌ.	This ambitious young man has a brilliant future ahead of him.
لا تَعرِفُ الحُكُومَةُ كَيْفَ تَتَصَرَّفُ أَمامَ العَجْزِ المالِيِّ الكَبِيرِ.	The government does not know how to act in the face of a large fiscal deficit.
تَوَقَّفْتُ طَوِيلًا أَمامَ مُشْكِلَتِي.	I stopped long in front of my problem.
أَمامَ القِمَّةِ العَرَبِيَّةِ أَهَمُّ القَضايا المِحْوَرِيَّةِ فِي المِنْطَقَةِ.	The Arab summit will deal with the most important issue in the region.

أَمامَ can be followed by pronoun suffixes, as follows:

أَمامَ + هُما	أَمامَهُما		أَمامِي	أَمامَ + أَنا
أَمامَ + نَحْنُ	أَمامَنا		أَمامَكَ	أَمامَ + أَنْتَ
أَمامَ + أَنْتُمْ	أَمامَكُمْ		أَمامَكِ	أَمامَ + أَنْتِ
أَمامَ + أَنْتُنَّ	أَمامَكُنَّ		أَمامَهُ	أَمامَ + هُوَ
أَمامَ + هُمْ	أَمامَهُمْ		أَمامَها	أَمامَ + هِيَ
أَمامَ + هُنَّ	أَمامَهُنَّ		أَمامَكُما	أَمامَ + أَنْتُما

قُدّامَ can be followed by pronoun suffixes, as follows:

قُدّامَ + هُما	قُدّامَهُما		قُدّامِي	قُدّامَ + أَنا
قُدّامَ + نَحْنُ	قُدّامَنا		قُدّامَكَ	قُدّامَ + أَنْتَ
قُدّامَ + أَنْتُمْ	قُدّامَكُمْ		قُدّامَكِ	قُدّامَ + أَنْتِ
قُدّامَ + أَنْتُنَّ	قُدّامَكُنَّ		قُدّامَهُ	قُدّامَ + هُوَ
قُدّامَ + هُمْ	قُدّامَهُمْ		قُدّامَها	قُدّامَ + هِيَ
قُدّامَ + هُنَّ	قُدّامَهُنَّ		قُدّامَكُما	قُدّامَ + أَنْتُما

خَلْفَ / وَراءَ

خَلْفَ and وَراءَ are synonyms, and they are both adverbs of place that mean 'behind':

قَضى السّارِقُ أَرْبَعَ سَنَواتٍ خَلْفَ القُضْبانِ.	The thief spent four years behind bars.

Locative adverbs

لَا أَعْرِفُ مَاذَا يُوجَدُ خَلْفَ أَسْوَارِ هَذِهِ البِنَايَةِ.	I do not know what is behind the walls of this building.
يُحِبُّ المُؤَلِّفُ أَنْ يَجْلِسَ وَرَاءَ الكَوَالِيسِ أَثْنَاءَ عَرْضِ المَسْرَحِيَّةِ.	The author likes to sit behind the scenes during the show.
لَا تَضَعِ الكُرْسِيَّ وَرَاءَ البَابِ حَتَّى لَا يَصْطَدِمَ بِهِ أَحَدٌ.	Do not put the chair behind the door so that no one hits it.

خَلْفَ and وَرَاءَ can be used figuratively. In the selected corpus, it has been noted that (وَرَاءَ) is used in more figurative contexts than in the literal sense:

تَقِفُ الحُكُومَةُ وَرَاءَ الأَزْمَةِ الحَالِيَّةِ وَعَلَيْهَا أَنْ تَتَحَمَّلَ مَسْؤُولِيَّةَ حَلِّهَا.	The government stands behind the current crisis and must take responsibility for resolving it.
وَرَاءَ سُلُوكِ الدِّبْلُومَاسِيِّ أَسْبَابٌ وَدَوَافِعُ عَدِيدَةٌ.	There are many reasons and motivations behind the diplomat's behavior.
هَلْ فَهِمْتَ المَعَانِي الكَامِنَةَ وَرَاءَ أَبْيَاتِ القَصِيدَةِ؟	Did you understand the meanings behind the verses of the poem?
وَقَفَتِ القُوَّاتُ المُسَلَّحَةُ خَلْفَ قَائِدِهَا فِي مُوَاجَهَةِ الرَّئِيسِ.	The armed forces stood behind its leader in the face of the president.

خَلْفَ can be followed by pronoun suffixes, as follows:

خَلْفَهُمَا	خَلْفَ + هُمَا		خَلْفِي	خَلْفَ + أَنَا
خَلْفَنَا	خَلْفَ + نَحْنُ		خَلْفَكَ	خَلْفَ + أَنْتَ
خَلْفَكُمْ	خَلْفَ + أَنْتُمْ		خَلْفَكِ	خَلْفَ + أَنْتِ
خَلْفَكُنَّ	خَلْفَ + أَنْتُنَّ		خَلْفَهُ	خَلْفَ + هُوَ
خَلْفَهُمْ	خَلْفَ + هُمْ		خَلْفَهَا	خَلْفَ + هِيَ
خَلْفَهُنَّ	خَلْفَ + هُنَّ		خَلْفَكُمَا	خَلْفَ + أَنْتُمَا

وَرَاءَ can be followed by pronoun suffixes, as follows:

وَرَاءَهُمَا	وَرَاءَ + هُمَا		ورائي	وَرَاءَ + أَنَا
وَرَاءَنَا	وَرَاءَ + نَحْنُ		وَرَاءَكَ	وَرَاءَ + أَنْتَ
وَرَاءَكُمْ	وَرَاءَ + أَنْتُمْ		وَرَاءَكِ	وَرَاءَ + أَنْتِ
وَرَاءَكُنَّ	وَرَاءَ + أَنْتُنَّ		وَرَاءَهُ	وَرَاءَ + هُوَ
وَرَاءَهُمْ	وَرَاءَ + هُمْ		وَرَاءَهَا	وَرَاءَ + هِيَ
وَرَاءَهُنَّ	وَرَاءَ + هُنَّ		وَرَاءَكُمَا	وَرَاءَ + أَنْتُمَا

تَحْتَ

تَحْتَ means 'below' and 'under', and it can be used figuratively:

اِخْتَبَأَتِ القِطَّةُ تَحْتَ الطَّاوِلَةِ.	The cat hid under the table.
وَافَقَ المُوَظَّفُ عَلَى القَرَارِ تَحْتَ ضَغْطٍ مِنْ رَئِيسِهِ.	The employee accepted the decision under pressure from his boss.
اِجْتَمَعَ المُوَاطِنُونَ تَحْتَ شِعَارِ وِحْدَةِ الأَدْيَانِ.	Citizens met under the banner of unity of religions.
اِنْتَشَرَتْ قُوَّاتُ الجَيْشِ في الشَّوَارِعِ تَحْتَ ذَرِيعَةِ حِفْظِ الأَمْنِ وَالأَمَانِ.	Army forces were deployed in the streets under the pretext of maintaining safety and security.

تَحْتَ in fixed expressions

تَحْتَ عُنْوَانِ	under the theme of	اِجْتَمَعَتِ الوُفُودُ المُشَارِكَةُ في المُؤْتَمَرِ تَحْتَ عُنْوَانِ إِعَادَةِ إِعْمَارِ العِرَاقِ.	The delegations participating in the conference met under the theme of the reconstruction of Iraq.
تَحْتَ شِعَارِ	under the banner of	تَجَمَّعَ المُعَارِضُونَ تَحْتَ شِعَارِ إِسْقَاطِ النِّظَامِ.	Opponents gathered under the banner of toppling the regime.
تَحْتَ إِشْرَافِ	under the supervision of	تَمَّتِ الإِنْتِخَابَاتُ تَحْتَ إِشْرَافِ القُضَاةِ.	The elections were held under the supervision of the judges.
تَحْتَ وَطْأَةِ	under the brunt of	عَانَى المُوَاطِنُونَ تَحْتَ وَطْأَةِ الأَزْمَةِ الإِقْتِصَادِيَّةِ الطَّاحِنَةِ.	Citizens suffered under the brunt of crushing economic crisis.
تَحْتَ رِعَايَةِ	sponsored by	عُقِدَ المُؤْتَمَرُ تَحْتَ رِعَايَةِ شَرِكَاتِ تَصْنِيعِ السَّيَّارَاتِ المَحَلِّيَّةِ.	The conference was sponsored by local car manufacturers.
تَحْتَ سَيْطَرَةِ	under the control of	تُعْتَبَرُ جَمِيعُ القَنَوَاتِ التِلِفِزِيُونِيَّةِ الرَّسْمِيَّةِ تَحْتَ سَيْطَرَةِ الدَّوْلَةِ.	All state television channels are under the state's control.
تَحْتَ الاِحْتِلَالِ	under occupation	تُحَدِّدُ اِتِّفَاقِيَّةُ جِنِيف وَضْعَ الأَرَاضِي الوَاقِعَةِ تَحْتَ الاِحْتِلَالِ.	The Geneva Convention defines the status of territories under occupation.
تَحْتَ تَأْثِيرِ	under the influence of	تَمَّ التَّصْوِيتُ عَلَى القَرَارِ تَحْتَ تَأْثِيرِ الضَّغْطِ الأَمْرِيكِيِّ.	The resolution was voted under the influence of US pressure.

Locative adverbs 163

تَحْتَ قِيَادَة	under the leadership of	فَازَ حِزْبُ المُعَارَضَة بِالإنْتِخَابَاتِ تَحْتَ قِيَادَةِ رَئِيسِهِ الشَّابِّ.	The opposition party won the election under the leadership of its young president.
تَحْتَ سِتَارِ / غِطَاءِ	under the guise of	قَامَتِ الحُكُومَةُ بِمُصَادَرَةِ أَمْوَالِ الأَغْنِيَاءِ تَحْتَ سِتَارِ مُحَارَبَةِ الفَسَادِ.	The government confiscated the wealth of rich people under the guise of fighting corruption.
تَحْتَ لِوَاءِ / رَايَةِ	under the banner of	اتَّحَدَتْ جَمِيعُ قَبَائِلِ العَرَبِ تَحْتَ رَايَةِ الإسْلَامِ.	All Arab tribes united under the banner of Islam.
تَحْتَ رَحْمَةِ	at the mercy of	يَعِيشُ الفِلَسْطِينِيُونَ تَحْتَ رَحْمَةِ قُوَّاتِ الإحْتِلَالِ الإسْرَائِيلِيِّ.	Palestinians live at the mercy of the Israeli occupation forces.
تَحْتَ ذَرِيعَةِ	under the pretext of	قَمَعَ الرَّئِيسُ جَمِيعَ مُعَارِضِيهِ تَحْتَ ذَرِيعَةِ المَخَاوِفِ الأَمْنِيَّةِ.	The president repressed all his opponents under the pretext of security concerns.
تَحْتَ تَصَرُّفِ	at the disposal of	يَجِبُ أَلَّا تَكُونَ جَمِيعُ مَوَارِدِ الدَّوْلَةِ تَحْتَ تَصَرُّفِ الجَيْشِ.	All state resources must not be at the disposal of the military.
تَحْتَ خَطِّ الفَقْرِ	below the poverty line	يَعِيشُ أَكْثَرُ مِنْ نِصْفِ اليَمَنِيِّينَ تَحْتَ خَطِّ الفَقْرِ.	More than half of Yemenis live below the poverty line.

تَحْتَ can be followed by pronoun suffixes, as follows:

تَحْتَ + أَنَا	تَحْتِي			تَحْتَ + هُمَا	تَحْتَهُمَا
تَحْتَ + أَنْتَ	تَحْتَكَ			تَحْتَ + نَحْنُ	تَحْتَنَا
تَحْتَ + أَنْتِ	تَحْتَكِ			تَحْتَ + أَنْتُمْ	تَحْتَكُمْ
تَحْتَ + هُوَ	تَحْتَهُ			تَحْتَ + أَنْتُنَّ	تَحْتَكُنَّ
تَحْتَ + هِيَ	تَحْتَهَا			تَحْتَ + هُمْ	تَحْتَهُمْ
تَحْتَ + أَنْتُمَا	تَحْتَكُمَا			تَحْتَ + هُنَّ	تَحْتَهُنَّ

فَوْقَ

فَوْقَ means 'over' or 'above', and it can be used figuratively:

إرْتَفَعَتِ الأَعْلَامُ فَوْقَ جَمِيعِ المَبَانِي الحُكُومِيَّةِ.	The flags rose above all government buildings.

Locative adverbs

اِحْتِفَالًا بِالزِّفَافِ، حَمَلَ الشَّبَابُ العَرِيسَ فَوْقَ الأَعْنَاقِ.	In celebration of the wedding, young men carried the groom over the heads.
تَجَمَّعَتِ الطُّيُورُ فَوْقَ فُرُوعِ الأَشْجَارِ.	Birds gathered above the branches of the trees.
تَسَامَى فَوْقَ مُشْكِلَاتِهِ وَاسْتَطَاعَ تَحْقِيقَ النَّجَاحِ.	He overcame his problems and succeeded.

فَوْقَ in fixed expressions

فَوْقَ سِنِّ / عُمْرِ	over the age of	يَنْبَغِي أَنْ يَقُومَ بِالتَّصْوِيتِ كُلُّ مَنْ هُمْ فَوْقَ سِنِّ الثَّامِنَةَ عَشْرَةَ.	All persons over the age of eighteen should vote.
فَوْقَ كُلِّ شَيْءٍ	paramount	قَالَ الرَّئِيسُ فِي خِطَابِهِ إِنَّ مَصْلَحَةَ البِلَادِ وَأَمْنَهَا فَوْقَ كُلِّ شَيْءٍ.	In his speech, the president said that the country's interests and security are paramount.
فَوْقَ ذَلِكَ كُلِّهِ	above all	تَتَمَيَّزُ مُنْتَجَاتُ شَرِكَتِنَا بِالإِبْتِكَارِ وَالتَّمَيُّزِ وَالجَوْدَةِ، وَفَوْقَ ذَلِكَ كُلِّهِ تَتَمَيَّزُ بِالأَسْعَارِ المُنَاسِبَةِ.	The products of our company are characterized by innovation, excellence, quality and, above all, they are characterized by the right prices.
فَوْقَ رُؤُوسِ	over the heads of	حَلَّقَتْ طَائِرَاتُ الجَيْشِ فَوْقَ رُؤُوسِ حَاضِرِي العَرْضِ العَسْكَرِيِّ.	Army aircraft flew over the heads of those attending the military parade.
فَوْقَ أَكْتَافِ	over the shoulders	حُمِلَ المُطْرِبُ فَوْقَ الأَكْتَافِ.	The singer was carried over the shoulders.

فَوْقَ can be followed by pronoun suffixes, as follows:

فَوْقَهُمَا	فَوْقَ + هُمَا	فَوْقِي	فَوْقَ + أَنَا
فَوْقَنَا	فَوْقَ + نَحْنُ	فَوْقَكَ	فَوْقَ + أَنْتَ
فَوْقَكُمْ	فَوْقَ + أَنْتُمْ	فَوْقَكِ	فَوْقَ + أَنْتِ
فَوْقَكُنَّ	فَوْقَ + أَنْتُنَّ	فَوْقَهُ	فَوْقَ + هُوَ
فَوْقَهُمْ	فَوْقَ + هُمْ	فَوْقَهَا	فَوْقَ + هِيَ
فَوْقَهُنَّ	فَوْقَ + هُنَّ	فَوْقَكُمَا	فَوْقَ + أَنْتُمَا

Locative adverbs 165

دَاخِلَ

دَاخِلَ means 'inside', and it can be used figuratively:

تَمَّتْ مُنَاقَشَةُ بُنُودِ القَانُونِ الجَدِيدِ دَاخِلَ البَرْلَمَانِ.	The terms of the new law were discussed within Parliament.
حُبِسَ السَّارِقُ دَاخِلَ قَفَصِ الاتِّهَامِ أَثْنَاءَ المُحَاكَمَةِ.	The thief was locked inside the dock during the trial.
لَا أَعْرِفُ مَاذَا يُوجَدُ دَاخِلَ الصُنْدُوقِ.	I do not know what's inside the box.
يَتَمَتَّعُ كِبَارُ المَسْؤُولِينَ بِالحِمَايَةِ لِأَنَّهُمْ دَاخِلَ النِظَامِ.	Senior officials enjoy protection because they are part of the regime.

دَاخِلَ can be followed by pronoun suffixes, as follows:

دَاخِلَهُمَا	دَاخِلَ + هُمَا		دَاخِلِي	دَاخِلَ + أَنَا
دَاخِلَنَا	دَاخِلَ + نَحْنُ		دَاخِلَكَ	دَاخِلَ + أَنْتَ
دَاخِلَكُمْ	دَاخِلَ + أَنْتُمْ		دَاخِلَكِ	دَاخِلَ + أَنْتِ
دَاخِلَكُنَّ	دَاخِلَ + أَنْتُنَّ		دَاخِلَهُ	دَاخِلَ + هُوَ
دَاخِلَهُمْ	دَاخِلَ + هُمْ		دَاخِلَهَا	دَاخِلَ + هِيَ
دَاخِلَهُنَّ	دَاخِلَ + هُنَّ		دَاخِلَكُمَا	دَاخِلَ + أَنْتُمَا

خَارِجَ

خَارِجَ means 'outside', and it can be used figuratively:

انْتَظَرْتُ المُمَثِّلَ خَارِجَ المَسْرَحِ.	I awaited the actor outside the theater.
بَعْدَ الانْتِخَابَاتِ تَجَمَّعَتِ الأَحْزَابُ الصَّغِيرَةُ خَارِجَ البَرْلَمَانِ.	After the elections, small parties gathered outside Parliament.
هَلْ يُمْكِنُكُمُ التَّفْكِيرُ خَارِجَ الصُنْدُوقِ؟	Can you think outside the box?
أَقَامَ عَلَاقَةً مَعَ امْرَأَةٍ خَارِجَ إِطَارِ الزَّوْجِيَّةِ.	He established a relationship with a woman outside wedlock.

خَارِجَ can be followed by pronoun suffixes, as follows:

خَارِجَهُمَا	خَارِجَ + هُمَا		خَارِجِي	خَارِجَ + أَنَا
خَارِجَنَا	خَارِجَ + نَحْنُ		خَارِجَكَ	خَارِجَ + أَنْتَ
خَارِجَكُمْ	خَارِجَ + أَنْتُمْ		خَارِجَكِ	خَارِجَ + أَنْتِ
خَارِجَكُنَّ	خَارِجَ + أَنْتُنَّ		خَارِجَهُ	خَارِجَ + هُوَ

خَارِجَهُمْ	خَارِجَ + هُمْ		خَارِجَهَا	خَارِجَ + هِيَ
خَارِجَهُنَّ	خَارِجَ + هُنَّ		خَارِجَكُمَا	خَارِجَ + أَنْتُمَا

إِزَاءَ

إِزَاءَ means 'facing' and 'in front of', and it can be used figuratively in the sense of 'toward'. It has been noted that in current media, it is used more figuratively than literally, and it is used often in contexts of expressing attitudes:

نَتَمَنَّى أَنْ يَكُونَ المَوْقِفُ الأَمْرِيكِيُّ إِزَاءَ قَضِيَّةِ السَّلَامِ حِيَادِيًّا.	We hope that the American position on the issue of peace will be neutral.
أَعْلَنَتِ الأُمَمُ المُتَّحِدَةُ عَنْ قَلَقِهَا إِزَاءَ أَوْضَاعِ حُقُوقِ الإِنْسَانِ فِي المِنْطَقَةِ.	The UN has expressed concerns about the human rights situation in the region.
اتَّخَذَتِ الحُكُومَةُ خُطُوَاتٍ جَادَّةً إِزَاءَ تَحْسِينِ الوَضْعِ الاِقْتِصَادِيِّ فِي البِلَادِ.	The government has taken serious steps toward improving the country's economic situation.
الْتَزَمَتِ الحُكُومَةُ الصَّمْتَ إِزَاءَ التَّقَارِيرِ الدَّوْلِيَّةِ الأَخِيرَةِ حَوْلَ القَمْعِ السِّيَاسِيِّ.	The government has been silent about recent international reports on political repression.

إِزَاءَ can be followed by pronoun suffixes; however, it is not used commonly with pronoun suffixes in current media.

تِجَاهَ

تِجَاهَ means 'toward', and it can be used figuratively. Similar to 'إِزَاءَ', it is used often in contexts of expressing attitudes:

قَرَّرَتِ الحُكُومَةُ تَبَنِّي مَوْقِفٍ مُحَافِظٍ تِجَاهَ إِيرَانَ.	The government has decided to adopt a conservative stance toward Iran.
تَطِيرُ الفَرَاشَاتُ تِجَاهَ الضَّوْءِ.	Butterflies fly toward the light.
لَمْ تَتَّخِذْ دُوَلُ المِنْطَقَةِ خُطُوَاتٍ فَعَّالَةً تِجَاهَ إِعَادَةِ إِعْمَارِ العِرَاقِ.	The countries of the region have not taken effective steps toward the reconstruction of Iraq.
لَا تَشْعُرُ الحُكُومَةُ بِالمَسْؤُولِيَّةِ تِجَاهَ الأَزَمَاتِ اليَوْمِيَّةِ الَّتِي يُوَاجِهُهَا المُوَاطِنُونَ وَلَا تَتَدَخَّلُ لِحَلِّهَا.	The government does not feel responsible for the daily crises faced by citizens and does not intervene to resolve them.

تِجَاهَ can be followed by pronoun suffixes, as follows:

تِجَاهَهُمَا	تِجَاهَ + هُمَا		تِجَاهِي	تِجَاهَ + أَنَا
تِجَاهَنَا	تِجَاهَ + نَحْنُ		تِجَاهَكَ	تِجَاهَ + أَنْتَ

Locative adverbs

تِجَاهَكُمْ	تِجَاه + أَنْتُمْ		تِجَاهَكِ	تِجَاه + أَنْتِ
تِجَاهَكُنَّ	تِجَاه + أَنْتُنَّ		تِجَاهَهُ	تِجَاه + هُوَ
تِجَاهَهُمْ	تِجَاه + هُمْ		تِجَاهَهَا	تِجَاه + هِيَ
تِجَاهَهُنَّ	تِجَاه + هُنَّ		تِجَاهَكُمَا	تِجَاه + أَنْتُمَا

جَانِبَ

جَانِبَ means 'beside', and it can be used figuratively:

أَوْقَفْتُ سَيَّارَتِي جَانِبَ الرَّصِيفِ.	I stopped my car beside the pavement.
لَمْ أَجِدْ طَاوِلَةً خَالِيَةً، هَلْ يُمْكِنُنِي أَنْ أَجْلِسَ جَانِبَكَ؟	I could not find a vacant table; can I sit next to you?
وَجَدْتُ الحَقِيبَةَ جَانِبَ السَّيَّارَةِ البَيْضَاءِ.	I found the bag beside the white car.
وَقَفْتُ جَانِبَ صَدِيقِي.	I stood next to my friend.

جَانِبَ in fixed expressions

Producers improve the quality of products as well as reduce their prices.	يَعْمَلُ المُنْتِجُونَ عَلَى تَحْسِينِ جَوْدَةِ المُنْتَجَاتِ إِلَى جَانِبِ تَقْلِيلِ أَسْعَارِهَا.	as well as	إِلَى جَانِبِ
Beside teaching, my colleague works in translation.	بِجَانِبِ التَّدْرِيسِ، يَعْمَلُ زَمِيلِي فِي التَّرْجَمَةِ.	beside	بِجَانِبِ
Support was provided to victims by UN organizations.	تَمَّ تَقْدِيمُ الدَّعْمِ لِلضَّحَايَا مِنْ جَانِبِ مُنَظَّمَاتٍ تَابِعَةٍ لِلْأُمَمِ المُتَّحِدَةِ.	by	مِنْ جَانِبِ
For his part, the minister announced the increase in salaries of employees in the ministry.	مِنْ جَانِبِهِ، أَعْلَنَ الوَزِيرُ عَنْ زِيَادَةِ رَوَاتِبِ العَامِلِينَ فِي الوِزَارَةِ.	for his part	مِنْ جَانِبِهِ
On one side, my friend wants to enhance his skills, and on the other side, he wants to earn some money from his summer vacation work.	مِنْ جَانِبٍ يُرِيدُ صَدِيقِي أَنْ يُعَزِّزَ مَهَارَاتِهِ وَمِنْ جَانِبٍ آخَرَ يُرِيدُ كَسْبَ بَعْضِ المَالِ مِنَ العَمَلِ فِي العُطْلَةِ الصَّيْفِيَّةِ.	on one side, and on the other side	مِنْ جَانِبٍ وَمِنْ جَانِبٍ آخَرَ

168 *Locative adverbs*

جانِبَ can be followed by pronoun suffixes, as follows:

جانِبَهُمَا	جانِبَ + هُمَا		جانِبِي	جانِبَ + أَنَا
جانِبَنَا	جانِبَ + نَحْنُ		جانِبَكَ	جانِبَ + أَنْتَ
جانِبَكُمْ	جانِبَ + أَنْتُمْ		جانِبَكِ	جانِبَ + أَنْتِ
جانِبَكُنَّ	جانِبَ + أَنْتُنَّ		جانِبَهُ	جانِبَ + هُوَ
جانِبَهُمْ	جانِبَ + هُمْ		جانِبَهَا	جانِبَ + هِيَ
جانِبَهُنَّ	جانِبَ + هُنَّ		جانِبَكُمَا	جانِبَ + أَنْتُمَا

وَسْطَ

وَسْطَ means 'in the middle of' or 'among', and it can be used figuratively:

تَمَّ عَقْدُ جَوْلَةٍ جَدِيدَةٍ لِلْمُفَاوَضَاتِ وَسْطَ أَجْوَاءٍ يَسُودُهَا التَّوَتُّرُ.	A new round of negotiations was held in a tense atmosphere.
جَلَسْتُ وَسْطَ التَّلَامِيذِ لِأَقُصَّ عَلَيْهِمْ قِصَّةً جَمِيلَةً.	I sat in the middle of the pupils to tell them a beautiful story.
خَرَجْنَا لِلتَّمْشِيَةِ وَسْطَ الغَابَةِ.	We went out for walks in the forest.
وَصَلَ المُمَثِّلُونَ إِلَى قَاعَةِ العَرْضِ وَسْطَ تَصْفِيقِ الجَمَاهِيرِ.	The actors arrived at the showroom amid applause from the audiences.

It is worth noting that these are not all the adverbs of place in Arabic. There are many adverbs of place that have not been included here, as they do not function as semi-prepositions, and therefore, they fall outside the scope of this publication, for example (حَيْثُ, حَيْثُمَا, أَيْنَ).

7 Analysis of examples of errors by students

Introduction

The question of dealing with second-language learners' errors has long been a subject of debates among linguists. Errors and their correction are considered an integral part of the learning process. Consideration of psychological factors in the acquisition of a second language, such as the interference of first-language habits in the learning of the second language, has added another dimension to the subject. A most important outcome of the various studies of errors is enabling teachers to identify areas of challenge faced by their learners so that they can give special attention to and highlight the importance of those areas, and they may in time be able to predict the types of errors that require further attention in an attempt to help learners remedy them (Corder, 1981).

Learners' errors can be attributed to various factors, such as interlingual influence from the first language to the second language, as well as intralingual influences. Another contributing factor that leads to errors is the overall system of the second language, especially when it differs greatly from that of the first language. Contrastive linguistics often attributes errors made by learners of a second language to unintentional transfer of the systems or the rules of the mother tongue.

Examples of errors by students

In this section, we highlight selected typical errors of Arabic prepositions by some non-native speakers of Arabic. We provide examples of typical errors of students from a corpus of two hundred written essays containing examples which were collected over a period of three years from students studying Arabic with modern languages.

We are focusing on written samples by students at intermediate and advanced levels because it is very difficult to isolate the errors that beginners make with regard to the appropriate use of prepositions from students' overall errors involving other aspects of second-language learning, such as the correct use of tenses, word order, sentence structure and agreement.

The participating students at the advanced level have studied Arabic in class for six hours per week, in addition to an estimated seven hours of self-study a week over two to three years of study at their home institutions. Additionally, students at the advanced level have also spent at least four months of formal study in Arabic-speaking countries. Students at the intermediate level have studied Arabic in class for six hours per week, in addition to an estimated seven hours of self-study a week over a period of one-and-a-half years, with no experience abroad yet. Almost all these students are native speakers of English, although a very small percentage is heritage Arabic learners of Arab descent. The latter minority of students may have some knowledge of spoken Arabic but have no exposure to formal written Arabic.

We extracted short phrases and sentences from the corpus where the errors in the use of the prepositions are overt and clearly apparent. This is due to the fact that students' errors in the corpus are not only restricted to the use of prepositions in isolation but also involve various other aspects of Arabic grammar. We also focused on examples where the errors appear frequently, instead of focusing on isolated, infrequent errors. Also, we eliminated spelling mistakes, as they are not indicative of any patterns of typical errors in students' writing. We have focused primarily on students' writing in Arabic, with a special emphasis on the use of the most frequently used Arabic prepositions.

Learners of Arabic often make errors when using prepositions, whose use is considered as one of the most confusing aspects of language acquisition in general. Most of the preposition errors are due to interference from the mother tongue. We found in the corpus that the students either avoided using certain prepositions in their writing or substituted one preposition for another or added a preposition in a sentence when it was not required. In the following section, we highlight some of the errors made by students and provide correct versions and translations of the examples.

We have divided the types of errors made by these students into three different categories: deletion, substitution or addition of prepositions. We highlight possible factors which may have influenced the students' use of certain prepositions in place of others and the deletion of prepositions in certain contexts, as well as adding them unnecessarily in certain instances.

Deletion of prepositions

Students sometimes fail to add a preposition when required, as the equivalent English expression does not require a preposition whereas the Arabic equivalent does. For example, *obtain* in English corresponds to (حصل على); *enjoy* in English

Analysis of examples of errors by students 171

corresponds to (استمع ب) or (تمتع ب); *miss* in English corresponds to (اشتاق إلى).
Examples of this type of error and their corrections and translations can be found in the following table.

Error	Correction	Translation
أشتاق بلدي	أشتاق إلى بلدي	I miss my country.
حصل لقب	حصل على لقب	He obtained the title.
أريد أن استمر هذا العمل	أريد أن استمر في هذا العمل	I want to continue this work.
النساء العربيات لا يتمتعن الحرية	النساء العربيات لا يتمتعن بالحرية	Arab women do not enjoy freedom.
يحظى سكان بعض المناطق في العراق نوعية حياة أحسن من مناطق أخرى	يحظى سكان بعض المناطق في العراق بنوعية حياة أحسن من مناطق أخرى	Residents of some areas of Iraq have a better quality of life than others.
أتطلع لرؤيتك والاستمرار دراستي العربية	أتطلع لرؤيتك والاستمرار في دراستي للعربية	I am looking forward to seeing you and continuing my Arabic studies.
التقدم التكنولوجي يسمح لنا معرفة الأخبار بسرعة وسهولة	التقدم التكنولوجي يسمح لنا بمعرفة الأخبار بسرعة وسهولة	Technological advances allow us to know the news quickly and easily.
لم استمع حرارة الطقس	لم استمع بحرارة الطقس	I did not enjoy the hot weather.
شعرت آمنة	شعرت بالأمان	I felt safe.
الاحتفال عيد ميلادي	الاحتفال بعيد ميلادي	celebrating my birthday
ولكنهم يستمرون العمل	ولكنهم يستمرون في العمل	But they keep working.
انضم الأردن تحالف أمريكا ضد داعش	انضم الأردن إلى تحالف أمريكا ضد داعش	Jordan joined America's alliance against ISIS.
لا يثق العلمانيون الحركات الإسلامية	لا يثق العلمانيون بالحركات الإسلامية	Secularists do not trust Islamic movements.
انتهيت السنة الخارجية	انتهيت من السنة الخارجية	I finished the year abroad.
فاز نجيب محفوظ جائزة نوبل	فاز نجيب محفوظ بجائزة نوبل	Naguib Mahfouz won the Nobel Prize.

172 *Analysis of examples of errors by students*

Error	Correction	Translation
يخاف انتشار الأفكار المتشددة في البلد	يخاف من انتشار الأفكار المتشددة في البلد	He fears the spread of radical ideas in the country.
لا تؤثر أحد آخر	لا تؤثر على أحد آخر	Do not affect anyone else.
يحافظ التوازن بين القوى المختلفة	يحافظ على التوازن بين القوى المختلفة	maintains the balance between different forces
أشدد أهمية القضية	أشدد على أهمية القضية	I stress the importance of the issue.
يشير الشعر الذكاء في المجتمع العربي	يشير الشعر إلى الذكاء في المجتمع العربي	Poetry indicates the intelligence in Arab society.
يساعد في التذكير الثقافة والتراث	يساعد في التذكير بالثقافة والتراث	helps recall culture and heritage
التحامل الفلسطينيين	التحامل على الفلسطينيين	prejudice against the Palestinians
بالنسبة اللغة العربية	بالنسبة إلى اللغة العربية	for the Arabic language
معرفتي اللغة العربية	معرفتي باللغة العربية	my knowledge of Arabic
اغتنموا الفرصة لينقلبوا الشاه	اغتنموا الفرصة لينقلبوا على الشاه	They seized the opportunity to overthrow the Shah.
لم أتنبأ المستقبل	لم أتنبأ بالمستقبل	I didn't predict the future.
كانت تجربة مثيرة الاهتمام	كانت تجربة مثيرة للاهتمام	It was an interesting experience.
من المستحيل التشكيك شرعية الملك	من المستحيل التشكيك في شرعية الملك	It is impossible to question the legitimacy of the king.
يضحي خروفًا في العيد	يضحي بخروف في العيد	He sacrifices a lamb in the feast.
لا يسمح أي مجموعة متشددة بأن تفرض آراءها	لا يسمح لأي مجموعة متشددة بأن تفرض آراءها	No militant group is allowed to impose its views.
حصلوا الخيول من غنائم الحرب	حصلوا على الخيول من غنائم الحرب	They got horses as the spoils of war.
تستطيع السيطرة مناطق كبيرة من البلد	تستطيع السيطرة على مناطق كبيرة من البلد	can control vast areas of the country
القدرة على التحدث لغتين مفيدة جدًا	القدرة على التحدث بلغتين مفيدة جدًا	The ability to speak two languages is very useful.

Analysis of examples of errors by students 173

Error	Correction	Translation
يطالب المسلمون الاعتراف بثقافتهم في قرطبة	يطالب المسلمون بالاعتراف بثقافتهم في قرطبة	Muslims demand the recognition of their culture in Cordoba.
تستخدم للتعبير مشاكلهم	تستخدم للتعبير عن مشاكلهم	It is used to express their problems.
تتمتع المرأة أيضًا حقوق الميراث والطلاق	تتمتع المرأة أيضًا بحقوق الميراث والطلاق	Women also enjoy inheritance and divorce rights.
كانت الدراسة صعبة ولكني استمتعتها	كانت الدراسة صعبة ولكني استمتعت بها	The study was difficult, but I enjoyed it.
يلمح أننا قد تأخرنا	يلمح إلى أننا قد تأخرنا	He hints that we are late.
ما زال يؤثر السياسة المغربية	ما زال يؤثر على السياسة المغربية	It still affects Moroccan politics.
هرب الرجل أي عقاب على جريمته	هرب الرجل من أي عقاب على جريمته	The man escaped any punishment for his crime.
كيف تتمكن البلاد القيام بالتنمية	كيف تتمكن البلاد من القيام بالتنمية	how can the country achieve development
يعود تاريخ المدينة أكثر من 5000 سنة	يعود تاريخ المدينة إلى أكثر من 5000 سنة	The city dates back more than 5,000 years.

Students sometimes overuse iḍāfa constructions at the expense of deletion of certain prepositions, this is understandable as iḍāfa constructions imply the meaning of the preposition *of*, without being explicit.

Error	Correction	Translation
تكسب 85% أرباحها من صادرات النفط	تكسب 85% من أرباحها من صادرات النفط	earns 85% of its profits from oil exports
60% عدد السكان يستخدمون الإنترنت	60% من عدد السكان يستخدمون الإنترنت	60% of the population uses the internet.
أغلبية ساحقة النساء لا يعرفن حقوقهن	أغلبية ساحقة من النساء لا يعرفن حقوقهن	An overwhelming majority of women do not know their rights.
جزء التراث العربي	جزء من التراث العربي	part of the Arab heritage
كانت هناك موجة اللاجئين اليهود	كانت هناك موجة من اللاجئين اليهود	There was a wave of Jewish refugees.

174 *Analysis of examples of errors by students*

Error	Correction	Translation
سنرى نسبة أعلى السعوديين في المستقبل	سنرى نسبة أعلى من السعوديين في المستقبل	We will see a higher percentage of Saudis in the future.
خمسين بالمئة اللاجئين السوريين	خمسين بالمئة من اللاجئين السوريين	Fifty percent of Syrian refugees.
تستطيع المرأة أن تفتح حساب البنك	تستطيع المرأة أن تفتح حسابًا في البنك	A woman can open a bank account.
أهم جزء السنة الخارجية هو التعرف على الشعب	أهم جزء من السنة الخارجية هو التعرف على الشعب	The most important part of the year abroad is getting to know the people.
آخر شهر وقتي في الأردن	آخر شهر من وقتي في الأردن	the last month of my time in Jordan
معرفتي العربية كانت مفيدة جدًا	معرفتي بالعربية كانت مفيدة جدًا	My knowledge of Arabic was very useful.
هي مزيج الأديان والمعتقدات المختلفة	هي مزيج من الأديان والمعتقدات المختلفة	is a combination of different religions and beliefs
لعبت كرة القدم مع مجموعة البنات والشباب	لعبت كرة القدم مع مجموعة من البنات والشباب	I played football with a group young people.
استفدت من مستوى عالٍ التعليم	استفدت من مستوى عالٍ من التعليم	I benefited from a high level of education.
كمثال وجود الإسلاميين في الأردن	كمثال على وجود الإسلاميين في الأردن	As an example of the presence of Islamists in Jordan.
أهم عشر سلالات الخيول	أهم عشر سلالات من الخيول	top ten breeds of horses
جزء لا يتجزأ المجتمع اليوم	جزء لا يتجزأ من المجتمع اليوم	an integral part of today's society
النحت رمز عبادة الأصنام	النحت رمز لعبادة الأصنام	Sculpture is a symbol of idolatry.
ليس عندهم مال لدفع الرعاية الصحية	ليس عندهم مال للدفع للرعاية الصحية	They have no money to pay for health care.
هناك استخدام مفرط الوقود الأحفوري	هناك استخدام مفرط للوقود الأحفوري	There is excessive use of fossil fuels.
قصر الحمراء هو مثال رائع التراث العربي	قصر الحمراء هو مثال رائع للتراث العربي	The Alhambra is a wonderful example of Arab heritage.

Error	Correction	Translation
توزيع منصف التمثيل السياسي	توزيع منصف للتمثيل السياسي	equitable distribution of political representation
أبرز مثال تدخل السعودية في سياسة البحرين	أبرز مثال على تدخل السعودية في سياسة البحرين	the most prominent example of Saudi intervention in Bahrain's politics
أحببت لقاء الناس وفرصة الاستماع قصصهم	أحببت لقاء الناس وفرصة الاستماع إلى قصصهم	I loved meeting people and the opportunity to hear their stories.
عاقبوهم شرب الكحول	عاقبوهم على شرب الكحول	They punished them for drinking alcohol.
مشاركة النساء إشارة العصر الجديد	مشاركة النساء إشارة إلى العصر الجديد	Women's participation is an indication of the new age.

Other errors involving deletion of prepositions can emerge from a lack of competence in collocation. Certain prepositions collocate with certain words. There is usually no logic in this collocation, and students need to learn these collocations and use them as Arabic speakers do.

Error	Correction	Translation
بالرغم افتتاح هذه المتاحف	بالرغم من افتتاح هذه المتاحف	despite the opening of these museums
بالنسبة التنمية المستدامة	بالنسبة إلى التنمية المستدامة	for sustainable development
إضافة ذلك	إضافة إلى ذلك	moreover
لا بد العودة إلى أصول الفن الإسلامي	لا بد من العودة إلى أصول الفن الإسلامي	It is necessary to return to the origins of Islamic art.
ستمهد الطريق تحسين وضع المرأة	ستمهد الطريق لتحسين وضع المرأة	It will pave the way for improving the status of women.
حين أن الأردن قد قطع شوطًا طويلًا	في حين أن الأردن قد قطع شوطًا طويلًا	While Jordan has come a long way
وبدلاً الدراسة في فلسطين، سافرت إلى الأردن	وبدلاً من الدراسة في فلسطين، سافرت إلى الأردن	Instead of studying in Palestine, I traveled to Jordan.
كانت غنية الثقافة والنشاط	كانت غنية بالثقافة والنشاط	It was rich in culture and activity.

Analysis of examples of errors by students

Error	Correction	Translation
على الرغم الأهمية الإقليمية للبلد	على الرغم من الأهمية الإقليمية للبلد	Despite the regional importance of the country,
الجدير بالذكر	من الجدير بالذكر	it is worth mentioning
بالنظر تأثير البدو على المجتمع المعاصر	بالنظر إلى تأثير البدو على المجتمع المعاصر	With regard to the influence of the Bedouins on contemporary society,
أكثر تسامحًا الأديان الأخرى	أكثر تسامحًا مع الأديان الأخرى	more tolerant of other religions
لا ينبغي الشخص أن يرفض القهوة	لا ينبغي للشخص أن يرفض القهوة	A person should not refuse coffee.
يجب صاحب البيت وجيرانه أن يتجمعوا	يجب على صاحب البيت وجيرانه أن يتجمعوا	The owner and his neighbors must gather.
مادبا قريبة الصحراء	مادبا قريبة من الصحراء	Madaba is close to the desert.
تاريخ خاص اللبنانيين	تاريخ خاص باللبنانيين	a history unique to the Lebanese

Substitution of prepositions

Students sometimes substitute one preposition for another. This is mainly due to direct translation from English which often results in the use of the wrong Arabic preposition. In English, certain verbs collocate with certain prepositions, while in Arabic, the same verbs collocate with other prepositions. For example, *buy with* in English corresponds to (اشترى ب); *adhere to* in English corresponds to (تمسّك ب); *interested in* in English corresponds to (اهتم ب); *known for* in English corresponds to (يُعرف ب). Examples of this type of error and their corrections can be found in the lists that follow.

Substitution of البَاء

Error	Correction	Translation
في المقارنة	بالمقارنة	in comparison
فضّلوا التكلم في الفرنسية	فضّلوا التكلم بالفرنسية	They preferred to speak in French.
أن أتكلم في العامية	أن أتكلم بالعامية	to speak in colloquial Arabic

Analysis of examples of errors by students

Translation	Correction	Error
all lessons in Arabic	كل الدروس بالعربية	كل الدروس في العربية
in the same way	بنفس الطريقة	في نفس الطريقة
The tribes are very proud of their heritage.	القبائل فخورة جداً بتراثها	القبائل فخورة جداً عن تراثها
He drives a sports car he bought with oil money.	يقود سيارة رياضية اشتراها بأموال النفط	يقود سيارة رياضية اشتراها مع أموال النفط
The Middle East is associated with violence.	يرتبط الشرق الأوسط بالعنف	يرتبط الشرق الأوسط مع العنف
in comparison with other countries	بالمقارنة مع بلدان أخرى	في المقارنة مع بلدان أخرى
We find that Western people cling to old ideas.	نجد أن الشعب الغربي يتمسك بالأفكار القديمة	نجد أن الشعب الغربي يتمسك إلى الأفكار القديمة
Jordanians are known for their hospitality.	يُعرف الأردنيون بضيافتهم	يُعرف الأردنيون لضيافتهم
because the government equips them with few resources and investments	لأن الحكومة تجهزهم بموارد واستثمارات قليلة	لأن الحكومة تجهزهم مع موارد واستثمارات قليلة
compared to Abu Dhabi	بالمقارنة مع أبو ظبي	بالمقارنة إلى أبو ظبي
famous for imprisoning opposition	مشهورة بسجن المعارضين	مشهورة لسجن المعارضين
The first step was taken by establishing Masdar City.	خطت الخطوة الأولى بإنشاء مدينة مصدر	خطت الخطوة الأولى مع إنشاء مدينة مصدر
This kind of art amazes people.	هذا النوع من الفن يدهش الناس	هذا النوع في الفن يدهش الناس
marrying her daughters to Jordanian men	تزويج بناتها من/برجال أردنيين	تزويج بناتها مع رجال أردنيين
She participated in the revolution with courage.	شاركت في الثورة بشجاعة	شاركت في الثورة مع شجاعة
We try to understand the country by ourselves.	نحاول أن نفهم البلد بأنفسنا	نحاول أن نفهم البلد لأنفسنا
interested in modernizing education	مهتمة بتحديث التعليم	مهتمة في تحديث التعليم

178 Analysis of examples of errors by students

Substitution of اللَّام

Error	Correction	Translation
عاش في مصر في فترة قصيرة	عاش في مصر لفترة قصيرة	He lived in Egypt for a short period.
الصورة النمطية من روسيا	الصورة النمطية لروسيا	the stereotypical image of/about Russia
قبول متزايد عن دور النساء	قبول متزايد لدور النساء	increasing acceptance of the role of women
نتيجة على ذلك	نتيجة لذلك	As a result,
الدين عنده تأثير مهم	الدين له تأثير مهم	Religion has an important influence.
كان عند القبائل دور مهم	كان للقبائل دور مهم	Tribes had an important role.
التهديدات المحتملة في التنمية الاقتصادية	التهديدات المحتملة للتنمية الاقتصادية	the potential threats to economic development
البُعد السلبي من دور الدين	البُعد السلبي لدور الدين	the negative aspect of the role of religion
نتيجة من سنوات الدعاية	نتيجة لسنوات الدعاية	as a result of years of propaganda
أقول إليك	أقول لك	I tell you
انتهزت الفرصة إلى السفر	انتهزت الفرصة للسفر	I took the opportunity to travel.
نهاية إلى الصراع	نهاية للصراع	end of the conflict
وسيلة إلى السيطرة	وسيلة للسيطرة	means of control
وسيلة إلى المحافظة	وسيلة للمحافظة	a way to maintain
"عائد إلى حيفا" من غسان كنفاني	"عائد إلى حيفا" لغسان كنفاني	'Returning to Haifa' by Ghassan Kanafani
بسبب دراستي في اللغة الإسبانية	بسبب دراستي للغة الإسبانية	because of my study of Spanish

Substitution of الكَاف

Error	Correction	Translation
الإمارات لديها نفس الثراء من الولايات المتحدة	الإمارات لديها نفس الثراء كالولايات المتحدة	The UAE has the same wealth as the United States.
عدم الذهاب إلى نفس المقاهي من الرجال	عدم الذهاب إلى نفس المقاهي كالرجال	not to go to the same cafes as men

Analysis of examples of errors by students 179

Substitution of عَنْ

Error	Correction	Translation
الصورة النمطية من روسيا	الصورة النمطية عن روسيا	the stereotypical image of/ about Russia
التقاليد في هذا البلد مختلفة من التقاليد في بريطانيا	التقاليد في هذا البلد مختلفة عن التقاليد في بريطانيا	Traditions in this country are different from the traditions in Britain.
فضلاً الى	فضلاً عن	as well as
وزارة السياحة مسؤولة بتوزيع التراخيص	وزارة السياحة مسؤولة عن توزيع التراخيص	The Ministry of Tourism is responsible for the distribution of licenses.
تتحمل كل المسؤولية للسياسة الخارجية	تتحمل كل المسؤولية عن السياسة الخارجية	They shoulder all responsibility for foreign policy.
هناك عزلة من البلد	هناك عزلة عن البلد	There is isolation from the country.
البحث على منزل جديد	البحث عن منزل جديد	the search for a new home
سأخبرك بالسنة الماضية	سأخبرك عن السنة الماضية	I'll tell you about last year.
حاول أن يحقق أهدافه بطريق العنف	حاول أن يحقق أهدافه عن طريق العنف	He tried to achieve his goals through violence.

Substitution of فِي

Error	Correction	Translation
تطوعت لمنظمة غير حكومية	تطوعت في منظمة غير حكومية	I volunteered for a nongovernmental organization.
نعيش بفترة ذات مغزى تاريخي	نعيش في فترة ذات مغزى تاريخي	We live in a period of historical significance.
من رأيي	في رأيي	in my opinion
ينحصر الى الحياة اليومية.	ينحصر في الحياة اليومية	confined to everyday life
مع سياقه التاريخي	في سياقه التاريخي	in its historical context
للختام	في الختام	in conclusion
مع السياق التاريخي	في السياق التاريخي	in the historical context

Analysis of examples of errors by students

Error	Correction	Translation
قررت الحكومة الاستثمار بالسياحة	قررت الحكومة الاستثمار في السياحة	The government decided to invest in tourism.
بالخاتمة	في الخاتمة	in conclusion
ساهم بزعزعة السياسة اللبنانية	ساهم في زعزعة السياسة اللبنانية	He contributed to the destabilization of Lebanese politics.

Substitution of مَعَ

Error	Correction	Translation
تكيف البدوي على المجتمع الحديث	تكيف البدوي مع المجتمع الحديث	Bedouin adaptation to modern society
بالمقارنة إلى أبو ظبي	بالمقارنة مع أبو ظبي	compared to Abu Dhabi
بالمقارنة إلى الغرب	بالمقارنة مع الغرب	compared to the West

Substitution of مِنْ

Error	Correction	Translation
قلق الجمهور عن المتطرفين	قلق الجمهور من المتطرفين	public concern about extremists
استفدنا بفرصة السفر	استفدنا من فرصة السفر	We took advantage of the travel opportunity.
بسبب انتشار الهروب في الدول المجاورة	بسبب انتشار الهروب من الدول المجاورة	because of the prevalence of escape from neighboring countries
في جهة واحدة	من جهة واحدة	on one hand
جزء مهم في التراث العربي	جزء مهم من التراث العربي	an important part of the Arab heritage
هذا النوع في الفن يدهش الناس	هذا النوع من الفن يدهش الناس	This kind of art amazes people.
تزويج بناتها مع رجال أردنيين	تزويج بناتها من رجال أردنيين	marrying her daughters to Jordanian men
نستثني أحزاباً عن الديموقراطية	نستثني أحزاباً من الديموقراطية	We exclude parties from democracy.

Substitution of إلَى

Error	Correction	Translation
وصلنا في الأردن	وصلنا إلى الأردن	We arrived in Jordan.
يقاتل حزب الله في سوريا في جانب بشار الأسد	يقاتل حزب الله في سوريا إلى جانب بشار الأسد	Hezbollah is fighting in Syria on Bashar Assad's side.

Substitution of عَلَى

Error	Correction	Translation
شجّعه للرياضة	شجّعه على الرياضة	He encouraged him to do sport.
تعودت إلى الطقس	تعودت على الطقس	I got used to the weather.
حصل الإسلاميون الى معاملة سيئة.	حصل الإسلاميون على معاملة سيئة.	Islamists were treated badly.
فضلت المغرب من الأردن	فضلت المغرب على الأردن	I preferred Morocco to Jordan.
بسبب اعتماد المجتمع من العادات	بسبب اعتماد المجتمع على العادات	because of the community's dependence on customs
من الرغم	على الرغم	although
بناءً من التجارب	بناءً على التجارب	based on experiences
شكراً لرسالتك	شكراً على رسالتك	Thanks for your letter.
أنفقت الحكومة أكثر من بليون دولار في الفن	أنفقت الحكومة أكثر من بليون دولار على الفن	The government spent more than one billion dollars on art.
رد إلى الاضطرابات السياسية في المنطقة	رد على الاضطرابات السياسية في المنطقة	response to political turmoil in the region
ممنوع للمهاجرين أن يغيروا وظائفهم	ممنوع على المهاجرين أن يغيروا وظائفهم	Migrants are not allowed to change jobs.
من الرغم من أن	على الرغم من أن	although
تدريب للمهن	تدريب على المهن	professional training

Addition of prepositions

Students sometimes add to a sentence a preposition which is not used in Arabic. Intralingual transfer can be one of the factors when learners add prepositions to verbs or nouns that do not require prepositions, such as confusing the verb (زَارَ) 'to visit', which does not require a preposition, and (سَافَرَ) 'to travel', which requires the preposition (إلى). Another contributing factor can be direct translation from English or even influences from colloquial Arabic for students who are familiar with colloquial dialects. A common error that students make in this regard is the use of the Arabic word for *think*. We can translate *think* into Arabic in two ways: (فَكَّرَ), which means 'to think', and (اِعْتَقَدَ), which means 'to believe'. The former is commonly used in colloquial Arabic, while the latter is only used in Modern Standard Arabic. Students often generalize the use of (فَكَّرَ) to mean both, as is the case in colloquial Arabic. Moreover, in English the verb *think* collocates with the preposition *of*, unlike the Arabic verb that takes a direct object. As a result, some students make mistakes like the ones illustrated in the following.

Addition of البَاء

Error	Correction	Translation
يفكر الغربيون بأن الإسلام	يعتقد الغربيون أن الإسلام	Westerners think that Islam

Addition of اللَّام

Error	Correction	Translation
اجتاح للمغول أراضيهم	اجتاح المغول أراضيهم	The Mongols invaded their lands.
عملت في خدمة للنزلاء	عملت في خدمة النزلاء	I worked for the guests.
أنواع أماكن للعبادة مثل الكنائس	أنواع أماكن العبادة مثل الكنائس	types of places of worship such as churches
ليس من الممكن لمناقشة دور الدين في المجتمع اللبناني دون الإشارة إلى السياسة	ليس من الممكن مناقشة دور الدين في المجتمع اللبناني دون الإشارة إلى السياسة	It is not possible to discuss the role of religion in Lebanese society without reference to the politics.
بفضل للاستثمارات الكبيرة	بفضل الاستثمارات الكبيرة	thanks to the large investments

Analysis of examples of errors by students 183

Error	Correction	Translation
تنتقد الحلفاء للسعودية	تنتقد حلفاء السعودية	She criticizes the allies of Saudi Arabia.
انتخبوا له	انتخبوه	They voted for him.
تبلغ لنا	تبلغنا	reach us
لمقاومة للقوات الحاكمة	لمقاومة القوات الحاكمة	to resist the ruling forces
يدعمون لهذه الجهود	يدعمون هذه الجهود	They support these efforts.
هذه العشيرة ستنتخب له	هذه العشيرة ستنتخبه	This clan will elect him.
سأنصح لكل الطلاب الجدد	سأنصح كل الطلاب الجدد	I will advise all new students.

Addition of الكَاف

Error	Correction	Translation
يمثل كمنصة للقومية العربية	يمثل منصة للقومية العربية	It represents a platform for Arab nationalism.

Addition of مِن

Error	Correction	Translation
أغلبية من الوقت	أغلبية الوقت	the majority of the time
إحدى من الصور النمطية	إحدى الصور النمطية	one of the stereotypes
إحدى من أهم المشاكل	إحدى أهم المشاكل	one of the most important problems
ستكون من أغلبية الشباب بدون مهارات أو مؤهلات مناسبة	ستكون أغلبية الشباب بدون مهارات أو مؤهلات مناسبة	The majority of young people will be without appropriate skills or qualifications.
درست أغاني من ماجدة الرومي	درست أغاني ماجدة الرومي	I studied the songs of Majida El Roumi.
أريد أن أقضي كل من الوقت مع أسرتي	أريد أن أقضي كل الوقت مع أسرتي	I want to spend all the time with my family.
السفر إلى أماكن مختلفة خارج من العاصمة	السفر إلى أماكن مختلفة خارج العاصمة	travel to different places outside the capital

Error	Correction	Translation
خارج من الصف، سافرت عبر المغرب	خارج الصف، سافرت عبر المغرب	Outside the class, I traveled through Morocco.
هو عضو من التيار الوطني الحر	هو عضو التيار الوطني الحر	He is a member of the Free Patriotic Movement.

Addition of *في*

Error	Correction	Translation
دخل في الجامعة	دخل الجامعة	He went to university.
في كل بلاد في العالم العربي	في كل بلاد العالم العربي	in every country of the Arab world
الإمارات من أغنى بلدان في العالم	الإمارات من أغنى بلدان العالم	The UAE is one of the richest countries in the world.
أفقر مناطق في البلد غنية	أفقر مناطق البلد غنية	The poorest areas of the country are rich.
لا يسيطر الدين على السياسة مثل في البلاد الأخرى	لا يسيطر الدين على السياسة مثل البلاد الأخرى	Religion does not control politics like other countries.

Addition of *إلى*

Error	Correction	Translation
زرت إلى الأردن	زرت الأردن	I visited Jordan.
يبلغ عدد اللاجئين المسجلين إلى حوالي خمسة ملايين	يبلغ عدد اللاجئين المسجلين حوالي خمسة ملايين	The number of registered refugees is about five million.
يطلب من المرأة إلى تغطية شعرها	يطلب من المرأة تغطية شعرها	The woman is asked to cover her hair.

Addition of *عَلَى*

Error	Correction	Translation
يمنع الإسلام على تمثيل الأشخاص	يمنع الإسلام تمثيل الأشخاص	Islam prohibits the representation of persons.

Conclusion

Prepositions have always been a challenging aspect for learners of Arabic as a foreign language. This challenge can be faced by understanding the functions of Arabic prepositions and how they differ in usage from English. Learners also should try to learn collocations, rather than separate words, so as to learn the correct ways in which prepositions are used. Moreover, teachers should point out to students errors they make in the use of prepositions, and learners should endeavor to learn from these errors. Learners should also be careful not to generalize their first-language knowledge and apply it to Arabic without thinking. Following is a glossary of verbs that collocate with prepositions.

Glossary of common verbs with prepositions

This glossary includes a bilingual list of common Arabic verbs with prepositions and particles and their English translations. All the Arabic verbs are presented in the past tense conjugated with *he*, as this is considered the simplest form of the verb, which corresponds to the infinitive in English. The English translation is the present-tense infinitive form. The selected verbs are ordered alphabetically so as to allow the verbs that appear with different prepositions to appear together, for example:

| hate, dislike | رَغِبَ عَنْ |
| desire, like | رَغِبَ فِي |

It should be noted that this is not a comprehensive list of all Arabic verbs and prepositions, but a list of verbs that we consider to be common and that students of Arabic as a foreign language are likely to come across or may need to use in their careers.

permit	أَبَاحَ لِ
begin, start from	اِبْتَدَأَ مِنْ
stay away from	اِبْتَعَدَ عَنْ
be slow in	أَبْطَأَ فِي
keep, retain	أَبْقَى عَلَى
report	أَبْلَغَ عَنْ
make available	أَتَاحَ أَمَامَ / لِ
unite with	اِتَّحَدَ مَعَ
be consistent with	اِتَّسَقَ مَعَ
contact	اِتَّصَلَ بِ
lean on	اِتَّكَأَ عَلَى
accuse of	اِتَّهَمَ بِ

Glossary of common verbs with prepositions

come to, arrive at	أَتَى إِلَى
bring, provide, supply	أَتَى بِ
finish off, destroy	أَتَى عَلَى
reward	أَثابَ عَلَى
influence, impact	أَثَّرَ عَلَى / فِي
burden with	أَثْقَلَ بِ
burden	أَثْقَلَ عَلَى
praise	أَثْنَى عَلَى
answer	أَجابَ عَلَى
permit	أَجازَ لِ
force to	أَجْبَرَ عَلَى
agree on	اِجْتَمَعَ عَلَى
meet up with	اِجْتَمَعَ مَعَ / بِ
rent from	أَجَرَ مِنْ
evacuate	أَجْلَى عَنْ
agree on (collectively)	أَجْمَعَ عَلَى
finish off	أَجْهَزَ عَلَى
surround	أَحاطَ بِ
refer to	أَحالَ إِلَى
need	اِحْتاجَ إِلَى
watch out for	اِحْتاطَ مِنْ
deceive	اِحْتالَ عَلَى
protest against	اِحْتَجَّ عَلَى
be cautious of	اِحْتَرَسَ مِنْ
keep	اِحْتَفَظَ بِ
celebrate	اِحْتَفَلَ بِ
celebrate, welcome	اِحْتَفَى بِ
seek refuge from	اِحْتَمَى مِنْ
include	اِحْتَوَى عَلَى
be reluctant to, abstain from	أَحْجَمَ عَنْ
feel	أَحَسَّ بِ
allow	أَحَلَّ لِ

188 *Glossary of common verbs with prepositions*

tell about	أَخْبَرَ عَنْ
conclude	اِخْتَتَمَ بِ
be concerned with	اِخْتَصَّ بِ
abbreviate to	اِخْتَصَرَ إِلَى
abbreviate as	اِخْتَصَرَ فِي
kidnap from	اِخْتَطَفَ مِنْ
mingle with	اِخْتَلَطَ بِ
disagree about	اِخْتَلَفَ عَلَى
differ from	اِخْتَلَفَ عَنْ
disagree with	اِخْتَلَفَ مَعَ
be alone with	اِخْتَلَى بِ
lead to	أَخَذَ إِلَى
accept	أَخَذَ بِ
reproach, blame	أَخَذَ عَلَى
study under, learn from	أَخَذَ عَنْ
start, begin	أَخَذَ فِي
take from, take out of	أَخَذَ مِنْ
delay	أَخَّرَ عَنْ
take out from	أَخْرَجَ مِنْ
subdue	أَخْضَعَ لِ
err	أَخْطَأَ فِي
fail	أَخْفَقَ فِي
violate	أَخَلَّ بِ
evacuate	أَخْلَى مِنْ
insert	أَدْخَلَ عَلَى
list, add	أَدْرَجَ عَلَى
insert, include	أَدْمَجَ فِي
lead to	أَدَّى إِلَى
obey, accede to	أَذْعَنَ لِ
relieve of	أَرَاحَ مِنْ
want for	أَرَادَ لِ
be related, connected to	اِرْتَبَطَ بِ / مَعَ
collide with	اِرْتَطَمَ بِ

Glossary of common verbs with prepositions

ascend to	اِرْتَفَعَ إِلَى
be based on	اِرْتَكَزَ عَلَى
send to	أَرْسَلَ إِلَى
force	أَرْغَمَ عَلَى
be crowded with	اِزْدَحَمَ بِ
abuse	أَسَاءَ إِلَى
bestow upon	أَسْبَغَ عَلَى
be upset about	اِسْتَاءَ مِنْ
replace by	اِسْتَبْدَلَ بِ
invest in	اِسْتَثْمَرَ فِي
respond to	اِسْتَجَابَ إِلَى / لِ
turn into	اِسْتَحَالَ إِلَى / لِ
possess, seize	اِسْتَحْوَذَ عَلَى
inquire about	اِسْتَخْبَرَ عَنْ
use for	اِسْتَخْدَمَ لِ
extract from	اِسْتَخْرَجَ مِنْ
belittle	اِسْتَخَفَّ بِ
extract from	اِسْتَخْلَصَ مِنْ
infer from	اِسْتَدَلَّ عَلَى
be guided by	اِسْتَدَلَّ بِ
be relieved from	اِسْتَرَاحَ مِنْ
go on with	اِسْتَرْسَلَ فِي
be guided by	اِسْتَرْشَدَ بِ
surrender to	اِسْتَسْلَمَ لِ
borrow from	اِسْتَعَارَ مِنْ
seek help from	اِسْتَعَانَ بِ
marvel about	اِسْتَعْجَبَ مِنْ
be prepared with	اِسْتَعَدَّ بِ
be prepared for	اِسْتَعَدَّ لِ
inquire about	اِسْتَعْلَمَ عَنْ
be surprised	اِسْتَغْرَبَ مِنْ
be absorbed in	اِسْتَغْرَقَ فِي
benefit from	اِسْتَفَادَ مِنْ

ask about	اِسْتَفْسَرَ عَنْ
inquire about	اِسْتَفْهَمَ عَنْ
resign from	اِسْتَقَالَ مِنْ
settle in	اِسْتَقَرَّ فِي
decide on	اِسْتَقَرَّ عَلَى
inquire about	اِسْتَقْصَى عَنْ
attract to	اِسْتَقْطَبَ إِلَى
succumb for	اِسْتَكَانَ إِلَى / لِ
receive from	اِسْتَلَمَ مِنْ
enjoy	اِسْتَمْتَعَ بِ
draw from	اِسْتَمَدَّ مِنْ
continue	اِسْتَمَرَّ فِي
adhere to, seize	اِسْتَمْسَكَ بِ
be based on, to rest on	اِسْتَنَدَ إِلَى
belittle	اِسْتَهَانَ بِ
be guided by	اِسْتَهْدَى بِ
begin with	اِسْتَهَلَّ بِ
import from	اِسْتَوْرَدَ مِنْ
capture, overtake	اِسْتَوْلَى عَلَى
hurry to	أَسْرَعَ بِ / فِي
base on	أَسَّسَ عَلَى
regret, feel sorry for	أَسِفَ عَلَى / لِ
result in	أَسْفَرَ عَنْ
expatiate	أَسْهَبَ فِي
contribute	أَسْهَمَ بِ
contribute to	أَسْهَمَ فِي
praise	أَشَادَ بِ
point to, indicate	أَشَارَ إِلَى
spread a rumor about	أَشَاعَ عَلَى
clash with	اِشْتَبَكَ مَعَ
participate in, share	اِشْتَرَكَ فِي
buy with	اِشْتَرَى بِ
ablaze with	اِشْتَعَلَ بِ

Glossary of common verbs with prepositions

work in	اِشْتَغَلَ بِ
include	اِشْتَمَلَ عَلَى
be famous for	اِشْتَهَرَ بِ
supervise	أَشْرَفَ عَلَى
feel sorry for	أَشْفَقَ عَلَى
be disgusted with	اِشْمَأَزَّ مِنْ
affect by	أَصَابَ بِ
insist on	أَصَرَّ عَلَى
accompany to	اِصْطَحَبَ إِلَى
run into, crash with	اِصْطَدَمَ بِ
collide with	اِصْطَدَمَ مَعَ
listen to	أَصْغَى إِلَى
suffer	أُصِيبَ بِ
light with	أَضَاءَ بِ
add to	أَضَافَ إِلَى
go on strike	أَضْرَبَ عَنْ
be forced to	اُضْطُرَّ إِلَى
overthrow	أَطَاحَ بِ
elongate	أَطَالَ فِي
close, surround	أَطْبَقَ عَلَى
brief about, on	أَطْلَعَ عَلَى
be aware of	اِطَّلَعَ عَلَى
name	أَطْلَقَ عَلَى
return to	أَعَادَ إِلَى
help with	أَعَانَ عَلَى
get accustomed to	اِعْتَادَ عَلَى
assault	اِعْتَدَى عَلَى
apologize for	اِعْتَذَرَ عَنْ
object to	اِعْتَرَضَ عَلَى
acknowledge, admit	اِعْتَرَفَ بِ
be proud of	اِعْتَزَّ بِ
resort to	اِعْتَصَمَ بِ
depend on	اِعْتَمَدَ عَلَى

look after	اِعْتَنَى بِ
admire	أُعْجِبَ بِ
prepare for	أَعَدَّ لِ
express	أَعْرَبَ عَنْ
give	أَعْطَى لِ
absolve from	أَعْفَى مِنْ
announce	أَعْلَنَ عَنْ
raid	أَغَارَ عَلَى
faint	أُغْمِيَ عَلَى
mention	أَفَادَ بِ
benefit from	أَفَادَ مِنْ
wake up from	أَفَاقَ مِنْ
open with	اِفْتَتَحَ بِ
be proud of	اِفْتَخَرَ بِ
be separate from	اِفْتَرَقَ عَنْ
lie about	اِفْتَرَى عَلَى
lack	اِفْتَقَرَ إِلَى
overdo	أَفْرَطَ فِي
spoil by	أَفْسَدَ بِ
spoil for	أَفْسَدَ عَلَى
express	أَفْصَحَ عَنْ
lead to	أَفْضَى إِلَى
escape with	أَفْلَتَ بِ
escape from	أَفْلَتَ مِنْ
succeed	أَفْلَحَ فِي
base on	أَقَامَ عَلَى
reside with	أَقَامَ مَعَ
feed on	اِقْتَاتَ عَلَى
quote from	اِقْتَبَسَ مِنْ
get close to	اِقْتَرَبَ مِنْ
borrow from	اِقْتَرَضَ مِنْ
be associated with	اِقْتَرَنَ بِ
ration	اِقْتَصَدَ فِي

Glossary of common verbs with prepositions

be restricted to	اِقْتَصَرَ عَلَى
be brief about	اِقْتَضَبَ فِي
deduct from	اِقْتَطَعَ مِنْ
be convinced of	اِقْتَنَعَ بِ
venture, brave, dare	أَقْدَمَ عَلَى
acknowledge, admit	أَقَرَّ بِ
swear by	أَقْسَمَ بِ
swear to	أَقْسَمَ عَلَى
suffice	اِكْتَفَى بِ
stress	أَكَّدَ عَلَى
to return, revert to	آلَ إِلَى
adhere to, commit to	اِلْتَزَمَ بِ
insist on	أَلَحَّ عَلَى
insist to	أَلَحَّ فِي
commit to	أَلْزَمَ بِ
be characterized by	اِمْتَازَ بِ
extend to, stretch to	اِمْتَدَّ إِلَى
stretch from	اِمْتَدَّ مِنْ
to brim with	اِمْتَلَأَ بِ
abstain from	اِمْتَنَعَ عَنْ
to order	أَمَرَ بِ
to catch	أَمْسَكَ بِ
shower	أَمْطَرَ بِ
do carefully	أَمْعَنَ فِي
enable	أَمْكَنَ لِ
hope for	أَمَلَ بِ / فِي
believe in	أَمَنَ بِ
severe from	اِنْبَتَرَ عَنْ
be emitted, be resurrected	اِنْبَعَثَ مِنْ
be impressed by	اِنْبَهَرَ بِ
commit suicide by	اِنْتَحَرَ بِ
affiliate to, join	اِنْتَسَبَ إِلَى
extricate, save from	اِنْتَشَلَ مِنْ

benefit from	اِنْتَفَعَ بِ / مِنْ
move to	اِنْتَقَلَ إِلَى
take revenge	اِنْتَقَمَ مِنْ
belong to	اِنْتَمَى إِلَى
result in	اِنْتَهَى إِلَى
end with	اِنْتَهَى بِ
align with	اِنْحَازَ إِلَى
descend, derive from	اِنْحَدَرَ مِنْ
deviate from	اِنْحَرَفَ عَنْ
descend to	اِنْحَطَّ إِلَى
be deceived by	اِنْخَدَعَ بِ
get involved in	اِنْخَرَطَ فِي
be lowered, dip	اِنْخَفَضَ إِلَى
be listed, classified under	اِنْدَرَجَ تَحْتَ
slip between	اِنْدَسَّ بَيْنَ
barge into	اِنْدَفَعَ إِلَى
mix with	اِنْدَمَجَ فِي
be amazed at	اِنْدَهَشَ مِنْ
warn	أَنْذَرَ بِ
be annoyed	اِنْزَعَجَ مِنْ
be in harmony with	اِنْسَجَمَ مَعَ
withdraw	اِنْسَحَبَ مِنْ
get detached from	اِنْسَلَخَ مِنْ
separate from	اِنْشَطَرَ عَنْ
be (pre)occupied with	اِنْشَغَلَ بِ
be distracted from	اِنْشَغَلَ عَنْ
split from	اِنْشَقَّ عَنْ
leave	اِنْصَرَفَ عَنْ
join	اِنْضَمَّ إِلَى
apply to	اِنْطَبَقَ عَلَى
set off from	اِنْطَلَقَ مِنْ
be isolated from	اِنْعَزَلَ عَنْ
bear to	اِنْعَطَفَ إِلَى

Glossary of common verbs with prepositions 195

be reflected on	اِنْعَكَسَ عَلَى
indulge in	اِنْغَمَسَ فِي
open up to	اِنْفَتَحَ عَلَى
be alone with, unique	اِنْفَرَدَ بِ
be separated from	اِنْفَصَلَ عَنْ
spend	أَنْفَقَ عَلَى
save from	أَنْقَذَ مِنْ
be divided into	اِنْقَسَمَ إِلَى
be cut off	اِنْقَطَعَ عَنْ
be absorbed in	اِنْهَمَكَ فِي
find	اِهْتَدَى إِلَى
be guided by	اِهْتَدَى بِ
be interested in	اِهْتَمَّ بِ
present to	أَهْدَى إِلَى
neglect	أَهْمَلَ فِي
inspire	أَوْحَى لِ
be about to	أَوْشَكَ عَلَى
give a lift, lead to	أَوْصَلَ إِلَى
beckon to	أَوْمَأَ إِلَى
reveal to	بَاحَ إِلَى
reveal, disclose	بَاحَ بِ
rush into, do promptly	بَادَرَ إِلَى
hurry with	بَادَرَ بِ
begin with	بَاشَرَ بِ
sell to	بَاعَ إِلَى
exaggerate	بَالَغَ فِي
decide on	بَتَّ فِي
search for	بَحَثَ عَنْ
look into, discuss, research	بَحَثَ فِي
began with	بَدَأَ بِ
start, begin	بَدَأَ فِي
declare innocent from	بَرَّأَ مِنْ
justify by	بَرَّرَ بِ

excel, surpass	بَرَزَ عَلَى
stand out in	بَرَزَ فِي
excel at	بَرَعَ بِ / فِي
prove	بَرْهَنَ عَلَى
be clear, free of	بَرِئَ مِنْ
announce (good news)	بَشَّرَ بِ
send to	بَعَثَ إِلَى
send, delegate	بَعَثَ بِ
send from	بَعَثَ مِنْ
get away from	بَعُدَ عَنْ
come, start early	بَكَّرَ فِي
report	بَلَغَ عَنْ
base on, build on	بَنَى عَلَى
explain for	بَيَّنَ لِ
repent	تَابَ عَنْ
be affected by	تَأَثَّرَ بِ
trade	تَاجَرَ بِ / فِي
be late for	تَأَخَّرَ عَنْ
be late in	تَأَخَّرَ فِي
be based on	تَأَسَّسَ عَلَى
long for	تَاقَ إِلَى
become adapted to	تَأَقْلَمَ مَعَ
ensure	تَأَكَّدَ مِنْ
be composed of	تَأَلَّفَ مِنْ
conspire against	تَآمَرَ عَلَى
contemplate	تَأَمَّلَ فِي
dress up for	تَأَنَّقَ فِي
go slowly about	تَأَنَّى فِي
astray from	تَاهَ مِنْ
exchange with	تَبَادَلَ مَعَ
brag about	تَبَاهَى بِ
disown	تَبَرَّأَ مِنْ
donate to	تَبَرَّعَ إِلَى

Glossary of common verbs with prepositions

donate	تَبَرَّعَ بِ
adopt as	تَبَنَّى كَ
be slow, sluggish	تَثَاقَلَ فِي
respond to	تَجَاوَبَ مَعَ
disregard, forgo	تَجَاوَزَ عَنْ
spy on	تَجَسَّسَ عَلَى
be clear in	تَجَلَّى فِي
wrong, hurt	تَجَنَّى عَلَى
roam	تَجَوَّلَ فِي
ally with	تَحَالَفَ مَعَ
be prejudiced against	تَحَامَلَ عَلَى
converse with	تَحَاوَرَ مَعَ
deceive	تَحَايَلَ عَلَى
speak in	تَحَدَّثَ بِ
speak with	تَحَدَّثَ مَعَ
be liberated from/of	تَحَرَّرَ مِنْ
grieve over	تَحَسَّرَ عَلَى
be allergic to	تَحَسَّسَ مِنْ
improve at	تَحَسَّنَ فِي
check	تَحَقَّقَ مِنْ
demonstrate (a trait)	تَحَلَّى بِ
be passionate about	تَحَمَّسَ لِ
change, convert into	تَحَوَّلَ إِلَى
change, convert from	تَحَوَّلَ عَنْ
bias for	تَحَيَّزَ لِ
bias with	تَحَيَّزَ مَعَ/ إِلَى
conspire with, call	تَخَابَرَ مَعَ
graduate from	تَخَرَّجَ مِنْ/ فِي
specialize in	تَخَصَّصَ فِي
do away with, get rid of	تَخَلَّصَ مِنْ
miss, lag behind	تَخَلَّفَ عَنْ
abandon	تَخَلَّى عَنْ
flock to	تَدَاعَى عَلَى

interfere with	تَدَخَّلَ فِي
audition for	تَدَرَّبَ عَلَى
make progress	تَدَرَّجَ فِي
be grumpy about	تَذَمَّرَ مِنْ
retreat to	تَرَاجَعَ إِلَى
retreat from (a stance)	تَرَاجَعَ عَنْ
retreat from (a place)	تراجع مِنْ
be lenient about	تَرَاخَى فِي
translate into	تَرْجَمَ إِلَى
translate from	تَرْجَمَ مِنْ
frequent	تَرَدَّدَ عَلَى
hesitate	تَرَدَّدَ فِي
nominate himself for	تَرَشَّحَ لِ
grow	تَرَعْرَعَ فِي
leave to	تَرَكَ إِلَى/ لِ
be concentrated in	تَرَكَّزَ فِي
coincide with	تَزَامَنَ مَعَ
marry	تَزَوَّجَ مِنْ
fall	تَسَاقَطَ عَلَى
rise above	تَسَامَى عَلَى / عَنْ
be lenient with	تَسَاهَلَ فِي / تَسَاهَلَ مَعَ
cause	تَسَبَّبَ فِي
cover up	تَسَتَّرَ عَلَى
rush, haste	تَسَرَّعَ فِي
overcome, prevail	تَسَلَّطَ عَلَى
sneak through	تَسَلَّلَ عَبْرَ
receive from	تَسَلَّمَ مِنْ
distract, entertain (oneself) from	تَسَلَّى عَنْ
be pessimistic about	تَشَاءَمَ مِنْ
be tangled, clash with	تَشَابَكَ مَعَ
suspect, doubt	تَشَابَهَ عَلَى
quarrel with	تَشَاجَرَ مَعَ
share	تَشَارَكَ فِي

consult about	تَشَاوَرَ حَوْلَ
hold to	تَشَبَّثَ بِ
be saturated with	تَشَبَّعَ بِ
emulate	تَشَبَّهَ بِ
be strict about	تَشَدَّدَ فِي
doubt	تَشَكَّكَ فِي
long for	تَشَوَّقَ إِلَى
befriend	تَصَادَقَ مَعَ
collide with	تَصَادَمَ مَعَ
wrestle, fight with	تَصَارَعَ مَعَ
emanate from	تَصَاعَدَ مِنْ
reconcile with	تَصَالَحَ مَعَ
confront	تَصَدَّى لِ
manage	تَصَرَّفَ فِي
behave like	تَصَرَّفَ كَ
suffer from	تَضَرَّرَ مِنْ
touch upon	تَطَرَّقَ إِلَى
intrude on	تَطَفَّلَ عَلَى
aspire to, look forward to	تَطَلَّعَ إِلَى
pretend	تَظَاهَرَ بِ
complain about	تَظَلَّمَ مِنْ
get to know	تَعَارَفَ مَعَ
deal with	تَعَامَلَ مَعَ
coexist with	تَعَايَشَ مَعَ
become tired of	تَعِبَ مِنْ
stumble on	تَعَثَّرَ بِ / فِي
be amazed about, wonder	تَعَجَّبَ مِنْ
be difficult for	تَعَذَّرَ عَلَى
be exposed to	تَعَرَّضَ لِ
crave, be avid for	تَعَطَّشَ لِ
stop, become idle	تَعَطَّلَ عَنْ
be attached to	تَعَلَّقَ بِ
pledge	تَعَهَّدَ بِ

be accustomed to	تَعَوَّدَ عَلَى
overlook	تَغَاضَى عَنْ
become an expatriate	تَغَرَّبَ عَنْ
get over	تَغَلَّبَ عَلَى
penetrate	تَغَلْغَلَ فِي
absence from	تَغَيَّبَ عَنْ
boast	تَفَاخَرَ بِ
agree on	تَفَاهَمَ عَلَى
negotiate with	تَفَاوَضَ مَعَ
contemplate	تَفَكَّرَ فِي
be unique in, alone with	تَفَرَّدَ بِ
excel	تَفَوَّقَ عَلَى
meet	تَقَابَلَ مَعَ
fight with	تَقَاتَلَ مَعَ
retire	تَقَاعَدَ عَنْ
be lazy, inactive	تَقَاعَسَ عَنْ
propose to	تَقَدَّمَ إِلَى/ لِ
got ahead of, progress	تَقَدَّمَ عَلَى
make progress in	تَقَدَّمَ فِي
approach	تَقَرَّبَ مِنْ
be disgusted at	تَقَزَّزَ مِنْ
abide by	تَقَيَّدَ بِ
lazy	تَكَاسَلَ عَنْ
cover up	تَكَتَّمَ عَلَى
speak about	تَكَلَّمَ عَنْ
speak with	تَكَلَّمَ مَعَ
adapt	تَكَيَّفَ مَعَ
stutter	تَلَعْثَمَ فِي
linger in	تَلَكَّأَ فِي
enjoy	تَمَتَّعَ بِ
result in	تَمَخَّضَ عَنْ
lie on	تَمَدَّدَ عَلَى
rebel against	تَمَرَّدَ عَلَى

Glossary of common verbs with prepositions

exercise, practice	تَمَرَّنَ عَلَى
cling to, adhere to	تَمَسَّكَ بِ
be able to	تَمَكَّنَ مِنْ
evade, escape	تَمَلَّصَ مِنْ
complete	تَمَّمَ لِ
slow down	تَمَهَّلَ فِي
compete about	تَنَازَعَ عَلَى
abdicate	تَنَازَلَ عَنْ
be in harmony with	تَنَاغَمَ مَعَ
compete on	تَنَافَسَ عَلَى
compete with	تَنَافَسَ مَعَ
discuss	تَنَاقَشَ حول/ فِي
discuss with	تَنَاقَشَ مَعَ
contradict	تَنَاقَضَ مَعَ
predict, forecast	تَنَبَّأَ بِ
disavow	تَنَصَّلَ مِنْ
deny knowledge of	تَنَكَّرَ لِ
be complacent about	تَهَاوَنَ فِي
evade	تَهَرَّبَ مِنْ
exist with	تَوَاجَدَ مَعَ
hide from	تَوَارَى عَنْ
communicate with	تَوَاصَلَ مَعَ
colluded with	تَوَاطَأَ مَعَ
agree to	تَوَافَقَ عَلَى
agree in	تَوَافَقَ فِي
agree with	تَوَافَقَ مَعَ
dawdle	تَوَانَى فِي /عَنْ
be anxious about	تَوَتَّرَ مِنْ
head toward	تَوَجَّهَ إِلَى
get involved in	تَوَرَّطَ فِي
mediate between	تَوَسَّطَ بَيْنَ
beg, implore	تَوَسَّلَ إِلَى
arrive at	تَوَصَّلَ إِلَى

ablaze with		تَوَقَّدَ بِ
depend on		تَوَقَّفَ عَلَى
refrain from		تَوَقَّفَ عَنْ
ablaze with		تَوَهَّجَ بِ
revolt, rise against		ثَارَ عَلَى
take revenge on		ثَأَرَ مِنْ
maintain, adhere to		ثَبَتَ عَلَى
fix to		ثَبَّتَ عَلَى
discourage		ثَبَّطَ عَنْ
dissuade, divert from		ثَنَى عَنْ
bring		جَاءَ بِ
grant		جَادَ بِ
grant to		جَادَ عَلَى
argue about		جَادَلَ فِي
wrong, oppress		جَارَ عَلَى
roam		جَالَ فِي
answer, reply		جَاوَبَ عَلَى
coward		جَبُنَ عَنْ
take seriously		جَدَّ فِي
attract to		جَذَبَ إِلَى
draw, bring upon		جَرَّ عَلَى
strip off, dispossess		جَرَّدَ مِنْ
dare, venture		جَرُؤَ عَلَى
run, head for		جَرَى إِلَى
befall, happen		جَرَى لِ
pity, mourn		جَزَعَ عَلَى
worry about		جَزَعَ مِنْ
reward		جَزَى عَلَى
sit on		جَلَسَ عَلَى
combine		جَمَعَ بَيْنَ
decorate with		جَمَّلَ بِ
be inclined to		جَنَحَ إِلَى
deviate, depart from		جَنَحَ عَنْ

Glossary of common verbs with prepositions 203

declare, voice loudly	جَهَرَ بِ
equipped with	جَهَّزَ بِ
be ignorant about	جَهِلَ بِ / عَنْ
deviate from	حَادَ عَنْ
obtain, win	حَازَ عَلَى
preserve, maintain	حَافَظَ عَلَى
trial for	حَاكَمَ عَلَى
interfere with, come between	حَالَ بَيْنَ
block, withhold	حَبَسَ عَنْ
lock, confine	حَبَسَ فِي
decree	حَتَّمَ عَلَى
hide, obscure from	حَجَبَ عَنْ
deny access	حَجَرَ عَلَى
keep away from	حَجَزَ عَنْ
limit	حَدَّ مِنْ
insist on	حَدَا بِ
talk about	حَدَّثَ عَنْ
stare at	حَدَّقَ فِي
warn against	حَذَّرَ مِنْ
delete from	حَذَفَ مِنْ
excel at	حَذِقَ فِي
forbid	حَرَّجَ عَلَى
liberate from	حَرَّرَ مِنْ
be keen on	حَرَصَ عَلَى
incite, provoke	حَرَّضَ عَلَى
forbid to	حَرَّمَ عَلَى
deprive of	حَرَمَ مِنْ
begrudge/envy	حَسَدَ عَلَى
fill, stuff with	حَشَا بِ
jam, squeeze in	حَشَرَ فِي
limit, restrict to	حَصَرَ فِي / بِ
obtain	حَصَلَ عَلَى
immunize, protect	حَصَّنَ مِنْ

urge to	حَضَّ عَلَى
come to	حَضَرَ إِلَى
lower, decrease	حَطَّ مِنْ
ban	حَظَرَ عَلَى
gain, own, enjoy	حَظِيَ بِ
surround	حَفَّ بِ
be entitled to	حَقَّ لِ
investigate	حَقَّقَ فِي
interrogate	حَقَّقَ مَعَ
sentence to	حَكَمَ بِ
sentence	حَكَمَ عَلَى
tell	حَكَى لِ
absolve	حَلَّ مِنْ
descend upon	حَلَّ عَلَى
arrive, set in	حَلَّ فِي
like	حَلَا لِ
dream of	حَلَمَ بِ
adorn, decorate with	حَلَّى بِ
bring	حَمَلَ إِلَى
force	حَمَلَ عَلَى
be pregnant by	حَمَلَ مِنْ
long for	حَنَّ إِلَى
sympathize with	حَنَّ عَلَى
be furious, resentful	حَنِقَ عَلَى
divert, change to	حَوَّلَ إِلَى
divert from	حَوَّلَ عَنْ
risk	خَاطَرَ بِ
fear	خَافَ مِنْ
know	خَبَرَ بِ
seal, conclude	خَتَمَ بِ
be embarrassed about	خَجَلَ مِنْ
go against	خَرَجَ عَلَى
came out to	خَرَجَ إِلَى

Glossary of common verbs with prepositions

leave, exit	خَرَجَ مِنْ
dedicate for	خَصَّ بِ
allocate for	خَصَّصَ لِ
occur to	خَطَرَ لِ
plan	خَطَّطَ لِ
ease	خَفَّفَ مِنْ
be hidden from	خَفِيَ عَلَى
be free from	خَلا مِنْ
conclude	خَلَصَ إِلَى
mix with	خَلَطَ بِ
impart to	خَلَعَ عَلَى
persist	دَأَبَ عَلَى
revolve around	دَارَ حول
defend	دَافَعَ عَنْ
owe (something)	دانَ بِ
owe (someone)	دانَ لِ
get into	دَخَلَ فِي
access	دَخَلَ إِلَى
plot against	دَسَّ عَلَى
call for	دَعَا إِلَى
curse	دَعَا عَلَى
support with	دَعَمَ بِ
pay for, push for	دَفَعَ لِ
bury in	دَفَنَ فِي
knock	دَقَّ عَلَى
scrutinize	دَقَّقَ فِي
indicate	دَلَّ عَلَى
prove	دَلَّلَ عَلَى
come close to	دَنَا مِنْ
marvel at	دَهَشَ مِنْ
melt in	ذَابَ فِي
remind of	ذَكَّرَ بِ
go to	ذَهَبَ إِلَى

be distracted	ذُهِلَ عَنْ
like	رَاقَ لِ
bet	رَاهَنَ عَلَى
exceed	رَبَا عَلَى
pat, caress	رَبَّتَ عَلَى
associate with	رَبَطَ بِ
link between	رَبَطَ بَيْنَ
feel sorry for	رَثَى لِ
favor	رَجَّحَ عَلَى
bring back	رَجِعَ بِ
return to	رَجِعَ إِلَى
stone with	رَجَمَ بِ
welcome	رَحَّبَ بِ
move to	رَحَلَ إِلَى
leave	رَحَلَ عَنْ
return to	رَدَّ إِلَى
fail	رَسَبَ فِي
nominate for	رَشَّحَ لِ
accede to	رَضَخَ لِ
accept	رَضِيَ بِ
be pleased with	رَضِيَ عَنْ
hate, dislike	رَغِبَ عَنْ
desire, like	رَغِبَ فِي
be kind to	رَفَقَ بِ
have sympathy for	رَقَّ لِ
mount on	رَكَّبَ عَلَى/فِي
focus on	رَكَّزَ عَلَى
rely on	رَكَنَ إِلَى
symbolize	رَمَزَ إِلَى/لِ
aim	رَمَى إِلَى
throw at, accuse	رَمَى بِ
promote	رَوَّجَ لِ

Glossary of common verbs with prepositions

exceed	زَادَ عَلَى/عَنْ
increase	زَادَ فِي / مِنْ
pair, marry	زَاوَجَ بَيْنَ
force, squeeze into	زَجَّ بِ
rebuke, scold	زَجَرَ عَنْ
march toward	زَحَفَ عَلَى
be abound in	زَخَرَ بِ
be proud of	زَهَا بِ
abandon, withdraw from	زَهَدَ فِي
pair of	زَوَّجَ مِنْ
supply with	زَوَّدَ بِ
decorate with	زَيَّنَ بِ
prevail	سَادَ عَلَى
rush, haste	سَارَعَ فِي
contribute	سَاعَدَ بِ
help with	سَاعَدَ فِي / عَلَى
convey	سَاقَ إِلَى
ask about	سَأَلَ عَنْ
be bored of	سَأَمَ مِنْ
contribute to	سَاهَمَ فِي
bargain for	سَاوَمَ عَلَى
equate with	سَاوَى بِ
make equal	سَاوَى بَيْنَ
swim in	سَبَحَ فِي
cover, conceal	سَتَرَ عَنْ
record, register in	سَجَّلَ فِي
draw to	سَحَبَ إِلَى
mock, ridicule	سَخِرَ مِنْ
be pleased with	سُرَّ بِ
daydream	سَرَحَ فِي
steal from	سَرَقَ مِنْ
burgle	سَطَا عَلَى

be happy with	سَعِدَ بِ
seek	سَعَى إِلَى / نَحْوَ
rely on, be assured about	سَكَنَ إِلَى / لِ
dispossess, take from	سَلَبَ مِنْ
escape, be safe from	سَلِمَ مِنْ
accept	سَلَّمَ بِ
greet	سَلَّمَ عَلَى
surrender to	سَلَّمَ لِ
entertain	سَلَّى عَنْ
forget	سَلَا عَنْ
rise above	سَمَا عَلَى
allow to	سَمَحَ بِ
allow for	سَمَحَ لِ
lend an ear	سَمِعَ لِ
heard of	سَمِعَ بِ
name	سَمَّى بِ
avail for	سَنَحَ لِ
overlook	سَهَا عَنْ
facilitate for	سَهَّلَ عَلَى
control	سَيْطَرَ عَلَى
participate	شَارَكَ فِي
make similar	شَبَّهَ بِ
obscure	شَبَّهَ عَلَى
encourage	شَجَّعَ عَلَى
charge, load	شَحَنَ بِ
stress	شَدَّدَ عَلَى
deviate	شَذَّ عَنْ
begin to	شَرَعَ فِي
feel	شَعَرَ بِ
love	شُغِفَ بِ
occupy with	شَغَلَ بِ
trouble	شَقَّ عَلَى
doubt	شَكَّ بِ / فِي

Glossary of common verbs with prepositions

complain to	شَكَا لِ
complain about	شَكَا مِنْ
thank for	شَكَرَ عَلَى
question	شَكَّكَ بِ
testify	شَهَدَ بِ
attest to, testify against	شَهِدَ عَلَى
scandalize	شَهَّرَ بِ
approve	صَادَقَ عَلَى
reconcile	صَالَحَ بَيْنَ
save, protect from	صَانَ عَنْ
show patience toward	صَبَرَ عَلَى
wake up	صَحَى مِنْ
be issued in	صَدَرَ فِي
be issued by	صَدَرَ مِنْ/ عَنْ
turn away from	صَدَفَ عَنْ
certify	صَدَّقَ عَلَى
announce	صَرَّحَ بِ
announce to	صَرَّحَ لِ
spend on	صَرَفَ عَلَى
distract from	صَرَفَ عَنْ
board	صَعَدَ إِلَى
forgive	صَفَحَ عَنْ
be suitable, fit for	صَلَحَ لِ
insist on	صَمَّمَ عَلَى
shoot at	صَوَّبَ عَلَى
vote on	صَوَّتَ عَلَى
vote for	صَوَّتَ لِ
be full of	ضَجَّ بِ
be bored of	ضَجَرَ مِنْ
laugh at	ضَحِكَ مِنْ
sacrifice	ضَحَّى بِ
pressurize	ضَغَطَ عَلَى
stray	ضَلَّ عَنْ

excel at	ضَلَعَ فِي
include with	ضَمَّ إِلَى
guarantee to	ضَمِنَ لِ
restrict	ضَيَّقَ عَلَى
go around	طَافَ حَوْلَ
demand	طَالَبَ بِ
apply to	طَبَّقَ عَلَى
happen	طَرَأَ عَلَى
expel	طَرَدَ مِنْ
knock	طَرَقَ عَلَى
challenge	طَعَنَ فِي /عَلَى
oppress	طَغَى عَلَى
overlook	طَلَّ عَلَى
ask	طَلَبَ مِنْ
divorce	طَلَّقَ مِنْ
paint	طَلَى بِ
aspire to	طَمَحَ إِلَى
covet	طَمَعَ فِي
enable	طَوَّعَ لِ
surround	طَوَّقَ بِ
win	ظَفَرَ بِ
denounce	عَابَ عَلَى
return to	عَادَ إِلَى
return with	عَادَ بِ
live with	عَاشَ مَعَ
punish with	عَاقَبَ بِ
punish for	عَاقَبَ عَلَى
treat with	عَالَجَ بِ
treat from	عَالَجَ مِنْ
suffer	عَانَى مِنْ
fill with	عَبَّأَ بِ
care about	عَبَأَ بِ
play with, manipulate	عَبَثَ بِ

Glossary of common verbs with prepositions 211

cross to	عَبَرَ إِلَى
express	عَبَّرَ عَنْ
obscure	عَتَّمَ عَلَى
find	عَثَرَ عَلَى
be unable to	عَجَزَ عَنْ
rush, hurry	عَجَّلَ بِ
offer	عَرَضَ عَلَى
expose to	عَرَّضَ لِ
be known for	عُرِفَ بِ
introduce	عَرَّفَ عَلَى
attribute	عَزَا إِلَى
play (an instrument)	عَزَفَ عَلَى
dislike	عَزَفَ عَنْ
isolate from	عَزَلَ عَنْ
attribute to	عَزَى إِلَى
storm	عَصَفَ بِ
be kind to	عَطَفَ عَلَى
forgive	عَفَا عَنْ
comment on	عَقَّبَ عَلَى
be bent on	عَكَفَ عَلَى
tower over	عَلَا عَنْ
comment on	عَلَّقَ عَلَى
know of	عَلِمَ بِ
tend to	عَمِدَ إِلَى
be full of	عَمَرَ بِ
follow	عَمِلَ بِ
work on, pursue	عَمِلَ عَلَى
generalize to	عَمَّمَ عَلَى
be blind to	عَمِيَ عَنْ
be concerned with	عُنِيَ بِ
trust with	عَهِدَ إِلَى
compensate	عَوَّضَ عَنْ
hinder from	عَوَّقَ عَنْ

appoint as	عَيَّنَ كَ
be absent from	غَابَ عَنْ
leave to	غَادَرَ إِلَى
exaggerate	غَالَى فِي
feed, nurture	غَذَّى بِ
drown in	غَرِقَ فِي
be angry at	غَضِبَ مِنْ
cover with	غَطَّى بِ
plunge, dive into	غَطَسَ فِي
forgive	غَفَرَ لِ
disregard, be distracted from	غَفَلَ عَنْ
cover, flood with	غَمَرَ بِ
win	فَازَ بِ
be abundant in	فَاضَ بِ
open to	فَتَحَ لِ
search for	فَتَّشَ عَنْ
kill	فَتَكَ بِ
be happy with	فَرِحَ بِ
impose on	فَرَضَ عَلَى
finish	فَرَغَ مِنْ
furnish, cover	فَرَشَ بِ
be scared of	فَزِعَ مِنْ
interpret	فَسَّرَ بِ
fail	فَشَلَ فِي
dismiss from	فَصَلَ مِنْ
explicate	فَصَّلَ فِي
notice, understand	فَطِنَ إِلَى
think about, of	فَكَّرَ فِي
be surprised by	فُوجِئَ بِ
lead against	قَادَ ضِدَّ
compare with	قَارَنَ بِ
suffer from	قَاسَى مِنْ
measure against	قَاسَ عَلَى

Glossary of common verbs with prepositions

say to	قَالَ لِ
undertake	قَامَ بِ
be based on	قَامَ عَلَى
barter for	قايض بِ
barter between	قايض بَيْنَ
barter with	قايض مَعَ
arrest	قَبَضَ عَلَى
receive money from	قَبَضَ مِنْ
accept	قَبِلَ بِ
accept as	قَبِلَ كَ
kill with	قَتَلَ بِ
estimate	قَدَّرَ بِ
be able to	قَدَرَ عَلَى
present to	قَدَّمَ إِلَى
came to	قَدَمَ إِلَى
prefer, advance	قَدَّمَ عَلَى
knock on	قَرَعَ عَلَى
present to	قَدَّمَ إِلَى / لِ
divide into	قَسَّمَ إِلَى
separate, divide	قَسَّمَ بَيْنَ
aim for, head toward	قَصَدَ إِلَى
underperform	قَصَّرَ فِي
fail to act	قَصَّرَ عَنْ
sentence	قَضَى بِ
destroy, eliminate	قَضَى عَلَى
be less than	قَلَّ عَنْ
decrease	قَلَّصَ مِنْ
worry about	قَلَقَ عَلَى
be content with	قَنَعَ بِ
suffer from	كَابَدَ مِنْ
strive for	كَافَحَ مِنْ أَجْلِ
strive against	كَافَحَ ضد
dedicate to	كَرَّسَ لِ

dress, cover	كَسَا بِ
uncover	كَشَفَ عَنْ
tell	كَشَفَ لِ
stop, abstain from	كَفَّ عَنْ
disbelieve in	كَفَرَ بِ
assign to	كَلَّفَ بِ
lie in	كَمَنَ فِي
take refuge	لَاذَ بِ
blame for	لَامَ عَلَى
resort to	لَجَأَ إِلَى
follow	لَحِقَ بِ
remark	لَفَتَ إِلَى
call	لَقَّبَ بِ
allude to	لَمَحَ إِلَى
die of	مَاتَ بِ
be full of	مَاجَ بِ
lean toward	مَالَ إِلَى
extend to	مَدَّ لِ
praise as	مَدَحَ بِ
pass by	مَرَّ بِ
pass by	مَرَّ عَلَى
walk to	مَشَى إِلَى
go away with	مَضَى بِ
proceed in	مَضَى فِي
stay in	مَكَثَ فِي
enable	مَكَّنَ مِنْ
enable to	مَكَّنَ لِ
fill with	مَلَأَ بِ
be bored of	مَلَّ مِنْ
deprive of	مَنَعَ عَنْ
bestow upon	مَنَّ عَلَى
be afflicted by	مُنِيَ بِ
promise	مَنَّى بِ

Glossary of common verbs with prepositions

stop, prevent from	مَنَعَ مِنْ
pave the way for	مَهَّدَ لِ
excel at	مَهَرَ فِي
become deputy	نَابَ عَنْ
call for	نَادَى بِ
compete for	نَافَسَ عَلَى
emanate from	نَبَعَ مِنْ
excel in	نَبَغَ فِي
survive	نَجَا مِنْ
succeed in	نَجَحَ فِي
carve	نَحَتَ فِي
deputize	نَدَبَ لِ
regret	نَدِمَ عَلَى
remove	نَزَعَ مِنْ
descend to	نَزَلَ إِلَى
leave, descend	نَزَلَ مِنْ
ascribe to	نَسَبَ إِلَى
coordinate	نَسَّقَ بَيْنَ
coordinate with	نَسَّقَ مَعَ
emerge from	نَشَأَ عَنْ
advise	نَصَحَ بِ
advise	نَصَحَ لِ
say, utter	نَطَقَ بِ
look at	نَظَرَ إِلَى
exile	نَفَى مِنْ
move to	نَقَلَ إِلَى
rise from	نَهَضَ مِنْ
migrate to	هَاجَرَ إِلَى
descend to	هَبَطَ إِلَى
abandon to	هَجَرَ إِلَى
threaten with	هَدَّدَ بِ
aim for	هَدَفَ إِلَى
escape through	هَرَبَ عَبْرَ

escape from	هَرَبَ مِنْ
perish with	هَلَكَ بِ
congratulate for	هَنَّأَ بِ / عَلَى
dominate	هَيْمَنَ عَلَى
confront with	وَاجَهَ بِ
balance	وَازَنَ بَيْنَ
sustain	وَاظَبَ عَلَى
trust	وَثِقَ بِ / فِي
authenticate as	وَثَّقَ كَ
become compulsory	وَجَبَ عَلَى
inherit from	وَرِثَ عَنْ / مِنْ
distribute to	وَزَّعَ عَلَى
expand	وَسَّعَ فِي
brand as	وَسَمَ بِ
describe as	وَصَفَ بِ
arrive to, at, in	وَصَلَ إِلَى
promise	وَعَدَ بِ
provide for	وَفَّرَ لِ
sign	وَقَّعَ عَلَى
fall upon	وَقَعَ عَلَى
fall in	وَقَعَ فِي
stand behind	وَقَفَ خَلْفَ / وَرَاءَ
stand against	وَقَفَ ضِدَّ
stand with	وَقَفَ مَعَ
protect from	وَقَى مِنْ
enter, access	وَلَجَ إِلَى
endow, gift to	وَهَبَ لِ

Answer key

Chapter 2

I

    1 Destination or direction of movement
    2 Location
    3 The manner of undertaking an action
    4 Transitivity – location
    5 Ascribing or specifying
    6 Role
    7 Time
    8 possession
    9 Manner
    10 Beneficiaries

II

1 ل
2 ل
3 ب-ل
4 ل
5 ب-ل
6 ب-ك
7 ل-ك
8 ب
9 ب-ل
10 ل

III

1–C   تُنَادِي الأُمَمُ الْمُتَّحِدَةُ بِتَسْوِيَةٍ نِهَائِيَّةٍ لِقَضِيَّةِ السَّلَامِ فِي الشَّرْقِ الأَوْسَطِ.
2–E   عَقَدَ الْبَرْلَمَانُ جَلْسَةً طَارِئَةً لِمُنَاقَشَةِ تَطَوُّرَاتِ الأَزْمَةِ الاِقْتِصَادِيَّةِ.
3–A   اِلْتَحَقَ أَحْمَدُ زُوَيْل بِكُلِّيَّةِ الْعُلُومِ بِجَامِعَةِ الإِسْكَنْدَرِيَّةِ.
4–B   أَصْبَحَتِ الْغَرْدَقَةُ مَقْصِدًا لِعَدَدٍ هَائِلٍ مِنَ السَّائِحِينَ.
5–D   تَكَلَّمَ الْعَرَبُ عَنِ النَّفْطِ كَسِلَاحٍ يُسْتَخْدَمُ فِي الْحِفَاظِ عَلَى مَصَالِحِ الْعَرَبِ فِي الْمُجْتَمَعِ الدَّوْلِيِّ.

IV

1   The Arabic translation of the book appeared for the first time in 1904.
2   The father loves his children, and he is strongly attached to them
3   This dancer looks like a beautiful butterfly.
4   As everyone knows, the book is composed of three parts.
5   Compensations were paid to the victims.

V

1   لِمَاذَا تَدْرُسُ اللُّغَةَ الصِّينِيَّةَ؟
2   قَدَّمَ الرَّئِيسُ لِلْفَرِيقِ جَوَائِزَ.
3   تُكَافِحُ مُعْظَمُ الشُّعُوبِ الْعَرَبِيَّةِ لِتَأْمِينِ لُقْمَةِ الْعَيْشِ.
4   أُؤَكِّدُ لَكَ بِأَنَّ الْكِتَابَ فِي الْمَكْتَبَةِ.
5   كَأَنَّ الْمَاضِيَ الْجَمِيلَ عَادَ.

Chapter 3

I

1   To indicate what something is made of
2   Used with a verb denoting liberation
3   To indicate deviation
4   To provide a reason and account for the action
5   Used with a verb expressing manner, state or condition
6   To designate a departure from a place.
7   To designate a location
8   To denote *per*
9   To designate a location
10 Used with a verb that denotes forgetfulness

II

1   ها
2   ها
3   هم

Answer key   219

4	كُم
5	ه
6	ها
7	ها
8	ه
9	كَ
10	ها

III

1	في
2	من
3	من
4	من
5	عن
6	عن
7	عن
8	من
9	عن
10	عن

IV

1	من
2	في
3	عن
4	في
5	من
6	عن
7	في

V

1–B عَلَينا أَنْ نَضعَ خُططًا اسْتراتيجِيَّةً لِكي نَتَمَكَّنَ مِنَ التَّقْليلِ مِنَ الأوْقاتِ العَصيبةِ التي نَتَعرَّضُ لها

2–C هُناكَ جُهودٌ عَرَبِيَّة جَماعِيَّة هائِلَة في عِدّة اتّجاهاتْ، وتأْتي المَسْألةُ العِراقِيّة كآخِرِ التَّطوراتِ التي فَجَرَتْ أكْثَرَ مِنْ قَضِيَّةٍ تَمَسّ أوْضاعاً عَرَبِيَّةً ودَوْلِيَّةً

3–E تَتَمَيَّز هَذِه الأنْشِطَةُ بالشَّموليَّة كَما تَتَمَيَّز بالاسْتِمْراريّة حتَّى يَتِمَّ تَحْقيقِ أهْدافِها.

4–A أُسِّسَ المُنْتَدى بِهَدفِ إيجادِ مُلْتَقى يَجْتَمِعُ فيهِ المُفَكِّرونَ والباحِثونَ مِنْ أَهلِ العِلْمِ والفِكْرِ.

5–D هُناكَ جُهودٌ عَرَبِيَّةٌ جَماعِيَّةٌ هائِلَةٌ في عِدّة اتّجاهاتٍ

VI

1. زَارَنِي صَدِيقِي ومَعَهُ طَبَقٌ مِنَ الحَلْوَى العُمَانِيَّةِ.
2. تَقَعُ الجَامِعَةُ عَلَى بُعْدِ عَشَرَةِ كِيلُومِتْرَاتٍ مِنْ مَرْكَزِ المَدِينَةِ.
3. إِنَّ الأزمَةَ المَادِّيَّةَ الآنَ دَفَعَتِ الكَثِيرَ مِنَ الشَّرِكَاتِ إِلَى التَّضْحِيَةِ بِالْإِسْتِثْمَارَاتِ طَوِيلَةِ الأمَدِ.
4. تَأَخَّرَ القِطَارُ عَنْ مَوْعِدِ وُصُولِهِ المُقَرَّرِ بِنِصْفِ سَاعَةٍ.
5. قَضَيْنَا عُطْلَةَ الصَّيْفِ فِي مِصْرَ.

VII

1. We met at the university campus.
2. He absented himself from attending the party for family reasons.
3. Media outlets need to get rid of the use of stereotypes.
4. A lot of children died during the Iraq War.
5. The celebrations will take place during the next few days.

Chapter 4

I

1. Exception
2. Time passed since an event
3. Obligation
4. Locality (figuratively)
5. Recipient
6. Direction of movement
7. Time passed since an event
8. Probability
9. Exception
10. Exception

II

1. عَدَا
2. عَلَى
3. إِلَى
4. مُنْذُ
5. مُنْذُ
6. عَلَى
7. عَدَا
8. إِلَى
9. مُنْذُ
10. عَدَا

Answer key 221

III

1 عَدَا
2 مُنْذُ
3 عَلَى
4 عَلَى
5 إِلَى
6 إِلَى
7 مُنْذُ
8 عَدَا
9 رُبَّ
10 عَدَا

IV

1–B   لَمْ يَحْصُلِ الرَّئِيسُ عَلَى غَالِبِيَّةٍ كَبِيرَةٍ فِي الِانْتِخَابَاتِ الْمَاضِيَةِ.

2–A   شَهِدَ الْيَمَنُ حُرُوبًا عَدِيدَةً عَلَى أَرْضِهِ مُنْذُ سُقُوطِ الْمُلْكِيَّةِ وَخُرُوجِ الِاسْتِعْمَارِ.

3–E   لَا يُمْكِنُ تَنَاوُلُ الوَضْعِ الدَّاخِلِيِّ فِي الْبَلَدِ دُونَ الْإِشَارَةِ إِلَى الْعَدَالَةِ الِاجْتِمَاعِيَّةِ.

4–C   وَافَقَ الْجَمِيعُ عَلَى إِنْشَاءِ خَطِّ الْأَنَابِيبِ عَدَا الْقَبَائِلِ الَّتِي تَسْكُنُ فِي الصَّحْرَاءِ.

5–D   الْمُنَاخُ الْمُعْتَدِلُ فِي الْمِنْطَقَةِ شَجَّعَ عَلَى الِاسْتِقْرَارِ وَعَلَى الْأَنْشِطَةِ الزِّرَاعِيَّةِ.

V

1 Matches will be held from August 16 to 24.
2 Republicans control the Congress.
3 Over time, the press has proved its independence from government in democratic countries.
4 The government plans to raise electricity prices for household consumption of more than 500 kilowatts per month.
5 For two years, the United States has been allowed to export textiles to Egypt.

VI

1   يَجِبُ أَنْ نَقُومَ بِاتِّخَاذِ الْخُطُوَاتِ الْعَمَلِيَّةِ الْمَطْلُوبَةِ مِنْ أَجْلِ إِشْرَاكِ الْفِئَاتِ الْمُهَمَّشَةِ.

2   جَلَسَ أَخِي عَلَى يَسَارِي.

3   رَأَيْنَا قَوَارِبَ تُبْحِرُ عَلَى مِيَاهِ الْبُحَيْرَةِ.

4   مُنْذُ مَا قَبْلَ الْإِسْلَامِ، كَانَتِ الْقَبَائِلُ الْعَرَبِيَّةُ تَتَصَارَعُ مَعَ بَعْضِهَا الْبَعْضِ.

5   تَمَّ قُبُولُ الْهُدْنَةِ عَلَى شَرْطِ إِطْلَاقِ سَرَاحِ الْأَسْرَى مِنَ الْجَانِبَيْنِ.

Chapter 5

I

1–E	كُنْتُ رَفِيقَتَهُ حَتَّى فَارَقَ الْحَيَاةَ
2–D	سَهِرْنَا لَيْلَةَ أَمْسِ حَتَّى الصَّبَاحِ
3–A	سَافَرَت بِالسَّيَّارَةِ حَتَّى وَصَلَت أَبوظَبِيّ
4–C	لَا أَعُودُ مِنَ الْعَمَلِ حَتَّى تَغْرُبَ الشَّمْسُ
5–B	سِرْتُ مِنَ الْعَمَلِ حَتَّى الْمَطْعَمِ

II

1. دَرَسْتُ النَّحْوَ الْعَرَبِيَّ حَتَّى الصَّبَاحِ.
2. أَكَلْنَا الدَّجَاجَةَ حَتَّى شَبِعْنَا.
3. قَرَأَ عَلِيٌّ الْكِتَابَ حَتَّى صَفْحَةِ الْخَاتِمَةِ.
4. اِنْتَظَرْتُهُ حَتَّى السَّاعَةِ السَّادِسَةِ مَسَاءً.
5. مَكَثْنَا أَمَامَ الْبَيْتِ حَتَّى وَصَلَتْ هِنْدٌ.

III

1. The soldiers fought until victory.
2. I listened to the judge until the end of the judgment.
3. The guests came, except Sarah.
4. God forbid to betray my partner at work.
5. I watched the film until the end.

Bibliography

ʿAbbās, H. (1996). *Al-Naḥw Al-Wāfī (Comprehensive Syntax) 4 Vols* (13th ed.). Cairo: Dār Al-Maʿārif.
ʿAbdel Nasser, M. (2013). The Polysemous Nature of Some Arabic Prepositions. *International Journal of Linguistics*, 5(2), 66–86.
al-Farahīdī, A.K.I.A. (2003). *Kitāb al-ʿAyn*. Beirut: Dār al-Kutub al-ʿIlmīyah.
al-Ghalāyīnī, A.M. (1994). *Jāmiʿ al-Durūs al-ʿArabīyah*. A.A.M. Khafājah (Ed.). Sidon-Beirut: Manshūrāt al-Maktabah al-ʿAṣrīyah.
Alhawary, M. (2009). *Arabic Second Language Acquisition of Morphosyntax*. New Haven: Yale University Press.
Alhawary, M. (2016). *Arabic Grammar in Context* (Languages in Context Series). London and New York: Routledge.
al-Khūlī, M.A. (1998). *al-Tarākīb al-Shāiʿah fī al-Lughah al-ʿArabīyah: Dirasah Iḥṣāʾīyah*. ʿAmmām: Dār al-Falāḥ lil-Nashr wa-al-Tawzīʿ.
al-Suyūṭī, J.A.D.A.R. (1909a). *Kitāb Hamʿ al-Hawāmiʿ sharḥ Jamʿ al-Jawāmiʿ fī ʿIlm al-ʿArabīyah* (1st ed.). Cairo: Maṭbaʿat al-Saʿādah.
al-Suyūṭī, J.A.A.A.R. (1909b). *Bughyat al-Wuʿāt fī Ṭabaqāt al-Lughawīyīn wa-al-Nuḥāht*. Cairo: Maṭbaʿat al-Saʿādah.
Al-Warraki, N.N. (1994). *The Connectors in Modern Standard Arabic*. Cairo and New York: The American University in Cairo Press.
Ammār, M.I. (1998). *al-Akhṭāʾ al-Shāiʿah fī Istiʿmālāt Ḥurūf al-Jarr* (1st ed.). Riyad: Dār ʿĀlam al-Kutub lil-Ṭibāʿah wa al-Nashr wa al-Tawziʿ.
Arberry, A.J. (1996). *The Koran Interpreted*. New York: Simon & Schuster.
Baalbaki, R. (2007). *The Early Islamic Grammatical Tradition* (The Formation of the Classical Islamic World). Aldershot: Ashgate Publishing Limited.
Badawi, E., Carter, M., and Gully, A. (2014). *Modern Written Arabic: A Comprehensive Grammar* (2nd ed.). (Routledge Comprehensive Grammars). London and New York: Routledge.
Bahloul, M. (2007). *Structure and Function of the Arabic Verb*. London and New York: Routledge.
Beeston, A.F.L. (2006). *The Arabic Language Today* (Georgetown Classics in Arabic Language and Linguistics). Washington, DC: Georgetown University Press.
Bernards, M. (2017). *Changing Traditions: Al-Mubarrad's Refutation of Sībawayh and the Subsequent Reception of the kitāb* (Studies in Semitic Languages and Linguistics). Leiden: Brill.
Brustad, K., Al-Batal, M., and Al-Tonsi, A. (2004). *Al-Kitaab fii Taʿallum al-ʿArabiyya: Pt. 1: A Textbook for Beginning Arabic* (2nd ed.). Washington, DC: Georgetown University Press.
Buckley, R. (2004). *Modern Literary Arabic: A Reference Grammar*. Beirut: Librairie du Liban.

Bibliography

Buckwalter, T., and Parkinson, D. (2011). *A Frequency Dictionary of Arabic*. London: Routledge.

Cachia, P. (1973). *The Monitor: A Dictionary of Arabic Grammatical Terms; Arabic-English, English-Arabic*. Beirut: Librairie du Liban.

Cantarino, V. (1974–1976). *Syntax of Modern Arabic Prose* (3 Vols.). Bloomington and London: Indiana University Press.

Carter, M.G. (1981). *Arab Linguistics: An Introductory Classical Text with Translation and Notes*. Amsterdam: Benjamins.

Carter, M.G. (2004). *Sībawayhi*. New York: I.B. Tauris.

Carter, M.G., and Marogy, A.E. (2012). *Foundations of Arabic Linguistics: Sībawayhi and Early Arabic Grammatical Theory* (Studies in Semitic Languages and Linguistics). Leiden and Boston: Brill.

Corder, S.P. (1974). The Significance of Learners' Errors. In Richards, J. (Ed.), *Error Analysis: Perspectives on Second Language Acquisition* (pp. 19–28). London: Longman Group Limited.

Corder, S.P. (1981). *Error Analysis and Interlanguage*. Oxford: Oxford University Press.

Dickins, J., and Watson, J.C.E. (1999). *Standard Arabic: An Advanced Course*. Cambridge: Cambridge University Press.

Elgibali, A., and Nevenka, K. (2008). *Media Arabic: A Course Book for Reading Arabic News*. Cairo: The American University in Cairo Press.

Ellis, R., and Barkhuizen, G. (2005). *Analysing Learner Language* (Oxford Applied Linguistics). Oxford: Oxford University Press.

Esseesy, M. (2010). *Grammaticalization of Arabic Prepositions and Subordinators: A Corpus-based Study*. Leiden: Brill.

Fischer, W., and Rodgers, J. (2001). *A Grammar of Classical Arabic* (3rd ed.). New Haven: Yale University Press.

Gully, A. (1995). *Grammar and Semantics in Medieval Arabic: A Study of Ibn-Hisham's 'Mughni l-labib'*. Richmond, Surrey: Curzon Press.

Gully, A. (1997). Taḍmīn, "Implication of Meaning," in Medieval Arabic. *Journal of the American Oriental Society*, 117(3), 466–480.

Ḥasan, A. (1960). *Al-Naḥū al-Wāfī maʻa Rabṭihi bi-al-'Asālīb al-Rafīʻa wa al-Hayāt al-lughawīya al-Mutajaddida* (4 Vol.). Cairo: Dār al-Maʻārif.

Haywood, J. (1965). *Arabic Lexicography: Its History, and Its Place in the General History of Lexicography* (2nd ed.). Leiden: E.J. Brill.

Haywood, J., and Nahmad, H. (2005). *A New Arabic Grammar of the Written Language*. Aldershot, Hampshire: Lund Humphries.

Holes, C. (1987). *Language Variation and Change in a Modernising Arab State: The Case of Bahrain* (Library of Arabic Linguistics, Monograph 7). London and New York: Kegan Paul International.

Holes, C. (2004). *Modern Arabic: Structures, Functions and Varieties* (Rev. ed.). Washington, DC: Georgetown University Press.

Hospers, J.H. (1974). *A Basic Bibliography for the Study of the Semitic Languages, Vol. II*. Leiden: Brill.

Ibn, A.A.A.-R., Rifāʻī, Q.-S., and Ibn, M.M.A.A. (1987). *Sharḥ Ibn ʻAqīl ʻalá Alfīyat ibn Mālik*. Beirut: Dār al-Qalam.

Ibn al-Sarrāj, A.B. (1985). *Kitāb al-'u Uṣūl fī al- Naḥw*. A.A.H. al-Fatlī. (Ed.). Beirut: Muʼassassat al-Risāla.

Ibn Fāris, A.A.Q. (1972). *Muʼjam Maqayīs al-Lughah Vol 2*. A.S.M Hārūn (Ed.). Beirut: Dār al-Fikr.

Ibn Hishām, A.A. (1964). *Mughnī al-Labīb*. Beirut: Al- Maktaba al-ʻAṣrīya,

Ibn Jinnī, A.A.F.U. (2001). *al-Khaṣā'is*. Beirut: Dār al-Kutub al-ʻIlmīyah.

Ibn Jinnī, A.A.F.U. (2013). *Sirr Ṣinā'at al-I'rāb*. M.H.M.H.I. Shāfi'ī and A.R. Shiḥāt (Eds.). Beirut: Dār al-Kutub al-'Ilmīyah.

James, C. (1998). *Errors in Language Learning and Use: Exploring Error Analysis* (Applied Linguistics and Language Study). London: Longman.

Khalīl, and al-Farāhīdī, A.A.R.A.H.I.A. (1988). *Kitāb al-'Āyn*. M. al-Maḫzūmī and I. al-Sāmarrā'ī (Eds.). Baghdad: Dār al-Rašīd.

Levin, A. (1987). The Views of the Arab Grammarians on the Classification and Syntactic Function of Prepositions. *Jerusalem Studies in Arabic and Islam*, 10, 342–367.

Levin, A. (1994). Sībawayhi's Attitude to the Spoken Language. *Jerusalem Studies in Arabic and Islam*, 17, 204–243.

Levin, A. (1998). *Arabic Linguistic Thought and Dialectology*. Jerusalem: Hebrew University Press.

Louchene, N.E.N. (2006). *Ḥurūf al-Jarr fī al-'Arabīyah: Bayn al-Muṣṭalaḥ wa-Alwaẓīfah*. Alexandria: al-Maktab al-Jami'ī al-Hadīth.

Marogy, A.E. (2010). *Kitāb Sībawayhi: Syntax and Pragmatics*. Boston: Brill.

Marogy, A.E. (2012). *The Foundations of Arabic Linguistics: Sibawayhi and Early Arabic Grammatical Theory*. M.G. Carter (Ed.). (Studies in Semitic Languages and Linguistics). Leiden: Brill.

Mubarrad, I.Y. (1923). *al-Kāmil fī al-lughah wa-al-adab*. Cairo: Maṭba'at al-Sa'ādah.

Al-Murādī, B.A.D.A.H.Q. (1992). *la-Jun al-Dānī fī Ḥurūf al-Ma'ānī* (1st ed.). F. Qabā and M.N. Fādil (Eds.). Beirut: *Dār* al-kutub al-'ilmīyah.

Owens, J. (1984). *A Short Reference Grammar of Eastern Libyan Arabic*. Wiesbaden: Otto Harrassowitz.

Owens, J. (1988). *The Foundations of Grammar: An Introduction to Medieval Arabic Grammatical Theory*. Amsterdam: Benjamins.

Owens, J. (2006). *A Linguistic History of Arabic*. Oxford: Oxford University Press.

Owens, J. (2013). *The Oxford Handbook of Arabic Linguistics*. Oxford: Oxford University Press.

Peled, Y. (2008). *Sentence Types and Word-order Patterns in Written Arabic: Medieval and Modern Perspectives* (Studies in Semitic Languages and Linguistics). Leiden: Brill Academic Pub.

Rummānī, A.I. (2008). *Kitāb Ma'ānī al-Ḥurūf*. Beirut: Dār wa-Maktabat al-Hilāl lil-Ṭibā'ah wa-al-Nashr.

Ryding, K.C. (2005). *A Reference Grammar of Modern Standard Arabic*. Cambridge: Cambridge University Press.

Ryding-Lentzner, K. (1977). *Semantic and Syntactic Aspects of Arabic Prepositions*. Ph.D. dissertation. Georgetown: Georgetown University.

Shartūnī, R. (1961). *Mabādi' al-'Arabīyah fī al-Ṣarf wa-al- Naḥū*. Beirut: al-Maṭba'ah al-Kāthūlīkīyah.

Shawqī, Ḍ. (1968). *Al-Madāris al-Naḥwiyya*. Cairo: Dār al-Ma'ārif.

Sībawayhi, 'Amr ibn 'Uthmān, and Hārūn, 'Abd al-Salām Muḥammad. (1988). *Al-Kitāb. (Kitāb) Sībawayhi Abī Bishr 'Amr Ibn 'Uthmān Ibn Qanbar*. Vol. 1. Cairo: Maktabat al-Khānjī.

Spillner, B. (2017). *Error Analysis in the World: A Bibliography*. Sprachwissenschaft, Berlin: Frank & Timme.

Stetkevych, J. (1970). *The Modern Arabic Literary Language: Lexical and Stylistic Developments*. Chicago: University of Chicago Press.

Suleiman, Y. (1999a). *The Arabic Grammatical Tradition: A Study in ta'līl*. Edinburgh: Edinburgh University Press.

Suleiman, Y. (Ed.). (1999b). *Arabic Grammar and Linguistics*. Surrey: Curzon.

Versteegh, C.H.M., and Mushira, E. (2005). *Encyclopedia of Arabic Language and Linguistics*. Leiden: Brill.

Versteegh, C.H.M., and Versteegh, K. (2014). *The Arabic Language*. Edinburgh: Edinburgh University Press.

Versteegh, K. (1994). The Notion of "Underlying Levels" in the Arabic Linguistic Tradition. *Historiographia Linguistica*, 21(3), 271–296.

Versteegh, K. (1997a). *Landmarks in Linguistic Thought, Vol. III: The Arabic Linguistic Tradition*. London and New York: Routledge.

Versteegh, K. (1997b). *The Arabic Linguistic Tradition*. London and New York: Routledge.

Watson, J. (1999). The Syntax of Arabic Headlines and News Summaries. In Suleiman, Y. (Ed.), *Arabic Grammar and Linguistics*. Surrey: Curzon.

Wehr, H. (2008). *A Dictionary of Modern Written Arabic – Arabic–English*. J. M. Cowan (Ed.). Beirut: Librairie du Liban.

Wightwick, J., and Gaafar, M. (2018). *Arabic Verbs and Essentials of Arabic Grammar* (3rd ed.). New York: McGraw-Hill Education.

Wright, W. (1896). *A Grammar of the Arabic Language*. Translated from the German of Caspari and Edited with Numerous Additions and Corrections. Vol. 2. Cambridge: Cambridge University Press.

Wright, W. (1966). *Lectures in the Comparative Grammar of the Semitic Languages* (2nd ed.). Amsterdam: Philo Press.

Wright, W. (1967). *A Grammar of the Arabic Language (Combined Volume)* (3rd ed.). Cambridge: Cambridge University Press.

Yaʿqūb, I. (1995). *Mawsūʿat ʾUlūm al-Lughah al-ʿArabīyah*. Beirut: Dār al-Jīl.

Zajjājī, A.Q.A.A.R. (1959). *al-ʾĪḍāḥ fī ʿIlal al-Naḥw*. M. al-Mubārak (Ed.). Cairo: Dār al-ʿUrūba.

Zubaydī, M.I.A. (1954). *Ṭabaqāt al-Naḥwīyīn wa-al-Lughawīyīn*. M. Ibrāhīm (Ed.). Cairo: Al-Khanjī.

Index

إِلَى: in context 98; in fixed expressions 106–107; functions of 99–101; notes on translation 103–104; notes on usage 101–103; with interrogatives and conjunctions 104–106; with pronoun suffixes 104
عَلَى 107; in context 108; in fixed expressions 116–121; functions of 108–110; notes on the usage of 110–113; notes on translation 114; with interrogatives and conjunctions 115; with pronoun suffixes 114–115
خَلَا / عَدَا: functions of 122–124; with pronoun suffixes 124
مُنذ 124–125; functions of 125–126
رُبَّ 126; functions of 127
البَاء: in context 11–12; description of 11; fixed expressions with 22–28; functions of 12–20; with interrogatives and conjunctions 21–22; with pronoun suffixes 20–21
اللَّام 29; in context 29; fixed expressions with 38–39; functions of 30–33; interrogatives and conjunctions 37; notes on translation 36; notes on usage 33–35; with pronoun suffixes 36–37
الكَاف: in context 39–40; notes on usage 41, 44; usage of 40
وَاو وبَاء وتَاء القَسَم 44
حَتَّى: in context 130–131; functions of 131–133; vs. إِلَى 131
حَاشَا 133; in context 134–135

adverbial objects 144
adverbs 15, 131, 132; of place 137–138, 157–168; of time 136–137, 156–159
al-Khuli, M.A. 2–3
Arabic, colloquial 182
Arabic learners 161, 185

Arabic particles 1
Arabic prepositions 1–2; case marking of prepositional phrases 7–9; classifications of 4; constructions involving 4–7; definition of 2; for foreign-language learning 10; functions of 3; importance of 2–3; locative adverbs 9–10

Basra school 1
Buckley, R. 5

Cantarino, V. 12
Corder, S.P. 169

errors, by students 169; addition of prepositions 182–184; deletion of prepositions 170–176; examples of 169–170; in students' writing 161; substitution of prepositions 176–182; types of 160, 161

foreign-language learning, importance of prepositions 10

genitive nouns 138

intralingual transfer 182
intransitive verbs 14

Kufa school 1–2

learners, of Arabic 161, 185
learners' errors: addition of prepositions 182–184; deletion of prepositions 170–176; examples of 169–170; substitution of prepositions 176–182
locative adverbs 5, 136; adverbs of place 137–138, 159–168; adverbs of time

136–137, 156–159; categories of 136–137; examples of 137

Modern Standard Arabic (MSA) 2, 182

nominal sentences 5
noun phrases 57
nouns 3, 5, 8, 9, 60, 130, 132, 158, 182; categories of 1; plural genitive form of 49, 59

one-letter prepositions 10

particles 1, 2
possession 144, 147
prefixes 149
prepositional phrases 5
prepositions 2, 3, 8, 11, 19, 51, 131, 134; addition of 182–184; deletion of 170–176; foreign-language learning, importance in 10; quasi-redundant 4; redundant 4; substitution of 176–182; true 4, 69; use of 185; *see also* four-letter prepositions; one-letter prepositions; three-letter prepositions; two-letter prepositions
pronouns 20, 59, 60, 131
pronoun suffixes 5, 57, 143, 146, 147, 151, 153, 154, 156, 160, 161, 163–165

quasi-redundant prepositions 4

redundant prepositions 4
relative pronouns 5, 59
Ryding, K.C. 10, 138
Ryding-Lentzner, K. 136

semi-prepositions 8, 9–10, 49, 136, 138, 159
semi-redundant prepositions 126
spatial contexts 146, 153–155
spatial functions 148
suffixes, pronoun 5, 57, 143, 146, 147, 151, 153, 154, 156, 160, 161, 163–165
superlative constructions 52

temporal contexts 98, 107, 140–141, 146, 153, 154
temporal functions 30, 99, 148
three-letter prepositions: عَلَى 98–106; إِلَى 107–115; خَلَا 122–124; مُنْذُ 124–126; رُبَّ 126–127
transitivity 12
true prepositions 4, 69
two-letter prepositions: عَنْ 47–69; مِنْ 69–79; فِي 79–93; كَي 93–95

verbs 1, 16, 17, 48, 51, 53, 54–55, 112–113, 130–132, 135, 182, 185; intransitive 14; present-tense 56

Wright, W. 2, 12